ART IN THE PRE-HISPANIC SOUTHWEST

Issues in Southwest Archaeology
Edited by John Kantner

Mission Statement

Issues in Southwest Archaeology is dedicated to publishing volumes that critically evaluate current archaeological research in the US Southwest and Northwest Mexico. The books consider topics that are pervasive themes both in the archaeology of the region but also in contemporary anthropological inquiry, such as ethnicity, gender, migration, and violence. Written by leading scholars in the field, the volumes discuss more than just what archaeologists know about the prehistory of the Southwest; they also consider issues that impact the practice of archaeology today, including the roles of cultural resource management, oral history, and cultural property rights. Each contribution to the series is guided by the research interests and theoretical perspective of the author, but each book is ultimately synthetic, comparative, and fully engaged in broader anthropological interests.

Books in the Series

ART IN THE PRE-HISPANIC SOUTHWEST

An Archaeology
of Native American Cultures

RADOSŁAW PALONKA

LEXINGTON BOOKS
Lanham • Boulder • New York • London

Published by Lexington Books
An imprint of The Rowman & Littlefield Publishing Group, Inc.
4501 Forbes Boulevard, Suite 200, Lanham, Maryland 20706
www.rowman.com

86-90 Paul Street, London EC2A 4NE

British Library Cataloguing in Publication Information Available

Library of Congress Cataloging-in-Publication Data

Names: Palonka, Radosław, author.
Title: Art in the pre-Hispanic Southwest : an archaeology of Native American cultures /
   Radosław Palonka.
Description: Lanham : Lexington Books, [2022] | Series: Issues in Southwest archaeology
   | Includes bibliographical references and index. | Summary: "This book examines the
   development of pre-Hispanic Native American cultures in the American Southwest
   and Mexican Northwest from the Paleoindian period until the appearance of the first
   Europeans in the sixteenth century through studies of settlements, rock art, and pottery
   iconography"— Provided by publisher.
Identifiers: LCCN 2022011918 | ISBN 9781793648730 (cloth) | ISBN 9781793648747
   (ebook) | ISBN 9781793648754 (paper)
Subjects: LCSH: Indian art—Southwest, New. | Indians of North America—Material
   culture—Southwest, New.
Classification: LCC E78.S7 P35 2022 | DDC 970.01/1—dc23/eng/20220513
LC record available at https://lccn.loc.gov/2

For Ada and Weronika

Contents

List of Figures

List of Tables

Preface

I HAVE BEEN FASCINATED by the Southwest (formerly the part of the famous Wild West) since childhood. At that time, I did not expect that this world, so colorfully described by adventure books and westerns, had so much more to offer than merely an otherwise intriguing and ever vivid cowboy culture (a concept that is alive and well today) and fights with Native Americans. However, as it turned out, this region had become a vibrant home for some of the most developed and complex Native American cultures north of Mexico long before the arrival of Christopher Columbus and the first Europeans to America at the end of the fifteen century. It was actually an entire civilizational area created by the agricultural communities of the Pueblo, Hohokam, Fremont, Mogollon/Mimbres, and Casas Grandes cultural traditions, who lived in large settlements or proto-towns and whose artificial irrigation systems were comparable to those known in ancient Peru, Egypt, and the Middle East.

This book marks an attempt to explore, to some extent, the most important questions concerning this extraordinary world of Native Americans who, in the arid and inhospitable regions of the semideserts and plateaus of the Southwest that is the border between today's southwestern United States and northern Mexico, were able to organize themselves into well-functioning organisms creating supra-regional structures or in some cases—I use this term with no hesitation—even proto-states. Yet, it was not a world free from conflict, turbulence, collapse, and migration from one area to another. It was also particularly sensitive to changes in the natural environment and climate, which heavily impacted the fairly delicate ecosystems, often determining the existence and shaping, to some extent, of the cultural face of this region. These environmental influences were particularly discernible at the end of the thirteenth century AD in the Ancestral Pueblo world, which flourished in the northern part of the Southwest, but they weren't limited to this period or culture.

This book also presents some aspects of ancient beliefs, including their expression through intricately decorated pottery and rock art iconography—that is, paintings and petroglyphs covering the canyons walls, cliff shelters, and alcoves, as well as individual rocks and boulders. Changes in pottery and rock art iconography over time correlate with shifts in the natural environment and climate, the transition from the Ice Age to the Holocene, and the appearance of agriculture. Special emphasis is also devoted to the rock art from Paleoindian and Archaic periods and later Hohokam, Casas Grandes, Fremont, Mogollon/Mimbres, and Pueblo cultural traditions.

Acknowledgments

ALTHOUGH THE PROCESS of writing the book took almost two years, the materials for it had been gathered over many years as the result of several scholarship visits thanks to grants from the Fulbright Commission, Tokyo Foundation, and the Kosciuszko Foundation and to American universities during my doctoral studies. These academic relationships led to consultations and observations related to the research methodology used by American scientists and direct participation in their archaeological projects. Certain theories, theses, and thoughts presented in this publication were also shaped to a large extent thanks to participation in conferences and symposia in Europe and, above all, in the United States. Direct contact with contemporary Pueblos, Navajos, Apache, and Utes and other descendants of the pre-Hispanic cultures that were archaeologically studied and described in this book were instrumental to this work, especially in terms of their rich oral traditions.

In 2011, thanks to the generous suggestion by one of my PhD dissertation reviewers, Prof. William D. Lipe, consultations with another advisor, Dr. Mark D. Varien, and support from the Institute of Archaeology and the Faculty of History of the Jagiellonian University in Krakow, Poland, as well as many American researchers, I began the first Polish archaeological project in the US Southwest. This research focused on the reconstruction of sociocultural changes and settlement structure and documentation of rock art at one Puebloan community consisting of around forty sites and located in the Central Mesa Verde region of southwestern Colorado. Initially these studies were funded by universities, private companies, and American partners, primarily the US Bureau of Land Management and the US Consulate General in Krakow. Subsequently these studies were funded by the National Science Center, Poland, within the scope of the SONATA and SONATA BIS grants (UMO-2013/11/D/HS3/01879 and UMO-2017/26/E/HS3/01174) and remain so to this day.

This publication would not have been created without the help and generous support of many people and numerous institutions. At this juncture, I would like to thank all those without whom it would not have been possible to write this book. First of all, I would like to thank my wife and daughter, who allowed me to steal a lot of valuable family time and devote it to this work. I would also like to thank my parents, including my father, who introduced me to the world of books and movies about Native Americans when I was a child. This book is dedicated to them. Many thanks for Kasey Beduhn for encouraging me to write this book for Lexington Books and for Dr. John Kantner, the Issues in Southwest Archaeology series editor for his support and review; additional great thanks for anonymous reviewers for their engagement and invaluable help for improving the book.

It would have been impossible to create this publication without the favor and support of successive deans at the Faculty of History of the Jagiellonian University. Field research in particular, as well as collecting the materials necessary for this publication, was also made possible thanks to the support of Polish and American archaeologists, including my mentor, Professor Janusz Kozłowski and the reviewers of my PhD dissertation, professors William Lipe (Washington State University), Aleksander Posern-Zieliński (Adam Mickiewicz University in Poznań) and Mark Varien (Crow Canyon Archaeological Center). Many thanks to Paul Fish and Barbara Mills (University of Arizona, Tucson) and Michele Hegmon (Arizona State University, Tempe) for their enormous mentoring support related to my PhD thesis and subsequent consultations and cooperation; I also thank the Colorado research and educational institutions—the Crow Canyon Archaeological Center and the Canyons of the Ancients National Monument—and their employees for the omnifarious and varied assistance they have provided over many years; a big thank you to Vince MacMillan. Also my deepest gratefulness to Bridget Ambler, Linda Farnsworth, Kristin Kuckelman, Ricky Lightfoot, Scott Ortman, Donna Glowacki, Tom Windes, James Kayser, Cory Breternitz, Bob Brunswig, Polly and Curtis Schaafsma, Wendy Weston and the Weston family (Navajo), Beki Hammond (Ute), Hopi consultants from the Hopi Cultural Preservation Office, including Leigh Kuwanisiwma, Lee Wayne Lomayestewa, Ronald Wadsworth, Garry Nicholas, Joel Nicholas, Delwyn Tawvaya, and Kevin James Crook and many other people.

Michał Znamirowski deserves a special mention, whose work on the graphic design of the book, assistance at every stage during the composition of this publication and participation in the project in Colorado cannot be overestimated. I would also like to thank Maria O'Meara for her linguistic corrections and smoothing of the text. I would also like to thank my neighbor, Maria, for her kind prayers and who, especially in the last, very difficult months of writing this book, gave me sympathy and support in this demanding work, and also often reminded me of other important matters in life.

Krakow (Poland), 24.06.2021

Pre-Hispanic and the Early-Historic Southwest   1

North American Southwest: Cultural and Geographical Context

THE NORTH AMERICAN SOUTHWEST that comprises the border of the US Southwest and adjacent parts of northern Mexico is not only a geographical concept, as the name may suggest, but an archaeological and anthropological one as well. It is, perhaps above all, a cultural term. Its broad definition encompasses the characteristic desert and semi-arid landscape of cacti and prickly pears and vast sandstone plateaus/ mesas crisscrossed by canyons, as well as pre-Hispanic, historic, and modern cultures, including the highly developed agricultural Native American societies that thrived in this difficult environment and climate long before the arrival of Europeans. Today, the term *Southwest* is alive and well in colloquial American discourse, reflecting the division of the United States into parts or areas of economic, geographic, landscape, cultural, and touristic importance.

The cultural region of the Southwest was designated by scientists during the first decades of the twentieth century, along with a general division into so-called cultural regions and areas in North America and Mesoamerica (Trigger 1989; Willey and Sabloff 1993). The criteria for the division, based mainly on the archaeological and ethnographic research at that time, were similarities and differences in geography and the natural environment, as well as cultural and technological determinants, along with the degree and level of civilizational development pertaining to individual indigenous cultures. Moreover, the Southwest was also the first region to receive a full archaeological, cultural-historic, and chronological study, which later constituted a model for similar studies of other cultural areas in the New World (Cordell 1997:67–100; Willey 1966).

The center of the Southwest region comprises the central and southern parts of the states of Utah and Colorado, the entire states of Arizona and New Mexico, adjacent parts of southeastern California and Nevada, with parts of west Texas bordering New Mexico to the east. Archaeologically, however, the Southwest as it is most widely understood extends beyond the territory of the present-day United States and overlaps the states of Sonora and Chihuahua—northern provinces of Mexico (e.g., Cordell 1997; Plog 1997). This is a simplification, but it is often used by many American researchers, to emphasize the vastness of this territory and the kind of cultural unification existing there, especially visible in the pre-Hispanic and protohistoric period.

There is, however, an even broader concept of the Southwest, the so-called Greater Southwest, defined as the area from the city of Durango in southern Colorado to the city of Durango in the state of the same name in Mexico, and from the town of Las Vegas in New Mexico to the famous Las Vegas, Nevada (Cordell 1997:3–6; Plog 1997:12–13). The latter definition is, of course, again a simplification, but researchers still use it, especially to emphasize the territorial extent of this area and the fact that its southern regions are located far beyond the southern border of the present-day United States, which again illustrates that former cultural areas transcended today's political boundaries.

The well-known thesis that modern administrative and political boundaries do not fully reflect the cultural divisions of the past is particularly underlined in the case of the Southwest. Some territory belonging to tribes and cultures was divided between the United States and Mexico in the mid-nineteenth century. Today, some peoples such as the Tohono O'odham (formerly known as the Papago) still live on both sides of the US-Mexico border. Nowadays the rights of native societies to freely cross the border are even more restricted than in the past, including by the construction of a wall (or rather sections of walls and barbed wire, separated by natural barriers) separating Mexico from the United States. As for the Tohono O'odham, still many members of the population of this tribe in Mexico make, for example, an annual pilgrimage to the mission of San Xavier del Bac in southern Arizona, founded in the eighteenth century, and many of the 25,000 people from this group living today in Arizona make pilgrimages to the city of Magdalena in the Mexican state of Sonora (usually in memory of Saint Francis of Assisi and Francis Xavier). Obviously, this causes many problems and conflicts, including when it comes to the possibility for Native Americans to freely cross the border both for religious reasons and in order to participate in traditional ceremonies, as well as to visit their families. In addition, it necessitates cooperation between these tribes and agents of the American and Mexican governments in part because of immigration that takes place through reservations that overlap the US and Mexican border. Archaeology and anthropology related to the Native American economic situation intertwine here with the politics of these two countries and regions, and not for the first time.

One of the characteristic features of the Southwest region is its striking natural environment, a landscape that includes unique rock formations and terrain, as well as a distinct climate. Although it is customary to think of this region as fairly homogeneous in terms of nature—deserts/semideserts and scant vegetation and plateaus and canyons most readily spring to mind when imagining this area—the true picture of its geological structure, fauna and flora, and the natural environment as a whole is very diverse. For example, the deserts and semiarid areas of Arizona and New Mexico contrast with the high mountain ranges crossing them, covered with dense spruce, piñon pine and juniper forests, as well as the picturesque sandstone plateaus known as *mesas*. Likewise, the Colorado Plateau (north and mid-Southwest) which generally receives more precipitation than the rest of the Southwest, is extremely varied. These differences were present in the past, and they influenced the formation of different cultures in the region, in terms of their level of technological development, social organization, and beliefs, which are explored in more detail in chapter 2.

Although the individual cultures and tribes of the Southwest differed quite significantly from one another, particularly during the pre-Hispanic period that marked the beginnings of agriculture (or even slightly earlier) we can distinguish several features common to this area. First, there was the economic, cultural, political, and territorial domination of peoples with an agricultural economy. These included, first and foremost, the Pueblo, Hohokam, Mogollon/Mimbres, Casas Grandes cultures and, in part, the Fremont culture and others cultures (figure 1.1); Chapters 4 to 8 of this book are devoted to them. They formed great cultural provinces, together covering virtually the entire Southwest, leaving only some ecological niches and land available to hunter-gatherer communities. Ultimately however, this balance shifted dramatically in favor of the hunter-gatherer peoples and the areas they occupied due to two factors: environmental, climate, and social changes that affected almost the entire Southwest from the thirteenth and fourteenth centuries AD and the arrival of Europeans in this area soon after.

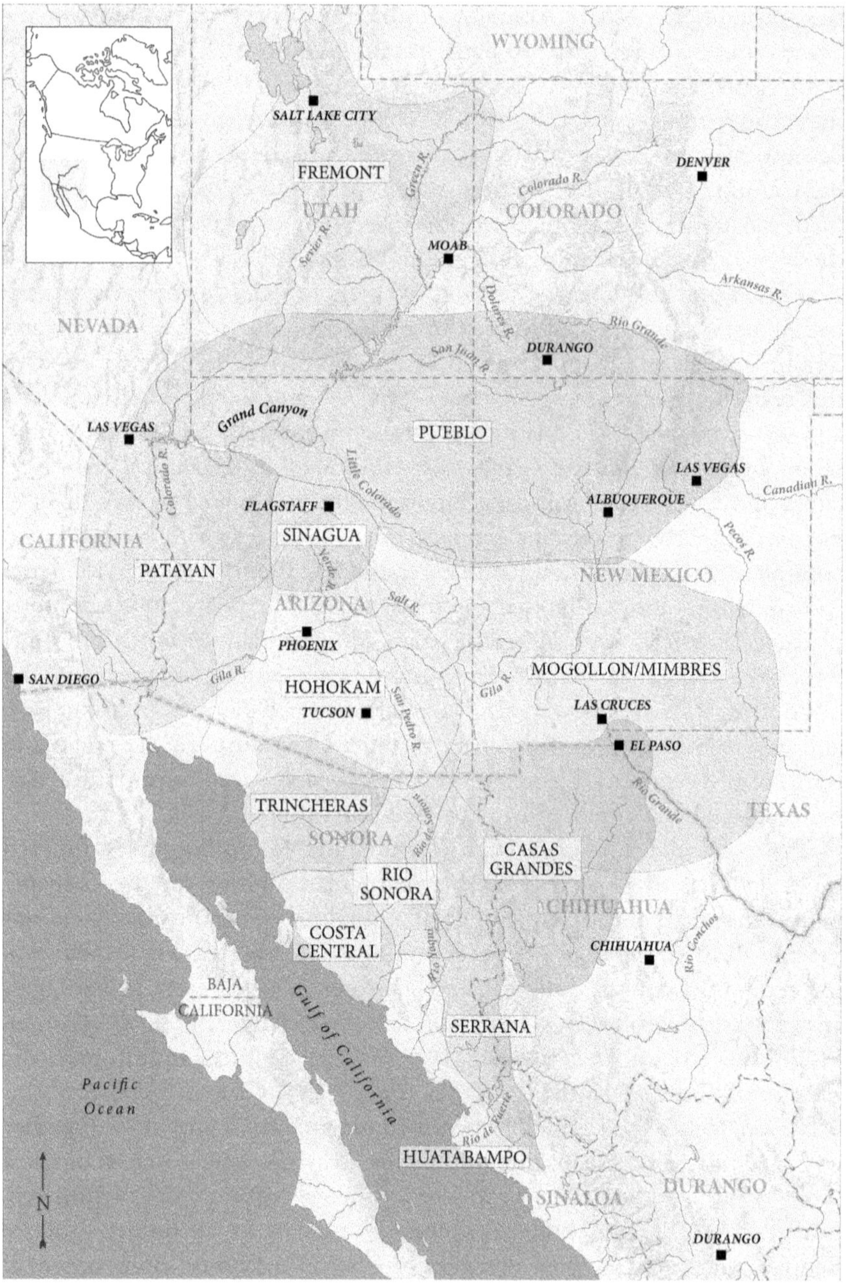

Figure 1.1. North American Southwest and the most important agricultural and semi-agricultural cultures and cultural traditions of the pre-Hispanic period. Compiled by Radosław Palonka and drawing by Michał Znamirowski.

The agricultural peoples developed complex water management to successfully grow crops in arid and semiarid lands. These systems were comprised of irrigation canal systems, canyon and mountain terraces, and dams. The Hohokam culture of the deserts of southern Arizona took artificial irrigation to its apogee, with its size and efficiency now compared to the irrigation and cultivation systems of ancient Peru and even the Middle East. The agricultural economy and some form of the "Neolithic Revolution" that also occurred in the Southwest (see chapter 3 of this book), facilitated a gradual demographic growth and the emergence of large settlements (figure 1.2a), sometimes—as in the case of the Pueblo, Mimbres/Mogollon, and Casas Grandes traditions—even proto-urban centers with the population of over a thousand or more in one such settlement. In the Pueblo, Mogollon, and Casas Grandes cultures and traditions, complex stone or adobe and multistory residential buildings were constructed, sometimes, as in the case of the Hohokam culture, built on high earth and stone platforms.

Before the arrival of Europeans, another common feature of agricultural communities was their know-how in the production of high-quality pottery, usually thoroughly fired and richly decorated with painting and other forms of decoration (sometimes polychrome ceramics). There was also manufacture of other elements of material culture, such as intricately made jewelry consisting primarily of turquoise and other stones, minerals, and shells. The technology of silver processing was adopted from the Spaniards and is practiced today, notably by Pueblo and Navajo peoples. Shells were often imported from distant areas, including from the Gulf of California and the Gulf of Mexico, evidence of long-distance trade.

Another important characteristic of most cultures within this region including hunter-gatherer communities was the creation of rock art—paintings (pictographs) and petroglyphs that were likely initiated in the Paleoindian period. Rock art was usually located in highly exposed places—on canyon walls, individual boulders or sometimes in caves or rock alcoves and shelters. In this way, entire rock art galleries (figure 1.2b) sprang up, often adjacent to, or overlapping, each other. These galleries were created over time by different cultures and tribes. This expansive artwork characterized the region to such an extent that in the 1970s, National Geographic called the Southwest the "Wild Louvre" because of the sheer wealth of rock art there. A significant part of this book is focused on rock art in various Native American societies in the pre-Hispanic Southwest.

Due to climatic and social changes, the late pre-Hispanic (protohistoric) and early-historic period, from the thirteenth to the fifteenth century AD, witnessed the restriction of areas occupied by agricultural communities, while hunter-gatherer communities quickly swept into the depopulated regions (e.g., Adler et al. 1996; Kohler et al. 2009; Nelson and Schachner 2002; Palonka 2011). These new inhabitants included Athapaskans (Apache and Navajo), who had migrated from the far north of the North American continent (from the area of today's Canada), as well as communities speaking Numic languages, such as Ute, Shoshone, and Comanche who arrived from the west—California and/or Nevada; the ninth (final) chapter of this book is devoted to these societies. Some agricultural cultures, such as the Hohokam and Mogollon, had been in decline before Spaniards came to the Southwest, while the Puebloan cultural tradition survived and is an example of cultural continuity from at least the beginning of the first millennium BC until today.

When considering the cultural transformations of the Southwestern communities, one should also recall the significant role played by the highly developed centers in the Mesoamerican area. At the beginning, these contacts were related to conveying the practice of agriculture from Mexico. Later the influence is visible in material culture such as copper bells, cacao cultivation, parrot feathers and live birds transported for their colorful feathers over great distances as well as in the architecture and layout of settlements, for example, in the form of characteristic groups of buildings around plazas and patios, as well as the presence of ballcourts, platform mounds, or sometimes characteristic colonnades in Pueblo architecture. Social and religious influences also can be observed, for example, in the changing iconography of pottery and rock art. It is worth pointing out that these influences ran in both directions. In all likelihood, most of the turquoise used to make objects, in the Aztec Empire was transported from the Southwest, while some Aztec beliefs pinpoint the place from where their ancestors came, perhaps somewhere in the Southwest.

Cultural relations between Mesoamerica and the Southwest in the late pre-Hispanic period were related to the well-functioning trade and exchange between the two areas, which was also one of the characteristic features of the pre-Hispanic world (e.g., Ericson and Baugh 1993; Lekson 1999, 2018; McGuire 1980; Nelson et al. 2017). This trade probably contributed to the development of individual settlement-cities as well as entire regions in the Southwest, including Ancestral Puebloan settlements in Chaco Canyon, New Mexico; the Mimbres culture of southern Arizona and New Mexico; the Hohokam culture of southern Arizona; and the Casas Grandes tradition from the northern states of Chihuahua and Sonora in today's Mexico. The most important trade routes ran from the world

Figure 1.2. Cliff Palace, the largest Ancestral Pueblo cliff dwelling located in Fewkes Canyon in the Mesa Verde National Park, southwestern Colorado (a) and (b) Newspaper Rock near today's Monticello in Utah, with petroglyphs from different periods (primarily historic Ute). Photos by Radosław Palonka.

of the Pueblo, Mimbres, and Hohokam cultures to northwest and central Mexico, and expanded in other directions toward California, Texas, Oklahoma, Kansas, and beyond.

Individual societies from the Southwest also traded with the peoples inhabiting other territories, such as hunter-gatherer groups from the southern Great Plains—from whom they obtained, among other items, bison meat, skins, and bones—as well as with communities living in coastal areas, from whom they procured decorative shells and other items. An extensive network of trade relations also extended to individual territories and provinces within the Southwest and included both sedentary and agricultural cultures as well as hunter-gatherers at vastly different stages of economic and social development.

These two worlds—farmers and hunter-gatherers—engaged in conflicts and devastating warfare as often as they traded with each other, as illustrated by highly suggestive ethnohistoric records (written sources from the first period of contact with, and presence of, Europeans in this area). Ethnohistoric sources are extremely important as they often relate to matters that are later described by professional ethnography, but they have an advantage because they depict Native American communities when they came into first contact with the Spaniards when they were yet to be transformed by the influences of European cultures.

Clash of Cultures and Conquest in the Southwest

In the sixteenth century, the Spaniards appeared in the Southwest, and from that moment the cultural face of this region was dramatically transformed forever. It should be noted however, that many indigenous communities in this part of North America survived this period of contact and conquest, and to this day maintain many of their traditions, beliefs, and identities. Native Americans of the Southwest had contact with the Spanish conquistadors and missionaries as early as in the 1530s and 1540s, although these relations were not constant during the sixteenth century and it seems that not all native societies of the area were involved to the same extent, at least in the beginning. Permanent settlement of the Spaniards in the Southwest was only recorded from 1598, when Juan de Oñate established one in the northern Rio Grande Valley region of what is now New Mexico.

During this first period, the Spaniards seem to have made the most frequent contact with various Pueblos living in the Rio Grande Valley, in western New Mexico and to some extent in northern Arizona. From the seventeenth century onward, Apache, Navajo, Utes, and other communities of the Southwest appear more frequently in written Spanish sources. The period of Spanish domination (New Spain, as a part of the Spanish Crown with its capital in Mexico City) lasted in the Southwest until 1821, and from then until 1846/48, when Mexico gained independence. After the revolution, it was controlled by Mexico. In 1848, after the war won by the United States against Mexico, the areas of today's states of Arizona, Utah, New Mexico, Colorado, California, Nevada, and Texas fell under the US rule, and this has been the status quo until today.

As mentioned above, large Spanish expeditions arrived in the Southwest in the first half of the sixteenth century (figures 1.3, 1.4). These quests were drawn by tales from the Spanish conquistador Álvar Núñez Cabeza de Vaca who had survived the shipwreck of a 1528 expedition led by Pánfilo de Narváez to explore the south and southeast of North America. Cabeza de Vaca brought with him to Mexico the legend of the mysterious seven golden cities of Cíbola and Quivira, which were thought to be wealthy native cities somewhere north of Mexico. His information fueled fantastic tales that were already circulating and encouraged Antonio de Mendoza, viceroy of New Spain, to organize further expeditions. An expedition led by the Franciscan Marcos de Niza in 1539 confirmed the revelations brought by Cabeza de Vaca, and yet another exploration led by Francisco Vásquez de Coronado followed in 1540–1542. These expeditions set out from the territory of central Mexico along the Sierra Madre Occidental and reached the territory of present-day New Mexico and Arizona and as far as Kansas in the case of the Coronado expedition. These explorers encountered various native settlements along the way, including the Hopi and Zuni pueblos, and possibly the Apacheans in the Great Plains (e.g., Flint and Flint 2005; Kessell 2002; Spicer 1962).

Inspired by Marcos de Niza's travels, the Coronado expedition had more lasting significance than that of de Vaca's due to the descriptions and chronicles recorded throughout as well as the influence it had on the native cultures of this region. In February 1540 Coronado set out north from the city of Compostela in Mexico. His journey may have followed trade routes that had existed during the pre-Hispanic period and that were still largely functioning after the arrival of the Spaniards (e.g., Flint 2005; Flint and Flint 2005).

These first expeditions gave the Spanish in Mexico numerous descriptions of newly "discovered" territories, including depictions of nature, rivers and mountain ranges, and other geographical features, as well as the first and quite extensive characterization of individual native societies of the Southwest. These accounts were made primarily by chroniclers accompanying the expeditions, generally missionaries or officers. Chroniclers Pedro Castañeda and Juan Jaramillo accompanied Coronado and created detailed records of many sites and native societies from the Grand Canyon to the Kansas plains. For the part of the Southwest within US borders, these descriptions referred to the agricultural Pueblo groups that lived

Figure 1.3. The painting showing the arrival of the Spanish conquistadors' expedition led by Coronado to Hawikuh Pueblo of Zuni and a meeting with Native Americans (a) and (b) part of Zuni Pueblo from the end of nineteenth century. Similar pueblos may have been encountered by Spanish conquistadors in the sixteenth century. Painting by William Hartmann (a) and (b) by Edward Curtis/Library of Congress Collection [# 90715428].

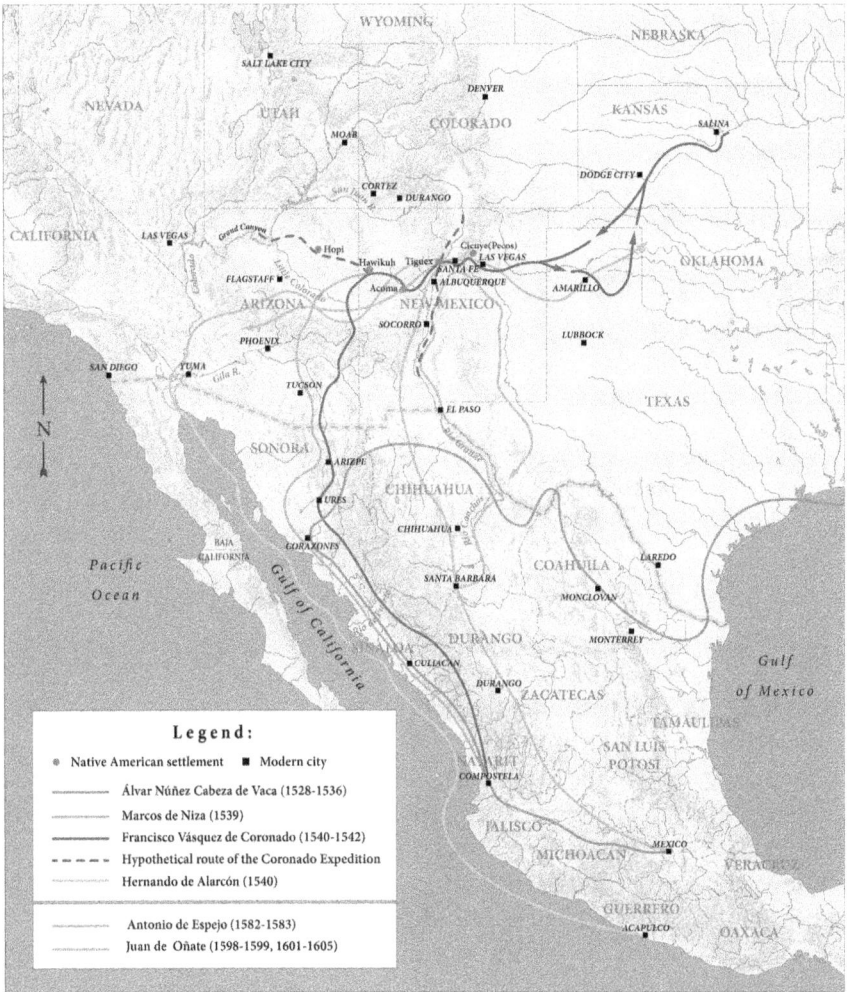

Figure 1.4.   Map showing the routes of Spanish expeditions to the Southwest in the first and second half of the sixteenth century. Compiled by Radosław Palonka on various sources and drawing by Michał Znamirowski.

along the Rio Grande Valley, and those to the west, such as Acoma, Zuni, and Hopi. The conquistadors also mentioned peoples with a different type of economy, hunters who, unlike the Pueblo people, did not live in permanent settlements; identified today as the Apache and Navajo, these communities were collectively referred to by the Spaniards as *Querechos*.

After the Coronado expedition, there were no other Spanish entradas to the Southwest for nearly forty years. It was only in the years 1581–1591 that three more rather small expeditions to the Southwest (e.g., Simmons 1979:178–79) set out, including three Franciscans headed by Father Agustín Rodríguez and a small army unit led by Francisco Sánchez Chamuscada that traveled along the Rio Grande River and reached some Pueblo groups in New Mexico in 1581. The following year (1582), another expedition set out under the leadership of Antonio de Espejo. The 1598 expedition led to the establishment of the first permanent Spanish settlement in the Southwest under the command of Juan de Oñate, sometimes known as the "last conquistador"; de Oñate was a Mexican aristocrat who married the granddaughter of Hernán Cortés. This settlement, San Juan de los Caballeros, was established near the community of Ohkay Owingeh (San Juan Pueblo) at the mouth of the Chama River, a major tributary to the Rio Grande in northern New Mexico. The de Oñate expedition numbered at least four hundred soldiers, colonists, missionaries, and Mexican natives (e.g., Simmons 1979:179). After establishing the settlement, de Oñate and his nephew Vincent de Zaldívare, organized six expeditions lasting until 1605 that explored areas from the Great Plains to the mouth of the Colorado River in the Gulf of California (albeit incorrectly describing California as an island).

Descriptions and written sources from this period act as a kind of "window" through which one might glimpse a fragment of native peoples' history at the moment of their first contact with Europeans. Subjected to appropriate criticism and research, these records are an invaluable source of information about Native American cultures and a foundation for analogies and comparisons to historical and modern native societies from the Southwest. Chronicles and other records from the period also tell a great deal about the reasons for different Spanish expeditions, establishing frameworks of relations and the beginning of the deep cultural, social, and demographic changes that affected the Native American communities of this region and have made a lasting impression on the cultural face of the Southwest region.

Early Scientific Exploration and Contemporary Research Challenges

Most of the Southwestern territory was discovered relatively late by Euro-Americans (as Spaniards only theoretically controlled some of the northern part of the Southwest). The same can also be said of Euro-American scientific knowledge and research of this region. The first American expeditions were primarily military quests, but these missions were often accompanied by scientists who described, drew, and photographed a world unknown to them. Cartographers and surveyors played an important role, creating maps of areas thus far scarcely known to Europeans. These American military and geographic expeditions were organized beginning in the 1850s, including those led by William H. Emory (1848) and J. H. Simpson (1850) (Cordell 1997; https://pubs. Usgs.gov/circ/c1050/surveys.htm). The desire to learn about deposits of natural resources and the geology of new areas was of primary importance, and officially became one of the reasons for the establishment in 1879 of the United States Geological Survey—an American scientific and research agency.

Soon after, the first scientific institutions began to appear in the Southwest. The University of Colorado at Denver (Colorado's first university) and Boulder were founded in 1884 and 1886, respectively. Meanwhile in 1883, the Arizona State Museum was established followed two years later by the University of Arizona in Tucson, the first university in Arizona. Through their anthropology and archaeological schools and departments, both universities began to set the bar for research in the Southwest, along with other research facilities in the East, such as Harvard University, Pennsylvania State University, and the Smithsonian Institution. Researchers working in the Southwest developed many elements of modern research methodology valid not only for this region, but used throughout American archaeology; here too lie the foundations of modern absolute dating methods (see chapter 2 for the dendrochronology example).

The Southwest was, and still is, a region that offers fascinating monuments of nature, as well as many places where one can actually touch the Native American past and where the descendants of pre-Contact cultures still live in the same place as their ancestors. Undoubtedly, all of this was and remains a kind of magnet attracting the first ethnographers and archaeologists, as well as amateurs of archaeology and tourists; this was in line with the growth of tourism in this region (a similar interest in adventure tourism arose in Europe at the same time). In the late nineteenth and early twenty centuries, many "archaeologists-ethnographers" in the Southwest laid the foundations for the modern archaeology of this area and developed standards, some of which remain valid until today (e.g., Cordell 1997:67–100; Lekson 2008). One of the most important figures in the late nineteenth century was Adolph Bandelier. Starting in 1880, Bandelier spent about twelve years alternating between archaeological excavations and ethnographic research in the Southwest. Others include Frank Hamilton Cushing, leader of the first official archaeological expedition to the Southwest, the so-called Hemenway Expedition (1886–1889), Byron

Cummings, Jesse W. Fewkes, Edgar L. Hewett, Walter H. Hough, Cosmo and Victor Mindeleff, James Stevenson, and the Finnish-Swedish scientist Gustaf Nordenskiöld. More than one hundred years ago, these pioneering researchers of Southwestern native cultures conducted excavations in summer and ethnographic studies of living Native American communities in autumn and winter.

In the first three decades of the twentieth century, a new generation of researchers emerged, including Nels Nelson, Alfred L. Kroeber, Franz Boas, Alfred V. Kidder, Emil Haury, Harold S. Gladwin, Harold S. Colton, and others who developed a chronological and cultural framework for the Southwest as well as the wide use of stratigraphy that remain largely in use today. After the invention of absolute dating methods, including dendrochronology or ^{14}C methods, the relative chronologies they proposed were updated and expanded, but they remain a yardstick to which most researchers still refer.

After World War II, the archaeology and anthropology of the Southwest, and the whole of North America, were subject to global currents and trends occurring in this field. Lewis R. Binford exerted a great influence on researchers investigating cultures of the Southwest; although he worked at several universities in the region, he himself never conducted any fieldwork in the area. Some of most important aspects that shaped modern anthropology and American archaeology in the reconstruction of pre-Hispanic and early historic Native American cultures from this region are summarized below.

Many modern archaeological research projects in the United States are carried out not only by academic institutions but also through so-called rescue or contract archaeology as it is often called in the United States. Rescue contractors explore areas related to road construction and development and dams and large water reservoirs that often flood entire valley systems, irretrievably destroying many archaeological sites. The beginning of large-scale contract projects dates back at least to the 1950s (e.g., Cordell 1997).

Since the 1970s, rescue research has fallen within the scope of so-called Cultural Resource Management (CRM), a broadly understood program of research and management of cultural heritage along with natural resources in the United States, including their protection and conservation; the term was first coined by archaeologists and National Park Service personnel (e.g., Fowler 1982; Lipe 1974). The inception of Cultural Resource Management (CRM) led to a spike in demand for archaeologists in government institutions, parks and national monuments, universities, as well as in the private sector.

Riding the wave of CRM's creation, new standards (mainly for academic archaeology) were also developed, including in the form of so-called Conservation Archaeology, which was largely the brainchild of William D. Lipe (e.g., Lipe 1974), one of the leading researchers of Southwestern archaeology. This trend assumes the least possible physical interference with a given site, which in practice comes down to test-pit and limited excavations or just field surveys. The strategy behind this sampling method is to save part of the site for the future when better and less-invasive research techniques emerge. Large-area and whole-site studies are still conducted, mostly in the domain of rescue archaeology and occasionally academic research. Today, one can clearly see the preference of surveys or noninvasive research over the traditional excavations and exploration of the entire sites.

Numerous contract archaeology and rescue research projects have been carried out in the Southwest and are still ongoing. Some well-known, long-term projects began in the 1970s and 1980s. In addition to collecting an extremely large amount of data, these initiatives strive to answer research questions and even set new trends in empirical and interpretative approaches. These projects include the Glen Canyon Project in northern Arizona; the Black Mesa Archaeological Project in northeastern Arizona, one of the longest-lasting and largest archaeological projects in the entire United States (1967–1983); Southern Arizona's Salt River Project; the Central Arizona Project; the Transwestern Pipeline Project; and the Dolores Archaeological Program (DAP) in southwestern Colorado connected with the construction of the McPhee Reservoir in the late 1970s–early 1980s (Cordell 1997:184–85); to mention just a few.

At the same time, academic archaeology has played a major role, periodically organizing "field schools"—that is, field internships for students—archaeology. Large numbers of volunteers and avocational archeologists also frequently participate in archaeological research, assisting the professional archaeologists both during field work and in subsequent laboratory analyses (see also https://www.saa.org/about-archaeology/archaeology-law-ethics).

Currently, the widespread use of modern technologies has yielded a tremendous influence on the development of modern archaeological and anthropological research on the history of Native American cultures in the United States. As in other disciplines, computers began to be used by the 1970s. Today, new equipment and software drive modern methods of data collection, analysis, and reconstruction accelerating the pace and precision of discovery. These new technologies allow for ultra-precise documentation of architecture (for individual walls and buildings, as well as entire sites), rock shelters, and elements of the surrounding landscape and rock art. Computer-based virtual reconstructions are also often used in contemporary exhibitions and the creation of interactive programs involving visualizations displayed on monitors and touch screens, which younger and older people can use to navigate and almost even touch the past.

The large-scale application of new technologies, such as photogrammetry and 3D laser scanning, has catalyzed enormous progress in terms of the speed and precision with which many sites are documented. Analysis of images from 3D scanning, photos taken from the air using unmanned aerial vehicles (drones), satellite and aerial images (which have been applied for quite some time) and airborne laser scanning known as LIDAR (Light Detection and Ranging) offer tremendous potential for discovery that could not have been imagined even twenty years ago. These methods are being applied in several important studies initiated in the Southwest including the reconstruction of ancient roads of the Pueblo culture associated with Chaco Canyon in New Mexico (e.g., Friedman et al. 2017), the analysis of settlement and demographic changes in settlements of Jemez (Walatowa) Pueblo (Liebmann et al. 2016), various GIS-based viewshed studies (e.g., Kantner and Hobgood 2016), and other studies involving digital archaeology methods (e.g., Palonka et al. 2021).

US Legislation and Heritage Protection in the Southwest

American legislation protects monuments of the past differently than the majority of European countries. Laws that protect archaeological and historical heritage in the United States generally apply only to state and government property, while most regulations (other than those regarding human remains and in other rare cases) do not apply to private property. State and federally owned lands are vast, and national parks and national monuments administered by federal and state sectors contain a large number of discovered and as yet unregistered archaeological sites, yet many such places are also located on private land.

The Antiquities Act was the first legislative act under which the federal government undertook the responsibility to care for archaeological monuments. Passed in 1906 with the establishment of the well-known Mesa Verde National Park in Colorado, the Antiquities Act has since protected many thousands of archaeological sites, including the spectacular Ancestral Pueblo cliff dwellings—see figure 1.2a). Even earlier, some groups of sites and places had been brought under legal protection. The involvement of local and influential residents or newcomers who often appreciated their value was of great significance; one such example is the Goodman Point Pueblo in the southwestern part of Colorado, a large site put under protection as early as 1889 and which later became part of the famous Hovenweep National Monument (Coffey and Kuckelman 2006).

After the Antiquities Act, the Historic Sites Act was adopted in 1935. It obligated the National Park Service (the United States federal agency managing national parks) to identify and protect the most historically important places. Today, the US Bureau of Land Management, another government institution apart from the National Park Service, plays a major role in the management of some legally protected areas (including national monuments), especially in the western part of the United States, and has numerous field offices and local museums that conduct research in the areas under their jurisdiction.

In the second half of the twentieth century, additional acts and regulations were passed, including the National Historic Preservation Act in 1966, with subsequent amendments resulting in, among other things, financial resources for the protection of many historic sites. The enactment of the National Environmental Policy Act in 1969 required the examination of areas under development, for example the construction of roads or water reservoirs, with the obligation to take into account the cultural, historical, and environmental value of such locations. This act allowed archaeologists to conduct rescue research in areas imminently subject to irreversible changes.

The 1970s brought additional changes and special funding from federal institutions, resulting in more consistent funding for much of the ongoing archeological and ethnographic research and ensuring better protection for archaeological sites on federal territory or Native American reservations that are at risk of destruction or development. The Archaeological and Historic Preservation Act of 1974 and the Archaeological Resources Protection Act of 1979 were passed, and the so-called National Register of Historic Places was established in 1966 further strengthening these protections. However, the

Native American Graves Protection and Repatriation Act, adopted in 1990 is the most important act dealing with the ownership of possessed artifacts and potential cooperation with Native Americans (see more below).

This federal legislation is further supplemented with regulations and statutes in each state, and even in individual large cities, reflecting both the specificity of the local archaeology as well as the presence or absence of living descendants of the cultures being archaeologically studied, along with other factors. As mentioned above, these laws rarely apply to privately owned lands, meaning that archaeological sites located beyond protected areas such as parks or nature reserves, and outside areas owned by the country or a particular state, are only minimally protected or even not at all. In addition, the collection of artifacts is very popular in the United States, fueling a fairly well-developed antiquities market. This has led to the destruction and looting of archaeological sites to obtain individual items, such as, for example, beautifully decorated ceramic vessels or stone blades that are highly valued by collectors.

Various operations run by the state, the scientific community and museum workers as well as private and nonprofit organizations are working to crack down on this trade. These actions include lobbying for changes in the law as well as additional legislative amendments. The last dozen or so years have also witnessed specific government financial incentive programs—usually by lowering taxes for land owners—in exchange for the protection and professional documentation of sites.

Established in the 1970s, the Mimbres Foundation supports private attempts to protect archaeological sites and antiquities. Founded by Steven LeBlanc, the foundation's mission was initially to prevent the plundering of Mimbres sites on the border of Arizona and New Mexico. In 1980, LeBlanc joined with Mark Michel to found the Archaeological Conservancy organization, which has so far protected over five hundred archaeological sites, mostly through donations or purchase of the property from private owners. These founders (as in the case of the Mimbres Foundation) set themselves the goal of raising funds to purchase particularly important archaeological sites from private hands when possible. The Conservancy's activities later spread to the rest of the United States and were followed by other organizations and associations. Archaeology Southwest, for example, raises major funding from private sponsors, government grants, and smaller contributors to preserve archaeological sites and to support an expansive educational mission emphasizing the need to protect and preserve archaeological and historical heritage.

Unfortunately, to this day, it is often the case that treasure hunters and looters plunder many places in search of Native American artifacts. In the Southwest, sites of the Mimbres culture have suffered most, followed possibly by those of the Pueblo culture. Sadly, the activities of illegal treasure hunters plague not only the Southwest, but also Central and South America.

Archaeologists and Native Americans—the Modern Face of American Archaeology

In the United States, archaeology is considered a subfield within cultural anthropology, itself at the nexus of the humanities and the social sciences, in juxtaposition to its position in many European universities where archaeology is treated more as a historical or natural science, although all of these sciences could form a field of research on human communities (e.g., Catacchio 1986:53–54; Palonka 2005). The academic teaching of archaeology at most American universities takes place primarily in anthropology departments; only a handful of universities include archaeology within departments of history or organized as stand-alone departments. To emphasize the importance of archaeology as an anthropological science, the phrase "American archaeology is anthropology or it is nothing" (Willey and Phillips 1958:2) was coined as early as the 1950s; not long after, Lewis R. Binford repeated and developed this thesis in his famous article "Archaeology as Anthropology" published in *American Antiquity* (Binford 1962:217).

This positioning of archaeology as an anthropological science is related to the fact that in many places in North America (especially in the Southwest), Native American cultures exhibit centuries if not millennia of cultural continuity. This is reflected in their continuous occupation of the same territories, the survival of many elements of material culture, the continuity of iconography found in ceramics and rock art, and in the numerous religious customs that reflect deep historical connections. From the beginning of scientific research in the Southwest, the Ancestral Pueblo

Figure 1.5.   Examples of field consultations conducted at an Ancestral Pueblo site with rock art in southwestern Colorado with representatives of the Hopi Cultural Preservation Office (HCPO). These consultations concerned the interpretation of the relations between the architecture, landscape, and rock art in terms of information from traditional tribal knowledge. Photos by Michał Znamirowski.

culture was of considerable interest because of this cultural continuity and the survival of many traditions, beliefs, and rituals, including dances and ceremonies. This was in stark comparison to the cultures and Native American tribes of the east of the continent, most of which had been displaced or annihilated. Initially archaeologists and ethnographers worked quite closely with the indigenous Southwest societies, observing their everyday life, and documenting it in paintings, sketches, and photos. They were also admitted to many religious ceremonies (e.g., Downer 1997:23–34).

However, what were initially relatively positive relations between the world of science and indigenous cultures deteriorated over time. In the second half of the twentieth century in particular, the relationship between various Native American groups and archaeologists eroded, largely due to concerns over the excavation of cemeteries and the analysis of native burials, as well as disputes over who has the right to interpret and write the history of individual Native American cultures: non-native scientists or those directly concerned—that is, the descendants themselves. Attitudes toward human remains as well as grave goods and sacred objects would become one of the main causes of conflict between the archaeological community and the Native world. Archaeologists have often disregarded the voice of local tribes, even if their connections with the archaeologically studied site or culture is documented. Disputes between the two groups began to arise and intensify, not only in the Southwest but among descendant communities in other countries, such as Maori in New Zealand and Aboriginal groups in Australia.

In the 1960s and 1970s, individual representatives of the world of Western science began to realize that the right to the history, or its interpretation, of peoples, tribes and cultures still living today cannot be appropriated, especially when faced with clear opposition of individual communities. Concerns over this kind of exploitation eventually resulted in the most far-reaching law regarding respect for the rights of Native Americans, the 1990 passage by Congress of the Native American Graves Protection and Repatriation Act (https://www.nps.gov/nagpra/), or NAGPRA. The law regulates disputes over the disturbance of human remains, thus research on cemeteries or individual graves is currently rarely carried out except in areas at risk of destruction. However, as with other statutes, the law applies to national and federal lands, and to private land only when human remains are found there.

NAGPRA also obligated federal institutions and government agencies to return, or repatriate, museum collections consisting of human remains and funerary objects of a sacred and cultural nature (although this was sometimes rather difficult to define completely). These repatriations are done after consultation with representatives of the Native American societies to determine whether the collections can be positively affiliated with a given tribe or nation. Even the largest museums and universities in the United States, such as the Smithsonian Institution, the University of Penn-

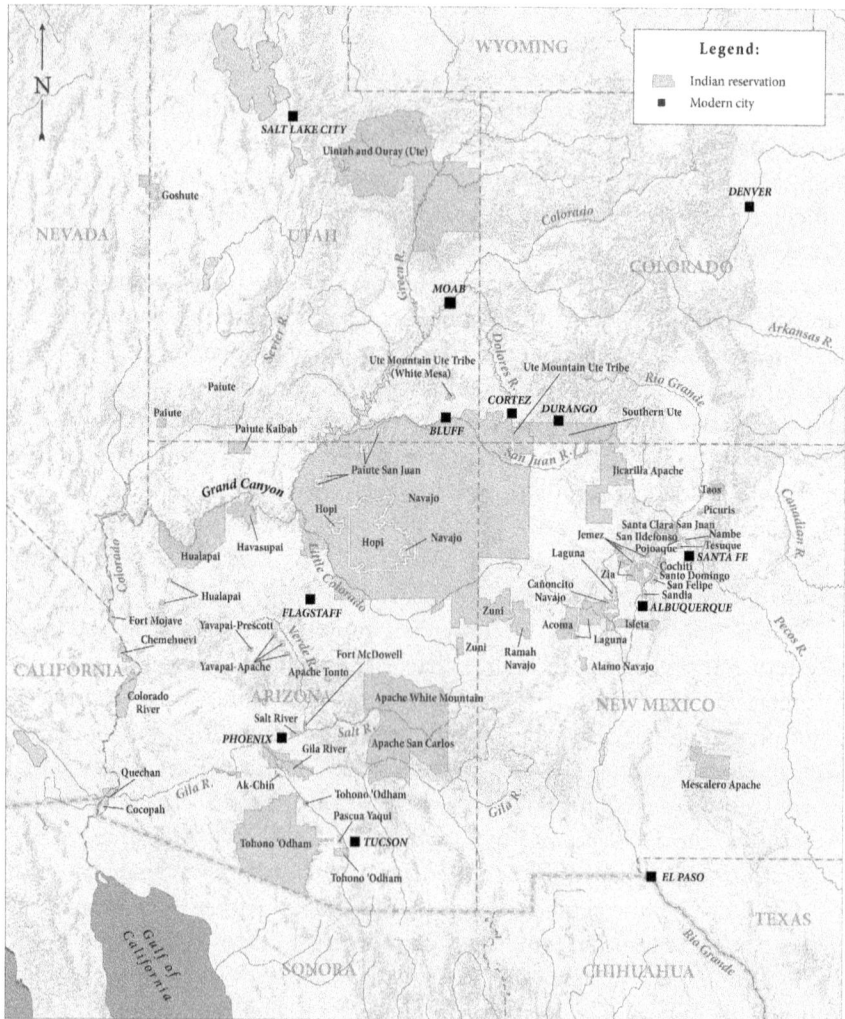

Figure 1.6.   A map showing the location of Native American reservations in the US Southwest, largely coinciding with the areas of native cultures, where they were found by Spanish conquistadors. Compiled by Radosław Palonka and drawing by Michał Znamirowski.

sylvania, and the Field Museum in Chicago, are not exempt from such returns. This process is often accompanied by reburials of human remains with special ceremonies.

The changes that have occurred over the past decades, including the shift in the attitudes of archaeologists, as well as the laws themselves, would not have achieved much if there had been no positive response in Native American communities.

Still, many controversial issues remain to be fully resolved. Many publications especially starting in the 1990s describe both the challenges that remain but also the enormous potential of mutual cooperation when taking account of the native point of view (e.g., Deloria 1997; Dongoske et al. 1997; Nabokov 1996; Swidler et al. 1997; Watkins 2014a, 2014b).

Today, collaboration between archaeologists and Native communities in the Southwest is routinely implemented in many research projects. The first such archaeological–Native American project is thought to have taken place in 1975 and was conducted with the Pueblo of Zuni. These collaborations often start with the initial design of the research project and continue through the subsequent interpretation of results and publications. These partnerships offer a great opportunity for a fuller understanding of the Native American past through the collaborative integration of information preserved in indigenous oral traditions, with their wealth of knowledge passed down from generation to generation (e.g., Mason 2000; Ortiz 1969; https://www.crowcanyon.org/).

The Geography, Climate, and Environment of the Southwest

GEOGRAPHICALLY, THE SOUTHWEST REGION extends from the central-southern parts of the states of Utah and Colorado, through the southeastern and eastern parts of Nevada and California, covering all of Arizona and New Mexico, and as far south as the adjacent areas of the north of Mexico (the northern parts of the states of Sonora and Chihuahua). To the east, the region extends to the extreme western side of Texas and the border of the southern Great Plains (figure 2.1).

Distinct regions differing in natural environment, climate, topography, and the diversity of historic cultural groups can be distinguished within the Southwest. Today, the center of the Southwest encompasses four American states: southern parts of Utah and Colorado along with Arizona and New Mexico which border them from the south. Taken together, they form the region popularly known as the Four Corners.[1] Recently, the term "International Four Corners" has also been used to denote the borders of Arizona and New Mexico on the American side and the states of Sonora and Chihuahua on the Mexican side. In the pre-Hispanic period, Four Corners was inhabited primarily by groups belonging to the Ancestral Pueblo and Fremont worlds, while during the Protohistoric period, the center of cultural development shifted south to the central and southern parts of Arizona and New Mexico. Here the highly organized communities of the Hohokam, Pueblo, and Mogollon/Mimbres cultures had developed earlier, in tandem with Casas Grandes/Paquimé cultural tradition in the northern parts of Mexican state of Chihuahua.

The American Southwest lies mostly in the dry climate zone along with varieties of climates and microclimates typical of upland and mountain areas. The climate of this region is generally very dry, although there is

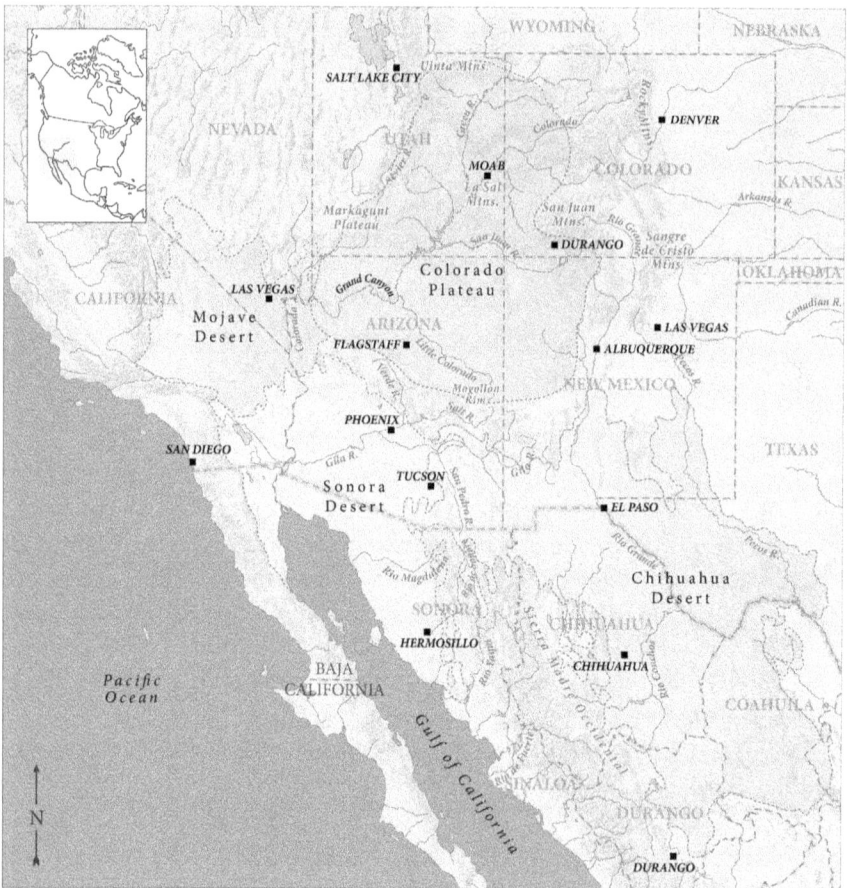

Figure 2.1. Map of the North American Southwest with the most notable physical and geographical provinces, rivers and mountain ranges marked. Compiled by Radosław Palonka and drawing by Michał Znamirowski.

more rain and humidity in the higher mountain ranges. Precipitation is not evenly distributed throughout the entire territory. The middle and eastern areas of the region receive more—an average rainfall of even 500 mm per year, whereas rainfall in the desert areas in the western and southern area of the Southwest is far less, and does not exceed 150–200 mm and can be even lower.

Two areas with distinct patterns of rainfall concentration, or "rainy seasons," can be distinguished in the Southwest (Cordell 1997). The western part of the region—Arizona, southern Utah and Nevada, southwestern Colorado, eastern California, and Mexican Sonora are characterized by the distinct rainy seasons—summer (July–August) and winter (December–March), reaching its peak in February. These rainy seasons are formed by air masses moving from the Gulf of Mexico in the summer and from the Gulf of California and the Pacific in the winter. In contrast, the eastern part of the Southwest, mainly New Mexico, most of south-central Colorado, western Texas, and most of Mexico's Chihuahua state, there is one rainy season during the summer months of June and July which is also related to air currents from the Gulf of Mexico. Summer rainy seasons in both western and eastern subregions are often marked by short-term, violent storms which periodically fill dry stream beds for brief periods and carry a high risk of damage to crops and present challenges for properly irrigating the soil for growing food crops. The frequent destruction of cars, bridges, and structures swept away by the resulting floods demonstrates the destructive power of these storms.

Central and North-Central Areas: The Colorado Plateau

Although, in popular imagination the Southwest conjures up desert landscapes crisscrossed by canyons, in reality it is not so homogeneous and includes four distinct physical and geographical provinces. The central and north-central part of the Southwest (including the Four Corners region) is located in the Colorado Plateau, a vast area encompassing 337,000 square kilometers that covers western Colorado, eastern and southern Utah, northern Arizona, and northwest New Mexico. Most of the Colorado Plateau is hemmed in by mountain ranges, including the Rocky Mountains and the San Juan Mountains of Colorado and New Mexico, the Uinta Mountains and the La Sal Mountains of Utah, and the Mogollon Rim Range in Arizona. Most of the Plateau lies higher than 1,520 meters above sea level (ASL) with some peaks rising over 3,500 meters above sea level, or higher. These high-altitude locations attract more rainfall than other parts of the Southwest.

Nearly 90 percent of the Colorado Plateau is located in the basin of the Colorado River and its tributaries, including the Green, San Juan, Little Colorado, and Gila rivers. The Colorado River, the region's largest, flows through the Grand Canyon. Characteristic landscape in this area consists of horizontally arranged sandstone formations that create small plateaus—*mesas* in Spanish— interspersed with many steep, plunging canyons (figure 2.2). Mesas often erode into even smaller forms, such as free-standing steep *buttes* or even needles and isolated pinnacles that remain from the aeolian

Figure 2.2.   Examples of different geological and land features on the Colorado Plateau: (a) mesas, buttes, and needles in Monument Valley on the Utah-Arizona border and (b) lower part of Sand Canyon, Colorado, view toward Sleeping Ute Mountain. Photos by Radosław Palonka and Michał Znamirowski.

and rain erosion of sandstone formations. In the past, the bedded sandstone provided an excellent and relatively easy-to-process building material for the people living in this region. Mountainous areas resulting from high volcanic activity were a source of obsidian, much desired by many pre-

Hispanic and historic Native American communities from the Southwest and Mexico (e.g., Dolan et al. 2017; Shackley 2005).

The Colorado Plateau is rich in other raw materials, including hard coal that was once mined to fire pottery in the pre-Hispanic period. More recently, coal, natural gas, oil, and uranium (particularly during the Cold War arms race) have become important sources of fuel. Changes in US policy regarding exploitation of these resources across the entire Southwest pose a serious threat to entire complexes of archaeological sites, even within legally protected national parks and national monuments including Bears Ears National Monument and Grand Staircase-Escalante National Monument, both in Utah, among others. These changes made by the Trump administration in 2017 have provoked numerous protests from the archaeological community, including members of the Society for American Archaeology—SAA—and other scientists and conservationists, many Native American tribes, as the areas affected by these plans lie within places that are sacred for Native Americans, where individual indigenous groups often still celebrate their traditional ceremonies. In early October 2021 newly elected president, Joe Biden, restored the boundaries of these two Monuments to protect and respect Native Americans rights and cultural heritage. This order additionally expanded protections for the Northeast Canyons and Seamounts National Monument (the marine national monument on the New England coast).[2]

The Colorado Plateau itself is diverse in terms of geological structure, landform, and environmental and climatic conditions. In many northern areas, the relatively high elevation and resulting increased rainfall, humidity and stable climate supported the formation of complex cultures. For example, the great Ancestral Pueblo culture settlements of a "proto-urban" character in Chaco Canyon lasted several centuries, as did this culture's later "boom" in the Mesa Verde region, located on the border of Utah and Colorado and in the adjacent parts of Arizona and New Mexico.

In addition to the physical and geographical features described, the southern border of the Colorado Plateau marks the southern end of the sagebrush growing area, one of the most common plants on this plateau. Further to the south, this vegetation is replaced by increasingly common species of cactus and prickly pears.

The Rocky Mountains

To the north and east, the Colorado Plateau is bordered by another sub-region of the Southwest, the southern province of the Rocky Mountains which encompasses the ranges of the San Juan Mountains and the Sangre de Cristo Mountains in southern Colorado and northern New Mexico. Rising to a height of about 4,300 meters above sea level, these ranges are rich in natural resources, as they abound in coniferous and deciduous forests which provided building materials in the past, ample game—mainly deer, elk, mountain sheep, and bears—and large deposits of mineral resources such as igneous rocks such as basalt and obsidian and various types of flints, galena, turquoise, and malachite, which were used by many Native American groups during the pre-Hispanic period and later to craft weapons and jewelry.

As the source of many rivers and tributaries, these mountains were, and still are, critically important for the entire Southwest in terms of water supplies and water management. They determined the existence and survival of many native groups and communities in the past as well as in the present day.

These rivers include the San Juan River, flowing into the Colorado River, and the Dolores River, also the famous Rio Grande, which flows into the Gulf of Mexico. Other major rivers, like the Colorado, flow into the Gulf of California. The path of the rivers is determined by the Continental Divide of North America which runs along an imaginary north-south line along the peaks of mountain ranges in the western part of the continent and divides the Pacific and the Atlantic basins.

Western and Southern Deserts Areas

The western and southern areas of the Southwest, which encompass the central and western parts of Arizona and New Mexico, are flat often semi-arid deserts and valleys surrounded by numerous jagged and relatively small mountain ranges essentially running along a north-south line, hence the English name for this area is the Basin and Range Province. The area in the north extends as far as the states of Idaho and Oregon (on its western side), while its eastern and southern ends are included in the Southwest. The characteristic mountain ranges of this Southwestern subregion include the Sierra Ancha or Sierra Madre Occidental in Mexico. Lower in elevation than the Rocky Mountains, or even the San Juan Mountains and therefore more accessible, these areas were often inhabited by various groups of people including during the pre-Hispanic period, and generally did not restrict or interfere with travel between different areas.

The climate of this area is largely determined by winds that sweep in from the Pacific side. Moisture carried by these winds is largely blocked and "collected" by mountain ranges in California such as the Sierra Nevada, forming a "rain shadow" to the east, making the area extremely dry. Some of the rivers flowing into this subregion end up in ephemeral and periodic lakes or even in the dry bottoms of former lakes, sometimes with large deposits of salt mined in the pre-Hispanic period. Such "dry" or seasonal lakes are referred to as *playas* in the Southwest, and most commonly *barriales* in Mexico. However, several large rivers flowing through this region (Colorado, Gila, Salt, Yaqui, and Conchos) and their tributaries have, in the past, facilitated the emergence of complex social and settlement structures in this area related to extensive systems of artificial irrigation and the construction of watering channels, for example, by the Hohokam societies of southern Arizona.

The Mojave and Sonora are the two largest deserts in this region. The Mojave Desert, which receives very little rainfall—in the range of 15 to 150 mm per year depending on the area—stretches from southern California and southern Nevada to southwestern Utah. The average altitude of this desert is about 610–1520 meters above sea level, but some of this area, for example Death Valley, lies in a depression with its lowest point at 86 meters below sea level. Another important desert, located on the border of central and southwestern Arizona, California, and northern Mexico is the Sonoran Desert (figure 2.3) measuring nearly 311,000 square kilometers with an average annual rainfall of less than 150–200 mm.

Eastern Area and the Great Plains

The westernmost area of the Great Plains lies in the fourth physical and geographical subregion within the Southwest, or more precisely in its eastern part. This was the least exploited and inhabited by the Native American societies culturally related to the Southwest, nevertheless it was important in the context of the eastern settlements of the Pueblo groups and Apachean societies, as well as for the trade relations between the Pueblo and Hohokam cultures and the tribes of the Great Plains. This region comprises the relatively high (1828–2133 m above sea level) Raton area in northeastern New Mexico with numerous plateaus, the Pecos River valley in the eastern part of the state, and the Llano Estacado territory (600–1524 m above sea level) on the northeastern border between New Mexico and northwestern Texas. The above-mentioned Pecos and the Cimarron River are the most important rivers running through this region. The ultra-dry climate coupled with suitable geological conditions resulted in the formation of large salt deposits, eagerly exploited by the

Figure 2.3.   Typical vegetation in the Colorado Plateau: (a) ponderosa pine in the Sleeping Ute Mountain range (approx. 2,800/3,000 m ASL) and (b) piñon pine, juniper, and yucca in the Mesa Verde National Park (approximately 2,000 m ASL); and (c) typical landscape in lower elevations in the Sonoran Desert including Saguaro cacti, near Tucson, Arizona. Photos by Radosław Palonka.

Ancestral Puebloans and other groups from the Southwest. Important trade commodities from the hunters of the Great Plains were bison meat, skins, and bones, as well as various kinds of stones and flints, including from the Edwards Plateau in Texas, while products of the agricultural settlements— corn and pottery—were transported to the Great Plains.

Such a climate imposes significant constraints on agriculture, which has always been concentrated near rivers or in higher altitudes where more humidity could be expected. Pueblo culture settlements extended to a maximum altitude of about 2,200–2,500 meters above sea level, which correlates with the upper limit of where maize can be grown. At 2,190–2,200 meters above sea level there are too few frost-free days; successful cultivation of maize requires at least 120 frost-free days per year for cultivation (Adams and Petersen 1999:26–28; Erdman et al. 1969:57). Above this limit, it is sometimes possible to grow maize, but it depends on the place, the microclimate, and the characteristics of the natural environment.

Flora and Fauna

The vegetation of the Southwest varies by subregion. The wood of many species—juniper, ponderosa pine, piñon pine—was used to construct houses. The seeds and nuts of these plants were harvested and eaten. Food and drink including alcoholic beverages were prepared from cactus flowers, leaves, and fruit, and many plants were also used in herbal medicine; juniper for example is still often used today. Yucca was used to make many everyday objects, such as baskets, containers, items of clothing, sandals,

Figure 2.4. Examples of artifacts made of yucca (a); (b) woven basket (besides yucca also from willow), southeastern Utah; (c) a three-color bag, most likely dated to 1000 BC–400 AD, southeastern Utah; (d) pair of sandals (the soles), Canyonlands National Park, Utah. Photos by Radosław Palonka (a) and Edge of the Cedar Mesa Museum.

ropes, and other items (figure 2.4). Wood was harvested for fuel and for making various types of equipment and utility items.

For the Pueblo, Apache, Navajo, O'odham, and Ute communities, among others, knowledge of the use of herbs and plants for making necessary things, as well as in medicine, rituals, etc., was intrinsic to ancient traditions, (e.g., Chapoose et al. 2012; Stoffle et al. 1999; Native American Ethnobotany Database: http://naeb.brit.org/).

In addition to their purely economic significance to the various indigenous communities of the Southwest, some of the fauna were instrumental in their beliefs, ceremonies, and rituals. Birds, notably parrots, turkeys, and eagles, as well as some cat species, such as mountain lions and bobcats, show up in paintings and petroglyphs—as do deer, mountain sheep (figure 2.5), and bison (in the Great Plains and in the northern and eastern parts of the Southwest), dating as far back as the Paleoindian and Archaic periods. They can also be found in images recorded by the later agricultural cultures of Pueblo, Mogollon, and Hohokam, and also by the Ute, Apache, and Navajo. These images might be related to so-called hunting magic, but that is likely not the only explanation for the images of animals appearing on the rocks. Sometimes they were depictions of clan symbols, as well as vitality and rebirth, such as in the case of the stylized bear's paw in the rock art of the Utes. The turkey (*Meleagris gallopavo*) was one of the most important birds for many Native American communities in North America, including the Southwest. Domesticated in Pueblo communities around the seventh century AD, the turkey often formed the basis of the meat diet for this culture (e.g., Driver 2002; Van West and Dean 2000).

Most domesticated crops depended solely on rainfall (so-called dry-land farming), the technique that was practiced widely in pre-Hispanic times in the Southwest. Such crops were widely cultivated in the Pueblo culture but were characterized by major unpredictability in terms of harvest. This necessitated the use of artificial irrigation which was developed during this time. Before the arrival of the Europeans, the Hohokam culture of southern and central Arizona created an impressive system of irrigation channels in the American Southwest—the largest artificial watering and irrigation system north of Peru—for farmland as well as terraces and dams. On a smaller scale, other ancient farming cultures devised canals and artificial reservoirs and a highly complex system of water supply to farmlands, and groups of residential buildings—a characteristic feature of the Casas Grandes cultural tradition in Chihuahua, northern Mexico (e.g., Cordell 1997; Doolittle 1992; Plog 1997). The remains of these structures have often survived in fairly good condition to this day, so much so that the

Figure 2.5. Mountain sheep (a) and (b) depictions of mountain sheep hunting in historic Ute rock art in Arches National Park, Utah. The presence of horses indicates the petroglyphs were made in the historic period. Photos by Radosław Palonka.

canals of the pre-Hispanic Hohokam culture were even incorporated into the modern water and sewage network in the city of Phoenix, Arizona at the beginning of the twentieth century.

Thanks to the preservative properties of such a dry and hot climate, many artifacts made of these plant-based materials—wooden structures and parts of buildings, baskets, and textiles—have been conserved in archaeological sites. This organic material would not have survived in such remarkable condition in other environments (besides wet). The preserved wooden beams were used mostly for the construction of houses and wood was used largely for roofing in the form of beams (*vigas*) and decking (*latillas*) or as roof supports in pithouses (figure 2.6a); they also allow for dendrochronological dating and thus the creation of precise chronologies of individual cultures and entire areas. (In the Southwest, this method works best for the Pueblo culture that thrived mainly in the Colorado Plateau.)

Dendrochronology, reading annual tree ring increments and comparing (overlapping) the calibrated scales of such increments in modern trees with historic trees from antiquity, can date the time of tree cutting within an accuracy of one year (and sometimes even a specific season of the year), and thus indicate the probable time when a given building was constructed. The Southwest has a very well-established chronology based on tree ring dates for at least the last two thousand years. The common building material in the Southwest was piñon pine, ponderosa pine, Douglas fir, for which appropriate scales and chronological curves were established a relatively long time ago, while other trees, such as the juniper, also commonly used in the construction of houses, had to "wait" for their chronology until just few decades ago (Thomas Windes, oral communication, 2016).

In addition, a lot of information may be obtained from the rings about the former climate, primarily regarding the quantity and intensity of rainfall or periods of drought (e.g., by analyzing the thickness of individual rings for a given year). Such data are extremely important for the reconstruction of and reasons for human migrations, such as for the Ancestral Pueblo culture and the Mesa Verde region on the border of Colorado and Utah (Dean and Van West 2002; Van West and Dean 2000; Varien et al. al. 2007). To reconstruct the Southwest's climate, the study of pollen profiles, geomorphology, and region-specific analysis of rodent and packrat nests, are of key significance since they convey a wealth of information from the past about the flora and the environment located relatively close to such nests. Packrat nests that were built hundreds or even thousands of years ago have survived to our times in the arid climate of the region. In order

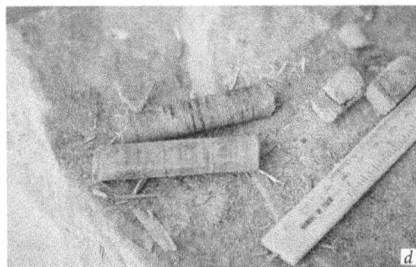

Figure 2.6. Examples of the methods of taking wood samples for dendrochronological dating: (a) involving cutting entire fragments of wooden beams at Pueblo Bonito (Chaco Canyon, New Mexico); (b) Thomas Windes and Radosław Palonka extracting cores from wooden beams at site 5MT1807 (Crescent House) in Colorado; (c) plugging the holes left after removing with visible numbers of samples; (d) cores extracted and later dated in the Laboratory of Tree-Ring Research at the University of Arizona. Photos by Radosław Palonka and Michał Znamirowski.

to correlate them with absolute chronology and calendar dates, individual layers in such nests are most often dated using radiocarbon methods.

Dendrochronology, on the other hand, is mainly used in the study of Pueblo, Fremont, and Mogollon cultures, where it enabled the development of ultra-precise chronologies for the functioning of individual settlements and entire settlement micro- and macro-regions. This method is less often applied in the chronology of the Hohokam culture, where researchers rely more on the radiocarbon, and sometimes also the archaeomagnetic, method. A pioneer in the development of the dendrochronology method in the Southwest in the 1920s and 1930s in the University of Arizona was the astronomer A. E. Douglass, and hence dendrochronology as a science spread globally. By 1930 Douglass had managed to compile dendrochronological dates for many settlements in the Mesa Verde region and Chaco Canyon. These were the first absolute calendar dates obtained for any prehistoric archaeological site in the world (Plog 1997:30–31).

Native Americans' oneness with the natural world—their intimate relationships with the weather, landscape, seasons, and natural resources shaped their cultures over centuries up to today. In the following chapters, we will explore in more detail how their economies, architecture, art, technology, religious rituals, and rich societies reflect their responses to, respect for, and knowledge of their environment.

Notes

1. This name arose because the boundaries of these four states intersect at right angles at one point. The Four Corners proper is located in the Navajo Nation Reservation and today features a viewing point for tourists to stand where the four states meet.

2. Another scene of these efforts for protecting the natural environment and native cultural heritage (things that are strictly connected together in many places in the Southwest and in North America generally) were the protests related to the construction of a pipeline (the so-called Dakota Access Pipeline) passing, among other heritage sites, the Sioux Standing Rock Preservation in South Dakota. The Sioux protested, in their opinion, the possibility of water pollution (including in the Missouri River) and the potential destruction of many sacred sites including cemeteries. In 2020, due to a court decision, the launch of the pipeline was suspended due to the threat to the environment and the need to investigate the matter. In July 2021 the Biden administration due to the several-years protest by various Native American communities (including Rosebud Sioux Tribe/Sicangu Lakota Oyate, Fort Belknap Indian Community/Assiniboine/Nakoda, and Gros Ventre/Aaniiih tribes), environmentalists, and landowners also canceled the Keystone XL pipeline project (designed for bringing oil from Canada's western tar sands to US refiners).

Mammoth and Bison Hunters   **3**
The Paleoindian and Archaic Periods

⊞

Migration to the New World and the First People in the Southwest

THE APPEARANCE OF THE FIRST HUMANS in the New World is one of the most difficult events to reconstruct in the history of North and South America, and it poses some of the most fascinating questions across modern scientific disciplines: anthropology, archaeology, genetics, linguistics, climatology, paleobotany, and others. When did the first people come to America? From where? Who were these First Americans, ancestors of contemporary Native Americans? What was their heritage and what cultural elements did they bring with them from their homelands to the New World? These are just a few questions that are being pursued. Answers to these questions and many theses offered by scientists often evoke strong emotions in the scientific and Native American communities.

Additionally, serious discrepancies in the interpretation of this initial period in the history of human cultures in the Americas, known as the Paleoindian period, occur in the research community, notably among American and European scholars who look at the settlement of America from slightly different perspectives. Two main theories regarding the chronology of when people appeared in the New World have emerged (e.g., Dillehay 2009; Fiedel 1992; Goebel et al. 2008; Kozłowski 1999, 2004). A major distinction between these two theories is the date of these first human arrivals. The "pre-Clovis" theory suggests that human arrivals began as early as forty thousand years ago, while the "Clovis-first" theory posits that humans did not appear in the New World until about thirteen thousand years ago.[1]

Evidence now suggests that the process of migration from Asia to America was not fueled by a desire to discover new lands but was motivated by a natural tendency to follow the migrating animals that people hunted. As glaciers advanced and retreated, these routes shifted but generally they led from northeastern Asia and Siberia (Chukotka) to Alaska and further south along the coasts or through the interior of the continent. The land bridge between Asia and America, which existed during the last Ice Age, is called Beringia (the present-day Bering Sea).

In its broadest sense, Beringia stretched from the Lena River Basin in Northeast Russia to the Mackenzie River in Canada. During the last glaciation of the Upper Pleistocene, Beringia emerged at least three times—at about seventy thousand, thirty-two thousand, and eighteen thousand years ago (sometimes slightly different dates are given: one hundred to ninety-four thousand, seventy-four to sixty-two thousand, and twenty-eight to eighteen or thirteen thousand years ago). During these times, people could cross the area connecting the two continents via dry land. The maximum extent of Beringia fell around twenty-one thousand years ago (e.g., Elias and Brigham-Grette 2007). Beringia, Chukotka, and the part of Alaska with the Yukon River basin are thought to have been ice-free at all times.

About 14,900–13,500 years ago, the road through Beringia divided into two possible routes: a north-south land corridor between two glaciers—the Cordilleran in the west and the Laurentian in the east (figure 3.1a) when the glaciers began to melt, and a second route along the coasts and shores of western North America (e.g., Goebel et al. 2008; Heintzman et al. 2016; Potter et al. 2017) running farther south, including to the Southwest and beyond. It is possible that some kind of land or ice connection between Asia and America existed throughout the entire Ice Age.

The latest research comprised of radiocarbon dating and DNA research on bison remains from this period (Heintzman et al. 2016) reveal that the corridor between the glaciers "widened" from the south, starting about 13,500 years ago (perhaps earlier, as previously noted), and so migrating animals moved south to north (and not from north to south as once assumed). However, it is likely that the entire corridor between the glaciers was ice-free around 13,000 years ago (which coincides with the emergence of the Clovis culture) and only then allowed the free movement of migratory animals and people along the route within the North American continent.

The appearance of Beringia was accompanied by a drop in the sea and ocean level by fifty meters at which point a narrow isthmus appeared. During the period of maximum glaciation the ocean/sea level was even

120 meters below today's sea level; at that time, a strip of land and ice nearly one thousand kilometers wide and a about five thousand kilometers long "surfaced." Even today, the distance between Alaska and Chukotka is quite short (only about eighty kilometers at its narrowest point dotted by several islands on the way). Although the Bering Sea is not the calmest, many cases in the historic period of the Inuits and Aleutians describe how they traversed this distance in leather and wooden boats, *kayaks* and *umiaks*, thus this waterway should also be given serious consideration for later waves of human migration. These successive migratory waves are also visible both in archaeological and genetic data (e.g., Reich 2018).

The third most frequently cited migration route is the southern route that may have led from Southeast Asia and across the Pacific Ocean to South America. This nautical route would have involved covering great distances between strips of Southeast Asia, Australia, and possibly New Zealand as well as the coasts of South or Central America, a distance of about eight to nine thousand kilometers to Chile or Ecuador as the crow flies. In between lie islands scattered across the vast ocean, including Polynesian islands such as Easter Island, and the Galapagos islands closer to South America. Although these islands did not make the journey shorter, they may have made them easier as travelers could stop along the way.

Linguistic similarities between some languages from Polynesia and the North Native Americans appear to support the hypothesis of a trans-Pacific route, but even if we accept this theory, it may have encompassed only part of the migration wave, and probably did not represent all cultures in America. Furthermore, such migration may have originated in America and may have occurred long after the first people appeared in the New World.

Recently some American researchers have posited an alternative to the Beringia routes: a possible northern route, which may have run from Europe along the border between Spain and France westward along the ice shelves of the ice-bound North Atlantic Ocean to northeastern North America. Researchers Bruce Bradley and Dennis Stanford (Bradley and Stanford 2004; Stanford and Bradley 2012), associate this route with the potential migration of some of the Solutrean societies and connect it with the later Clovis culture from America. Although rather intriguing and potentially feasible, this theory is quite often challenged by European and American researchers and experts on Magdalenian and Clovis cultures (e.g., Kozłowski 2004; Straus 2000). Opponents draw attention to the lack of convincing similarities between the typical Solutrean and Clovis blades as well as the chronological hiatus between the decline of the Solutrean in

Europe (about 18,000 years ago) and the emergence of the Clovis culture in America (13,200 years ago); there are however sites in North America with chronologies that overlap these dates.

The oldest sites associated with the "long chronology" of America's settlement lie far south of the Southwest region. These include Pedra Furada (Boqueirão da Pedra Furada) and Lapa Vermelha IV in Brazil dated to 35–40,000 years ago and linked with traditions of using choppers, pebble tools and sometimes simple flakes. In addition, slightly younger sites in South America feature the first projectile points. These include El-Jobo and Taima-Taima in Venezuela and the Pikimachay Cave in Peru, probably from the period around 16/15–12,000 years ago and Monte Verde in southern Chile, whose levels are dated to the periods between 33,000 and 12,000 years ago and rarely contested by supporters of "Clovis-first" theory. Other sites much older than those found in the United States and Canada located in Central America are dated to a time horizon of around 33–35,000 years ago. They include sites on Lake Tlapacoya, the El Cedral site and the Valsequillo valley in Mexico (the latter site is dated, like Pedra Furada, to about 30–40,000 years ago), or El Bosque in Nicaragua, dated to around 35–18,000 years ago. Again these sites are mainly associated with communities using choppers pebble tools, wood tools (in the case of the Tlapacoya site) and stone-making technologies previously characteristic of Europe and Asia.

The oldest known archaeological sites in North America include a very well-dated group of Bluefish Caves in Alaska and the Meadowcroft overhang in Pennsylvania, both dating back to around 16,000–18,500 years ago, along with Cactus Hill (Virginia) and Topper (South Carolina) sites (e.g., Dillehay 2009). These are "flagship" sites for supporters of so-called long chronology. This evidence is also supported by the similarity of their material culture in the form of an inventory of flint and stone products—for example, projectile points and flakes from the so-called flat retouching technique—to those items found in cultures from northeastern Siberia, mainly the Dyuktai, Nenana, and Mesa cultures (Bandi and Kozłowski 1981; Gómez-Coutouly and Holmes 2018; Kozłowski 1999, 2004:527–28; Sikora et al. 2019).

The flint-making techniques from these sites suggest another wave of migration, one that occurred later than the oldest sites mentioned above from South and Central America. These waves are thought to have arrived from Asia. Other potential pre-Clovis sites from the Southwest and surrounding areas include Debra in Texas (about 15,000 years ago) and Pendejo Cave in New Mexico with dates ranging between 17,000 and

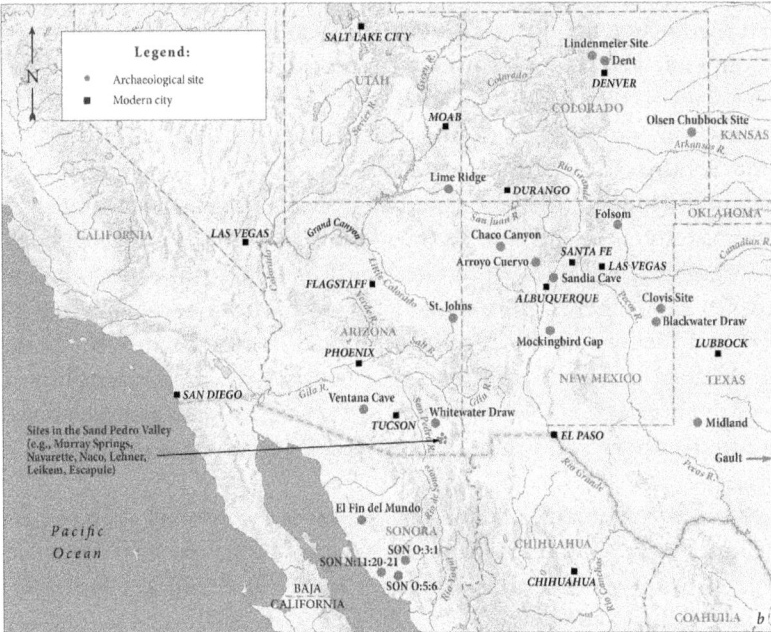

Figure 3.1. The earliest (pre-Clovis) sites from North and part of South America (a) and (b) selected sites from the Clovis and Folsom cultures in the North American Southwest mentioned in the book (after Cordell 1997:Fig. 3.1; Fiedel 2000:Fig. 1 and other sources). Compiled by Radosław Palonka and drawing by Michał Znamirowski.

12,000 years ago, but considerable doubts have also been raised as to the accuracy of their dating. Recent years have seen the discoveries of several more places that predate the classical Clovis culture by at least a thousand years; these include the thoroughly researched and dated Gault site in Texas, Manis in Washington, and the Paisley in Oregon (e.g., Haynes 2015; Heintzman et al. 2016; Williams et al. 2018).

The absence of earlier archaeological sites in the Southwest, and their scant quantity elsewhere in North America (north of Mexico and the Rio Grande River), has been explained by a variety of factors, but most likely this was due to the fact that for much of the Wisconsin glaciation, a vast tract of North America (from the central parts of Alaska to the area of the present-day Great Lakes and the US-Canadian border) languished under a thick layer of ice.[2] In addition, many sites that may have been on the Pacific coast are now underwater, because sea and ocean levels have risen increasingly since the last Ice Age, taking from a few to several kilometers of land. Underwater archaeology has yielded clear evidence at a certain distance from the modern coast line, where archaeologists have found numerous items from the Paleoindian period underwater. Although detailed reconnaissance in such an environment often presents many varied and unpredictable obstacles, it is a tremendously important direction for archaeology in the quest to uncover traces of the first Americans.

However, nowadays new and powerful evidence of human presence in the Southwest dated between 21,000 and 23,000 years ago was published in the journal *Science* (Bennett et al. 2021). In an analysis of fossilized footprints of people and animals (megafauna including mammoth, but also smaller animals as canids) at White Sands National Park in south-central New Mexico, investigators studied footprints from several stratigraphic layers and identified more than sixty human footprints mostly teenagers and children and less frequently those of large adults. Radiocarbon dating of ditch grass seeds (*Ruppia cirrhosa*, a species of the aquatic plant) that were found above and below the analyzed footprints was used to date the footprints.

Also, new, completely unknown, or once overlooked sources related to climate change and melting glaciers in Alaska and the Arctic have emerged. Some of these apply to the fringes of the Southwest—that is, the ice patches in Colorado's Rocky Mountains, as well as further north in Alaska. Research in these places has uncovered artifacts that literally "step out" of the ice after hundreds or thousands of years (similar to the famous finding of the Ötzi man in the Alps), due to, among other things, global warming. In the case of North America, these include artifacts from the

Clovis culture (e.g., Hare et al. 2012; Lee 2012; Robert Brunswig, oral communication, 2016). These finds bring some hope for new discoveries related to the appearance of the first people in America and for filling in the missing pieces of the jigsaw puzzle regarding human migration to the New World and the routes by which they later spread throughout both American continents. At the same time, the research raises alarms about the need for the protection and cataloging of these artifacts to prevent amateurs, treasure hunters, and tourists from getting their hands on them.

The Southwest in the Early Paleoindian Period

The climate and elements of the natural environment in the Southwest of the late Pleistocene are reconstructed in part on the basis of profiles of alluvial and other soils, lake sediments, (plant) pollen profiles, plant debris and other materials left by packrats (more on this in chapter 2), as well as permanent isotopes from bones and teeth and speleothems; archaeology also draws on the achievements of other sciences, including paleontology. As for the environmental and climatic conditions that prevailed in the Southwest at the end of the Pleistocene period, it is generally assumed that the entire region was cooler and wetter than it is today or has been in the last several thousand years. On the other hand, analyses of some lake sediments have revealed lower water levels than expected, and studies of micro- and macro-remnants of plants from packrats do not support the thesis of higher climate humidity but instead suggest a drier climate (e.g., Ballenger et al. 2017). There are also differences in the natural environment and certain ecological niches between the various regions within the Southwest. At the very end of the Pleistocene, an increase in precipitation in winter is also noticeable in the Southwest, with a simultaneous decrease in the amount of precipitation in the form of summer monsoons (Ballenger et al. 2017). In addition, the period between 12,900 and 11,600 years ago witnessed an even more severe cooling of the climate, confirmed by drillings from glaciers in Greenland, for example.

The Southwest marks an extremely important starting point for research on this culture and the appearance of the first people in America. This is the area where the first eponymous sites of Clovis and Folsom cultures were discovered in the 1920s and 1930s, such as Blackwater Draw near Clovis or Folsom, both in what is now New Mexico, and the Dent and Lindenmeier sites in Colorado. Here too the foundations for the archaeology of the Paleoindian period were laid. This research is largely conducted by units from Southwestern universities, including the University of Arizona in Tucson, Arizona State University in Phoenix-Tempe, the University of New Mexico in Albuquerque, and the recently created Center for the Study of the First Americans at Texas A&M University which is dedicated exclusively to this issue. The oldest traces left by people in the Southwest are the places where game was killed (*killing sites*) and quartered (*butchering sites*), and sporadic camps (figure 3.1b).

In a 2007 *Science* paper, Michael Waters and Thomas Stafford (Waters and Stafford 2007) reinterpreted the known ^{14}C radiocarbon dates and dates from new sites (including in the Southwest) and proposed a slightly younger and narrower dating of the Clovis culture to around 13,250–12,800 (calibrated dates) or 11,050–10,800 years ago (uncalibrated ^{14}C dates), suggesting an even shorter horizon of this culture's development (13,125–12,925 years ago). The Waters and Stafford dating of the Clovis culture has been widely debated and is now broadly accepted, but not all researchers agree with these findings, although the previous dating was not much different from that proposed by Waters and Stafford, ranging from around 13,450–12,800 years ago (11,500–10,900 uncalibrated) (e.g., Haynes 2008; Holliday 2000; Woodman and Athfield 2009). Projectile points and other products of the material culture of the Clovis can be found practically all over North America, free of ice at the time, and as far south as Central America (Mexico, Guatemala, Belize) and South America (there, a local variety of smaller blades called Fishtail blades).

The Clovis culture is part of the so-called Llano cultural horizon, shared by another—the Folsom culture, dated to 13/12–11 kya, although recently slightly more precise dates have positioned this culture at around 12,8–11,7 kya (e.g., Ballenger et al. 2017). Quite recently, new dates have emerged for the Folsom culture (after analyzing previous finds and taking into account the new radiocarbon dates) ranging from only about 12,6–12,2 kya (Surovell et al. 2016).

The stone inventory of both cultures is characterized by precisely crafted bifacial blades with an elongated shape and a slightly concave, thinner base, made with a technique called fluting (canelling) found only in the New World (figure 3.2). Clovis and Folsom hunters from the Paleoindian period tracked the great animals of the Ice Age, the Pleistocene megafauna including mammoths and mastodons in the Clovis culture and giant bison and caribou/reindeer in the Folsom.

People from these cultures hunted other species as well, depending on the availability of game in their territory. In the Pleistocene, about thirty-five species of megafauna lived in North America alone; practically all of them except the bison died out with the advent of the Holocene or even

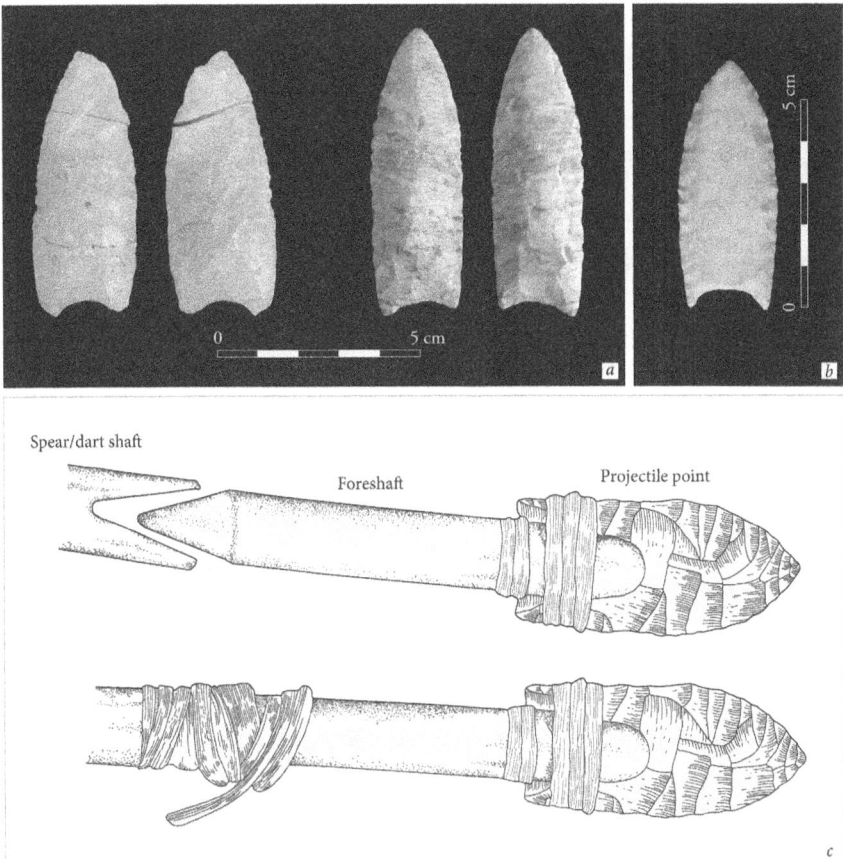

Figure 3.2.   Examples of Clovis blades from the Lime Ridge site in Utah (a, left) and Paleo-indian blade resembling Clovis points (a, right); (b) Folsom blade from unknown site in Utah-Colorado border; (d) technique how Clovis and Folsom blades were attached to a spear. Photos by Edge of the Cedar Mesa Museum and drawing by Przemysław Rosół.

immediately before this epoch of global warming. In South America, even more species—around fifty—became extinct. In addition to mammoths (*Mammuthus primigenius* and *Mammuthus columbi*), these now extinct species included mastodons (*Mammut americanum*), giant bison (*Bison antiquus*), horses (*Equus*), camelids (*Camelops*), tapirs (*Tapirus*), saber-toothed tigers (*Homotherium*), short-faced bears (*Arctodus*) and many others.

Scientists contest the nature and speed of this process (or one-off event) of megafauna extinction and whether it was caused by human activity (mass hunting) or more due to environmental and climatic changes. The theory that humans were completely responsible for the extinction of mammoths first emerged in the 1960s (Martin 1967) and was based partly on the assumption that Paleoindian hunters ate about 4.5–5 kilograms of meat per day and that they wasted a great deal of mammoth hunting food. Recently, however new data suggest that mainly weak or sick individuals were hunted because they could be easily isolated from the herd and killed (e.g., Kelly and Todd 1988); it is also somewhat difficult to imagine that the humans of that time would be responsible for "killing off" almost all species of Pleistocene megafauna, although of course it cannot be completely ruled out.

More and more data would appear to suggest that this extinction was fairly rapid after all (Haynes 2009). Furthermore, research on new sites and reinterpretation of older studies have yielded surprising results on the diet of the Clovis population, which at some sites has been demonstrated to have comprised a fairly large proportion of plants or meat of small animals, proving not only great diversity of their diet, but also that they may not have been solely dependent on the meat of hunted mammoths (e.g., Kelly and Todd 1988), as some researchers seem to still imply.

As for human activities that could have contributed to the mass extinction of the large animals of the Ice Age, there are two types of impact on the extinction of megafauna: the so-called *blitzkrieg*—that is, killing game via numerous hunts in a very short time, and *sitzkrieg*, which may have involved a slow yet systematic change in individual habitats and environmental niches, for example, by burning grass and the regular hunting associated with it (Haynes 2009:2). Researchers in recent years have also presented theories to explain the extinction of the Pleistocene megafauna by a cosmic catastrophe—the collision of an asteroid or comet, (e.g., Firestone et al. 2007). Although seriously considered by a large group of researchers, has not yet found unequivocal confirmation in the fossil evidence uncovered in the Southwest and beyond (e.g., Haynes et al. 2010). There are other theories as well, such as the potential introduction of germs and diseases by migrating hunters from Asia and their hunting companions, dogs (e.g., Fiedel 2000:61; 2005).

It was once thought that most of the sites from the Paleoindian period particularly the Clovis and Folsom cultures were found in the Southwest because this where the first sites related to these cultures were discovered, but now it is clearly observable that more such sites exist in the east of North America. In the Southwest, the Clovis and Folsom sites are concentrated in the southern part of the region (Arizona and New Mexico), although the first site to be discovered with Clovis and Folsom blades is Dent in Colorado (e.g., Brunswig 2007). There is also a fairly uneven distribution and density of Paleoindian sites in individual subregions of the Southwest, which are visibly sparser in the western part of the region.

There are many indications that the largest concentrations of sites from the early Paleoindian period in subregions of the Southwest do not always coincide with a similar intensity of usage by human groups in late Paleoindian cultures. Such a concentration of sites related to the Clovis and Folsom cultures is found in central and southern New Mexico, especially in the areas west of the Pecos River valley. Another such concentration occurs in the San Pedro River Valley in southern Arizona. Blades from the Paleoindian period, but without the characteristic fluting (often later than Clovis/Folsom) are, in turn, much more characteristic of the southern part of the Colorado Plateau and central and southern New Mexico, including the Rio Grande valley. The Southwest, as indicated in the previous chapters, is not and has never been homogeneous in terms of the natural environment, individual zones, and ecological niches, although the intensity of variety has also changed over time. Undoubtedly, environmental changes over time translated into the use of the natural environment to a different extent and scope by nomadic groups of hunter-gatherers from the Paleoindian period.

The presence of hunter-gatherer communities from the Paleoindian period was probably most closely related to various environmental niches. Finding evidence of these communities is largely influenced by the degree of current population density as well as agricultural and urban transformations (Prasciunas 2011:107). Our knowledge of the settlement picture, land use and potential Paleoindian population demographics also depends to a large extent on the intensity of research in particular areas and the number of publications. For example, it is clear that in the Mesa Verde region of southwest Colorado there are many more Paleoindian (especially late) sites than previously thought (e.g., Lipe and Pitblado 1999; Pitblado 1993, 1999). This corresponds to information contained in unpublished reports and single finds (Michael V. MacMillan oral information, 2016 and oral communication with other local people).

One of the most intriguing features of the Paleoindian cultures in the Southwest and adjoining areas is their initial presence at quite high altitudes, around 2,000 meters ASL, or even much higher. For instance, cultures in the Rocky Mountain range in Colorado are documented to have existed at altitudes of over 3,000–3,400 meters ASL, often in the high-altitude zone of yellow pine and certain species of evergreen oaks, as well as pine trees or junipers, and in the alpine tundra zone (Brunswig 2003, 2007:265–296; Pitblado 2003). Some high-altitude places, not only those in high-mountain areas, seem to have been chosen for their field exposure, because they ensured good visibility of the area—often 360-degree panoramic views—which undoubtedly helped in observing the movement of and hunting of game (e.g., Davis and Till 2014). Another characteristic feature of the Southwest, and also visible in other parts of North America, are the fairly well-documented trips of Clovis culture hunters over long distances—up to several hundred kilometers—in search of suitable raw materials such as flint and obsidian, to make blades and other tools.

The largest animals hunted by Clovis hunters were mammoths (figure 3.3) and mastodons. The mastodons were slightly smaller than the mammoths (about three meters tall, similar to Asian elephants, compared to mammoths that stood just over four meters). Mastodons had shorter and straighter tusks as compared to the strongly curved mammoth tusks, longer, flatter heads without the characteristic mammoth hump, and relatively small ears. Dental records show another major difference: the molars in

Figure 3.3.   Artistic reconstruction of a mammoth hunt in a natural trap (a swamp) by Paleo-indian hunters using spear thrower (*atl-atl*). Painting by Karina Znamirowska.

mastodons are "crown" sharpened, usually with several sharp ends in one tooth, adapted to eating small trees and grasses, not just grasses as in the case of mammoths or modern elephants, whereas the mammoths' molars are flat. These adaptations reflect their habitat and diet. The mammoths lived mainly in the steppe and grasslands areas while mastodons occurred more in the steppe/forests (more to the east of North America). The third important species of proboscidean in the New World was much smaller (up to about two meters at the withers) and widespread mainly in Central and South America, the so-called gomphothere (*Cuvieronius sp.*).

CLOVIS AND FOLSOM SITES IN THE SAN PEDRO VALLEY AND SONORA STATE The San Pedro River Valley in southern Arizona is characterized by a very high concentration of sites related to the earliest human cultures in the Southwest, especially in terms of mammoth remains and the places where they were hunted (e.g., Ballenger et al. 2017); this relatively well-studied area appears to be one of the largest concentrations of these animal remains in the world. Sites along the San Pedro River are located along thirty-five kilometers of this valley and its southern tributary, the Greenbush Draw River. Research and simulations for this area have shown that a population of 200–2,500 individuals could have existed there at any one time, depending on the environmental and climatic conditions (Ballenger 2010). Research and analysis of the sites in this region show that the occurrence of mammoths was limited mainly to the grasslands. Sites featuring hunted mammoths from the Clovis period tend to be in clusters, and were not, as was once believed, single units isolated from each other at considerable distances (Ballenger et al. 2017 after Haynes 2002). Interestingly, relatively large aggregation of sites related to the Clovis and Folsom cultures does not translate into the presence of other cultures and complexes from the late Paleoindian period, although the environmental conditions probably did not differ greatly in these two periods.

The Lehner Mammoth-Kill Site in the San Pedro River valley, the first well-dated Clovis site, contains well-documented mammoth hunting and killing areas and includes the largest accumulation of mammoth bones in the entire valley. At least thirteen specimens have been found here including a young mammoth in a roasting pit with two Clovis blades stuck in its ribs (Ballenger et al. 2017). The site has also yielded eleven other Clovis fluted blades, tools for butchering animal carcasses, a significant number of flakes, and traces of at least two hearths from which charcoals have been collected for dating. In addition to mammoths, the bones of a horse, tapir, several bison, a camel, a black bear, a turtle, several rabbits, and a bird were also found there. It was once thought that the accumulation of mammoth bones occurred over time as the result of at least a few hunts, but it is now more often believed to have been the result of a single hunt.

Another important place related to the Clovis and Folsom cultures of this area is the Murray Springs site. Located near the San Pedro River, Murray Springs (Haynes and Huckell 2007)—contains the remains of a camp as well as mammoth and bison hunting areas, which have in turn enabled the reconstruction of how hunting was conducted (see for example figure 3.3). The Murray Springs site is also very well recognized in terms of the stratigraphy and geology of the surrounding area. This is notable because, although in the case of the Clovis culture hundreds or even thousands of sites are mostly surface finds, while well-documented stratigraphy for camps, killing or butchering sites are rare. Very large accumulations of Pleistocene megafauna bones, mainly mammoths, have been found in several locations at this site. Also, places where flints and other rocks were processed, numerous Clovis blades, thousands of flakes, as well as processed bones and mammoth tracks and footprints have been discovered under the Younger-Dryas black mat layer—in other words, we can date this find to before approximately 12,700–12,800 years ago.

One of the most interesting relics from the Murray Springs site is a Clovis blade with a broken tip found at the killing area, while the tip was later located and collected about 130 meters away in the site's camp area. A tool made of mammoth bone with a hole at one end was also found there and has been interpreted as an object for straightening spears or as an *atl-atl* spear thrower (see below for a description of the thrower). Similar finds of spear throwers are recorded from the Old World and the European Paleolithic period, and are called *bâton de commandement* (e.g., Cordell 1997:Figure 3.6).

Sites with the remains of mammoths and Clovis blades (especially undamaged ones) are interpreted as places where these animals fell, but these blades were not found by the hunters, as there are no signs of human interference on the bones and no tools for butchering the animal carcasses (although after cutting and separating the meat from the skin, there were not always clear traces on the bones, as evidenced by ethnoarchaeological data) (e.g., Cordell 1997 after Frison 1988). Undamaged Clovis blades further support the theory the hunters had not found their prey, otherwise they would have undoubtedly removed their valuable tools. An example of such a site is the Escapule site, located near the Murray Springs site, on the banks of the Horsethief Draw, a tributary of the San Pedro River. Landowner Louis Escapule found mammoth bones here with two Clovis blades embedded in the ribs (Hemmings and Haynes 1969). No traces of butchering or other activities were subsequently found on the bones, indicating that the hunters had failed to find the animal when it died or the animal had survived the hunters' attack.

Three important sites in the San Pedro Valley related to human activity in the Early Paleoindian period are located near each other— the Naco (Naco Mammoth Kill Site), the Leikem and the Navarrete sites. At Naco, at least five distinctive Clovis blades were found between the remains of mammoths. In Leikem, located slightly north of Naco, researchers have revealed the remains of two mammoths (one with a Clovis blade), while the Navarrete site, just fifty meters from Naco, featured the remains of two more mammoths with a Clovis blade and possibly a bone tool (Ballenger et al. 2017).

Located in the present-day Tohono O'odham Reservation in the Sonoran Desert in southern Arizona is Ventana Cave, a famous site excavated in the 1940s by Emil W. Haury and Julian Hayden. In this multiphase site, the oldest layers were dated by radiocarbon methods to about 12,700–12,300 years ago. More certain traces of settlement from the Late Paleoindian and Archaic periods between 10,700 and 9,700 years ago (Cordell 1997; Huckell and Haynes 2003). Ventana Cave has provided significant data on hunting methods and techniques used by the Paleoindian and Early Archaic communities. Petroglyphs and rock paintings from later periods were left by various groups. Today the Ventana Cave site is under legal protection and has been entered into the National Register of Historic Places as a National Historic Landmark.

Another region that has piqued the interest of Paleoindian researchers in the past few decades is the southern Arizona and northern Sonora, Mexico (e.g., Ballenger et al. 2017; Sánchez and Carpenter 2012). In northern Mexican Sonora, only Clovis blades are found in the early Paleoindian period, suggesting that hunters associated with the Folsom culture did not venture further than the Sierra Madre Occidental mountain range, which probably constituted a barrier to the southwestern end of the Folsom culture in this part of the Southwest. Nor are Folsom blades recorded in the north of Chihuahua state, and there are very few (compared to Clovis blades) in southern Arizona either. Interestingly, the Clovis people in Sonora used only local materials to make blades, unlike other areas of North America.

So far, at least thirty or more surface and other Clovis culture sites have been discovered in Sonora in Mexico, with a large number located near watercourses at the foot of the western parts of the Sierra Madre

Occidental near present-day Hermosillo. Well-known sites include El Bajío, where nineteen Clovis blades and unfinished products were discovered along with traces of basalt and other raw mining material which resemble outcrops and mining sites from the Paleoindian period in eastern North America, as well as the SON O:3:1 site (the latter, together with El Bajío, covered a vast area of almost three-square kilometers each) and the SON N:11:20–21 site. It would appear that a large number of blades from this region were collected by amateurs and treasure hunters among the local residents without the knowledge of scientists.

One of the best researched sites in Sonora is El Fin del Mundo (Ballenger et al. 2017 after Sánchez et al. 2014), located at an altitude of 650 meters ASL in a mountain valley. Many Clovis products have been found there, including blades made of high-quality siliceous rocks as well as quartzite and rhyolite. El Fin del Mundo is a very important site in terms of chronology, as the dates obtained from it tend to fall around 13,500 years ago, which at this point is probably the oldest date related to the North American Clovis culture (similar dates were also obtained from Aubrey Clovis site and Gault site, both in Texas) (Ballenger et al. 2017; Sánchez and Holliday 2016); these data suggest the need to verify earlier dating and to move back the appearance of the Clovis culture some centuries earlier. The study of the El Fin del Mundo site has also revealed the remains of what are likely two different species of proboscidean, the aforementioned gomphothere (Sánchez et al. 2014)—a species more characteristic of the Central and South American regions whose presence this far north is a surprise.

CLOVIS-FOLSOM HORIZON IN THE CENTRAL AND NORTHERN SOUTHWEST AND ITS SURROUNDINGS Located in central Texas on the Edwards Plateau, the Gault site is one of the oldest sites linked to the Clovis culture. Some extremely well-documented tools and archaeological strata, from at least 2,500 years or more before the appearance of the Clovis culture, were discovered here; in an article published in *Science Advances* (Williams et al. 2018) the authors suggest, on the basis of luminescence dating/OSL, that the first humans may have appeared in Gault even as far back as 16,000 years ago (between 20,000 and 16,000 years ago, with a large number of samples dating in the range of 18,500 ± 1,500 years ago). Based on the analysis of stone finds, it can be concluded that the lithic (flake) technology, including the probable presence of microliths, was completely different than that of Clovis. This evidence may indicate that the Clovis blades evolved technologically from this tradition as well as that found at other sites from this time horizon including Monte Verde in

Chile, or that the Clovis population did in fact represent another wave of migration to the New World. These data provide another strong argument for the theory that the Clovis culture was not the first in the New World and that it spread more from the south of the present-day United States (based on absolute dates obtained and potential traces of following animals migrating from south to north, e.g., bison) (e.g., Sánchez and Holliday 2016), and not from the north as previously thought.

Dent and Lindenmeier are two flagship sites from the Early Paleoindian period in Colorado. Like many other Paleoindian sites, Lindenmeier (Wilmsen and Roberts 1978), was discovered in the 1930s in northern Colorado (north of Denver and near Fort Collins) on the outskirts of the Southwest and near the Rocky Mountain range. Some of the most abundant and best documented traces of hunting strategies primarily of the Folsom culture have been found here, including bison bones with arrowheads embedded in them as well as later traces of settlement from the Archaic period. In addition to bison, the remains of the hunted animals at this site also include rabbits, deer, antelopes, and wolves.

Located at the edge of the valley by a stream, the Lindenmeier site is relatively well preserved under a layer of more than three meters of later sediments. Discoveries related to the daily life of Folsom hunters include evidence of making and repairing flint tools, preparing food, and dressing leather. Abundant evidence suggests that many generations of Folsom visited the place periodically, possibly annually. Research at Lindenmeier has been ongoing since its discovery in 1924 (by the Coffin family) by the Smithsonian Institution and the Denver Museum of Nature & Science (formerly the Colorado Museum of Natural History in Denver). Since 2006, Jason LaBelle of Colorado State University in Fort Collins has been documenting and searching for new sites next to Lindenmeier, working to create a more detailed reconstruction of the settlement and presence of Paleoindian human groups in this region and in the wider context of the frontier of present-day Colorado and Wyoming (e.g., Deeringer 2012). Within a few years, LaBelle's team has managed to register nearly 300 new sites in the immediate vicinity of Lindenmeier alone, which will certainly herald a revision of the views held so far, including those on the density of this type of site and how the area was exploited by Paleoindian societies.

Bison seem to have been the most important prey for Folsom hunters, but they also hunted caribou, deer, mountain sheep and other smaller animals (Cordell 1997:96). Natural traps such as steep sand dunes were used to hunt bison. The animals were herded here, or into narrow ravines or around lakes and ponds, from where it would be difficult for them to escape. The rock cliff traps from which herded animals jumped seem to have been used less often. Though popular, the cliff trap theory can be contradicted by information from historic and contemporary observations of bison behavior, which would indicate that such traps are avoided by these (contrary to appearances) rather agile animals who would be able to execute an about-turn before reaching the abyss.

The effectiveness of such hunting probably also depended on the number of herds (e.g., Cordell 1997:94–96; Kelly and Todd 1988). Often the number of hunted specimens did not exceed twenty or so in a single hunt, although there are sites with more hunted bison, such as the Casper site in Wyoming, located near the Southwest, with the remains of seventy-four bison, which were herded onto sand dunes. Similar examples from the Southwest and its outskirts, such as the Jones-Miller site in Colorado show evidence of bison being herded into snowdrift traps and the remains of about 150 such animals, as well as the Olsen-Chubbuck site, also in Colorado, with traces of at least 143 hunted animals and possibly up to 191 individuals in one hunt in a shallow lake; there are also similar sites in Texas: Lipscomb (55 hunted animals) and Plainview with over 100 hunted bison.

Such large hunts appear to have been of a communal nature, bringing together many, probably dispersed, communities. These hunts could have been organized at certain times of the year, most commonly summer, but there is also evidence of hunting in winter. Whether such large collective hunts were held annually or at longer intervals remains unresolved. Some researchers have also suggested that for such large-scale hunts, large numbers of blades and spear points were specially produced, perhaps by specialized manufacturers producing "standardized" blades (Cordell 1997:95 after Bamforth 1991).

On the border of present-day New Mexico and Colorado and in the central-southern part of Colorado, the San Luis Valley seems to have been an area of extremely intense exploitation by hunter-gatherer groups from the Paleoindian period, including from the time when the Folsom culture thrived (these are mainly bison hunting places along with the accompanying butchering sites and base camps) as well as the later period up to the beginning of the Archaic period; here we can include some sites such as Linger, Zapata, and Stewart's Cattle Guard.

The Rio Grande basin, particularly its upper and middle region in New Mexico and north of El Paso, Texas, is one of the densest areas of Paleoindian sites in the Southwest, thus reflecting its intensive use during this period. There are many references to the Great Plains in terms of the inventory of artifacts that include similarities in their manufacturing process, hunting techniques, and the species of animals that were hunted, bison being the most prevalent here, even in the case of some Clovis sites. There are also more sites related to the Folsom culture and later Paleoindian/early Archaic cultures over the Clovis sites.

A particularly large number of sites from the Southwest—more than sixty—are located around the present-day city of Albuquerque in north-central New Mexico; nearly half of these are related to the Folsom culture. The remainder primarily involve complexes and cultures from the late Paleoindian period featuring blades without fluting (Ballenger et al. 2017); often these individual phases are stratigraphically separated and, fortunately, not always mixed. These sites are usually short-lived, ephemeral camps and bison-hunting places with stone raw materials identified more with the areas west of the Rio Grande valley than with the Great Plains. The Boca Negra Wash is one of the flagship sites in this area, associated with the Folsom hunters (e.g., Holliday et al. 2006). On the other hand, one of the largest Paleoindian sites in this region (and the entire Southwest) is the Mockingbird Gap Clovis, where research has yielded surprising results in terms of the presence of Clovis blades clearly smaller than at other sites of this culture (which is difficult to explain merely on the basis of the available data).

Located slightly further north, the Estancia Basin contains numerous sites from both the early and late Paleoindian period, including the Martin Folsom and the famous Lucy site. The latter is controversial since Sandia blades were found there, previously suspected as potentially older than Clovis blades (a theory that has now been completely rejected). However, research on the origin of raw materials from sites in the Estancia area shows that 70 to 95 percent of the raw materials including those at the Martin Folsom site where sourced outside the area, including a large proportion of the flints from the Edwards Plateau in Texas, confirming the trend at many Clovis and Folsom sites of making long-distance journeys for good quality raw materials—mainly silica rocks—for the production of blades.

In the Mesa Verde region, in southwestern Colorado and southeastern Utah, only about 40 sites from the Paleoindian period have been discovered so far—although it is one of the most famous archaeological regions in North America. On the other hand, ten times more (i.e., about 400) have been uncovered from the subsequent Archaic period (Lipe and Pitblado 1999:95–96). The vast majority of data, however, come from surface surveys and loose finds, with only a small part from regular excavations. In addition, there are rather few known sites from the early phase of the Paleoindian period. Their number increases with time until the Late Paleoindian period (Lipe and Pitblado 1999:101–102). The sparsity of early phase

Paleoindian sites may be due to the above-mentioned state of research and the collection of artifacts by private individuals and treasure hunters; also, most of these sites from this period in the area are grouped at an altitude of over 2,200 meters ASL.

One of the best-documented short-lived Clovis encampment and stone processing sites in the Mesa Verde region is Lime Ridge, located in southeastern Utah (Davis and Till 2014; Vance 2011). Lime Ridge lies on the edge of a terrace and offers a superb view of the adjacent canyon, as well as other areas. Situated at the foot of this terrace, the canyon was probably a place where game traversed between the lower and higher terrain, making this site important both for its habitat (at least at certain times) and for the possibility of observing migrating animals followed by hunts (Davis and Till 2014:23–24). Finds from this site include typical Clovis blades (see figure 3.2a), as well as scrapers, drills, and other tools made with flakes, as well as a lot of debitage left over from tool production. Most of the raw materials for these tools came from nearby, but some indicate expeditions and relations further afield, such as Pigeon Blood agate from central Utah and Wonderstone rhyolite, from deposits located in northern Nevada and Utah.

The Late Paleoindian Period and Transition to Holocene Cultures

The chronology of groups and cultural complexes from the so-called Late Paleoindian period in the Southwest (contemporaneous with or later than the Folsom culture) is much less well known and reconstructed, mainly because the different types of blades appear there primarily as mixed groups and are most often surface finds with no known stratigraphic context. There are just a few exceptions, including the Water Canyon site in western New Mexico, which features numerous bones from hunted bison (Ballenger et al. 2017).

In the Southwest, as in the Great Plains area, several cultural traditions of this late phase are distinguished, based primarily on various types of stone blades. These blade types include the Plainview, Agate Basin, Hell Gap (Jay), Cody, Scottsbluff, Eden (sometimes also called a subtype of the Cody complex, similar to the Firstview type) and Angostura types and cultures. Additionally, a much greater local diversity of selected cultures and cultural traditions can be observed.

After the Folsom culture vanished, three basic hunting techniques in the late Paleoindian cultures of the Southwest bear mentioning (Cordell

1997:96; Fowler 1988). The first, more present in the western part of the region, involved hunting small animals and fairly intensive gathering of wild plants. On the other hand in the eastern area of the region, hunting styles tended to be similar to those from the Great Plains (especially in mountain and intermountain areas)—in other words, a fifty-fifty split between hunting various species of animals and gathering wild plants and hunting bison when available. The third strategy focused primarily on bison hunting, but depended (at least in part, as in the Folsom culture) on the number of bison in a given year or period, which was directly related to the wet and dry seasons. In the case of drought, the bison population may have decreased drastically.

The basic hunting weapon (also used by Native American groups in battle) in the Early and Late Paleoindian period (e.g., Frison 1998), was a short spear used with the help of a thrower, which "extended" the hunter's arm and increased the projectile range. The spear-thrower was also used in periods much later than the Paleoindian period. This thrower, often called an *atl-atl* (the term comes from the Aztec language), was commonly used in both Americas, and is mentioned by conquistadors even in Mexico in the sixteenth century (Fiedel 1992:66). The *atl-atl* was a very effective weapon capable of penetrating the armor of the Spanish conquistadors; therefore, they often replaced iron armor with leather kaftans to protect against the obsidian blades, which were less able to penetrate such material. The known *atl-atl* throwers from Mexico and Peru, from the late pre-Hispanic period and the Spanish conquest were sometimes opulently decorated. Spear throwers were also present among the Paleolithic communities of Europe, and their appearance in America may be one of the indirect testimonies of human migration from Asia to America.

An *atl-atl* spear (see figure 3.2c) was shorter than a hand-thrown spear and usually consisted of two or three parts: a shaft, a projectile point (spearhead) and a replaceable part, also known in modern archery as a foreshaft, made of bone, horn, or wood (usually a hard variety). The spearhead was attached to the foreshaft and loosely connected to the shaft through it, so that if the blade was damaged, it could be easily replaced. The thrower itself, relatively small (40–70 cm long and 2–3.5 cm wide), was most often made of hard wood such as oak, and less often bone and horn. At the end of the thrower was a hook to support the spear, while the front featured a kind of grip for holding it. Often in the Southwest and throughout North America, this grip was made of two leather loops for inserting the index and ring fingers. In addition, there are small stones attached to the thrower (around its center, but not only) that probably acted as weights to ensure the accuracy, rather than greater range, of the shot (Raymond 1986). Some, carved in zoomorphic shapes, may have been types of amulets related to spirit guards, for example, which often appeared in the form of animals.

In the Southwest, this form of hunting and weaponry gradually (though not fully) disappeared with the appearance of bows and arrows. The appearance of the bow and arrow in the Southwest and other regions of central and southern North America has traditionally been dated to around the third to fifth centuries AD (Fiedel 1992), although new data may even point to a slightly later adoption in the south of the region, around 900 AD, while in the north it would have in fact been the period previously proposed (McBrinn and Vierra 2017, see there for further literature); however, we also know of small arrowheads from southern Arizona dating back to around 800 BC, which may suggest that bow and arrows were already present locally at that time.

The Oldest Examples of Mobile Art and Rock Art from the Southwest

Until recently, the emergence of rock, as well as mobile art among Paleoindian communities in both Americas has been discussed by many researchers. However, today we already know of at least a few places and even concentrations of such sites. The oldest rock art from America is often considered to be the petroglyphs and paintings from northeastern Brazil (e.g., from the Pedra Furada and Toca do Boqueirão rock shelters in the Serra da Capivara National Park, which are currently under the patronage of UNESCO), dated to around 12,000–10,300 years ago, or even perhaps 20,000 years ago (Guidon and Delibrias 1986; Neves et al. 2012; www.bradshawfoundation.com). These examples are included in the so-called the Northeastern tradition/*Nordeste Tradition* (e.g., Morales 2002; 2005), although it should be noted that some researchers question such an old chronology. In addition, paintings, and examples of preserved lumps of paints and pigments on rock flakes and tools have been found at sites in the Serra do Ererê and Serra de Paituna mountains near the present-day city of Monte Alegre in the lower Amazon basin (e.g., Davis 2016; Roosevelt et al. 1996). Furthermore, sites in the Caverna da Pedra Pintada or Painel do Pilão rock shelters, contain murals suspected to be linked with astronomical observations, which would set back known examples of such from human cultures by at least several thousand years. The dating of these sites ranges from 13,200–12,700 years ago; slightly younger dates (around 10,600 years ago) were obtained for sites from Argentina. Another example of rock art that is possibly this old (dated to ca. 12,500 years ago) was quite recently revealed in Amazonia Forest in Serranía de la Lindosa and the Chiribiquete National Park, Colombia, for example at the site called Cerro Azul (this was even called by *The Guardian* and other media as "the Sistine Chapel of the ancients").

There are also known examples of rock art from Mesoamerica and the Southwest of North America. Panels containing rock art from North America are dated to relatively old periods, such as the depiction of a California mountain sheep dated to about 19,000 ± 1,100 years ago (Rozwadowski 2009:61–62; Whitley 2000), but in this case there are question marks concerning the effectiveness of the dating method (modern techniques of petroglyph patina microstratigraphy analysis). Another example is a red paint painting in a so-called herringbone pattern from the Tecolote cave in the Mojave Desert, dated to around 9,300 years ago (Whitley 2000).

Recently, however, in the context of North America and the Southwest, the most frequently considered examples are concentrations of rock art in Nevada and in Utah, as well as mobile art—mainly stones with engraved decorations—from Texas, as well as from other parts of North America. These findings suggest that Clovis and Folsom hunters as well as representatives of later Paleoindian groups from North America probably painted or carved on rocks, and created so-called mobile art. Hunters from Paleoindian cultures, as in other parts of the world, adorned their bodies, as evidenced by, for example, finds of beads made of shells, bones, hematite or other rocks and minerals; so far, about one hundred such artifacts are known from the Clovis culture alone, from well-known sites like the above-mentioned Blackwater Draw and Lindenmeier, or others, such as Mockingbird Gap and Wilson-Leonard (Lemke et al. 2015:123, see there for further reading).

The Nevada sites in the Lahontan Valley, located about 1,200 meters above sea level on the western shore of Lake Winnemucca and near Pyramid Lake, are considered the oldest examples of rock art from North America. They consist of petroglyphs in the form of wavy lines, zigzags, circles, and cupules, creating fairly complex patterns and covering quite large areas of boulders and rocks on the lake shore. In the *Journal of Archaeological Science* and *Quaternary International* Larry V. Benson reported the dating of petroglyphs from Lake Winnemucca and Pyramid Lake (based on ^{14}C samples) as ranging from 10,200–9,700 years ago, and perhaps even about 14,800 years ago (Benson et al. 2012, 2013). If we accept the authenticity of this dating and other analyses, then these are undoubtedly the

Figure 3.4.   Examples of petroglyphs from Lake Winnemucca site in Nevada, considered by many researchers to be the oldest rock art in North America (a–c). Photos by Larry V. Benson.

oldest example of rock art that have been discovered in North America, if not the New World on the whole (figure 3.4).

Samples used to date this site were collected from and next to petroglyph sediments from at least fifteen places. These results were compared with the results of tests made on organic materials from the same site and from layers below the panels and beside the lake—human bones, hair, and textile fragments—which also date back to the Paleoindian period—about 11,000–10,400 years ago. In addition to radiocarbon studies, nine samples were analyzed according to strontium isotopes (popular for the study of human bones and tracking migration processes, and also used in the study of carbonate sedimentology), which correlated the location of petroglyphs at the Winnemucca Lake site with the historic rise and fall in water levels in the lake.

Some researchers link the petroglyphs of Winnemucca Lake with the so-called Great Basin Carved Abstract (GBCA) petroglyph style; examples of other sites in this style such as Long Lake in Oregon should be dated to the Archaic period (see below) (Cannon and Ricks 1986; Benson et al. 2013; Middleton et al. 2014). This style can probably be dated to between 12,000–8,000 years ago, primarily on the basis of finds from western North America, generally slightly west and north of the Southwest (e.g., Middleton et al. 2014). These potential early petroglyph sites (several dozen have been identified so far) are also characterized by the presence of a relatively large number of Paleoindian blades and areas for grinding wild plant seeds (Late Paleoindian/Early Archaic) in the vicinity of the rock art. The chronology of these sites is often established by dating the finds located directly below the rock art panels, but the petroglyphs or paintings are also dated directly, the latter via radiocarbon dating (^{14}C and AMS) as well as the CR method—that is, by analyzing the proportion of cations in the patina—and the so-called varnish microlamination method (VML), in terms of its microstratigraphy, in the case of petroglyphs.

Fascinating and intriguing though not commonly accepted methods are depictions of animals, most likely mammoths and bison, along with perhaps a camelid animal in at least one case, originating mainly from the southeastern part of present-day Utah (e.g., from the Upper Sand Island site near the city of Moab in the San Juan River Valley). They appear to have been accepted by some American and other researchers as authentic and originating from the Paleoindian period (e.g., Bednarik 2014; Malotki and Wallace 2011) but there are also some doubts about their authenticity and suggestions of their misinterpretation as they may represent other animals and could be dated for later periods (e.g., Gillam and Bednarik 2015). Such images of mammoths are also known from other parts of Utah and further west, including Mojave National Preserve, California, or Yellow Rock Canyon, Nevada, and other North American areas, albeit in limited quantities. There is a need for further studies that prove their dating of the Paleoindian period.

Well-dated examples of mobile art that were probably associated with beliefs and associated rituals have been found in several Clovis and Folsom sites. These include discoidal shells with intentional cuts and designs on the edges, as well as traces of ochre use perhaps only indirectly related to body decoration, for example, Blackwater Draw, Lindenmeier, Agate Basin and Butler. Ochre was used in a variety of contexts, including human burials. Ochre is known from sites of the Paleoindian period, including the Clovis culture, such as the Anzick 1, Gordon Creek, Browns Valley, Upward Sun River, and Horn Shelter sites; traces are also found on animal bones and in the context of camps and houses (Lemke et al. 2015), and traces of ochre mining from the Paleoindian period in Wyoming have been found (Frison 1988; Stafford et al. 2003).

Perhaps the most famous example of mobile art, possibly from the Paleoindian period, is an image of a mammoth carved on a mineralized mammoth bone from the Vero Beach site in Florida (figure 3.5a). This loose find was discovered by an amateur in 2006. From 1913 to 1916, the remains of fauna and people from the Paleoindian period had been excavated in this area. The artifact was dated to about 13,000 years ago (Lemke et al. 2015; Purdy et al. 2011). This mammoth bone carving is a spectacular find that has been described and published by the Smithsonian Institution and National Geographic, and most researchers confirm its authenticity (Purdy et al. 2011) based on, among other methods, electron microscopy analyses indicating that the mineralization at the base of the engravings is the same as on the rest of the bone; nevertheless there is a slight suspicion, reported by some scholars, that the image engraved on this bone may be a modern forgery on a genuinely old bone.

Other known examples of mobile art from the Paleoindian period in the Southwest and its surroundings are artifacts from the above-mentioned Gault site in Texas and associated with the Clovis culture, among others (Lemke et al. 2015; Malotki and Dissanayake 2018:60–67). At the Gault site, eleven stones and one bone with intentionally ornamented geometric designs in the form of perpendicular and parallel lines, zigzags, spirals, and others were discovered (figure 3.5b); researchers Bruce Bradley and Dennis Stanford discern animal outlines in some depictions, and a hunting scene in at least one case (Stanford and Bradley 2012:66). These artifacts are well documented stratigraphically and dated to the period of Clovis culture development. We know of about a hundred other artifacts from the Gault site (dated to the Paleoindian/Archaic period), but without such a detailed context; some of these were loose finds uncovered by amateur archaeologists and landowners before regular archaeological research was undertaken.

Decorations were carved on stones and tools made of limestone and various types of flints and bones; these are not large items, usually several

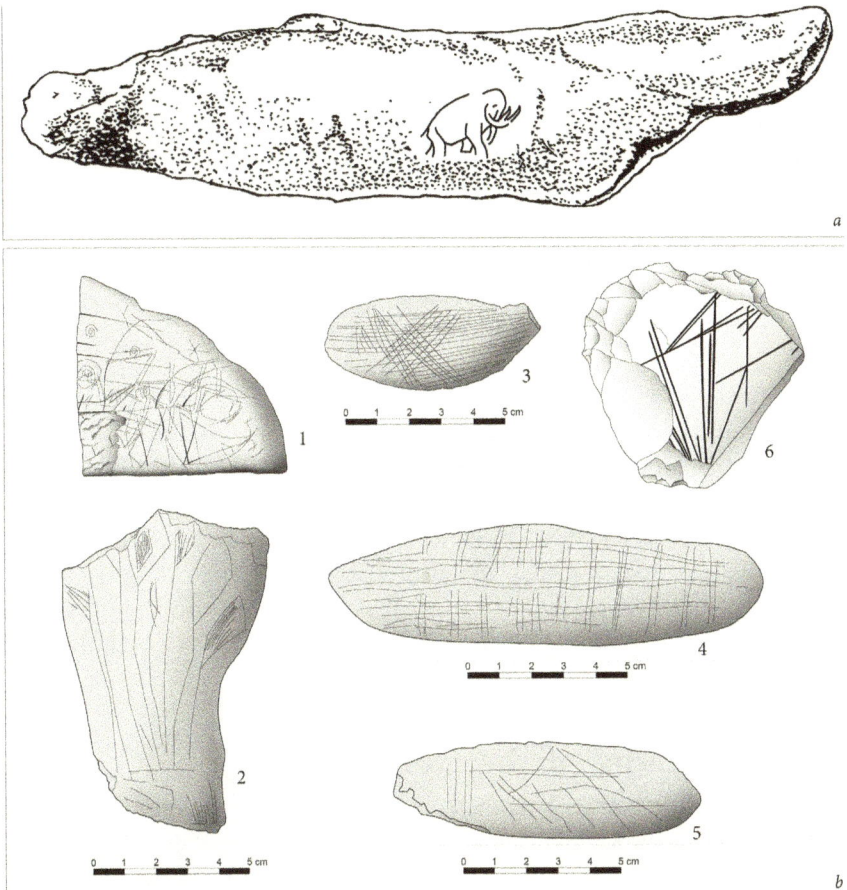

Figure 3.5.   A stylized drawing of a fossil mammoth bone with its image engraved, probably from the Paleoindian period from the Vero Beach site, Florida (a) and examples of carved stones from the Gault site in Texas (layers related to the Clovis culture). Drawings by Katarzyna Ciomek and Michał Znamirowski.

centimeters long and wide, sometimes larger, and slightly more than one centimeter thick. These relics were found in various locations at the Gault site, most often very close (5–10 cm) to the Clovis blades (one of which bears traces suggesting that it could have been used to make cuts on some stones). Two of these stone artifacts may in fact be associated with a later context—the first with the Folsom culture and the second with the transition complex between Paleoindian and Archaic periods, the so-called Dalton complex. The dating of the same context linked with the Clovis culture from the Gault site indicates a period of 12,990 ± 830 years ago (Lemke et al. 2015:117–19).

Decorated stones from the Gault site in Texas are just an example of mobile art recorded with increasing frequency both in the Southwest itself (e.g., engraved stones from Blackwater Draw and Wilson-Leonard—Lemke et al. 2015; Wernecke and Collins 2010) and its surroundings, as well as other parts of North America. They are mostly loose surface finds or poorly stratigraphically dated. It may be possible to include a spectacular find of thirty-six stones decorated with carving from Cedar Valley in Utah (now a private collection). These stones have been dated indirectly to about 8,000 years ago, mainly on the basis of similar and prominent motifs from the Hogup Cave site on the Great Salt Lake in Utah, as have similar items from Burton Gulch, Montana (Davis et al. 2009) also with double-sided designs. The latter are probably much older, dated to around 10,500 years ago. Carved stones from sites in Wyoming (Bighorn Basin), the East Wenatchee site in Washington state on the Northwest Coast, as well as the Sugarloaf and Shawnee-Minisink sites in the northeast of North America (Lemke et al. 2015:123–24) may also be related to the Clovis culture. Decorated bone tools have been found at the Murray Springs site in Arizona (Haynes and Huckell 2007).

The Beginning of the Holocene and the Archaic Period

The very term *Archaic* was coined in 1932 by William Ritchie (Fiedel 1992) and to this day is understood more as a certain state of development of Native American societies than a mere period in the history of their development. Basically, the Archaic period can be defined (Willey and Phillips 1958) as the time between the period of specialized Pleistocene megafauna hunts and the emergence of agriculture in an complex form, with greater settlement stabilization thanks to the specialization of the economy (e.g., fishing, gathering), the growing importance of plant gathering (although recent studies have shown that Clovis communities already used a wide variety of wild plants) and other factors, like the differentiation between stone and flint tools (compared to earlier periods), with products of slightly lower quality (in terms of the techniques of their production) than in the Paleoindian period.

The beginning of the Archaic period in North America was closely related to climate change (Fiedel 1992; Willey and Phillips 1958), above all to a shift in the extent of the ice sheet to the north, that marked an increase in the average temperature (by about 16°C) and, consequently, the complete flooding of the land connection between Asia and America when Beringia disappeared under water. The rise in temperature brought about a change in vegetation, the appearance of new environmental niches, and the extinction of the Pleistocene megafauna and their "replacement" by smaller animals. The human population at that time underwent transformations in many areas of their lives, as can be observed in the inventory of artifacts and modifications in the technology used to make hunting weapons. For example, stone points used in the Archaic period became smaller and much more varied, and were produced with more diverse techniques than before. In the Archaic period, mainly bison, deer and caribou were hunted.

The general periodization of the Archaic period is rather tricky, and researchers present different concepts (e.g., Fagan 2000; Fiedel 1992; Willey 1966), but the average chronology basically divides this epoch into three subperiods: the Early Archaic (8000–6000 BC), Middle Archaic (6000–3000 BC) and the Late Archaic (3000–1000 BC). This division however is more suited to the east of the continent than the west, where there is a greater spatial and chronological differentiation of individual cultural traditions. The end of the Archaic period differs widely from place to place, and in some places, such as parts of Nevada and California where hunter-gatherer communities including the historic Shoshones developed over a long time, it may have even lasted until the arrival of the Europeans.

It is generally accepted that the Archaic lasted in the American Southwest from 10,000 years ago to even around 500 BC (e.g., Cordell 1997; McBrinn and Vierra 2017). However, given such an extended chronological span, the Archaic period, in particular the earlier part of the epoch, is one of the least archaeologically and historically known periods in the history of Native American cultures of this region, as well as in the whole of North America due to the rather fragmentary material remains of mobile hunter-gatherer groups from this period. Evidence includes primarily flint and stone assemblages, a few traces of houses, hearths, and storage pits, as well as stones for grinding plant food. Additionally, research has tended to focus on developed agricultural cultures in this region whose traces remain in the form of well-preserved stone structures and buildings as in the case of the Pueblo or Mogollon cultures. This emphasis was driven by the interests of researchers and the general public that were focused on "more" fascinating problems and questions, such as the settlement of the New World. On the other hand, the late Archaic period in the Southwest is quite well studied, especially in the context of artificial irrigation and the appearance of the first crops that preceded the emergence of developed agricultural cultures in this region.

Cynthia Irwin-Williams (e.g., Irwin-Williams 1979) contributed greatly to the development of research on the Archaic, in particular the revelation that the beginning of the Archaic period in the Southwest marked a transition from hunting large mammals to a greater dependence on the gathering economy and hunting for smaller and different species of animals. These changes took place in its western part earlier than in the east. Radiocarbon dates which are fundamental for the periodization and dating of sites from the Archaic also suggest that in the Early Archaic, human groups were more present in the Colorado Plateau than in the southern area of the Southwest (McBrinn and Vierra 2017).

We should also thank Irwin-Williams for the categorization of the four main Archaic cultural traditions (see table 3.1): San Dieguito-Pinto, Oshara, Cochise, and Chihuahua. These were distinguished mainly—as in the case of cultures from the Paleoindian period—on the basis of similarities and differences in the projectile points technologies, hammerstones and stones for grinding seeds, nuts, and other plant parts (including *mano* and *metate* stones as well as various types of mortars, etc.). Additionally, the Archaic is often divided into Early, Middle, and Late Archaic, as mentioned above.

As in studies of communities at similar stages of cultural development in other parts of the world, research of the Archaic period in the Southwest has focused on the economy, the technology used for making stone tools and methods of exploiting the natural environment, including mobility, migration, and movements of individual groups. Notably such studies highlight relations between humans and the natural environment and the responses of individual Native American groups and communities to climate change. Less can be said about the spiritual and religious realm of these communities, although much research and debate on this subject has been stimulated by studying the rock art of this period, especially its middle and late phases.

The regional and time differences between individual traditions were caused by significant differences in the natural environment, including the availability of game according to the given region or even microregion, although for this period two large geographical and natural provinces of the Southwest that share similarities are sometimes generalized and referred to as a whole (McBrinn and Vierra 2017:233–34). The first is the northern area with varied landforms, more rainfall than in the south, low-lying grasslands and higher elevations with forests. The second area is the southern zone featuring less rainfall, valleys and mountain ranges, deserts, and

Table 3.1 Main Cultural Traditions in the Archaic Period in the Southwest

Cultural Tradition	Dating	Range of Occurrence and Characteristic Features
San Dieguito-Pinto (Western tradition)	6300–4300 BC	– Southern California, southern Arizona, and adjacent parts of Nevada – Primary features are Pinto Basin (straight-stemmed with concave bases) and Gypsum Cave (contracting stems and concave bases) projectile points and flake choppers and scrapers; stones for grinding seeds and plants (small *manos* and shallow-basin "*metates*") – Hunting hares, rabbits, mountain sheep, deer, and antelopes (confirmed reduction in deer hunting for the Mojave Desert for a greater diversity of animal species) – This tradition likely developed into many hunter-gatherer and farming communities inhabiting the Colorado River Basin
Oshara (Northern tradition)	6000/5500–200/400 BC Sometimes divided into phases: Jay (5500–4800 BC) Bajada (4800–3200 BC) San Jose (3200–1800 BC) Armijo (1800–800 BC)	– North-central New Mexico, south-central Colorado, southeastern Utah – Possible cultural continuation from the late Paleoindian period (Jay phase) – Differentiating between phases based on the typology of shouldered and stemmed points among other factors – Corn and pottery appear in the last (Armijo) phase – This tradition was the basis for the formation of the Ancestral Pueblo culture (Basketmaker period)
Cochise (Southern tradition)	8000/7500–200 BC Sometimes divided into phases: Sulphur Spring (Late Paleoindian/Early Archaic) Chiricahua (8000–6000 BC; alternative dating: 3500–1500 BC) San Pedro (1500–200 BC)	– Southeastern and eastern Arizona, southern New Mexico, northern Chihuahua, and Sonora – Stone tools for grinding plants in the Sulphur Spring phase, as nuts and plant seeds constituted a large share of the population's diet – In the Chiricahua phase a large amount of *mano* and *metate* stones, scrapers of various shapes and choppers, a fair number of side-notched points with concave bases – In the San Pedro phase, large side-notched knives, double-sided knives, and choppers, and *metate* stones with a deeper grinding bowl than in the Chiricahua phase – This tradition likely gave rise to the Mogollon culture
Chihuahua (Southeastern tradition)	6000–250 BC (phases: Keystone, Fresnal, Hueco)	– Frontiers of Arizona, New Mexico, Texas, and Mexico – A variety of notched and stemmed projectile points and stones for grinding, hammerstones and mortars (the most distinct tools are discoidal choppers, "one-handed" *manos*, *metates*) – Presence of maize and gourd in some sites

After Cordell 1997:107–111; Huckell 1996; McBrinn and Vierra 2017; Vierra et al. 2012.

semiarid vegetation, as well as forests at higher elevations. Lakes and reservoirs around which types of ecological and environmental niches formed, are also characteristic of the latter region. These differences translated into variations in hunting strategies, which are in turn manifested in the material culture such as different types of stone and flint tools.

Early Archaic (ca. 8000–6000 BC)

The Early Archaic is the least well-known period, although there are a number of fairly well-documented sites and finds from this period. Evidence of hunter-gatherers from the Early Archaic period may be observed at some sites from the Paleoindian period, though their presence may have been seasonal. Similarities in hunting techniques and many other cultural aspects suggest continuity, at least when it comes to the exploitation of the same areas. Perhaps these people were at least in part descended from the former "Paleoindian" populations. Some 9,000 years ago, new human groups are also thought to have come to the Southwest, possibly via two main routes (McBrinn and Vierra 2017:234): through the Colorado Plateau and through the Great Basin, which may correlate with the spread of groups who spoke Proto-Uto-Aztecan language(s) (e.g., Merrill et al. 2009); and from southern California to the southern parts of the Southwest. The reconstruction of these migration routes is based primarily on the similarities of lithics, mainly projectile points.

Stone and flint points clearly distinguish Archaic from Paleoindian communities. These began to vary in shape over time, but were generally squatter, thicker, and shorter than the fairly thin, finely machined, and standardized Clovis and Folsom blades or even those of late traditions during the Paleoindian period. At the sites from the Early Archaic, the presence of *manos* and *metates* for grinding seeds, nuts, etc. is clearly visible, although in some sites there is no such inventory at all. One example is Ventana cave in southern Arizona where, in addition to earlier traces from the Paleoindian period, Archaic points were found in the context of the cave being used as a ceremonial place related to hunting (Huckell 1996:330–31; McBrinn and Vierra 2017).

Other sites in the Colorado Plateau including Sudden Cave and Cowboy Cave have yielded numerous and varied artifacts, especially some very rare finds from this part of the Archaic period—woven baskets from Cowboy Cave include the oldest known basket from this region, which is completely preserved and dated to the years 6882 ± 113 BC), sandals of various types, as well as anthropomorphic figurines made of clay. Such figurines also appeared in several other sites in the area, see below).

Middle Archaic (ca. 6000–3000 BC)

Unlike the southern Southwest and the Rio Grande Valley north of Albuquerque, New Mexico, the Middle Archaic yields a surprisingly small number of archaeological sites in the Colorado Plateau except in the San Juan River Basin in northern New Mexico; researchers hypothesize that a settlement hiatus may have been caused by warming and the resulting droughts and overall drying of the natural environment in the north of the region. In turn, these environmental changes drove human migration to the vicinity of larger river valleys (McBrinn and Vierra 2017:236). The inventory of tools continues with Early Archaic forms, with an increasing visible dependence on certain plant species (e.g., piñon pine nuts) along with the hunting of small and large animals, usually in autumn or winter.

Other signs of stable settlement from those in agricultural communities. The largest Middle Archaic settlement in the Southwest known to date is probably the Keystone Dam site in El Paso, Texas. It consisted of about twenty houses, although was a multiphase settlement and only two or three houses were used at the same time. Nevertheless, the settlement clearly indicates stability and the relationship of groups with a given area.

Nevertheless, one can observe trips over long distances to obtain food, for example piñon pine nuts and raw materials for tools such as obsidian. Research on the distribution of obsidian has been conducted for sites in south-central Arizona, among others, showing that obsidian was obtained from sources located to the north at Kaibab Plateau, and west and south in the Sonoran Desert; these journeys were also pursued in this area in the Late Archaic (McBrinn and Vierra 2017 after Shackley 1996). On the other hand, studies on the acquisition of obsidian from several places in the Colorado Plateau indicate that it was transported from a distance of up to 200 kilometers. These trips may have aligned with hunting expeditions, and the acquisition of valuable raw materials for tools, including hunting points.

Points from the Middle Archaic are much more varied than previous ones. In the north of the Southwest, these include Pinto and San Jose blade types, while in the southern area, various forms of side-notched blades and blades with relatively poorly separated stems prevail. Perhaps these differences indicate different hunting techniques used by individual groups. It also seems that these points were made with long-term use in mind, as indicated by the repair and conversion of these points to new tools. The side-notched points were most likely designed in such a way that, after piercing the animal's body, the tip broke and would then remain in the animal, further injuring and weakening it, allowing the hunters to catch up.

The Tucson Basin in southern Arizona provides data confirming the alternating exploitation of lowland and highlands to obtain diverse plant nutrition, as well as for hunting, a phenomenon also later observed in the agricultural Hohokam culture, and even in the historic communities of the region, like the Akimel O'odham and Tohono O'odham). Taking into account the seasonality of these displacements and the economy, some researchers have suggested that such tactics, especially in the Tucson Basin, may have favored the subsequent adoption of agriculture in the area. Similar manners of obtaining food and exploiting lowland and mountain areas have been recorded during this and later periods in the Rio Grande Basin.

More data from this period helps to reconstruct various aspects of spiritual culture and probable beliefs. Animal figurines of mountain sheep and other animals made of shoots and plant fibers, mainly willow have been preserved at several sites in parts of the Southwest, (figure 3.6a). Examples of such split-twig figures come from cave sites in the Grand Canyon and sites in Utah on Green River, including in Straight Canyon (Coulam and Schroedl 2004; Schwartz et al. 1958). There are two styles of such figures based of their location and function. The first is the Grand Canyon style (figures from the Grand Canyon in Arizona, and from California and southern Nevada); the second is the Green River style from the vicinity of this river in southern Utah. In total, more than 400 such figurines produced in these two regional styles have so far been found within at least 30 sites in the Southwest, with radiocarbon dates ranging from approximately 2900 BC to 1250 BC (with the Green River split-twig figurines being made later, roughly from about 2150 BC to about 1500 BC), in the Middle and Late Archaic.

On the basis of ethnographic analogies, Coulam and Schroedl (2004:52–57) argue that these figurines were types of animal totems and testify to the existence of totemism among groups from these areas. Figures in the Green River style would tend to be used for social identification of the people with a given totem and are found in the residential structures, middens, as well as in burials, in particular those of children (e.g., Jett 1991). Figures made in the Grand Canyon style, specifically those from the Grand Canyon itself, were probably associated with a more complex form of totemism that involved visiting certain places (primarily caves), usually located within the territory of a family or clan, and with associated rituals such as initiation. Archaeological evidence confirms that the places where the figures were deposited were visited by multiple generations, over even hundreds of years, which would indeed be a manifestation of cultural continuity and elements of beliefs, rarely captured by archaeological research.

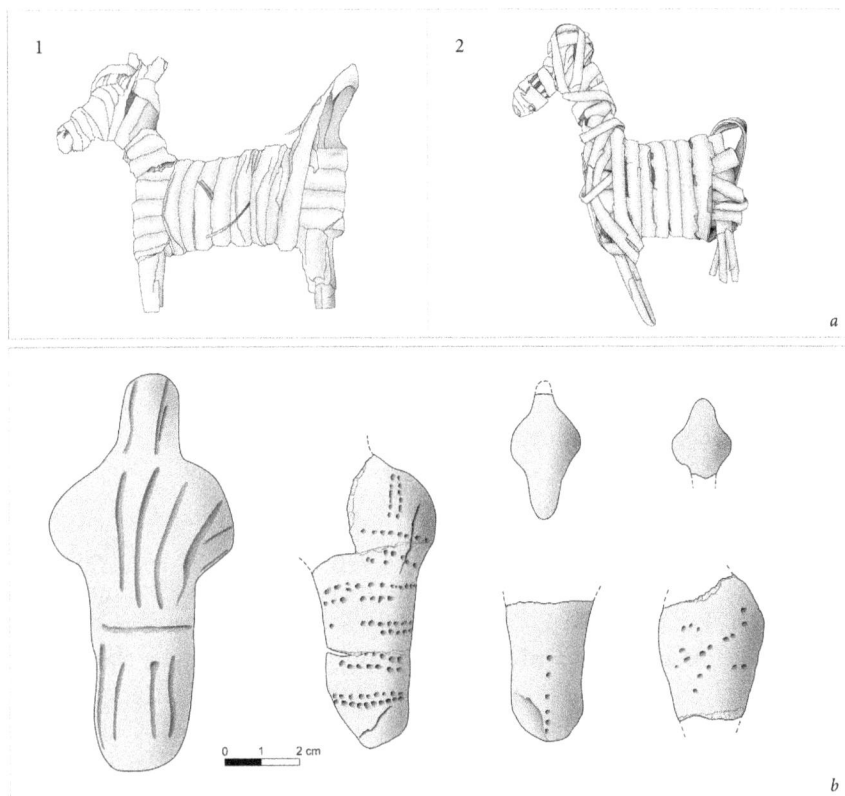

Figure 3.6. Drawings of the Archaic animal split-twig figures (including mountain sheep) from the Grand Canyon in Arizona and the Green River Basin in Utah (a) and (b) anthropomorphic unfired clay figurines from Utah and the Great Basin. Drawing by Katarzyna Ciomek.

Although these figures are often situated in the context of the Middle Archaic, chronologically they fit more closely with the next period—that is, the Late Archaic. From the Early, Middle, and Late Archaic, examples of anthropomorphic figures are known to have been made of unfired clay (figure 3.6b) (Coulam and Schroedl 1996). These figurines are grouped primarily in Utah at sites such as Cowboy Cave, Walters Cave and Sudden Shelter, as well as in parts of the Great Basin farther to the west. Outside of Utah, they are quite rare. These anthropomorphic figures are rather small, from three to eleven centimeters, and were probably made of a single piece of rolled clay and later smoothed, mainly in the lower part of the figures and on the "torso." They are referred to as the Horseshoe Shouldered style/type due to the shape of their rounded shoulders. They are decorated mainly on one side with incisions in the form of small cupules or points that sometimes form dotted lines. These figures often appear in the same contexts as additional conical objects from the same time frame, which are also made of unfired clay; these conical objects are small, from one to four centimeters in size, decorated with incisions or engravings (often dotted designs).

Even in the 1970s, these conical figures were judged to be related to the rock art of the Barrier Canyon style on the basis of similarities (Schroedl 1977); however, the Barrier Canyon style is probably much younger than the clay figurines. As for the interpretations of their functions, it is difficult to determine whether they served some religious practice or were perhaps made as toys for children which is less likely. Certainly, their resemblance to later rock art depictions is quite striking, which suggests that they could have performed similar functions related to rituals and beliefs.

Late Archaic (ca. 3000–1000 BC)

The Late Archaic period brings much greater diversity in the fields and spheres of culture, settlement, and economy of the individual communities than those that preceded it. This diversity is visible first and foremost in terms of far more stable settlements and, in certain regions of the Southwest (mainly in its southern part, including southern Arizona), in the cultivation of plants and the related construction of irrigation channels and later, the first pottery. Agriculture did not immediately dominate the traditional hunter-gatherer economy; rather, there appears to have been a long process as Native American communities in the area adopted agriculture as their primary economy. We witness many more expressions of beliefs and spiritual culture, including a variety of rock art styles that developed in particular parts of the Southwest. Researchers commonly associate the emergence rock art at so many sites with the aforementioned economic changes and possible subsequent shifts in the religious sphere (e.g., Cole 2004, 2009; Schaafsma 1980; Tipps 1994).

Rock Art in the Archaic Period: Middle Archaic, Barrier Canyon Anthropomorphic Style and Other Late Archaic Styles

Rock art from the Paleoindian period may have partially survived and continued in the Early and Middle Archaic period (up to 5,000 or 6,000 years ago) in the form of the Great Basin Carved Abstract (GBCA) present in a relatively large area, mainly in the northern Great Basin (in the vicinity of the Southwest). Sites related to this style from the Archaic period include Long Lake, Oregon, dated to about 7,000 years ago (e.g., Benson et al. 2013; Cannon and Ricks 1986). At this site the style was initially defined, and another example of this style is the Legend Rock site in Wyoming, with petroglyphs and charcoal paintings, dating to 7,000 years ago.

The rock art panels at Long Lake are set in groupings on a basaltic rock approximately four kilometers long. These are mainly geometric representations with a predominance of wavy and straight lines repeating and arranged in various configurations, as well as symbols similar to the "herringbone" motif or double V shape (in American terminology, the so-called Chevron motif), circles or concentric circles. When combined, these motifs create rather complicated patterns. Blades typical of the Early Archaic phase were also found near these panels. Similar petroglyphs, which can probably be included in the same style, are also found at Grimes Point in Nevada, very close to the Southwest border, and at other sites from the Great Basin and the frontier with the Southwest.

One of the late sites included in this style is Lava Beds in California, dating from about 5,000 to 6,000 years ago. Most of the rock art at this site is situated on a rock or hill called Petroglyph Point, which was once an island in the lake, and includes both petroglyphs and paintings. The paintings are located very close to the entrances to caves and shelters, and feature the color black made from charcoal mixed with animal fat, and white, a color most often obtained from white clay. The designs are primarily geometric motifs, such as straight and wavy lines, circles, and concentric circles with rays (perhaps solar representations), along with cupules, which could have served as mortars for crushing and grinding paints and mixing them with a binder such as fat or water. Here the historic Modoc and Klamath tribes lived, although in this case, considering the vast distance in time and migrations, we cannot speak of any ethnographic analogies. Unfortunately, the site also features many examples of contemporary vandalism and destruction in the form of modern graffiti including American and Japanese inscriptions that even predate World War II.

The presence of clay figures in the Middle Archaic corresponds somewhat with the presence of rock art from that period, but the clay figures are more common in the Late Archaic. The Barrier Canyon Style, also known as the Barrier Canyon Anthropomorphic Style, is one of the most important and widespread styles of Late Archaic rock art in the Southwest. This style developed in the central, western, and northern parts of the Colorado Plateau, mainly in the basin of the Colorado and Green Rivers, from northwest Colorado to eastern and southern Utah, and to the Grand

Canyon. Its southwestern tip is marked by the Escalante River basin in Utah, while the most northeastern point is the White River in Colorado (e.g., Cole 2004:8–9, Fig. 2.1a, Fig. 2.1b, Schaafsma 1994). The eponymous sites of this style are found in Horseshoe Canyon, which joins the Green River Canyon in central-eastern Utah. Horseshoe Canyon is home to the so-called Great Gallery that includes the famous Holy Ghost Panel and depictions of natural and supernatural human figures. The Gallery is sometimes called the Louvre of the Southwest (sometimes the name "Wild Louvre" is transferred to the entire Southwest due to the abundance of the rock art panels). The Great Gallery is located partly within the well-known Canyonlands National Park, in southeastern Utah, which today contains many archaeological and natural treasures including the largest number of Barrier Canyon rock art sites.

The dating of this style has changed over the course of archaeological research. It was once thought to have flourished in the Middle and Late Archaic from around 5000/4000 BC up to 1000/500 BC (e.g., Schaafsma 1994; Schroedl 1977). This assumption was based mainly on the similarities of the Barrier Canyon rock art representations to the clay figures described above and found in layers dated to the Middle Archaic, from the Cowboy Cave site, located near the Great Gallery in Horseshoe Canyon (figure 3.7) among others. However, more recent dating by chemist Marvin Rowe and his colleagues at Texas A&M University and others, puts its origin and development much later, around 2000/1900 BC–300/400 BC, still in the first or second millennium BC in the Late Archaic Period (Cole 2004; Ilger et al. 1995; Tipps 1994, 1995), These dates correspond to the development of hunter-gatherer societies at the end of the Archaic, as well as the transition to the agricultural Ancestral Pueblo culture (Basketmaker II period) and the beginning of the development of the Fremont culture, communities with a hunter-gatherer economy, that were also partly agricultural. This younger dating is based on radiocarbon dates (AMS and ^{14}C), and most panels in this style are dated indirectly from the sites next to them. Recently, new dating results for the Grand Gallery in Horseshoe Canyon (Pederson et al. 2014) again bring forward the age of these painted anthropomorphic figures to the period of 1–1100 AD, suggesting that by then, their creators may have all been the people of the Fremont culture; though this latter theory is not likely as, the Barrier Canyon style seems to have Archaic origins. Nevertheless, its cultural status is still debated and the discrepancies in terms of absolute dating will involve more research.

Barrier Canyon–style rock art, mainly paintings, and the petroglyphs that occur far less frequently, occur at fairly high altitudes, around 1,200–

Figure 3.7. The Great Gallery in Horseshoe Canyon (Canyonlands National Park, Utah) as an example of monumental Barrier Canyon style rock art (a) and (b) part of the Great Gallery. Photos from Wikimedia Commons, enhanced by Radosław Palonka and Michał Znamirowski.

2,100 meters above sea level (in a sense this is related to the above-sea-level location of the Colorado Plateau themselves) and are located primarily on the walls of canyons, but also in shelters and rock niches and on individual boulders, and often close to water sources—a common feature of rock art in the Archaic period in this region (e.g., Cole 2004). The Barrier Canyon style may be subcategorized into three main groups according to chronology and range of occurrence based on art style rather than absolute dating. These groups are in turn divided into seven local variants/styles: Canyonlands 1–3 associated with the Green River tributary to the Colorado River, eastern Utah, mainly the Canyonlands National Park area, San Rafael 1–2 in the San Rafael Desert and central-eastern Utah, and Book

Cliffs 1–2 in northeastern Utah and northwestern Colorado. Communities creating rock art in the Barrier Canyon style used different environmental niches, as did the later Fremont culture in the same territory. The placement of art was especially relevant for hunter-gatherer communities, and there are suggestions that the location of individual rock art panels may have been associated with marking important places or even marking the relations, social groups, or territories of individual groups or tribes. This theory is in some sense confirmed by the oral tradition of historic tribes of the Southwest, mainly Pueblo communities (e.g., Cole 2004; Young 1988). Rock art in the Barrier Canyon style as well as others in the Southwest should be considered in context with its location in the surrounding landscape for example as one of the elements of the sacred landscape. The art can also be interpreted in terms of the aesthetic location of individual panels in the vividly colorful setting of the red, orange, and yellow sandstone formations of this region, which stimulate the senses.

The most characteristic representations of the Barrier Canyon style are mainly paintings of trapezoidal and rectangular elongated anthropomorphic figures of significant size, often ranging from one meter to almost three meters tall giving the impression of being unrealistic or "supernatural" (often referred to as ghost-like) (Cole 2004, 2009; Schaafsma 1980; Tipps 1994). The figures were generally presented frontally with the body frequently similar to a rectangle, sometimes with only schematically marked rather short limbs, poorly distinguished anatomical features and, very rarely, sexual features or none at all. Facial elements are more common—for example, "bulging" eyes, possible masks and types of headgear resembling caps, decorations in the form of deer antlers that are reminiscent of shamanistic depictions, as well as types of traveling rugs or baskets. Though depictions of these characters are quite varied, they have some features in common including rounded shoulders and a more accurate representation of the upper and middle parts of the body than the lower ones, which usually end in a straight or rounded line or taper downward (Tipps 1994). The torsos of individual figures are generally not complemented by any decoration, but figures in a large group of these representations are filled with geometric elements such as dots, wavy and zigzag lines, spirals, and even depictions of ribs and other elements of the skeletons and sometimes small human and animal figures. It is theorized that sometimes children were shown together with adults on one panel due to the significant differences in the size of these representations; at times, these smaller figures are "inscribed" into larger ones.

Paintings are dominated by red-brown, red-orange, white, and then blue, green, yellow, and black, respectively. More than one color often appears in a given work, and character compositions generally consist of lines or dots, mostly in red and white. Some of these works even suggest that these communities may have had tattoos or worn body paintings. Petroglyphs, though rare, sometimes include representations of eyes, lips, contours of particular shapes, and painted representations. Specially prepared surfaces are found, usually in sandstone formations, in the form of rock that was smoothed and possibly painted in preparation for subsequent art work (Tipps 1994, see for further reading).

More "realistic" figures were shown in profile, without masks, headgear, or clothing. Often, they appear in action scenes—dancing, fighting, and hunting motifs, while some characters hold sticks, baskets and what may be plant-cutting tools. These "action" figures are often depicted accompanied by animals, generally mountain sheep, deer, dogs and coyotes, or foxes. Animals are usually shown in profile in a similar style to the "realistic" human figures, in varied sizes from 5 centimeters to even about 2 meters in height or body length. Known depictions of animals come from the Sego Canyon/Temple Mountain Wash in Utah, along the Colorado River near the city of Moab in Utah, the Horseshoe Gallery site, which also contains representations of both human and animal figures, and from other sites.

Although interpretation of rock art in any style is challenging, attempts have been made to read function and meaning of the Barrier Canyon style using contemporary understanding. It appears that this art was definitely intended for a wider audience because these genuine open-air galleries are usually located in easily visible and exposed places (e.g., Munson 2011:81–82); however the details could be seen only if someone is standing in the front of the panels, and the individual depictions are imposing and colorful. Many of these images have been interpreted as representations of deities, shamans, and perhaps family groups. Perhaps the most accepted and frequently cited interpretation is as evidence of shamanism (Cole 2004; Schaafsma 1994; Schroedl 1977; Tipps 1994). Features that support the shamanistic interpretation include face masks, bulging eyes, skulls, skeleton exposure, and so-called elements of transformation that suggest shamanistic trance, that is animals accompanying the shaman, elongation of the body, hands-wings, birds, claws instead of feet which symbolize the shaman's transformation into a bird and the journey to the other world(s).

Other rock art styles of the western part of North America from the Archaic period are iconographically and stylistically similar to the Barrier Canyon style and have some elements in common. These include the Glen Canyon Style 5 (Glen Canyon linear style), Grand Canyon Polychrome-Esplanade style, abstract geometric style and Lower Pecos styles as presented in table 3.2 and figure 3.8. Of course, the most features in common

Table 3.2. The Various Late Archaic Rock Art Styles from the Colorado Plateau and Texas, Similar to the Barrier Canyon Style and the Chihuahua Abstract Polychrome style

Style or Tradition	Dating	Range of Occurrence and Characteristic Features
Glen Canyon Style 5 Also known as the Glen Canyon linear style (Schaafsma 1980) and sometimes treated as part of the Palavuyu anthropomorphic style (McCreery and Malotki 1994)	1000–500 BC	– Mainly the southern Colorado Plateau – Rock art located near rivers (transport and trade routes), very clearly visible from a distance, possibly created by people who controlled or lived along these watercourses – Mostly petroglyphs, in contrast to the Barrier Canyon style; depictions of human figures and animals (generally mountain sheep and deer), the interiors of the figures usually filled with motifs of parallel, zigzag lines and patterns, as well as lines made from dots; figures from 20 cm to 1 m tall, often elongated and rectangle or oval in shape, usually grouped in rows – Head and ear decorations (plumes, often V-shaped head designs, perhaps horns, earrings), sometimes only the eyes and lips marked and formed from a series of cupules, single and multiplied lines on faces to make noses; arms sometimes present but often not; the characters seem to be wrapped or "restrained" in some material
Grand Canyon Polychrome-Esplanade Style	1000 BC (maybe earlier)–at the turning of era	– Western part of the Grand Canyon (Arizona and Utah), mainly on the Kanab Plateau – Perhaps the western variant of the Barrier Canyon style – Often accompanied by stone processing areas Mono- and polychromic paintings, the main colors are dark red, red, black, and creamy-white; the sizes of the depictions vary from a few cm to 2 m – Human figures featuring facial and bodily details created with lines, dots, stripes and quadrilaterals, rarely with arms but if present with hands raised upwards, palms depicted in detail, round or oval heads; some of the figures' torsos give the impression of "x-rays" or representations of "ghosts," some figures accompanied by snakes and wavy lines, dogs or coyotes, as well as birds and insects; smaller figures of people or animals on the shoulders of large figures; depictions of men with phalluses
Tradition of Abstract-Geometric Styles	The chronology is difficult to	– Nearly half of motifs in this style are geometric representations – Wide area of occurrence: from the Great Basin through the Southwest to the Rocky Mountains and the Great Plains

Style	Dating	Characteristics
Abstract styles from Arizona, Chihuahua, the upper Rio Grande Valley, and the plains of eastern New Mexico, as well as the abstract polychrome style from Chihuahua	specify precisely but the tradition probably originated before 1000 BC	– Petroglyphs as well as paintings (mono- and polychrome), with predominantly red, black, black-green, white, and cream colors – Mainly geometric and abstract representations, including wavy and zigzag lines, multiplied lines and *hachure* patterns, circles (possible solar motifs), dots creating more complex representations, the "spider's web" motif, schematic representations of plants including flowers, handprints, animal and bird tracks, rarely depictions of humans and animals
Lower Pecos Style Style from the lower area of the Pecos River	ca. 2200–1000 BC	– Mainly the territory of southwestern Texas – Paintings located in niches and rock shelters, filling almost the entire surfaces including part of ceilings of these shelters – Similarities to the Barrier Canyon style, including very large (up to 3 m), but also small (even several cm) slender anthropomorphic forms, painted with red and black, often accompanied by plants and animals; details paid to drawing – Similarities in material culture (tanged points, decorated stones, and figurines made of organic materials) probably testifying to the cultural relations of people representing the Barrier Canyon and Pecos styles – The most famous representation is the so-called White Shaman; its interpretation assumes a symbolic representation of peyote hunts and cultural continuity with historic native groups – Other important sites include Panther Cave, Black Cave and Halo Shelter, among many others
Chihuahua Abstract Polychrome style	Lack of precise dating (probably Late Archaic)	– Chihuahua Desert (southern New Mexico, western Texas and the northern part of the Mexican state of Chihuahua) – Multi-colored paintings (yellow, red, orange, black, and white are dominant) depicting abstract and geometric motifs and fairly schematic human figures – Comprised mainly of multiplied and closely spaced lines and zigzag lines, often forming "chains" and bands as well as linear grids; circles, ovals, solar disks and dots – There tends to be a lack of narrative scenes in this style, and the individual depictions do not connect into any coherent whole, unlike the Barrier Canyon style and other styles from the central and northern part of the Southwest at the time

After Cole 2004; Rozwadowski 2009; Schaafsma 1980, 1994; Tipps 1994.

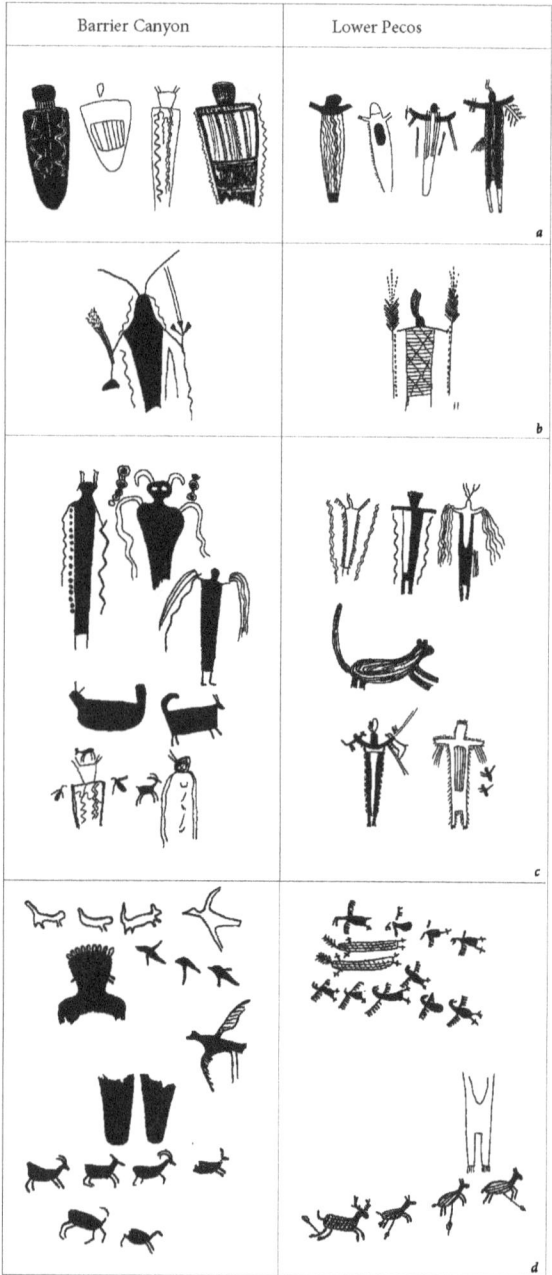

	Barrier Canyon	Lower Pecos

Figure 3.8. Comparison of anthropomorphic and other depictions in Barrier Canyon and Lower Pecos styles: (a) anthropomorphic representations with body decoration; (b) the characters holding the plants (possibly wild); (c) figures with wavy lines, also (separately) animals; (d) groups of animals (sometimes with associated anthropomorphs). Compiled by Radosław Palonka after Schaafsma 1994:Figure 132 and drawing by Magdalena Lewandowska.

can be distinguished between the styles within the Colorado Plateau, while the style from the Lower Pecos, although connected chronologically and somewhat stylistically with the Barrier Canyon style (Cole 2004:41–42; Schaafsma 1980), developed far away, in what is today Texas (and despite the similarities, there are many differences between Barrier Canyon and Lower Pecos styles). Yet another Late Archaic style on the southern fringes of the Southwest is the Chihuahua's Abstract Polychrome style (Schaafsma 1980:43–47) which does not, however, have many features in common with the Barrier Canyon style.

Some of the most spectacular examples of rock paintings are found in the lower part of the Pecos River valley in Texas. These were created at different times, with the Pecos River style being the oldest in this sequence and distinguished by Red Linear, Red Monochrome, and Historic Period, although traces of settlement in this region date back to the Paleoindian period. Research on this rock art has been conducted by many scientists, but studies and documentation using a wide range of modern technologies conducted by Carolyn Boyd (e.g., Boyd 2013, 2016) and her interdisciplinary team with the name SHUMLA (shumla.org) has possibly contributed the greatest achievements and publicity for these sites.

The Beginnings of Agriculture and the "Neolithic Revolution" in the Southwest

The origin of corn (*Zea mays*) agriculture is a characteristic feature of the Late Archaic in the Southwest. Corn agriculture emerged over a short period of time in several places in this area, first primarily in southern Arizona in the Tucson Basin, and also in the Colorado Plateau, and in northwestern and central New Mexico, including the Mogollon Mountains, the area of the present-day Zuni Reservation and on the border of Utah and Arizona (Matson 1991, 2008; McBrinn and Vierra 2017). The adoption of agriculture was probably a complex economic, cultural, and social process consisting of various factors, with a significant role played by changes in the climate and the natural environment happening independently of human activities.

From around 3900 BC, a more humid period began in the Southwest with less severe and warmer winters, culminating in 2500–50 BC when there were more frost-free days during a year and thus an extended growing season for plants. At the same time, a relatively high level of groundwater and the presence of periodically flooded river valleys are

recorded in the Late Holocene. According to many researchers, these factors culminated in the emergence of favorable conditions for the adoption
and development of agriculture in the Southwest (e.g., Merrill et al. 2009;
Vint and Mabry 2017:247–48). This period also coincided with the expansion of juniper and piñon pine forests to the Colorado Plateau (which
was already occurring before 3100 BC), providing a variety of nutrition
to supplement farming.

Sometimes the period of transition from hunter-gatherer communities to a productive and more stable agricultural economy is referred to in
American archaeology as the Early Formative period. In modern Southwestern terminology the most commonly used tag is the "Early Agricultural Period" (Vint and Mabry 2017:Table 12.1). In the twentieth century
the term *formative period* was often used to describe a certain stage in the
development of Native American communities, primarily as manifested by
the emergence of a more settled lifestyle, as well as the beginnings of pot-

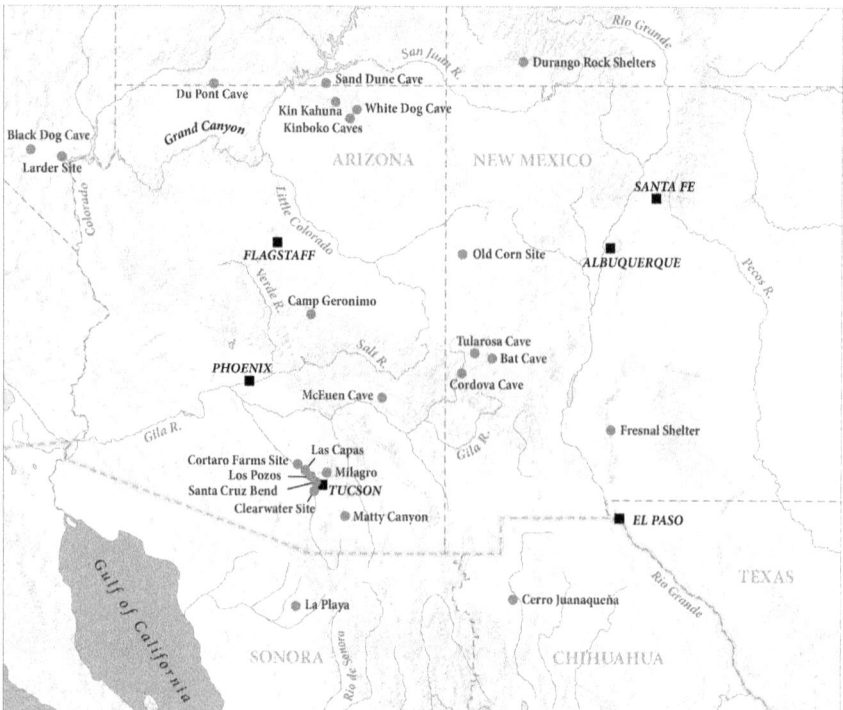

Figure 3.9. The oldest sites with domesticated plants in the Southwest primarily corn and
squash (after Matson 1991; Merrill et al. 2009; Vint and Mabry 2017:Figure 12.1). Compiled
by Radosław Palonka and drawing by Michał Znamirowski.

tery production and agriculture; the term came into use in the 1950s (e.g., Flannery 1968; Willey and Phillips 1958; Woodbury and Zubrow 1979).

It seems however, that in the case of the Southwest (e.g., Cordell 1997:223) the use of this term is not entirely suitable, mainly due to the rather harsh, dry climate and the tremendous diversity of nature within subregions, and the resultant degree of dependence on agriculture in individual communities and their need to combine agriculture with other methods of obtaining food. In the ancient or pre-Columbian Southwest, the model of living in small settlements observably functioned over a long time, along with periodic migrations that involved abandoning some areas and then occupying others often without returning to previous places.

Throughout the entire Southwest, the end of the Archaic, apart from the development of agriculture, coincided with the emergence and large-scale use of pottery and new household structures, such as pithouses, and permanent (or at least only seasonally moved) settlements associated with them. This mode of living formalized quite late, from 200 BC to 800 AD in areas of the Southwest, from the Grand Canyon to central New Mexico and from southern Utah and Colorado (the Cedar Mesa region and Dolores River basin) to the northern states of Sonora and Chihuahua in Mexico, although it could have happened earlier in different parts of this region.

The adoption of agriculture most likely arrived from what is now Mexico. The first and main crop in the Southwest was corn, which based on genetic studies and molecular biology, evolved from wild teosinte grass (*Zea mexicana* or *Zea perennis*) around 7000/8000 BC in southern Mexico (e.g., Cordell 1997; Matsuoka et al. 2002; see also most recent discussion for example at Roth 2016). Corn agriculture wended its way to the Southwest and Colorado Plateau several thousand years later, probably around 2200/2000 BC (or perhaps slightly earlier) most likely via the trade routes leading from the Oaxaca valley through the Tehuacán valley and the Tamaulipas region and further north (Merrill et al. 2009; Piperno and Flannery 2001). This dissemination of knowledge regarding the cultivation of corn and other crops in southern Arizona appears to have taken place from south to north along rivers and farther to the north for the Southwest region. This process most likely occurred in phases as varieties of corn were introduced and adapted to the climate of the region, and as agrarian techniques improved (Vint and Mabry 2017).

The fact that corn and the vast majority of other crops grown in the Southwest (some plants such as amaranth and barley may have been domesticated locally) came from Mexico is beyond doubt today. Controversies and disputes among researchers, however, focus on whether the spread of agriculture occurred through the adoption of discoveries via contact with groups from northern and central Mexico, or whether it was brought about by visitors from central Mexico who were colonizing southern and central Arizona, and later the Colorado Plateau located more to the north (e.g., Matson 1991; Vint and Mabry 2017). Some archaeologists and linguists including Jane Hill, interpret and associate the spread of agricultural knowledge in the Southwest with the expansion of peoples speaking languages from the Uto-Aztec, or rather the Proto-Uto-Aztecan (the so-called PUA) language family from Mexico (e.g., Hill 1999, 2001, 2002, 2017).

According to Hill, the population associated with the Proto-Uto-Aztecan languages around 4000 BC already inhabited a vast territory from the mountains of Sonora and Chihuahua in Mexico to the mountains and highlands of south-central Arizona. Their expansion from Mexico—the motherland of the population speaking these languages—is thought to have been associated with the pressure of overpopulation resulting, in a sense, from the success of agriculture, which translated into demographic growth in that area. During the period around 2000 BC, after the adoption of agriculture, this population in the Southwest would be divided into two groups—northern and southern—and according to Hill, the fact that this division took place after the adoption of agriculture proves that a more settled lifestyle drastically limited contact between different communities, which resulted in the differentiation seen in languages today. Apart from Hill's studies, archaeologist Peter Bellwood, also claimed expansion of the maize agriculture from Mesoamerica to the US Southwest as a consequence of the migration of Proto-Uto-Aztecan farmers (as part of his farming/language dispersal hypothesis) (e.g., Bellwood 1997, 1999).

These studies, however, assume the presence of Proto-Uto-Aztecan groups in the vicinity of the Southwest (see below) long before the adoption of agriculture (even ca. 6900 BC when they began to divide into subgroups and migrate to the Southwest (Merrill et al. 2009). Merrill et al. (2009) also suggest the subsequent, rather slow, migration of agriculture from Mexico (chain method, from group to group diffusion) but also Uto-Aztecans as main "helpers" in the adoption of farming practices.

The model proposed by Hill has been considered from various perspectives, including decorating styles, techniques used to make certain objects (points, *atl-atl* spear throwers, baskets, and sandals) (Mabry 2008), and in studies integrating archaeological data with the results of linguistic, genetic and paleoenvironmental studies (Merrill et al. 2009).

So, not everyone accepts Hill's theory, especially as it assumes that the Uto-Aztecan language originated in Mexico, while a number of researchers locate it somewhere in the Southwest or in the West of the United States, for example in the west-central Great Basin (e.g., Kemp 2006, for further reading; Merrill et al. 2009; see also Merrill 2012). Furthermore, some researchers hypothesize the spread of agriculture to the Southwest with the damper climate and more favorable conditions for agriculture (Carpenter et al. 2005), and divide the first farmers into groups, such as newcomers speaking Uto-Aztecan languages, and local people adopted agriculture from them (e.g., Matson 1991, 2002).

Genetic studies of ancient corn along with the study of human mitochondrial DNA (mtDNA) and the male Y chromosome are an important, perhaps decisive, consideration in these theories. These genetic studies trace the contribution of individual haplogroups and haplotypes in contemporary indigenous communities of the Southwest and Mexico speaking languages from the Uto-Aztecan family (Kemp 2006; Kemp et al. 2010; Malhi et al. 2003). These studies do not confirm the theory of the migration of Uto-Aztec peoples (or Proto-Uto-Aztec peoples) and the concurrent spread of agriculture to the Southwest.

William Doolittle and Jonathan Mabry postulate a more complex interpretation of the emergence of farming crops in the Southwest (Doolittle and Mabry 2006). Their research focuses on the large variety of environmental niches in the region, which is likely relevant to the faster or slower adoption of agriculture, and tends to dismiss the emergence of the agricultural economy as a one-off event from Mexico. Citing a significant amount of data, they claim that the local Archaic people were already practicing the local cultivation of certain crops about a thousand years before the arrival of maize in the Southwest; these are considerations that should be taken seriously, especially as many researchers confirm the presence of some domesticated endemic plants in the Southwest.

The "Neolithic Revolution" in the Southwest

The emergence of agriculture in the North American Southwest and the neolithization of this process in the Old World was a phenomenon whereby agriculture was adopted from influences outside, and not discovered locally, as it was in several large centers of neolithization throughout the world (but with few exceptions, see below).

Neolithic revolution is a term coined by British archaeologist Gordon Childe (Childe 1936) to refer to the gradual transition from an exclusively hunter-gatherer economy to one based on the cultivation of certain plant species and an agricultural economy. Today this process is more precisely referred to as the *Neolithic transition*. Neolithic transitions occurred independently in various parts of the world, including in the Middle East, Asia, and several parts of the Americas (see, for example, Price and Bar-Yosef 2011). In addition to changing the economy and human diet, the transition was also associated with demographic and social changes, primarily an increase in fertility which may indirectly indicate a certain nutritional stabilization and the number of births along with new social structures. In recent years, this term has been increasingly used by American researchers, including those from the Crow Canyon Archaeological Center and several universities (e.g., Washington State University) to highlight the role of the plant domestication process in the US Southwest (although these researchers often use different criteria than those in Europe to describe the general periodization of human cultures.)

The characteristics of the "Neolithic transition" in the North American Southwest are the same determinants of economic and social change as elsewhere in the world: an agriculture-based diet with appropriate food storage techniques, larger and permanent settlements (often over fifty people per settlement), population growth, social stratification, and the emergence of pottery and other types of tools. However, as recent studies show, this process probably took longer and was more regionally diverse in the Southwest compared to other places in the world (e.g., Kohler and Reese 2014). The most important element in this transition was the emergence of cultivated corn, while other components of "the Neolithic Package" (for example pottery or more permanent villages) appeared somewhat later or independently in different parts of the region.

The current state of research allows us to suppose that in the Southwest, the introduction of agriculture was not caused by a desire to boost food stocks, improve stability in obtaining food, or to rely mainly on food obtained from crops—the oldest forms of corn were very small and low in calories—but instead it was associated with a more varied diet (Vint and Mabry 2017, see there for further literature). Studies of bones of the early farmers in the Southwest show a strong dependency on wild plants and meat, and only the first millennium BC (as can be seen, for example, in the Basketmaker period of the Ancestral Pueblo culture) welcomed a change in this area. For a long time, gathering remained an important method of obtaining food, even in typically agricultural and developed communities in this area, helping to counterbalance the uncertain and quite unstable conditions of the natural environment and the changing climate of the Southwest.

It also seems that individual crops came to the Southwest separately, and not together in a kind of "bundle"; obviously, the primary plant was corn (maize). These crops spread throughout the region at different rates; for example, corn and squash sprang up in many places simultaneously practically as soon as they arrived in the Southwest. Gourds and later beans spread much more slowly.

The knowledge of the cultivation of corn (and often squash along with it) occurred almost simultaneously in several places in the Southwest, although the Tucson Basin is the region where agriculture with artificial irrigation in the form of water channels was first adopted and where we find most of its earliest evidence (e.g., Mabry 2008). Some of the first traces of maize cultivation are in the southern Arizona area (around 2000/2200 BC), and the first irrigation canals near present-day Tucson appeared sometime later. Interestingly, the available radiocarbon dates strongly suggest that irrigation canals were "invented" and used in the Sonoran Desert and the Southwest ca. 1250 BC; so before they were in Mexico, at least one century earlier if not more (Vint and Mabry 2017:253).

The most important sites featuring the remains of cultivated corn in this area are Milagro, Las Capas, Los Pozos, the entire complex of sites from this region and mainly the Santa Cruz River basin in southern Arizona, as well as Bat Cave, Cordova Cave, and Tularosa Cave in central-western New Mexico. As a rule, sites in Arizona were located in floodplain areas of low-lying river valleys. This seems to have been a pattern for situating the first multiphase sites related to agriculture, and the areas suitable for artificial irrigation became very valuable, as indicated, for example, by the Tucson Basin region. The second such pattern involves the above-mentioned cave sites from the areas higher in New Mexico. Another slightly different "model" are the settlements of the first farmers located in the hills—including the Cerro Juanaqueña site in the Mexican state of Chihuahua and a group of such sites from southern Arizona (Cordell 1997; Doelle 1999; Hard and Roney 2005; Vint and Mabry 2017).

Until recently perhaps the most famous site associated with the early farmers of the Southwest and traces of domesticated corn was Bat Cave in New Mexico, whose oldest corn-related strata were dated to around 2000 BC. However, some researchers claim that the verification of earlier studies and new dating have revealed that we should probably consider a much younger chronology, with traces of corn and squash cultivation from around 1000 BC, although some scientists still opt for older dates (Ford 1985; Matson 1991:247–51, see there for further reading; Roth 2016; Wills 1985, 1988). Despite the uncertainty as to the exact dating, this is one of the flagship sites of the second type (caves) alongside those established on a flat floodplain near rivers from the Late Archaic period and the Early Agricultural Period.

There are many known varieties and types of corn; in the Southwest alone, there are at least a few or a dozen; they differ in color, shape, size of the cobs and grains, as well as in taste. Other crops most likely to come to the Southwest from Mesoamerica are squash (*Cucurbita pepo*)-around 1100 BC (Roth 2016) and other cucurbits (*Cucurbitaceae*), which provide nutritious seeds, flowers, and pulp, and are also used as containers. Squash remains are found in pre-pottery sites almost wherever corn appears; until about 900 AD there was, practically speaking, one type of squash throughout the Southwest, but after that date many different types occurred, perhaps due to more frequent contact with the Mesoamerica.

The gourd (*Lagenaria siceraria*) appeared somewhat later in the Southwest (around 300 BC—Cordell 1997:135 after Ford 1981) which was well-suited for making various types of containers; its seeds are also highly nutritious. Remains of early gourds have been discovered from the Southwest—for example, from the Tularosa and Cordova caves—but because gourds are less tolerant to frost and cold spells than other crops, they are rarely found in the northern parts of the Southwest. There were also various types of beans (including common beans—*Phaseolus vulgaris*), estimated to have appeared sometime around 500/300 BC (in the Colorado Plateau only after 200 AD). A widely accepted theory is that beans, squash, and maize (called as "three sisters") complement each other in terms of essential amino acids, acting together as a substitute for animal protein. Furthermore their cultivation alongside each other in the same fields effectively protects against soil exhaustion and pests. Corn was—and still is in many Native American societies in North, Central, and South America—a very important component of beliefs and rituals.

Somewhere between 300 and 500 AD new Mesoamerican crops were grown, but unlike the first "wave" of corn and squash adopted by hunter-gatherer communities, these crops now found their way into the hands of farmers, enriching the "set" of crops. Here we can include, among others, cotton (*Gossypium hirsutum var.*), extremely important to weaving and trade for many pre-Hispanic communities in the Southwest, as well as new types of beans and squash plants, possibly from the Tehuacán Valley region (Cordell 1997).

Some plants were probably first domesticated in the Southwest (e.g., Roth 2016) including some types of beans, amaranth (*Amaranthus hypochon-*

driacus), agave (*Agave murpheyi* or *Agave parryi*) which was widely used both as food and for plant fibers for weaving and making cloth and sandals, a kind of small barley (*Horedeum pusillum*), so-called devil's claw (*Proboscidea parviflora var.*), and *Cleome serrulata*, also known as Rocky Mountain beeweed, which provided both nutritious edible parts and pigments to decorate ceramics. An interesting plant is tobacco; there are still disputes as to whether it was a plant grown in the Southwest (*Nicotiana rustica*) or whether wild tobacco (*Nicotiana trigonophylla*) was harvested, a practice followed by many native groups in this area, including the Hopis from Arizona.

Three or four phases of the Late Archaic connected with early agricultural communities (Cordell 1997; Vint and Mabry 2017) may be singled out:

1. no named phase (2100/2000–1200 BC) characterized by the oldest sites with domesticated plant remains (corn and squash) that includes sites: Bat Cave, Tularosa Cave, Cordova Cave, Milagro, Las Capas;
2. San Pedro phase (1200–800/400 BC) that was the final phase of the Late Archaic and when the agriculture spread to most of the Southwest (including to a greater extent the Colorado Plateau and the Rio Grande Basin) as well as the first irrigation canals appeared (including Las Capas in southern Arizona);
3. Early Cienega phase (800–400 BC), when agriculture occurred in the northern and eastern parts of the Colorado Plateau;
4. Late Cienega phase (400–50 BC) when agriculture finally expands throughout the majority of the Southwest.

Today researchers are uncovering promising data about cultivated corn dating it even from around 3700 BC at older sites from the Southwest, but they are yet to be published (Vint and Mabry 2017:249); a similar situation arose with the discovery two decades ago of the oldest irrigation channels from Las Capas in the Santa Cruz Valley in southern Arizona and other sites—e.g., La Playa in the Mexican Sonora—discoveries that have now been published and are officially included in the literature on the subject (e.g., Mabry 2008). These first "farmer" sites are grouped into certain enclaves and micro-regions, but there were many places where the hunter-gatherer economy continued to develop; the cultivation of corn and squash was not widespread in the entire Southwest region—especially in its northern and eastern parts—until the period of 1300/1200 BC—that is, the beginning of the San Pedro phase.

LAS CAPAS SITE Discoveries such as those at Las Capas (Mabry 2008; Tennesen 2009), near Tucson have yielded many phases of the existence of hunter-gatherers from the Archaic period (from about 2800 BC), as well as later settlements already associated with early farmers (from about 2100 BC), and an extensive network of irrigation channels from about 1250/1200 BC. These discoveries shed new light on how tightly organized the early Southwest farming communities were when it came to cultivating this environmentally challenging area. The Las Capas site is located on the former floodplain of the Santa Cruz River below the influx of its two tributaries and near the present-day city of Tucson. At this site, twelve Late Archaic/Early Agricultural irrigation channels have been discovered so far, ten of which have been radiocarbon dated from 1250 BC up to 750/500 BC (e.g., Mabry 2008) (figure 3.10a). At Las Capas, approximately fifty hectares have been surveyed by Desert Archaeology Inc. within a contract of archaeology research.

It is clearly visible that this site functioned for a very long time. Throughout this entire period, artificial irrigation was used and agriculture took hold permanently as the population managed to develop an effective model of farming in an inhospitable semi-arid climate. It proves that social changes taking place among the population, having until recently been based on a different economic model, did not necessarily lead to the emergence of hierarchical structures, but did give rise to a strong social and probably political organization, capable of running and maintaining the set of channels, irrigation systems, and plots over a fairly large area.

At the Las Capas site, there is a system of main channels supplying water from the river, second-rank canals that supplied water to the vicinity of cultivated fields, as well as third-rank canals distributing water directly to cultivated plots. The main canals were roughly 1.5 to 2 meters wide and 50–75 centimeters deep (Vint and Mabry 2017). The arable plots were rather small (about 4 × 6 m), fenced with low earth embankments. Such small farming fields (gardens) could have been irrigated more efficiently as it was easier to access them and distribute the water even when it was scarce; perhaps individual parts of such a system were intended for the cultivation of individual plants, and some plots could have even been used while others were excluded from cultivation at that time. The remains of some species of *crustaceans* and snails found in these channels suggest that water flowed in them for at least several months of the year, and the presence of other species indicates that the water must have been clean and running—that is, it did not stagnate and probably did not stay long in the channel in question.

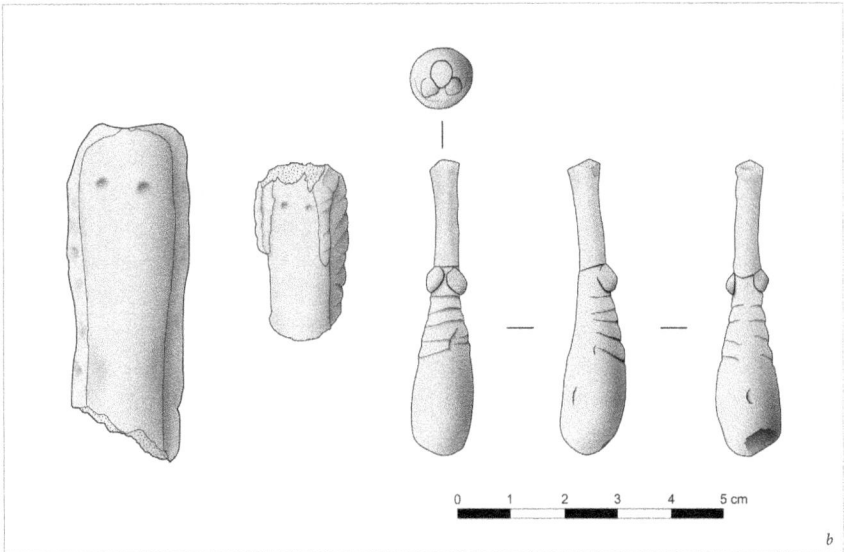

Figure 3.10. A fragment of the canal system from the Las Capas site (white, parallel lines represent small earth embankments for separating farming fields from water channels) (a); and (b) drawings of selected clay figurines from the Las Capas site as an example of mobile art from the Early Agricultural period. Photo by Radosław Palonka, drawings by Katarzyna Ciomek.

On the periphery of these irrigation canal systems, groups of two to four houses were located at fairly equal distances from each other with accompanying bell-shaped storage pits and other structures. At the end of the Early Agricultural Period, however, these storage pits were already located inside households, which resulted in greater protection against pests and theft of stocks, but also resulted in shorter storage in domestic conditions (Vint and Mabry 2017:259, see there for further reading).

In addition to canals, traces of agricultural practices and houses, processing sites and workshops and significant quantities of flint and stone artifacts (including a large collection of repaired tools), e.g. *mano* and *metate*, have been discovered at Las Capas. The techniques of making flint tools starting around 900 BC indicate a far-reaching similarity in southern Arizona and northern Sonora and may be evidence of the south–north population flow. Anthropomorphic clay figurines from the Las Capas site (figure 3.10b) are found in the context of houses and middens; perhaps they were associated with domestic rituals, many bearing traces of having been painted with hematite (also common in burials, most often in the form of inhumation in that period); some of these figurines were probably intentionally broken (Vint and Mabry 2017:258–59).

LA PLAYA SITE The site of La Playa in Sonora, Mexico, is similar in area to the Las Capas site in Arizona and from the same period. La Playa was studied extensively in the 1990s by Mexican archaeologists in collaboration with American researchers (e.g., Carpenter et al. 1999, 2005). La Playa was a multiphase site, with traces of human cultures from the Paleoindian to the Early Historic (Colonial) period. However, most of the data has been obtained from archaeological strata dating back to the Early Agricultural Period (1500 BC–200 AD). Discoveries at La Playa include ancient irrigation canals from that period that are faced with characteristic stone slabs and numerous bell-shaped pits for food storage, ovens/pits for roasting and baking food featuring the remains of corn, amaranth, cholla, prickly pear, sage, quinoa, and other plants, as well as animals such as deer, mountain sheep, hares, desert turtles and small rodents.

A large group of objects at the La Playa site are related to inhumation and cremation burials, but cremation begins to prevail there at the beginning of our era, similar to the practice in southern Arizona at that time. The dead were buried in a fetal position, often with one hand clasped to the knees and the other to the face. Little grave goods were used in the burials, but some skeletal graves contained fragments of hematite, usually placed on the limbs of the deceased. Analyses of the bones indicate that the population was fairly well-nourished and in relatively good health (Carpenter et al. 1999, 2005).

CERRO JUNAQUEÑA SITE A slightly different settlement and agricultural model is represented by the site of Cerro Juanaqueña in the Chihuahua state in northern Mexico. Like Las Casas and La Playa, it is an open site, but it is characterized by terraced residential buildings on the slopes and hilltop situated above the flood plain of the Rio Casas Grandes; small arable fields (a form of home gardening) were also located on these terraces. The site is dated to around 1150 BC (Hard and Roney 2005) and consists of nearly 500 terraces and over 100 circular stone and other structures. The fact that the houses were located here suggests an intentional defensive location, which, taken together with the aggregation and concentration of settlements, may indicate regional conflicts. Numerous artifacts were found in the context of the terraces including large stone *metate* and *mano*, as well as flint points, artifacts that are similar to those found in the Tucson Basin (Matson 1999).

The sites mentioned above and many other settlements from the time of transition from the Late Archaic to the Early Agricultural period formed the basis for the development of further, complex agricultural cultures. These include the Pueblo culture, which dates back to at least 1000/500 BC and continues to thrive today, the Hohokam which created an impressive network of irrigation channels for successfully farming the desert areas of central and southern Arizona, comparable to the irrigation systems of ancient Mesopotamia or Peru in the period between 450/500–1450 AD—and the Mogollon-Mimbres communities and the Casas Grandes (Paquimé) cultural tradition of northern Mexico. Within this set of complex agricultural societies, researchers often include the Fremont culture of what is now Utah. These cultures are part of the great circle of pre-Hispanic agricultural societies of the Southwest.

Notes

1. Calibrated (calendar) dates are presented everywhere in the book. In case of uncalibrated dates, they will be marked separately. The text also uses the abbreviation BC (Before Common Era), denoting dates calibrated (calendar) before our era, BP (Before the Present) to denote a date prior to 1950 (this date is taken as the limit for counting radiocarbon dates backwards) and kya for thousand years ago. "Pre-Clovis" (a term mainly used in North America) or "long chronology"—as it is more commonly referred to in Europe—dates the arrival of people in the New World and the oldest sites related to human cultures in America to around

thirty-five to forty thousand years ago. Apart from archaeological data, the results of genetic and, albeit indirectly, linguistic research also speak very clearly in favor of "long chronology." The "Clovis-first" or "short chronology" theory built on site dates—unchallenged by either side—suggest that the Clovis culture, the first Paleoindian human culture in America, did not appear in the New World until about thirteen thousand years ago.

2. Then similar conditions also prevailed in most of the area, the so-called The European Lowlands from Western Europe (northern France) to Central-Eastern Europe and further east.

3. This is completely different from the paleolithic rock art in the Franco-Cantabrian region in Western Europe, where many rock art galleries were located deep in the caves, likely with limited access for only some members of the society.

Architects, Artists, and Farmers of the Colorado Plateau   **4**
Ancestral Pueblo Culture

╫╫

MONG THE MANY CULTURES and communities that have shaped the cultural face of the North American Southwest, the Pueblo deserve special attention. In the pre-Hispanic period, the Pueblo occupied a large part of the Colorado Plateau—that is, the central and northern part of the Southwest. Having survived centuries of contact with Euro-Americans, the Pueblo culture still exists in modern Pueblo groups in Arizona and New Mexico. At its widest boundaries, the territory inhabited by Ancestral Pueblo societies included southern Utah and Colorado, and the northern and central parts of Arizona and New Mexico, extended to southeastern Nevada and periodically to western Texas where Pueblo enclaves are known to have existed in the historic period (figure 4.1).

Individual Pueblo groups developed in rhythms of cultural and social change and lived in different environmental niches; not all the areas where this culture emerged were inhabited simultaneously—some places were deserted, and the population moved to other areas. This cultural heterogeneity is still visible today. The most important subregions in the development of pre-Hispanic Pueblo culture include the Chaco Canyon region in northwestern New Mexico, which at one time exerted a powerful cultural influence on a large area of the Southwest; the Mesa Verde region located at the junction of Utah, Colorado, and New Mexico; the Kayenta region in northeastern and northern Arizona and the southern part of Utah (within this region, the Virgin Kayenta region is sometimes distinguished from the western parts of these two neighboring states and from southeastern Nevada); and, in the late pre-Hispanic (protohistoric) and historic period, the Tusayan region in northern Arizona including the area where Hopi have their reservation today. Additionally, during the pre-Hispanic

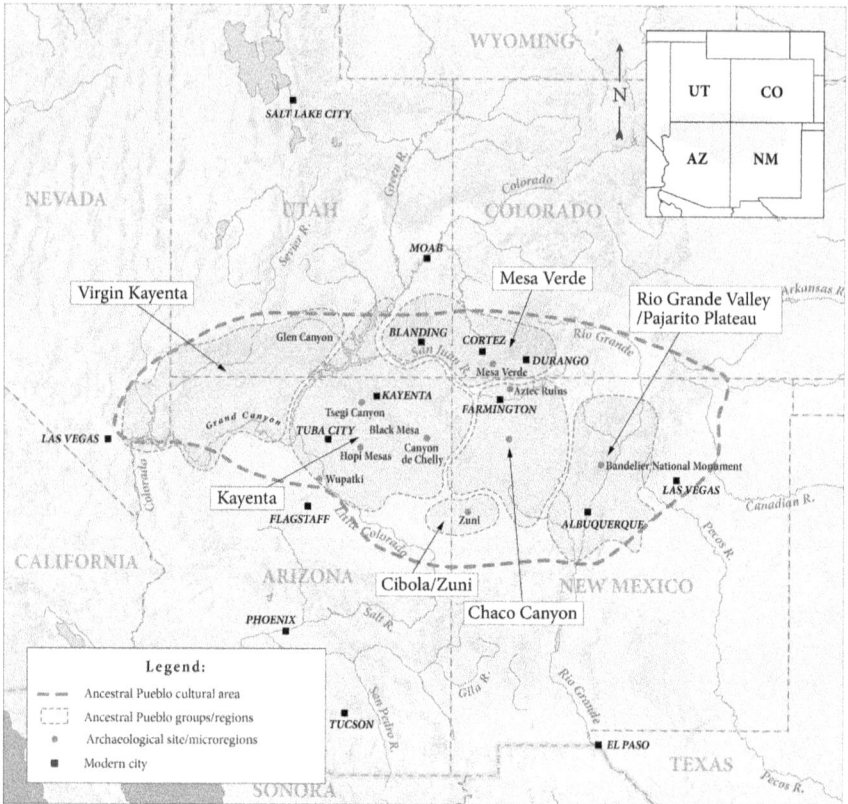

Figure 4.1. Map of the Ancestral Pueblo world with areas marked where various groups of this culture developed. Compiled by the author after various sources and drawing by Michał Znamirowski.

period and during the historic and modern periods, the Pueblo occupied the Cibola region in the western part of New Mexico and a large area of the Rio Grande River valley and its tributaries.

Due to the expansive thematic and chronological scope of this topic, this chapter focuses on the most important research issues and areas, with emphasis on the Mesa Verde and Chaco regions, where Ancestral Pueblo culture developed to a great extent during the pre-Hispanic period.

Unlike most of the complex farming traditions of the area, many of which disappeared even before the arrival of the Europeans, the Pueblo culture[1] has been developing since the beginning of the first millennium BC until now. Although quite diverse in terms of language—they are divided into five completely different linguistic groups—beliefs and the degree to which their traditions and identities have survived, today's Pueblo groups constitute a unique culture that is distinct from other groups in this region.

There are two main periods in the development of the Pueblo culture: the Basketmaker period (from around 1000/500 BC to ca. 700 AD), still without stone architecture and pottery, but predominantly agricultural, and the subsequent Pueblo period (from 700 AD until today) (e.g., Cordell 1997:Table 7.1, 164–65; Kidder 1927; Plog 1997:9). Many changes are observable from the very beginning of the latter period, notably the emergence of aboveground buildings made of sandstone or adobe, reaching heights of up to three and possibly four stories in later phases. In addition, there were changes in the economy, including the intensification of arable farming along with the domestication of turkey and new crops like cotton and extensive trade with other areas, for example, parts of Mesoamerica. A rich material culture in the form of decorated pottery, murals on building walls, and jewelry arose along with these sophisticated developments. These two periods, in turn, are divided into smaller phases and subperiods, defined slightly differently for individual groups and regions.

For many years, the chronology of the Pueblo culture was based on the so-called Pecos Chronology or Pecos Classification, adopted at the Pecos conference in 1927 (Kidder 1927). The periods of this classification are as follows: Basketmaker II (?–400 AD); Basketmaker III (400–700 AD); Pueblo I (700–900 AD); Pueblo II (900–1100 AD); Pueblo III (1100–1300 AD); Pueblo IV (1300–1600 AD); and Pueblo V (sometimes called also as historic period) is also distinguished, beginning ca. 1600 AD and lasting until today (Cordell 1997:164–67).

Today the Pecos Chronology is still referred to by local chronologies, although progress made through research on dating and the huge increase in new data have resulted in more distinct local chronologies. This multiplicity has resulted in a return to the traditional Pecos Chronology which still stands as a reference point. Also, in scientific literature, as well as in popular science and colloquial language, the term *Anasazi* was often used to describe the Ancestral Pueblo culture, although it is very rarely used today. Anasazi was a name used by archaeologists since the 1930s—a distorted English equivalent of the Navajo phrase meaning "Ancestral enemies" or "Enemies of our ancestors" because at the time, the Navajos often worked on excavations, and thus influenced the use of this term. Contemporary Puebloans regard the term as offensive and do not use it; rather they refer to their ancestors in various ways depending on the group. For example, the Hopi of northern Arizona speak of their ancestors as *Hisatsinom*, which in their language simply means the people who came before them. The commonly used term in English today is *Ancestral Pueblo*.

From Pithouses to the Beginnings of Pueblo Construction: The Basketmaker Period

The first noticeable period in the development of the Ancestral Pueblo culture is rooted in the Archaic—the so-called Basketmaker period. The term was used for the first time at the end of the nineteenth century (as Basket People and Basket Makers). A member of a Colorado cowboy and rancher family named Richard Wetherill pioneered research on this and other periods of the development of the Pueblo culture (Matson 1991:14). After several years of work with amateur and professional archaeologists including European scholar Gustaf Nordenskiöld, Wetherills became an expert and researcher of Pueblo culture, although he and his brothers and father were accused of conducting excavations for the sake of selling artifacts, a common practice at the time in the absence of regulations. It was only with Alfred Kidder and Samuel Guernsey in the 1920s and 1930s (e.g., Guernsey 1931; Kidder and Guernsey 1919) that thorough research was conducted on this period, along with systematization of the acquired knowledge.

Wetherills did rather accurately define the most important features of the community of this pre-ceramic period in the Pueblo culture including the presence of spear throwers (before bows and arrows), corn storage pits, burial pits, a large number of baskets, and sandals made of yucca and other parts of cloths made of leather, which differed from those of the later Pueblo period. Interestingly, this former cowboy and archaeology enthusiast was one of the first—if not the first—in the Southwest to use a stratigraphic distinction between layers (as well as between burials), to separate distinctive artifacts from the levels of the Basketmaker and later Pueblo periods (e.g., Matson 1991; Willey and Sabloff 1993).

In the first stage of this culture's development, individual Pueblo groups, most likely derived from the Oshara tradition (one of the four major cultural traditions of the Archaic period) were already leading a more settled lifestyle, and the basis of their existence was, as we assume today, largely agriculture (e.g., Matson 1991), although in the past, researchers have argued that corn crops were sporadic among the population of the Basketmaker II period. In phase II of the Basketmaker period, the culture split into two large groups, Eastern and Western. On the basis of differences in material culture and morphological skeletons, Richard Matson

(1991, 2002, 2008) proposed the theory that the population of the Western group was directly related to the San Pedro phase of the Late Archaic Cochise tradition, thus its descendants would be the communities of today's Western Pueblos (mainly Hopi, speaking a language of the Uto-Aztecan family); the Eastern group, on the other hand, is thought to consist of descendants of the population of the Archaic period who adopted agriculture from the Western group, and whose descendants today are the people of the Eastern Pueblo world from the Rio Grande valley, including groups that speak Tanoan languages. The territory occupied by this group is believed to extend from the area of today's Durango in the southwestern part of Colorado to the area south of Cuba in New Mexico and group in the upper reaches of the San Juan and Rio Puerco River basins.

Studies on the differentiation of these two groups have also been carried out on the basis of economies and various types of artifacts including, to a large extent, those made of organic materials found in huge quantities at sites from the Basketmaker period, and by using DNA samples (primarily mitochondrial DNA) from human remains and coprolites (fossils of humans excrements) (e.g., Matson 2008). Rich collections of organic artifacts were found in the first decades of the twentieth century, many of which were collected by Alfred Kidder and Samuel Guernsey, for example at the White Dog Cave and Kinboko Caves 1 and 2 sites on the Rainbow Plateau in northern Arizona (Geib and Spurr 2002).

Studies conducted on solid ^{12}C and ^{13}C carbon isotopes (Chisholm and Matson 1994; Matson and Chisholm 1991) and from human skeletons found at Cedar Mesa and Grand Gulch in southeastern Utah confirmed that the relatively small proportion of the ^{13}C isotope in bones from the Basketmaker period is very close to the percentage of this isotope in the bones of the Pueblo people from the Pueblo II and III periods, and is completely different from those of the Archaic period of the Oshara tradition. This dating in turn, proves that during the Basketmaker period, the amount of corn consumed, and thus dependence on it, was similar to later Pueblo periods, unlike that in Archaic hunter-gatherer communities. Researchers studying representative bones of the Basketmaker III community from the Mesa Verde region (e.g., Decker and Tieszen 1989) and coprolites from the Turkey Pen site in Utah dated to the Basketmaker II period (Aasen 1984; Lepofsky 1986), reached similar conclusions. These studies also indicate a high dependence on cultivated maize, which is confirmed by analyses from the Black Mesa in northern Arizona.

At the beginning of the Basketmaker II period, Ancestral Puebloans grew primarily corn and squash (early-stage beans were either not yet present at all or were only grown on a very small scale), and supplemented their diet with food from hunted animals (mainly deer, turkeys, hares, and rabbits, and—depending on availability—mountain sheep) as well as by foraging wild plants, including piñon pine nuts and other seeds, fruits, and nuts (Lipe 1999). The location of Basketmaker settlements near the most fertile lands does not differ significantly from the site location preferences in later periods. River floodplains seemed to be the most popular settlement sites at the time, with a gradual move toward fields situated in higher areas. Numerous groups of farmers probably displaced Archaic hunter-gatherer communities from attractive agricultural lands, as suggested by research on the area where Zuni Pueblo is today (Matson 2008).

As mentioned, the Basketmaker societies probably chose reasonably fertile areas with constant access to water. However research shows that for quite a long time this population group did not increase in number (Geib and Spurr 2002; Smiley 1997), one of the features of the so-called the Neolithic transition described in the previous chapter. A level population lasted until the improvement of agricultural technology and the introduction of crops into other areas without permanent access to water, but based on rainfall that had a rather high level of groundwater (so-called dry-land farming). Around the turn of the eras, the move to dry-land farming was accompanied by the appearance of larger population centers. Some researchers associate success in adopting and fully adapting agriculture, for example in the San Juan Valley (e.g., Robins 2002), with changes in social structure and the emergence of headmen who were able to successfully lead the adoption of agricultural processes and convince others to participate in this new economic model. There may have been a connection between the placement of rock art, especially monumental representations of anthropomorphic figures, and farmland (Robins 2002, see also below).

Despite the fact that the majority of the population of the Basketmaker II period preferred and engaged in agriculture, pottery was scarce in what was still the pre-ceramic period; the serious production of pottery started during the final phases of the Basketmaker III period. These examples confirm that the components of the "Neolithic package" did not coexist initially but emerged from different communities in the Southwest over time.

Gourds were used as basic containers in this period but above all were baskets—from which the name of the Basketmaker period originates. These baskets were woven from plant fibers and shoots, mainly yucca and others. On the basis of many cave findings including perfectly preserved fragments and entire baskets, it can be seen that the weaving was extremely dense, which, combined with waterproofing with resin, allowed them to serve as vessels for storing and carrying water and maybe even to boil it. Many everyday items such as nets, ropes, bags, and much more were woven and made from yucca and other plants.

A separate problem remains the question of whether the sites and areas that were occupied and used by hunter-gatherer communities were later inhabited by agricultural groups from the Early Agricultural period and by the populations of the Basketmaker period. The process seems to have unfolded differently in different territories. For example, as described in the previous chapter, the San Pedro Valley area around what is today the city of Tucson, witnessed a settlement continuum of some sort, with no apparent hiatus during this period. The situation may have been different in the Colorado Plateau, especially as the central part of this area contains quite a few sites from the Archaic period, in contrast to the Basketmaker II period and later (e.g., Matson 1991, 2008). Questions of continuous occupation have been studied in the Rainbow Plateau on the Arizona and Utah border (Geib and Spurr 2002), where the researchers considered the possible continuation of both settlement and material culture. The research sample consisted of twenty-seven sites, and radiocarbon dates obtained there indicated an absence of people in the area between the end of the Archaic period and the beginning of the Basketmaker period, a gap of approximately 400 years; the last known Archaic sites date from around 800 BC and are devoid of any traces of maize, whereas the first Basketmakers II settlements appear there no earlier than 400/300 BC, with extensive maize crops right from the outset. Suggestions about settlement discontinuation in this microregion do not necessarily correlate with other areas, but rather (as the authors suggest) point to the many ways in which humans adapt to the diverse environmental conditions of the Southwest.

In the Basketmaker II–III periods, the most commonly established settlements consisted of ten to twenty or so pithouses built according to a rectangular, square, or circular plan; sometimes these houses shared a kind of an adjoining small room (antechamber) (figure 4.2). The walls and roof of these structures were constructed with wooden beams and then covered with branches, earth and/or clay. The roof was usually supported by four vertical wooden poles. The interior of such a house was entered via a ladder leading to a roof opening or through a door in one of the house walls. The interior of the house contained a hearth dug into the ground, frequently accompanied by storage pits below the floor (generally a flattened, smooth earthen floor) as well as clay vessels and pits probably intended for supplies; shelves or earthen benches also ran around the walls, which were mostly faced with sandstone slabs. Additionally, there was a small hole in

Figure 4.2.   Cross-section through a typical pithouse with antechamber from the Basketmaker II–III periods (a) and (b) a photo of the reconstructed pithouse from the Step House in the Mesa Verde National Park, Colorado. Drawing by Michał Znamirowski (after Noble 2000:36 and other sources) and photo by Radosław Palonka.

the floor, the so-called *sipapu*, which, according to the beliefs of modern Pueblo people, is a mystical place from which their ancestors came from the underworld to the present or contemporary world (e.g., Plog 1997:21).

The Basketmaker period is known in various subregions where Ancestral Pueblo culture developed. In Chaco Canyon in modern-day northwestern New Mexico, Basketmaker III period settlements were usually located on plateaus (*mesas*) near the canyon; it is suspected that many undiscovered settlements also lie at the bottom of a wide canyon, probably

under alluvial sediments and the later Great Houses from the Pueblo period (Cordell 1997:190–91). Shabik'eschee village, one of the well-known
sites from this period, was first investigated in the 1920s by Frank H.
Roberts and later, in the 1970s, by archaeologists from the National Park
Service. At least nineteen pithouses and forty-five large storage pits located
outside of these houses were discovered, as well as one Great Kiva (Plog
1997:59–62), a building characteristic of the Pueblo period and at least two
rubbish (midden) mounds. The chronology of Shabik'eschee village spans
approximately 450 to 550 AD.

The houses at this site were quite large (18 sq. m on average), built
according to a circular or rectangular and square plan. The parts of the
walls below the surface of the ground were faced with sandstone slabs and
then plastered; in the central part of the house, a fireplace was set in the
ground or carved into the bedrock. Storage pits similar in construction to
pithouses were built in a bag-like or rectangular shape, with walls faced
with sandstone tiles, and roofs with openings through which food was
placed for storage. It is difficult to estimate how many households existed
at this site at one time, but they may have occupied most of the buildings.
The site could have been established and used by groups that met together
to collect pine nuts and other plants in the fall, and then, depending on
the success of the crops in the area, stayed or dispersed to smaller hamlets.
A small group, however, may have resided there permanently to guard
the food supply (Plog 1997:61; Wills 1991; Wills and Windes 1989). Few
burials are known from this site, including just one located under the floor
of the house.

Another well-known Basketmaker Period site is located in the Mogollon Mountains southwest of Chaco Canyon near today's Reserve. The
SU site features about thirty-five to forty pithouses, twenty-eight of which
were excavated and researched in the 1930s and 1940s by Paul S. Martin.
The dating of this site is very similar to the period of the Shabik'eschee
village and archaeologists often compare these two sites, although they
developed in areas of separate cultural and regional units. Houses at these
sites were constructed using similar techniques, but the SU walls were not
faced with stone slabs and there were no storage rooms directly adjacent
to the houses. SU houses were also larger on average than those from
Shabik'eschee and covered an average area of 38.6 square meters, more
than double the size of the settlement at Chaco Canyon, and most of the
storage pits were located inside the buildings.

The siting of storage pits either inside or outside houses may indicate
a transition from communal ownership (large outside storage pits as in

the case of Shabik'eschee village) to larger forms of private property and enrichment of individuals such as those at, the SU site. They may also indicate a transition from a hunter-gatherer economy to a typical agricultural one in different Pueblo groups, which would not be unusual among individual Pueblo groups that were developing quite rapidly at that time.

Some larger buildings may have performed special religious and social functions, or were home to the families of community leaders and may have also been used for collecting and storing food. During Basketmaker III period, palisades and fences made of wood and branches sometimes occur. In the Mesa Verde region in Colorado, defensive settlements of this type include the Knobby Knee, Gilliland, and Payne sites (Lipe and Varien 1999; Wilshusen 1999:180). Some large settlements from this period were located on the edges of mesas or in other places of limited accessibility, such as the Promontory, Bluff, and Connie sites. Such fortified, defensively located settlements certainly testify to the existence of some conflicts, but the defensive architecture in the form of wooden palisades surrounding the settlements was not particularly common.

During the Basketmaker III period in the Mesa Verde region, settlements were located on plateaus, often on their edges; caves and rock shelters were also used, and houses with an adjacent utility room were oriented toward the south. The first ceramics from this period were found on the border of Utah and Colorado. These examples are of the Chapin Grey type and pottery painted in the Chapin Black-on-White type. Taken together these vessels from the Mesa Verde region represent the beginning of a whole sequence of Pueblo pottery featuring black paint on a white vessel. Small arrowheads have also been observed in lithic assemblages, confirming that bows and arrows were already in use during this period alongside the *atl-atl* spear thrower, which was still in use for a long time.

In the Kayenta region, the Basketmaker period is known mainly thanks to large-scale rescue excavations that preceded the construction of roads and water reservoirs starting in the 1970s and 80s. These include the Glen Canyon Project and the Black Mesa, conducted in eponymous areas (Cordell 1997). The pithouses in the Kayenta area are mainly circular structures, and the first pottery found here includes sherds decorated with painting (Lino Grey and Lino Black-on-White), along with many examples of products made of organic materials such as mats, sandals, fishing nets and baskets, bags, and other containers. West of the Kayenta area is the Virgin region or Virgin-Kayenta comprised of areas of southeastern Nevada and the basin of the lower section of the Virgin and Muddy Rivers. The chronology of this region correlates with that of the Kayenta region (at least until the early Pueblo III period). Characteristic features during the Basketmaker period include pithouses lasting extremely late until the early Pueblo II period (ca. 1050 AD), with storage pits arranged in arched assemblies and possible split-twig figurines, similar to those from the Archaic period (Cordell 1997:197; Lyneis 1995).

In the northern part of the Rio Grande valley area, evidence of settlement during the Basketmaker period is quite sporadic as compared to other areas of Ancestral Pueblo homeland. The pre-ceramic period lasted here until at least around 600 AD, and even after this date, in the Developmental period, sites related to the Pueblo culture are relatively few and far between; only in the latter part of this period do they increase significantly in number.

San Juan Anthropomorphic–Style Rock Art from the Basketmaker Period

The Basketmaker III period features some very rare examples of clay figure production and perhaps figures created in the Basketmaker II period in the western part of the region in Utah. Rock art in the form of petroglyphs and paintings from the Basketmaker II–III period was located near settlements, and would become an integral part of the Pueblo culture over the centuries to come. In the first phases of the Pueblo culture, we can see two rock art styles (Schaafsma 1980:109)—which may have evolved from the Archaic Glen Canyon Linear Style (GCLS) and developed in the southern and southeastern part of Utah, although this continuity is under question now. Developed in the San Juan River drainage, the San Juan Basketmaker style is the most characteristic of the early phases of this culture. It is sometimes referred to as the San Juan Anthropomorphic style because of its predominant representations of anthropomorphic figures, both painted and petroglyphic. The Basketmaker communities appeared to continue a tradition of presenting large anthropomorphic figures in rock art, including the Barrier Canyon style (Cole 2009; Charles and Cole 2006; Schaafsma 1980).

The San Juan Basketmaker style features more paintings than petroglyphs; painted representations were usually located in rock shelters and caves. In addition to rock art, these places often yielded other remnants from that period, such as residential structures, storages, and graves. The dominant colors in these paintings were red and white, along with the occasional presence of other colors, such as yellow. Apart from anthropomorphic figures, other motifs in rock art painting from this period include hand prints and birds, for example in Canyon de Chelly and Canyon del Muerto in northeastern Arizona (Grant 1978; Schaafsma 1980). In these canyons, this art is also clearly visible at residential sites as well as those with other functions.

Characteristic features of San Juan Anthropomorphic style representations are large, frontally presented figures with broad shoulders and a rectangular or tapered (trapezoidal) torso (figure 4.3); as a rule, figures appear in pairs or in large numbers, often composed in bands where many are depicted in rows. In general, these figures' arms hang along their torso and feature clearly defined fingers and toes. Sometimes the torsos are decorated with items of clothing and jewelry, such as necklaces (often several semicircular cords and coils) and belts with tassels; sometimes made of multiple horizontal lines (in the case of paintings) as well as other representations inscribed, such as single or double/multiple wavy lines, animals, and human figures. The heads are usually quite small—outlined and entirely painted in or engraved with basic features—just a few facial elements (sometimes eyes or other parts), with hair or decorations depicted schematically in the form of plumes and types of antennae and multiple straight or semicircular lines directly next to the heads of many figures—and sometimes sexual characteristics.

One of the most spectacular depictions of petroglyphic anthropomorphic figures in this style may be seen at a site near the San Juan River in Butler Wash, Utah, where representations in the Glen Canyon style encounter the San Juan Basketmaker style alongside each other on the same panels. The dominant motif on one of the panels is a long row of very large anthropomorphic figures with the features described above, as well as representations of animals that are not very common at other sites, including mountain sheep and emphatically marked snakes, as well as single and pairs of handprints (Schaafsma 1980:115–16). Sometimes the human figures hold something in their hands, perhaps baskets or bags. Plants (probably yucca and unspecified fruit on types of branches) are presented separately. Additionally, *atl-atl* spear thrower motifs occur along with wavy lines, spirals, and numerous dots extending in a line, often set between individual figures. Masks with what is probably hair are also presented at this site as well as others in the area.

The depictions of characteristic anthropomorphic figures, often with birds (perhaps ducks) on their heads or arms, evoke associations of shamanistic interpretations, which would in turn place the San Juan Anthropomorphic style throughout the whole sequence and the continuation of shamanistic traditions and cultures of this southwestern region starting at

Figure 4.3.   Jakub Nawrot while doing photogrammetric documentation of Basketmaker anthropomorphs from the Sand Island Petroglyphs, near Bluff, Utah (a) and (b) enlargement of one of the depictions. Photos by Radosław Palonka.

least in the Archaic (e.g., Cole 2009; Schaafsma 1980, 1994). While this is the most accepted theory, Carol Patterson (e.g., Patterson 2018) has proposed that many of the themes interpreted as depictions of shamans may be identified with the dead or "ghosts," but in many cases they may be depictions of *kachina*,[2] intermediaries between the world of people and the world of spirits and ancestors who, according to the religion of some Pueblo groups (including the Hopi), are responsible for summoning rain and other necessities. These interpretations are based, among other things on ethnographic analogies from the nineteenth century (including Boas 1928; Cushing 1986; Stevenson 1890; White 1962) and refer mainly to certain groups of Pueblo on the Rio Grande and those speaking languages from the Keres group. This extremely intriguing interpretation requires further studies, as it would testify to the earliest known depictions of *kachina*, which—as is generally assumed—appeared only at the turn of the thirteenth and fourteenth centuries AD (see Schaafsma 1980 for more extended discussion; also Schaafsma 2000; Schaafsma and Taube 2006).

According to Michael Robins (e.g., Robins 2002) and others, these sophisticated and complex depictions of anthropomorphic figures and other San Juan Basketmaker style motifs from the Utah-Arizona border suggest that rock art was an emanation of a certain knowledge about the techniques of its making, reserved exclusively for a narrow group. In a broader sense, this art was an attempt to show the prestige and high social rank of the presented figures, as evidenced by both the monumentalism of these representations, as well as the body decorations, clothes, and weapons (e.g., *atl-atl* spears). Robins also closely links the rock art of this period with its location very close to settlements and probably farming areas. Furthermore, he assumes that the rights to own and exploit deposits of certain raw materials were marked by petroglyphs and paintings, as were the boundaries of territories belonging to individual groups, a common interpretation of this type of depiction in other areas of the Southwest and beyond.

In the western area where rock art occurred during the Basketmaker period, notably Snake Gulch, south of Kanab in Utah and adjacent parts of Arizona (e.g., Cole 2009:118; Schaafsma 1980:117–19), there are panels with slightly different anthropomorphic figures featuring large heads and trapezoidal or even triangular bodies, tapering sharply downward. These representations are usually painted in two dominant colors—red and white, with the most detailed treatment reserved for the upper parts of the body, the head with what looks like buns on either side, decorations (necklaces, often in several rolls) and possible cloths. Masks are sometimes depicted. Although the literature contains examples of such rock art, mainly from the southern part of Utah, extremely similar depictions in the form of petroglyphs were recently discovered in the Lower Sand Canyon and Sandstone Canyon in southwest Colorado in the Canyons of the Ancients National Monument (Palonka 2019a, 2021). These studies of the Sand-Canyon Castle Rock Archaeological Project recorded previously unknown or only partially documented triangular and trapezoidal anthropomorphic depictions from site 5MT264 (The Gallery) in the East Fork of Rock Creek Canyon and from site 5MT127 (Vision House) in Sand Canyon. We can classify them as eastern variants of the San Juan Basketmaker style and initially date them on the basis of analogies to other rock art of this type to the Basketmaker II period (or the beginning of the Basketmaker III period) (Cole 2009:117–43; Palonka 2019a, 2021; Schaafsma 1980:Map 3, 73, 109–21). Along with rock art from that period in Mancos Canyon, a few sites in the Mesa Verde National Park and near what is today Durango in southwest Colorado (Charles and Cole 2006; Cole 2009), these may be among the most southeastern variants of this style.

Interestingly, some of these panels are located in the center of much younger settlements (by about 800–1000 years) that feature stone architecture from the Pueblo III period (figure 4.4). It remains unclear as to why paintings and petroglyphs from earlier periods are located in thirteenth-century AD sites. Since these artworks are visible today (although some of them were uncovered after enhancement analysis), they must have been even more legible 800 years ago when the Ancestral Pueblo stone settlements were founded. An open question therefore remains as to whether the choice of the site was dictated by the presence of certain motifs and the symbolism emphasized by paintings and petroglyphs, or whether the reasons were more pragmatic, as it may have been well suited for living due to other reasons such as defense.

The easternmost sites featuring San Juan–style rock art are clustered near today's town of Bloomfield in northwestern New Mexico. They include petroglyphs with traces of painting in engraved parts and replicate the scheme of trapezoidal figures with lowered arms. Petroglyphs from the Bloomfield area are accompanied by hand motifs, also very common in rock art of this period as well as the later phases of Pueblo culture (up until the historic period). Prints were usually made by impressing a hand dipped in paint onto the rock; less often they were negatives created like a stencil by placing the hand on the rock and spitting paint from the mouth (for example through a tube). A commonly cited explanation for this motif based on ethnographic sources and contemporary Native American oral tradition is that they are signatures or a way of identifying a certain person—known to have been practiced in many parts of the world and in different periods of time including the European Paleolithic. There is no rock art at all further to the east, despite the fact that there are settlements related to the Basketmaker II period. The lack of rock art may be related to the division into the so-called Eastern and Western Basketmakers groups.

Eastern Basketmaker sites with rock art include the Navajo Reservoir District area where the Los Pinos Phase is not represented by rock art, but

Figure 4.4.   Rock art from the Basketmaker II period at site 5MT264 (The Gallery), Colorado (a–b) revealed partly due to the enhancement using DStretch software in the context of the Ancestral Pueblo sandstone architecture from the thirteenth century AD. Photo by Radosław Palonka and drawing after photo enhancement using DStretch software by Radosław Palonka and Katarzyna Ciomek.

Pueblo I Rosa–style rock art in his area (with estimated dates of ca. AD 700–900) (see also table 4.4) includes reduced and simpler Basketmaker-like representations of trapezoidal to triangular anthropomorphic figures (e.g., Schaafsma 1963). Possibly, this rock art had cultural/historical connections to the earlier and more complex Western Basketmaker rock art.

The Chaco Phenomenon: Monumental Architecture and the Political and Religious Domination of Chaco Canyon in the Ninth–Twelfth Centuries AD

The beginning of the Pueblo period witnessed fundamental changes in the material culture, economy, and social organization of Pueblo communities, which define this period and clearly distinguish it from the previous one. These differences include the large-scale use of pottery (although it should be noted that pottery was already known in the Pueblo corner of the world at the end of the Basketmaker III period), alongside continued popularity of containers made of organic materials, as can be observed in later periods as well as today. New plant species were introduced. Cotton cultivation began to play a very important role in the economy as it was associated with the development of weaving, which revolutionized large swathes of material culture, trade and, directly, clothing. Furthermore, turkey breeding became an important aspect of the economy. Turkey meat became the major source of animal protein in some later phases of the Pueblo period (although other animals including deer and rabbits continued to be hunted). Turkeys and parrots were also very important for their feathers which were used in ceremonies and rituals.

It seems that the most drastic change was the transition from pithouses to overground architecture that was constructed, depending on the period and region, of sandstone, or clay or mud layered sequentially and dried in the sun, so-called adobe; structures made of sandstone and adobe were connected using clay as mortar. The transition from pithouses to overground construction did not take place everywhere at the same time or at a uniform pace. Like other features of the Pueblo period, aboveground structures were not immediately visible everywhere, and spread across areas during the period running from 700 to 1000 AD (Cordell 1997:251). In some areas, such as the Mesa Verde region, pithouses were used for some time, initially accompanied by adjacent aboveground *jacal*-style structures—small buildings with a wall structure made of branches and covered with mud or clay—most often used as storage rooms. In other areas (such as places where the Mogollon culture developed), this transition occurred much more rapidly. Here, aboveground sandstone domestic and storage buildings were also accompanied by pithouses usually situated on their south side.

During the Pueblo period, multistory structures began to appear, today sometimes referred to as the first apartment blocks in North America;

located in places not easily accessed, some of them recall medieval European fortifications. Such pueblos were created by compact, adjoining complexes of buildings. Individual housing units and storage rooms were built side by side with touching walls. The upper floors were usually accessed using wooden ladders, and at the same time the upper floors had terraces and empty spaces on their roofs which were often the focal point of pueblo life. Traces of the former pithouses survived on the cusp of the Pueblo I and II periods in a new form of building—the kiva. A kiva is an all-purpose ritual room that served as a meeting place for celebrations and ceremonies (but in the pre-Hispanic times also as for a variety of daily activities such as cooking and sleeping). Kivas were constructed of stone in a circular or rectangular shape, often hidden underground. The wooden roof was supported by several wooden posts or stone pilasters.

In the Mesa Verde region at the time of the Pueblo II period, six pilasters—at that time niches—began to appear in the walls of the kiva), while in Chaco Canyon and outlier sites there were eight. Like a pithouse, the kiva interior was entered through a ladder leading from an opening in the roof. Shelves or benches ran around the walls of this underground structure (figure 4.5). Permanent elements of the kiva included a hearth and a small

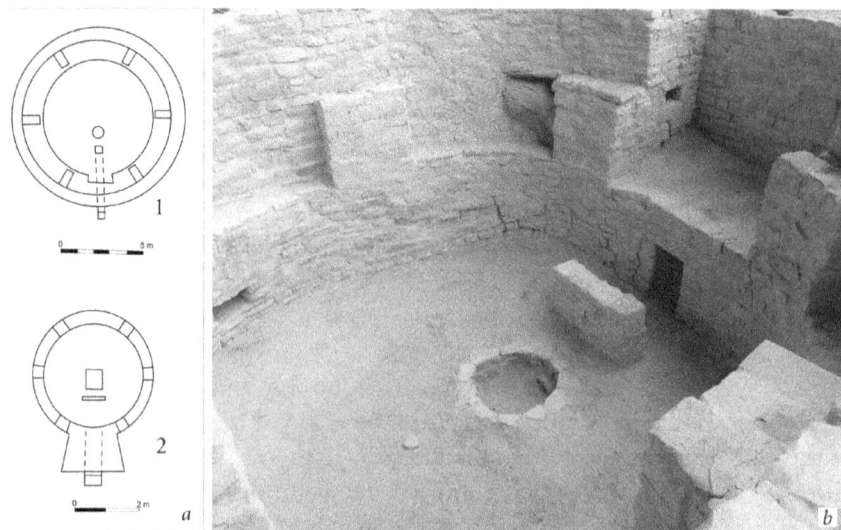

Figure 4.5.   Two types of kiva: (a) Chaco Canyon region (top) with six or eight stone pilasters supporting a wooden roof with an additional hearth and vent as well as one from the Mesa Verde region (bottom) with six pilasters, a "keyhole" layout, hearth, deflector and *sipapu* hole and (b) interior of a typical kiva from the Mesa Verde region (compiled and photo by Radosław Palonka, drawing by Anna Słupianek).

hole in the floor, the so-called *sipapu*. Two architectural features supported air circulation: a tunnel located on the south side through which the air entered and a stone wall called a deflector usually located south of the hearth.

The Ancestral Pueblo culture developed most fully at Chaco Canyon in northwestern New Mexico in the central San Juan River basin. From the mid-ninth century AD—that is, from the end of the Pueblo I period— large settlements featuring examples of the most monumental architecture of Pueblo culture in the pre-Hispanic period were built here; these centers thrived in the canyon until the beginning of the twelfth century (see table 4.1). Gradually, the influence of these sites extended to most of the central and northern parts of the Southwest, mainly in Pueblo culture areas, but others as well. All told, great settlements (so-called outliers) were established up to 250–300 kilometers from the center of Chaco, with architecture and a material culture very similar to the great town-settlements of the canyon itself, which functioned long after the fall of Chaco Canyon sites. Another characteristic feature of these centers was a developed system of long-distance trade, including with Mesoamerica, and the emergence of a kind of social hierarchy with a dominant elite, which was probably able to pass power from one generation to the next (e.g., Lekson 1999, 2008). However, it should be noted the most significant role of Chacoan societies in the southwestern cultural and political landscape continues to be debated today, and there is no broad agreement on its scale (e.g., Mills 2002; 2018, Schaafsma 2018; for current discussion, see also *Archaeology Southwest* 32, nos. 2–3, 2018 and *Antiquity* 364, no. 9, 2018).

Monumentalism and the relatively decent preservation of many sites in the canyon meant that they began to be described quite early (from the 1850s, from the time when the United States took the area from Mexico, or even earlier) and excavated; unfortunately, many shared the fate of other archaeological sites in the Southwest and were largely destroyed and looted by treasure hunters and the first amateur excavations. Professional research of various parts of the canyon was carried out following the end of the nineteenth century, both by several universities including the University of New Mexico, and by other research institutions and associations including the American Museum of Natural History, School of American Research, the Smithsonian Institution, the National Geographic Society, and the National Park Service (e.g., Cordell 1997; Lekson 2006, 2007).

Multistory buildings up to three and four stories high (often called Great Houses) are characteristic of the Ancestral Pueblo settlements from Chaco Canyon. These complexes featured adjacent walls that formed a compact row of housing units comparable to modern apartment buildings.

Table 4.1. Individual Phases of Cultural Development in Chaco Canyon

Pecos Chronology	Chaco Canyon Chronology	Major Characteristic Features
Late Pueblo III	Mesa Verde phase (1200–1300 AD)	– Reoccupation of many sites in the canyon but on a much smaller scale than in the earlier phases – Typical pottery: Mesa Verde Black-on-White and corrugated pottery with an admixture of crushed rock and pottery sherds
Pueblo III	McElmo phase (1140–1200 AD)	– A clear decline in population and building activity – Typical pottery: McElmo Black-on-White and corrugated pottery with an admixture of crushed rock, sherds, and sand
Early Pueblo III	Late Bonito phase (1090–1130/1150 AD)	– Building activity in the canyon itself is drastically decreased – The apogee of the development of outlier sites – Many outlier settlements founded in the northern San Juan Basin (Mesa Verde region) – An initial demographic increase, followed by a population decline at the end of this phase – Typical pottery: Chaco-McElmo Black-on-White, Gallup Black-on-White, corrugated pottery (with a sand admixture)
Late Pueblo II	Classic Bonito phase (1020/1040–1110 AD)	– Many new pueblos built in the canyon (so-called Great Houses), while older ones are extended (including Pueblo Bonito and Chetro Ketl) – Sites are founded beyond the canyon (outliers), mainly to the south, west and northwest of the canyon – Public architecture (plazas and large numbers of kivas, including Great Kivas) – Chaco Canyon becomes the dominant center politically, culturally, and religiously in the north and central part of the Southwest – A likely population decline (depending partly on the nature of a given settlement and today's interpretations) – Typical pottery: Gallup Black-on-White, corrugated pottery (with a sand and crushed trachyte rock admixture)
Late Pueblo I–Early Pueblo II	Early Bonito II phase (900–1020/1040 AD) Early Bonito I phase (850–925 AD)	– A surge in population growth compared to previous periods – The first large pueblos are constructed in the Chaco Canyon around 850/900 AD. These include Pueblo Bonito, Peñasco Blanco, Una Vida) and the Kin Bineola site 19 kilometers southwest of the canyon, i.e., parts of the settlements that would be expanded in subsequent phases – Common pottery types are: Red Mesa Black-on-White, Kiatuthlanna Black-on-White, Lino Gray, Kana'a Neckbanded, and corrugated pottery

After Cordell 1997; Lekson 2006; Windes 1984, 2003, 2007.

Individual units were connected by doors, and some units had direct access to courtyards or plazas. Those located on the upper floors had balconies or terraces. The upper floors were usually located at the back of the settlement, with access to outdoor spaces built on top of the roofs of lower-storied buildings in front. These formed multistoried terraces and small courtyards that could be accessed by back units, convenient places for communication and daily activities. This architectural model also functioned in smaller pueblos and in other areas; it has also survived to this day.

In Chaco Canyon and areas under its influence, individual Great Houses were inhabited by at least several hundred residents—perhaps even more than a thousand in some cases—and used for what may be over 300 years of continuous development. There are theories that some of these settlements, like Pueblo Bonito, were not typically residential, but could have functioned as places of ceremonies, and only groups of priests or representatives of the elite resided there (see below). In their final stages, these town-settlements either featured a D layout (or sometimes C or E shaped plans) or were rectangular (see table 4.2). Many of these settlements included so-called public architecture—that is, mainly plazas, usually surrounded by clusters of buildings or a wall, and Great Kivas, where large numbers from these settlements could gather for rituals and complex ceremonies, as shown by historic sources and similar uses of kivas by modern Puebloans today.

The development of settlements with monumental architecture continued from the beginning of the ninth century, or perhaps even slightly earlier, from the end of the eighth century (Plog et al. 2017). Although settlements like Pueblo Bonito and Peñasco Blanco were already up and running by then, they were still smaller in terms of number of rooms and population than contemporary sites in the Mesa Verde region. A significant shift in architecture and settlement size took place in Chaco Canyon at the turn of the tenth century, with housing and buildings emerging that were significantly larger than other structures of this type, and multistory buildings became the norm. The architecture itself acquired monumental features not only as multistory buildings, but also due to the thickness (up to 1–1.2 m) and massive structure of the walls (figure 4.6a,b), and the addition of more and more new rooms, which formed compact and massive blocks of buildings adjacent to each other.

The true apogee of the development of the above-mentioned sites and the foundation of many new ones dates from the beginning of the eleventh century. Dendrochronological studies carried out repeatedly at various sites in Chaco Canyon clearly show that the typical D-shaped layout was adopted by the settlements in the last phase of their development, as if this arrangement only became de rigueur at a certain point in time. However, some of them, for example a few of the latest ones, including Wijiji and Kin Kletso, were rather square and not D-shaped. In addition to periodization based on absolute dates, mostly by dendrochronology, various ceramic and architectural styles are assigned to them as well. As for the latter, Chaco Canyon features four or five main styles consisting in different facades (styles I–IV and style V—the McElmo style) (figure 4.6c), each of which was used in a specific period of time, generally quite briefly, although styles III and IV were used in the same period but at different sites (e.g., Cordell 1997; Lekson 2006, 2007; Vivian 1990; Vivian and Hilpert 2002:255–56).

In addition to large settlements, several hundred smaller sites have been recorded in the canyon although some appeared earlier and date to the eighth/ninth century AD. These small settlements did not exceed twenty households (Vivian and Hilpert 2002). Initially, housing in such settlements was interconnected via walls and connected housings formed a kind of arch facing the open space with an underground kiva. Over time, these sites were constructed around a rectangular plan, and kivas began to be built as an integral element of the buildings.

These settlements are grouped mainly in the southern part of the canyon south of the periodic Chaco Wash, often in site clusters located quite close to each other. The buildings there were single-story, and the roofs were constructed using wooden beams smaller than those used in the Great Houses; the pine and juniper—may have been obtained from nearby areas (Vivian and Hilpert 2002:223). Other elements characteristic of larger settlements, such as Great Kivas or enclosed plazas, are missing, though the plazas may still have been an element of their construction.

These small canyon sites may have been part of the settlement complexes associated with the nearby Great Houses. Perhaps they were inhabited by related groups, possibly extended families, or clans. On the other hand, some studies, for example those conducted at the small sites of Bc 50 and Bc 51, and comparative studies with larger settlements, suggest that the communities inhabiting the Great Houses and smaller settlements were two different groups, perhaps even on an ethnic and linguistic basis; this theory was proposed in 1939 by Clyde Kluckhohn (Kluckhohn and Reiter 1939), and later developed by Gordon Vivian and Gwinn Vivian (e.g., Heitman 2015; Vivian 1990) well-known researchers of the Ancestral Pueblo culture in Chaco Canyon.

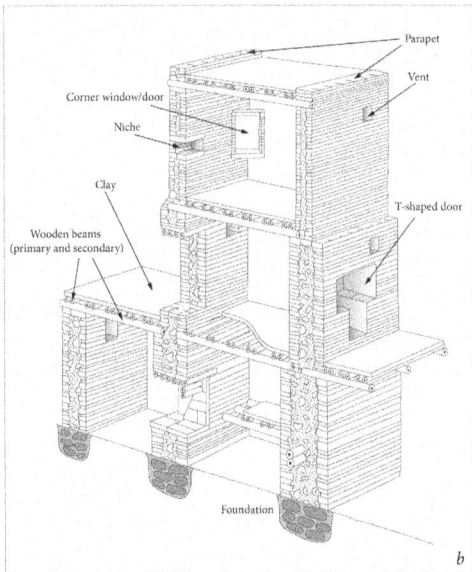

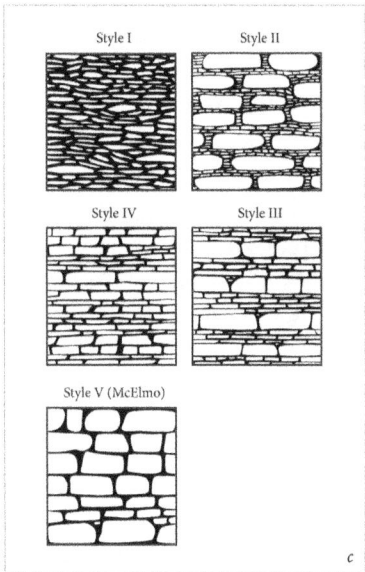

Figure 4.6.   Pueblo del Arroyo, Great House from Chaco Canyon built in the tenth–eleventh centuries AD (a); (b) schematic drawing of the layout of typical Great House multi-story buildings; (c) different styles of wall facing in Chaco Canyon and the outlier sites. Photos by Radosław Palonka and drawings by Magdalena Lewandowska and Anna Słupianek.

Pueblo Bonito—Beautiful Town in the Desert

The largest settlement in Chaco Canyon was Pueblo Bonito (Spanish: Beautiful Town or Beautiful Village), with about 800 residential and storage rooms (although estimates regarding the number of rooms vary greatly depending on the researchers and the method used), often rising up to three, or perhaps even four floors (with at least 350 rooms on the ground floor alone), thirty-five to forty-five kivas and two or three Great Kivas (figure 4.7). Estimated at over 300 years old, it was also one of the longest functioning and continuously inhabited Great Houses. The layout of the entire site at its final phase resembles a capital letter D, which repeats the schematic plan of other Great Houses, except that the shape of the letter D was formed by a row of single rooms separating the plaza from the outside, whereas the arc was the oldest and most built-up part of the Pueblo Bonito site. Many of the beams from the floors and ceilings were destroyed during amateur excavations and looting at the turn of twentieth century, some were used as fuel; but still many survived and were well dated dendrochronologically.

The northern part of the site consists of an arc of the highest housing units, which were terraced and faced south toward the plaza. The terraces formed the roofs of rooms with a smaller number of stories. The plaza was later divided by a wall into western and eastern sections, thus creating two plazas. Each plaza featured one Great Kiva, which often led to the assumption that these two parts of the pueblo were inhabited by two different social groups (e.g., Vivian and Hilpert 2002). To the south of the southern wall of pueblo lay two very large mounds—possibly garbage middens— which were later covered with clay. At least one and possibly two roads departed from Pueblo Bonito, one to the north, beyond the canyon, and a potential second route that may have led toward Casa Rinconada, the Great Kiva located in the southern part of the canyon.

The first known descriptions of Pueblo Bonito appear in reports from pioneering US military expeditions in the early 1850s; these included materials from an expedition led by Lieutenant James H. Simpson in 1850. A member of the Hayden Expedition (1874), William Henry Jackson created the first very detailed map and sketched reconstruction of the site which has been cited until today (e.g., Cordell 1997; Neitzel 2007:127–29; Plog 1997). Over the course of three years starting in 1896, the first excavations at this site were conducted as part of the Hyde Exploring Expedition by the American Museum of Natural History. Led by Neil Judd and sponsored by the National Geographic and the Smithsonian Institution, the second such large excavation project was conducted in the 1920s (1921–1927)

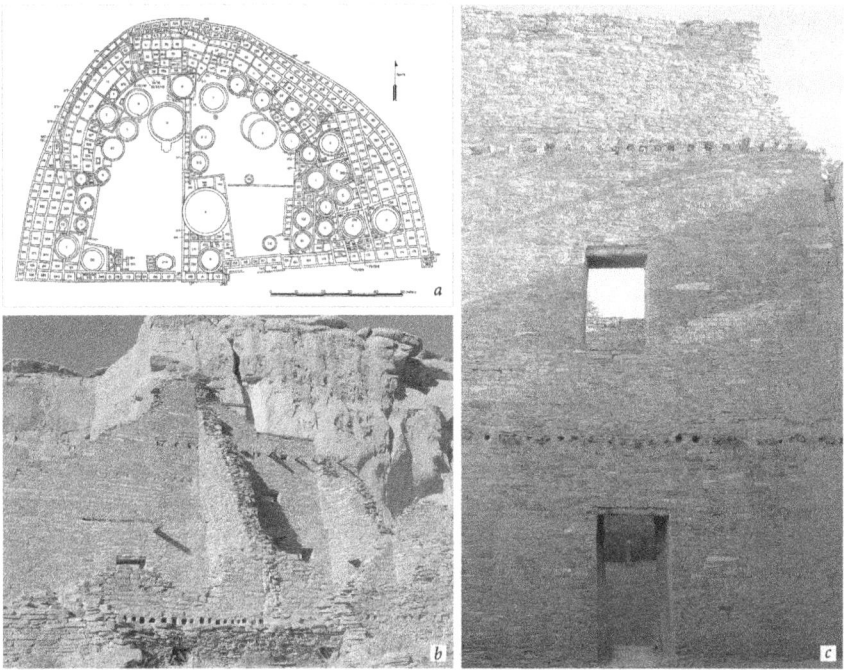

Figure 4.7.   Plan of Pueblo Bonito (a); (b) the northern part of the site; (c) one of the buildings in the central part of Pueblo Bonito with several floors shown by the remains of wood and beam sockets. Drawing by Thomas C. Windes and photos by Radosław Palonka.

(e.g., Judd 1954). More recent analyses have involved a reinterpretation of previous research and the conclusions drawn including research conducted by Stephen H. Lekson (including Lekson 1986, 2006, 2007). New dendrochronological studies by Thomas C. Windes (e.g., Windes 1984, 2003, 2007), have led to the establishment of dates of many buildings and completion of the chronological sequence of this site's development, placing the start of its construction at around 850 AD, or possibly even 828 AD, which is much earlier (at least fifty to seventy years) than previously suspected.

Several phases may be distinguished over the course of Pueblo Bonito's approximate 300 years of flourishing. Based on a large number of dendrochronological dates, Stephen Lekson has listed as many as six such stages or phases, (e.g., Lekson 1986; Neitzel 2007:Fig. 5.7), although some researchers distinguish three or four. The northern part of the site with housing in the form of an arc was erected first. Gradually new parts were added from the west, east, and south. Recent studies of Pueblo Bonito published in a special issue of the *Antiquity* journal (Crown and Wills 2018), provide details about these distinctions and confirm traces of a settlement from an earlier period (i.e., Basketmaker III), and include new data on the potential of agricultural production of the canyon which is larger than previously thought.

Various estimates mention the actual number of housing units and thus, how many people could have lived in Pueblo Bonito; most population estimates range from 400/500 people to even 2,000 (e.g., Plog et al. 2017:289). Other theories about demographics and therefore Pueblo Bonito's potential functions include a proposal that it could have been permanently inhabited by no more than 100 people by Thomas Windes (Windes 1984). Windes assumptions were based on counting the hearths and multiplying their number by the number of families that could use them. Even more far-reaching conclusions based on similar considerations and the lack of large midden (garbage) areas which usually accompany large sites, were proposed by Wesley Bernardini (Bernardini 1999), who suggested that only 70 people permanently lived in such a huge complex of buildings.

This theory of a very small population has been developed (e.g., Renfrew 2001; Toll 2006) with the supposition that a small group of people including priests and their entourage might have permanently resided there, with perhaps hundreds and thousands of people visiting periodically during holidays and ceremonies on pilgrimage as a kind of sanctuary which is similar to those in many countries today. This pilgrimage theory is also supported by the relatively small number of burials that have been discovered and around Pueblo Bonito, and the limited potential for agricultural production around its vicinity (although the latter issue seems unconvincing in the light of the latest research). However, Stephen Lekson, suggests that researchers who assume a small number of Pueblo Bonito inhabitants did not fully take into account the possibility of the existence of hearths on the upper floors which were largely destroyed by looters from the nineteenth century and the rather amateurish excavations that were also initiated at that time (Plog et al. 2017; Neitzel 2007).

Certainly, the data on Pueblo Bonito we have today are insufficient to clearly define the nature of this site. Most often, in addition to typically residential buildings (including houses for the social elite), Pueblo Bonito is associated with potential ceremonial roles and as a trade center for the collection and redistribution of exotic goods, related to a highly developed trade with Mesoamerica and other areas (e.g., Crown and Hurst 2009; Crown et al. 2015; Watson et al. 2015; Nelson 2002; Nelson et al. 2017).

This can be confirmed by the presence, among other things, of pottery rarely found at other sites, traces of cacao in some vessels, copper bells, and the skeletons of parrots, which may have been imported from the area of what is now southern Mexico and huge deposits of turquoise have also been discovered in the rich burials from this site.

A thorough analysis of the burials from Pueblo Bonito, was conducted by Nancy Akins (Akins 1986) as one part of the National Park Service's Chaco Project (www.chacoarchive.org). Akins distinguished two different groups of people buried there. The most remarkable were found in Room 33 located in the northwest area in one of the oldest parts of the site, dating back to the ninth century AD. A small room (2.0 m × 1.8 m and about 2.4 m high, with only one entrance, just 60 cm high), Room 33 contains fourteen skeletal burials with many grave goods. The room was probably intended to be a type of tomb from the outset (Price et al. 2017; www. chacoarchive.org).

The burials were located under the floor of this room, which was covered with wooden boards. The oldest burial from Room 33, dated to around 880 AD, is associated with a man who most likely died in a fight; furnishings of his grave consisted of, among other things, at least 12,000 beads and several hundred pendants made of turquoise and other minerals, and many artifacts made of shells, pottery, and other materials (Judd 1954:337–39); the grave rested on a platform of seventy centimeters of sand. Later thirteen other people were buried above the first, including another directly above the oldest burial. He was bestowed with approximately 6,000 turquoise beads and other gifts. Above him were laid six women and six other men. In addition to jewelry made of turquoise and other raw materials, trumpet shells, wooden flutes, pottery, and elaborate baskets were discovered, somewhat reminiscent of the wealth of the burials at the Casas Grandes/Paquimé site (see chapter 7 in this book). In total, the fourteen burials from this small room yielded over 30,000 items, 25,000 of which are beads and other turquoise jewelry—Plog and Heitman 2010). All told, these were the most elaborately equipped pre-Hispanic burials throughout the entire Southwest.

In the three rooms adjacent to Room 33 (Rooms 32, 53 and 56) twenty-five adult burials, all of them rich, were discovered. In Room 32, over 300 ceremonial wooden rods and a quiver with eighty-one arrows partially embedded in the ground were discovered. In the western part of this room, a layer of sand and black earth was discovered under the burial, layered again with sand and another layer of black earth, with some more sand on top (each layer was 2.5 to 12.5 cm thick—Plog and Heitman

2010). Skeletal mitochondrial DNA studies revealed a close matrilinear relationship of the deceased (e.g., Kennett et al. 2017). According to many researchers, these studies may prove the continuity of elite power that was held by the people from these burials during 300 years or more; ancestry could have been matrilinear, as is the case with most modern Pueblo groups. Later studies have additionally revealed the relationship of these skeletons with Pueblo populations living in the historic period and those who currently live on the Rio Grande as well as the Zuni group in western New Mexico.

A cluster of burials in the western part of the pueblo consists of four rooms dated about the same time as those described above—rooms 320, 326, 329 and 330 (Price et al. 2017); these rooms were originally used as storages and for accommodation. They revealed over eighty people including children were buried there over a long period of time. Compared to the grouping previously described, there were more women than men, and some rooms contained no men at all. Some people were buried in a supine position (lying on their back) with heads facing east. Others were in a fetal position and still others were buried as disarticulated skeletons. Bodies were sometimes placed on woven mats, and most commonly accompanied by numerous pieces of turquoise and sometimes jade jewelry, pottery, sometimes a dozen or so items, as well as fragments of textiles, projectile points, copper bells and artifacts made of bones and shells. Unfortunately, some burials were looted and grave goods were mixed up a long time ago. Some of the burials (possibly mummified ones) were explored during the first, unprofessional explorations and looting at the end of the nineteenth century (Judd 1954).

Extremely interesting research has been conducted on a rarely occurring genetic deficiency, polydactyly, consisting of the presence of an additional finger or toe, most often the first or fifth or sometimes growing from fingers or toes. At least three cases of polydactyly have been found in the Pueblo Bonito burials (Crown et al. 2016; Marden 2011); a six-digit motif—particularly six toes—is sometimes found in the iconography of rock art in Chaco Canyon examples just north of Pueblo Bonito, and beyond. Such representations have also been found in at least six examples of anthropomorphic pottery from the canyon where feet were shown in sandals, at least one clay figurine, and possibly other objects such as pendants.

The skeleton of a man from Room 330 in the Sand Canyon Pueblo in the Mesa Verde region dating from the second half of the thirteenth century AD, had six toes. According to Kristin Kuckelman (Kuckelman 2008), this evidence suggests potential genetic connections and transfer of power after the collapse of Chaco sites further north into the Mesa Verde region. Perhaps people with this type of genetic condition were awarded a special status and belonged to the social elite (although burials of such individuals are not always sophisticated, which would make this thesis questionable—Crown et al. 2016:427). It is also known that individuals and certain deities were depicted with six fingers or toes and perhaps treated with special attention at certain times and in particular communities in Mesoamerica, including Teotihuacan, the Zapotecs or in the Mayan Palenque (e.g., Crown et al. 2016 from Wrobel et al. 2012).

So far, no formal cemetery has been found next to Pueblo Bonito. All known burials come from rooms at this site, which may again indicate that the site was never occupied by a large group of people. It should be remembered, however, that the burials described above reflect only one group, most likely representatives of the highest social class/es. Interestingly, as in the case of Chaco Canyon, the Ancestral and historic Puebloans did not record such social differences and stratification. Various theories often speak of migrants from other parts of the Pueblo world such as those from the Mesa Verde region, who would lay the foundations for the social and cultural development of Chaco; however, this has not been confirmed either by the existence of such extensive social structures in Mesa Verde, or by the results of strontium isotope tests on the bones of people buried in Pueblo Bonito. These studies also indicate that the people from the social elite buried there were born and raised in Chaco itself or its immediate vicinity (Price et al. 2017).

Other Great Houses from Chaco

There were twelve to fourteen huge settlements, the so-called Great Houses, with up to several hundred buildings, such as Pueblo Bonito, Chetro Ketl, Pueblo del Arroyo or Pueblo Alto situated along over sixteen kilometers of the main part of Chaco Canyon; some of these are presented in Table 4.2 together with basic information on these sites. Some of these Great Houses from Chaco Canyon have fewer number of rooms and one of the smallest sites in this type is Casa Chiquita, with only about thirty to forty.

Many Chacoan sites feature architectural forms rarely found elsewhere or not at all at other Ancestral Pueblo sites and in other periods. These include Great Kivas, tower kivas that combine the architectural features of a kiva and a tower, and ceremonial plazas. Additional elements, perhaps referring directly to Mesoamerica, are the colonnade from Chetro Ketl and the platform mounds at Pueblo Bonito (e.g., Neitzel 2007; Lekson et al. 2007:166–70; Vivian and Hilpert 2002). An interesting example of such direct analogies may be offered by certain sites (e.g., 29SJ834 and 29SJ835), which were recently reconstructed as having been built on the flat tops of small hills with buildings situated on platforms and ramps leading to their tops, which closely resemble the pyramidal complexes from Mesoamerica (e.g., Stein et al. 2007).

Great Kivas emerged since the Basketmaker III period both in Chaco Canyon (the Shabik'eschee site) and in the Mesa Verde region, more to the north (e.g., Van Dyke 2007). However, most buildings of the Great Kiva type in Chaco Canyon are recorded in the mid- and late eleventh century and at the beginning of the twelfth century AD, with the best known at sites like Pueblo Bonito, Chetro Ketl (figure 4.8), Peñasco Blanco and Casa Rinconada. There are usually two or four Great Kivas in the Great Houses, although no such structures have been recorded (see table 4.2) at a few sites. Similar to smaller kivas, the Great Kivas were partially or completely located underground; they also partially duplicate elements of ordinary kiva architecture, such as the stone benches or shelves running around the walls, the presence of niches and a hearth usually located in the central-southern part of the building.

But there are also significant differences. In Great Kivas the hearth is usually located on a wall or platform much above the surface of the floor. There are also other architectural elements not found in smaller structures of this type, including four round depressions with stone discs for the pillars supporting the roof (in cases when the kiva was not roofed, these may have been symbolic places for pilasters), rectangular walls on both sides of the hearth raised about fifty to sixty centimeters above the ground (so-called *vaults*), in the vast majority of cases located along the north-south axis. The function of the *vaults* remains unknown but the theory most often cited is that they were drum bases on which a kind of membrane, possibly of wood, was stretched and then drummed with feet or large sticks (e.g., Vivian and Hilpert 2002). Another interpretation proposes that they were steam baths or sweat lodges of sorts, or storage areas where salt was stored for ceremonies related to cutting seedlings planted in spring (similar practices are still observed today during the Powamu ceremony, i.e., Hopi bean planting).

Another building type featured in the Chacoan architecture was the elevated or tower kiva, a kind of kiva with more than one story, though not necessarily bearing architectural features specific to kivas; sometimes the fireplaces were in the middle, as in the case of Kin Kletso, and the T-

Figure 4.8.   Chetro Ketl in Chaco Canyon, view from the plateau above the site (a); (b–c) a fragment of the settlement with a Great Kiva. Photos by Radoslaw Palonka.

shaped door was on the lower level (e.g., Kin Kletso, Chetro Ketl) or on the upper levels (Kin Ya'a). The elevated or tower kiva was often included in square rooms. They are characteristic of the late phases of the Pueblo culture in Chaco Canyon (eleventh and early twelfth century AD). There are fourteen such buildings in the canyon itself, and they are also known to have existed in outlier sites Salmon Ruins and Kin Klizhin. Their function is quite enigmatic; several theories mention, for example, their role in

Table. 4.2. Selected Great Houses from Chaco Canyon with the Most Important Characteristic Features

Name and Dating	Site Map (Schematic)	Main Characteristic Features
Chetro Ketl A few building phases, mainly mid-11th century AD		– 800 meters east of Pueblo Bonito – About 400–500 rooms, two and three story buildings, two Great Kivas in the plaza and a tower kiva within room suites, a type of terrace on the north side of the settlement wall (in the grouping of the tallest buildings) – Colonnade facing the plaza reminiscent of the architecture of some Mesoamerican centers – Several roads leading in and out of the site
Pueblo Alto 1020 AD–beginning of the 12th century AD (a few building phases)		– Built on a mesa north of Pueblo Bonito; location probably dictated by visual communication with other Great Houses (e.g., Una Vina, Peñasco Blanco, and Tsin Kletsin) – 120 dwelling and storage rooms and 18 underground kivas and no Great Kiva; probably single-story buildings – A row of rooms erected at the beginning of the 12th century AD "enclosing" the plaza and the site on the southern side – Several roads go from this site, mainly to the north including the so-called Great North Road
Pueblo del Arroyo Main (central) part of the site constructed from around 1060 AD, the side parts towards the end of the 11th century, some buildings from the beginning of the 12th century and later		– Approximately 200 m west of Pueblo Bonito, – The location in the middle of the canyon deviates from most of the Great Houses in its northern parts; near the periodic Chaco Wash holding a real risk of being washed away – 300 rooms, including 14 kivas with no Great Kiva; buildings up to three floors in height; D-shaped settlement layout – A concentric circle structure (the so-called tri-wall structure) to the west of the site (early 12th century AD) – A section of the road from Pueblo Alto leads to this site

Peñasco Blanco
Building started at the turn of the 10th century AD, with the main part of the site constructed from the middle to the end of the 11th century AD

- Approximately 5.5 km west of Pueblo Bonito on the Chacra Mesa and over the Chaco Wash and Escavada Wash watershed
- The site is connected by eye-contact to several sites located at the bottom of the canyon
- One of the first Great Houses built in the Chaco Canyon and one of only few located on its southern side
- One and two-story buildings, moving to single-story near the plaza
- Oval settlement plan, but retaining the "classic" layout of buildings consisting of a grouping of buildings adjacent to each other, a large plaza with two Great Kivas and a wall with rooms closing the plaza; two other Great Kivas outside the main part of the settlement
- At least two roads led to this site

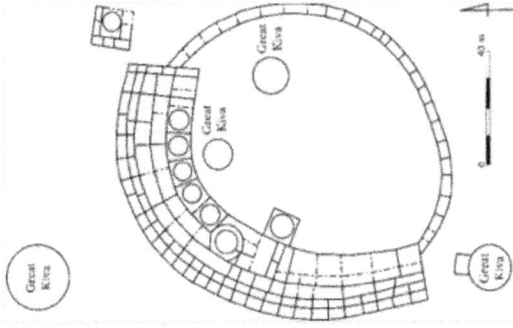

Una Vida
Building started from the mid-9th century AD similar to Pueblo Bonito

- About 5 km east of Pueblo Bonito close to the Fajada Gap and southern entrance to the Chaco Canyon
- Near the confluence of the Chaco Wash and Fajada Wash with water for artificial irrigation taken from Gallo Canyon about half a km away
- Settlement with an "asymmetrical" letter D layout
- 160 rooms of one or possibly two stories, probably two Great Kivas
- Eye-contact with Pueblo Bonito and possibly other sites

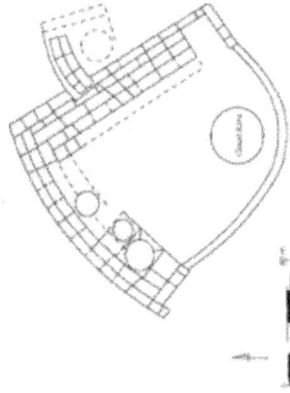

(Continued)

Table. 4.2. *(Continued)*

Name and Dating	Site Map (Schematic)	Main Characteristic Features
Hungo Pavi Two building phases: 1) Mainly ground-level rooms at end of the 10th—beginning of the 11th century AD 2) Upper stories added mid-11th AD century		– 3.2 km east of Pueblo Bonito in Mockingbird Canyon, Chaco Canyon branch – About 140 buildings, unexplored – D-shaped site plan, two-story buildings, a single-story arc-shaped row of buildings closes off the plaza on the south side – A Great Kiva and a tower kiva are the only kivas at this site
Wijiji A rather late site from the turn of the 12th century or beginning of the 13th AD, probably built in one building episode		– Approximately 8 km east of Pueblo Bonito – One of the easternmost Great Houses in Chaco Canyon – A lot of rooms in a relatively small area (very "tight" buildings); two kivas arranged symmetrically on both sides of the site; no arc closing the square from the south – No Great Kiva and no roads leading to this site; no midden area suggesting that perhaps the settlement was only temporarily inhabited by the Pueblo people

After Vivian and Hilpert 2002; Lekson 2006, 2007 and other sources. Compiled by the author and drawings by Anna Stupianek.

transmitting signals between sites or as symbolic *sipapu* sites (Kantner and Hobgood 2016; Vivian and Hilpert 2002:243).

The aspect of potential communication between such buildings and with other buildings and sites is quite intriguing. It would seem that at least some of the buildings and settlements located by the connecting roads are arranged in such a way as to allow eye contact with other sites. This siting therefore offered a means of communication between individual centers and even to isolated hills. Stone circles with evidence of charcoal and burnt stones, possible evidence of a religious function, have been found between tower kivas such as those at the sites of Kin Klizhin and Kin Ya'a (e.g., Vivian and Hilpert 2002:220-21). These geographic relationships are similar to those of the Great Houses located on mesas/plateaus (e.g., Pueblo Alto, Peñasco Blanco, Tsin Kletsin), from where it was possible to easily monitor the surrounding areas, even at a distance of several dozen kilometers. Communication and the transmission of signals could have been achieved by means of fire at night and smoke during the day. Archaeologists and rangers from the National Park Service have conducted several evening and night experiments using torches, which have largely confirmed these assumptions.

It must be admitted, however, that other interpretations of tower kivas (Kantner and Hobgood 2016) have recently emerged, suggesting that some of them, specifically the Kin Ya'a and Haystack, the two outlier sites, may have offered a means to communicate with settlements in the immediate vicinity rather than over long distances. These studies are based on thorough analyses of the geographic information system (GIS) and topography of the surrounding areas.

Yet another feature of Chacoan architecture was a structure in the shape of three concentric circles (tri-wall structure). They were usually made up of two circles with rooms that further surrounded the third, smallest circular structure. A similarly formed, complex building was the bi-wall structure. Most bi-wall structures are part of larger and adjoining complexes of buildings. Like the tower kivas, they are dated to the late period of when the Great Houses functioned in the eleventh and the beginning of the twelfth century AD, in architectural style V (McElmo style), and are known from sites like Pueblo del Arroyo or outlier Aztec Ruins. They are relatively common in the Mesa Verde region and it may have had some special significance there. Architecturally, the inner circle has kiva-like characteristics and was probably used for religious performances (Vivian and Hilpert 2002).

Chaco Astronomy and Rock Art

The monumental Chaco sites were built according to specific designs and site plans and featured the types of buildings and architectural styles briefly described above. The location and orientation of individual buildings, as well as entire sites, were tremendously important. To maximize solar heat in winter, most of the buildings (residential structures) faced southeast, presumably to capture the sun earlier in the mornings; other factors were also responsible for the specific placement of the buildings and structures such as access to water, although in the case of Chaco this factor did not seem to matter much. Research led by Anna Sofaer on the Solstice Project, (e.g., Sofaer 2007; https://www.solsticeproject.org/) focused on the fourteen Great Houses of Chaco Canyon in terms of their location in relation to certain astronomical phenomena. These studies revealed, among others, that the settlements in the canyon were located according to the strict cardinal directions (some almost perfectly aligned along the north-south axis) and the position of the sun at different stages and seasons—during the winter and summer solstices and the autumn and spring equinoxes—as well as the position of the moon, making the cardinal orientation of Great Houses more likely to be explained by nonfunctional reasons. To this day, solstices and equinoxes are of primary and secondary importance, respectively, for rituals practiced by modern Pueblo groups such as the Hopi and Zuni.

Earlier research by Sofaer led to the reconstruction of the function of petroglyph panels in the form of two spirals at the Fajada Butte site in the southern side of Chaco Canyon, the so-called Sun Daggers. There during the summer solstice from late morning to noon, the sun penetrates the spaces between three sandstone slabs and falls exactly in the center of the large spiral carved on the rock wall. During the autumn and spring equinoxes, the light falls on the right side of the large spiral and in the middle of the smaller spiral on the left side. In turn, during the winter solstice around 10:30 a.m., the sun's rays pass directly through two slabs and fall on both extreme parts of the spiral (figure 4.9a) (e.g., Sofaer et al. 1979, 1982). The team's later studies revealed the relationship of these spiraled panels to certain positions of the moon, which, according to Sofaer, translates into similar solar-lunar relationships in the location of buildings and entire sites. Sofaer's research on the Sun Daggers has become high-profile around the world, even leading to the filming of a documentary film about these discoveries by Robert Redford, although it must be admitted that not all researchers agree fully with her interpretations, especially regarding the moon.

Other studies have revealed that in some Chaco buildings the windows (mainly corner windows) and doors (e.g., in Pueblo Bonito) were located so that the rays of the sun fell through them, for example at sunrise during the summer or during the winter solstice. The same may be probably said for some Great Kivas, such as the Casa Rinconada, that were unroofed. In these structures, the niches built around the perimeter were also positioned to allow light to fall during solstices and equinoxes (according to the most common interpretation) (Cordell 1997; Malville 2008).

While Chacoan monumental architecture and social stratification have been well studied, rock art has not. Polly Schaafsma (e.g., Schaafsma 2018) points out that researchers have often excluded or even declined to examine the rock art from Chaco Canyon (maybe besides the Fajada Butte rock art) while analyzing, for example, the Chacoan social and religious organization, as well as the role of Chaco within the Southwestern region. Nevertheless, there is a lot of rock art to discuss.

The highest concentration of rock art panels in "downtown Chaco" is found between Kin Kletso and Chetro Ketl Great Houses and areas to the west. Most of the art is located on smooth south-facing canyon cliffs or walls on the north side of the canyon. The most common depictions include anthropomorphic stick-figures, "lizard men," humpback flute players, sporadic groups/rows of human figures holding hands in a way that suggests dancing, women sometimes featuring maiden hair whorls, hand- and footprints, sandal tracks, and a host of animals, sometimes in groups—mountain sheep, deer, mountain lions, macaws and other birds, and dogs. There are also various geometric and abstract motifs including spirals, circles and concentric circles, animal and bird tracks, wavy lines, and netlike motifs and textile patterns, the latter of which may be dated to later phases of the period of Chaco great architecture (Schaafsma 2018:51–57).

These images and their possible meaning may be similar to other contemporary Ancestral Pueblo rock art in the northern Southwest, for example, the depictions of two-legged bighorn sheep and many images of spirals (however, it should be noted that the spiral was one of the most common symbols in Ancestral Pueblo rock art). Chaco rock art was possibly associated with fertility, rain, moisture, clouds, and harvests through representations of flute players, scrolls, curlicues, and textile designs; all these confirm the homogeneity of beliefs and cosmology across the Colorado Plateau (Schaafsma 2013, 2018:61) and are fundamental Pueblo concerns tied with religion and its rituals even today.

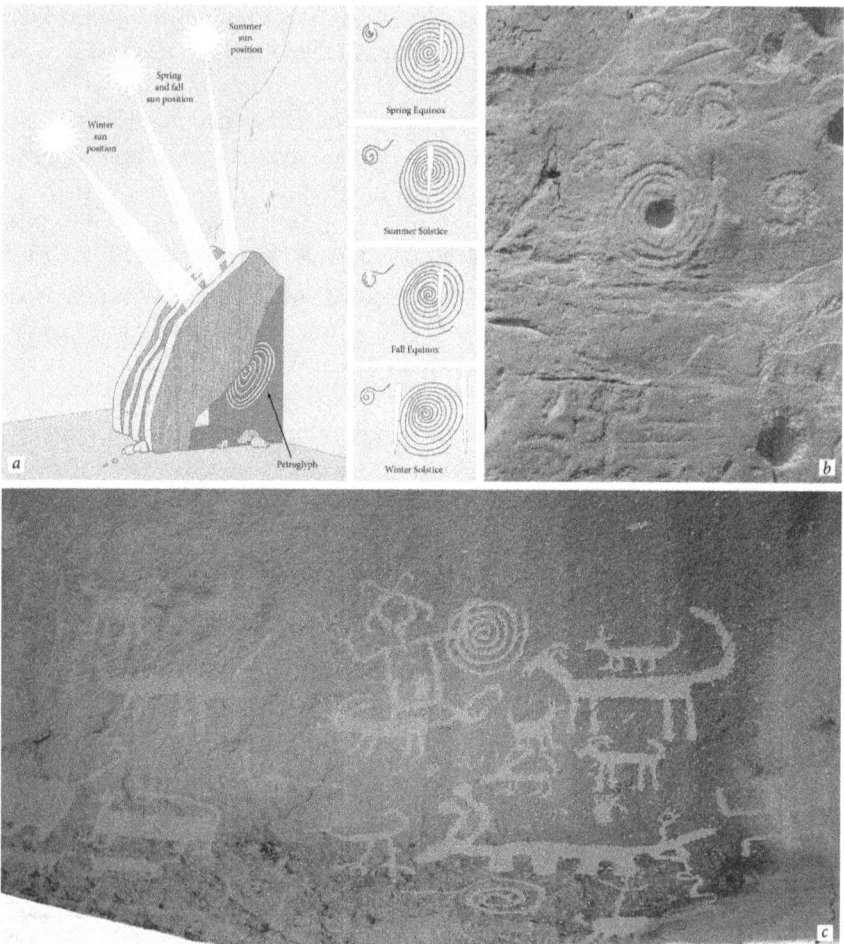

Figure 4.9.   Examples of Chaco Canyon rock art: (a) spirals at Fajada Butte connected with the astronomical observations; (b) depiction perhaps of a solar eclipse located between Pueblo Bonito and Chetro Ketl; and (c) a panel with anthropomorphic, geometric, and quadruped depictions at Una Vida Great House. Photos by Radosław Palonka, drawing by Michał Znamirowski.

Farming and Local and Long-Distant Trade as the Basis of the Chaco Economy

Studies have examined the potential of agricultural production and the ability to feed the thousands of people who potentially inhabited Chaco Canyon during its heyday. Managing the collection and distribution of water in this inhospitable territory was perhaps the key factor in the development of Great Houses and other settlements. Archaeologist R. Gwinn Vivian claims that the elites from Chaco were able to monopolize the extraction of water from the northern slopes of the canyon and, thanks to a system of irrigation canals and dams, could then distribute it for everyday needs as well as cultivation (e.g., Plog 1997:107). The highest rainfall is recorded in the canyon area during violent storms in the summer months, but water seeps through sandstone formations practically all year round. It is also clear that farmland in Pueblo Bonito was connected to this system of artificial water collection and distribution.

The latest research, including terrestrial and aerial laser scanning (LI-DAR) as well as geophysical surveys, confirms the existence of an extensive water management system and agriculture in Chaco itself together (e.g., Scarborough et al. 2018; Wills et al. 2018). These findings led to the documentation of irrigation channels running east-west just south of Pueblo Bonito which have been dated to around 1000 AD on the basis of radiocarbon dating from corn. These studies also show that water was collected from the surrounding plateaus as well as the intermittent overflow of the Chaco Wash and other periodic watercourses, mainly Escavada Wash, leading to the conclusion that Chaco Canyon and the immediate vicinity had much greater agricultural production potential than previously thought, and that the irrigation channels in their scale and complexity resemble enormous structures of this type from the Hohokam culture (see chapter 5).

Chaco Canyon and Ancestral Pueblo culture sites located therein have been characterized by an extraordinary richness of material culture and the manufacture of intricately decorated turquoise jewelry. These sites contain the largest deposits of semi-finished products and fully processed turquoise artifacts, mainly from burial contexts of all Southwest cultures. Additionally, they contain shells and raw materials such as bone and wood, elaborately painted ceramics, cylindrical vessels found only in this canyon, in which traces of cacao have been discovered, and intricately decorated baskets. A large number of exquisitely decorated items such as painted wooden flutes and shell trumpets, painted wooden figures, and objects in the shape of rectangular plates probably had some ritual and religious significance; the cylindrical pottery vessels indicate design influences from Mesoamerica, and the presence of shells imported from the Gulf of California demonstrates far-reaching trade.

Pottery from Chaco Canyon changed over time in form and, above all, decorative motifs. Several types of corrugated pottery for food preparation, often designed with finger and nail prints, as well as painted pottery, mainly black-on-white have been found. At sites in Chaco Canyon, there are at least two other types of painted pottery divided into smaller types: red ware, which was produced mainly in the western part of the Mesa Verde region (southeastern Utah), appeared in Chaco mainly between 700 and 1050 AD, along with smoothed brown ceramics (often with a black inner surface), that were imported primarily from the Mogollon area (central-eastern Arizona and western New Mexico) (e.g., Toll 2001, 2004). These brown and black ceramics prove extensive contact between people living in Chaco and other areas through extensive expeditions to these locations and visits from members of other cultures and societies to Chaco Canyon. More recently there are known ethnographic examples and photos of porters/merchants transporting large quantities of pottery on special platforms carried on their backs traveling through southern Arizona, Mexico, and mountainous areas of Guatemala, practices that are analogous to the situation in the pre-Hispanic Pueblo trade.

A great deal of pottery from Chaco Canyon and sites under its influence beyond the canyon has a characteristic design motif involving so-called *Dogoszhi*-style cross-hatching (figure 4.10a); the same style also appears on decorated items made of wood, stones, and textiles. Some scholars, such as Stephen Plog (Plog 2003), interpret this motif as a representation of the color of turquoise. Similar considerations were made for the pottery designs of the Mimbres culture (see chapter 6).

Chaco Canyon pottery (up to 50 percent of cases in the later periods of Chaco development) was not produced locally, as was the case with most pre-Hispanic cultures of the Southwest, but imported from remote areas, including the regions mentioned above, as well as from the Chuska Mountains and Valley in western New Mexico, from a distance of at least fifty-five to sixty kilometers or more, as was the wood used for building houses. Northeastern Arizona and the western part of New Mexico, west of the Rio Grande valley including the so-called Cibola region were other potential import sources for ceramic vessels. The origin of this pottery is evidenced by typological and archaeometric studies conducted on clay, as well as a small number of pits and kilns for firing ceramics in the canyon itself. The high level of imports primarily applies to the classical and later phases, which may in turn indicate the canyon's scarce resources of wood needed for firing ceramics and the possibility that food may have been transported in these vessels (Toll 2001, 2004).

The period between 1030 and 1100 AD seems to mark an intensification in imports of not only pottery, but also other products and raw materials, e.g., flint and stone (e.g., Toll 2004). The tendency to import

Figure 4.10.   Typical pottery forms and pottery with *Dogoszhi*-style decorative motif from the Una Vida, Pueblo Alto, and other sites (a) and (b) cylindrical vessels dated to approx. 1000–1125 AD, with traces of cacao. Drawing by Anna Słupianek, photo courtesy of the American Museum of Natural History Library (Image #ptc-3521).

products of material culture was also manifested in the import of raw materials, and even ready-made tools of stone, flint, chert, and, to a lesser extent obsidian (in the Classic Bonito phase) from far-flung areas. Yellow chert was imported from the region of today's Zuni reservation in western

New Mexico, green chert from the Mesa Verde region, and pink from the Chuska Mountains (called Narbonne Pass chert), the latter being very popular in some periods. Imported chert tools were primarily blades and various cutting tools, although the raw materials for their production could be found in the canyon itself and nearby, which is all the more surprising. However, it is assumed that the very heavy *metate* stones were made in situ from local stones. Obsidian was imported mainly from the outcrops in the Jemez Mountains (a known source of obsidian production in the pre-Hispanic period) and from the Mount Taylor mountain range south of Chaco; obsidian was used in Chaco Canyon mainly before 800 and after 1100 AD, while the interim period features relatively little (Toll 2001, 2004:36).

Interestingly, plants and animals were also imported into the canyon, probably due to the limited capability of feeding a large group of people with the resources of the canyon itself. It is believed that even some corn was harvested from further afield. Research on strontium isotopes in corn led by Linda Cordell and other scholars, shows that at least some of the Pueblo Bonito corn was also imported from the Chuska Mountains region from around Newcomb and the local Captain Tom Wash River, e.g., Toll 2004:38). These findings were based on studies in which they compared corn samples from historic Chaco Canyon sites and soil from known growing fields with modern crops and soil from the same fields. It is also assumed that some meat of the hunted animals—mainly rabbits, deer, and antelopes—must have also been imported from beyond the canyon, especially in the later phases of the canyon's occupation; the proportion of meat from hunted deer rose starting in the tenth century AD.

Large wooden beams were used to construct roofs and floors; because the canyon itself and its surroundings could not have supplied much wood, it appears to have been transported primarily from the Chuska Mountains and the Zuni Mountains in western New Mexico, a distance of about sixty to seventy-five kilometers from the canyon itself (e.g., Cordell 1997; Guiterman et al. 2016; Plog 1997; Vivian 1997b). Ponderosa pine, which today grows in some clusters near the central part of Chaco Canyon, may have been partially felled there (although local resources would probably not have satisfied all the demand). Fir and spruce which was also used in their buildings, did not naturally occur during the Ancestral Pueblo occupation of this area, so this lumber must have been imported from farther afield, the most likely places are again the Chuska Mountains and Mount Taylor.

Other traces of these relations in material culture include copper bells imported from north-central Mexico and parrots imported from tropical forests on the Mexico-Guatemala border, as well as northern Mexico (for more on importing parrots to the Southwest, see chapter 7). These artifacts are found in certain clusters and in several locations at the largest sites in Chaco.

Research led by Patricia L. Crown and W. Jeffrey Hurst (Crown and Hurst 2009), on the inner walls of the cylindrical pottery vessels (see figure 4.10b) show traces of theobromine, an organic chemical compound from the purine alkaloid group, occurring naturally in cacao beans. Traces of cacao so far from its source provides significant and fascinating evidence that the Pueblo people from Chaco most likely had direct contact with Mesoamerican elites. It seems that these vessels were used mainly in the period 1000–1125 AD and, interestingly, were found in clusters or deposits in just a few rooms in Chaco Canyon, mainly in Pueblo Bonito, as a result of excavations carried out in the 1890s. The analyses of vessel walls were made possible thanks to the fact that most of them were obtained during the first research expeditions from the turn of the twentieth century when vessels were usually not washed after being removed from the ground, thus allowing the preservation of traces of theobromine and other compounds.

Crown and Hurst's research was later expanded to include studies of a larger number of vessels (Washburn et al. 2011), mostly from richly furnished Chaco graves, and further extended to include analyses of vessels from a southern Arizona Hohokam site, Los Muertos. A larger chronological and territorial range was also analyzed (750–1400 AD, including the southern parts of Colorado and northwest New Mexico—Crown et al. 2015). These studies confirm the presence of theobromine and therefore cacao (after eliminating other potential plants that may have contained it) in vessels from rich burials and deposits. Traces of cacao have been found not only in cylindrical vessels, but in smaller amounts in jugs and certain forms of pots (in the case of these two groups of vessels—at small sites), and partially on vessels found in small sites, which is quite a surprising result because it shows the possibility of broader extent of cacao use. This is evidence of the transfer of certain behavior and perhaps elements of religion, involving the ritualistic drinking of cacao in Mesoamerica, to the Southwest and specifically to the town-settlements in Chaco Canyon and beyond.

All told, these examples show that trade supported every aspect of Pueblo material culture—food, pottery, tools, religious rituals, and construction.

Blue and Green Stones: Turquoise the Most Valuable Commodity

Huge amounts of turquoise are found at sites in Chaco Canyon itself, as well as beyond; turquoise occurs in larger quantities at Ancestral Pueblo sites after 900 AD (e.g., Thibodeau et al. 2012, 2018; Toll 2004). At the turn of the twentieth century, the largest quantity of turquoise artifacts in the Southwest was discovered in one of the burial rooms in Pueblo Bonito. The source of this turquoise is most likely mineral deposits located in Cerrillos, approximately 150–160 kilometers southeast of Chaco Canyon and from other sources (e.g., Hull and Fayek 2012:36). Some modern Pueblo groups from the Rio Grande refer to Cerrillos (Cerrillos Hills) in their oral tradition and claim that these mining sites were exploited by their ancestors, to whom they belonged. Furthermore, large amounts of turquoise were discovered at small sites in the canyon (both the raw material itself, as well as semi-finished and finished objects) together with lithic drills for making holes and decorative motifs (Toll 2004:38). The fact that turquoise had a special sacred meaning for the Ancestral Pueblo communities (and this is often the case today among contemporary Puebloans) is evidenced by the discovery of objects made of this material both in burials and in Great Kivas, for example, foundation offerings under the pilasters of kivas from the eleventh century AD and in special niches therein.

Theories have emerged about the importance of turquoise in supraregional trade, mainly with Mesoamerican centers that indeed could have obtained turquoise from the town-settlements in Chaco Canyon. Turquoise was widely used in the manufacture of jewelry and other items, especially in the post-classical period—that is, 900–1521 AD by Mixtecs and Aztecs (McEwan et al. 2006; Thibodeau et al. 2012)—but more recent studies of Mesoamerican artifacts made of turquoise (mainly analyses of lead and strontium isotope) have shown that, perhaps for a long period, the long-running theory may not be completely valid (Thibodeau et al. 2012, 2018) and that some Aztec turquoise relics may have been made of turquoise from native deposits located in Mexico and other parts of Mesoamerica.

Based on their examination of thirty-eight artifacts from Templo Mayor in Tenochtitlan and samples from elsewhere in the state of Puebla, Alyson M. Thibodeau and her coauthors (Thibodeau et al. 2018) suggest that the turquoise here originated from somewhere in western Mexico, or more likely (albeit unconfirmed due to the lack of a comparative base for turquoise deposits), from the provinces of Quiauhteopan (the eastern part of the state of Guerrero and adjacent parts of Puebla), Yautepec in western Oaxaca, and Tochpan in the northern part of Veracruz state. According to the information recorded in the so-called Codex Mendoza written around 1541–1542, these provinces paid the Aztecs a tribute in the form of turquoise, and perhaps a large part of this stone for the Mesoamerican elite originated in deposits in what is modern-day Mexico.

It should be noted that a fairly small sample (forty-odd artifacts in total) has been examined so far and comes from one place (Templo Mayor). Nevertheless, Cerrillos and other Southwestern turquoise mines are the most frequently cited as the most likely places from where turquoise was imported into Mesoamerica (e.g., Nelson 2003; Nelson et al. 2017). Other minerals or stone materials used in Chaco and other areas of the Ancestral Pueblo world for pendants and other jewelry include jade, hematite, and serpentine.

Outliers and Roads, Evidence of Chaco's "Domination" over the Southwest

In the period between the eleventh and thirteenth centuries AD, many centers—so-called outliers sprung up outside Chaco Canyon. The term "outliers" refers to sites of the Great House type with accompanying complexes of small settlements located beyond Chaco Canyon itself, but with visible elements of architecture—Great Kivas, plazas, roads—and material culture, notably pottery that were similar to those from the sites in the canyon itself. Outlier sites are often quite densely packed in a given area, but these individual sites and clusters—settlement microregions—are distant from each other with no traces of settlements between them (characteristically, these "no man's land" (or "everybody's land) areas feature relatively few or no settlements from earlier periods, e.g., Vivian and Hilpert 2002:176–77). The building and architectural styles are almost identical or even duplicates of certain types of buildings, and may have indirectly manifested the political, economic, and religious influence of Chaco Canyon.

Features that distinguish outliers from other sites in a given area (Cordell 1997) include the size of the site, the presence of buildings significantly larger than others within the site itself (residential buildings, kivas, Great Kivas), roads leading to the site or some places to transmit signals, and Chacoan ceramics, mainly Gallup Black-on-White type (decorated with hachured designs in Dogoszhi-style). Outliers closely related to the town-settlements of Chaco Canyon cover an area of over 100,000 square kilometers (Mills et al. 2018). There are about 200 known sites of this type that were built after 1025 AD, and the number of outliers from different periods probably totaled more than 300 (Lekson 2017), although some researchers differ slightly in this count by defining the concept of Great Houses and outliers differently. For example R. Gwinn Vivian and Bruce Hilpert (Vivian and Hilpert 2002) posit that there were no more than 100 such sites, although they do not rule out the possibility that there were more. However, most of sites have been very poorly researched, or merely registered, and others are located on private land making them even more difficult to record and study. A dozen or so outliers have been well excavated and published including Aztec Ruins, Salmon Ruin, Chimney Rock, Bluff Great House or Guadalupe Ruin, and Navajo Springs, but there are only unpublished reports from surveys and sketched site plans documenting the remainder.

The most significant large-scale projects on Chacoan outliers include The Chaco Project from 1976 (Powers et al. 1983) which explored outliers north of Chaco Canyon and a project that was initiated a year later exploring outliers south of Chaco (e.g., Vivian and Hilpert 2002:177).[4] Although dendrochronological dating of these sites is relatively scant compared to Chaco Canyon itself, most of them seem to have been built from the eleventh century AD on, although some were constructed earlier (e.g., Guadalupe Ruin site in New Mexico) (Cordell 1997; Lekson 2017; Lister and Lister 1987; Plog 1997; Vivian and Hilpert 2002). Interestingly, these sites continued to function long after the collapse of the sites in Chaco Canyon itself, even up to 150 years later.

Various interpretations regarding the function and significance of outlier sites have emerged, including theories about their establishment by the people of Chaco in a quest for areas that could be included in their trade zone and the acquisition of new land suitable for cultivation to provide food for the inhabitants of the large town-settlements in Chaco itself. This correlates well with Stephen Lekson's theory about the transfer of the alleged center of power from Chaco Canyon after the collapse of the Pueblo culture in the canyon itself—(e.g., Lekson 1999) to other regions of the Southwest. This power transfer possibly moved first to the Aztec Ruins and Salmon Ruins in the northern part of the New Mexico which ultimately collapsed following the depopulation of the entire Mesa Verde region in the thirteenth century AD. According to this theory power then moved farther south to Casas Grandes (Paquimé) in Chihuahua, Mexico, a distance of almost 1,000 km as the crow flies. Chronologically, it appears that Chaco outlier sites functioned between 850/900 and 1140 AD—the Aztec Ruins cluster of sites and Salmon Ruin between 1100 and 1275

AD, while the heyday of the Casas Grandes occurred between 1275 and 1450 AD. Lekson's theory is rather inspiring and evokes a reevaluation of previous views on egalitarian Pueblo communities. Further work that may confirm this theory should be based on new DNA research among other evidence.

The roads that linked many sites are one manifestation of the monumentalism of Chacoan architecture and the political and social organization and power of its social elite and religious leaders—these may have been the same people. Entire road systems connecting individual settlements and regions led from and to numerous Great House-type sites. The total length of known and assumed sections of Pueblo roads from the heyday of the Chaco Canyon settlements runs, according to various researchers, from several hundred to over two thousand kilometers. Most sections do not exceed ten to twenty kilometers, but longer ones of even about fifty to sixty kilometers are known to have existed and subsequent sections of road may have connected even more remote settlements, as far as one hundred kilometers away (e.g., Plog 1997:110). The most well-known road, the so-called Great North Road, runs from Pueblo Bonito and Pueblo Alto and directly north of Chaco Canyon. It appears that in the beginning most of the roads were built south and west of the canyon, and later north toward the Mesa Verde region.

Roads were constructed by removing the surface of earth and sand—often down to the bedrock—and using it to curb the sides with low earth embankments or stone and brick walls recessed ten to fifty centimeters above the surface. Roads usually ran in a straight line making the connection between settlements as short as possible, but they occasionally constructed along or around natural obstacles such as cliffs (e.g., Vivian 1997a, 1997b). Steps and stairs were often carved into the rocky slopes of canyons as sections of these roads and scaffolding may have been used on some sections. The width of the roads ranged from three to twelve meters (most often eight to twelve meters) and, although it is sometimes difficult to see them from the ground today, they are clearly visible from the air via aerial and satellite photos. New road sections have been identified quite recently with LIDAR scanning (Friedman et al. 2017).

Interestingly, some roads starting from large settlements ended abruptly after a few kilometers in places where there are few traces of any significant human presence. Sometimes several parallel and adjacent roads leave a settlement, later run in different directions, and rarely intersect; four such roads depart from Pueblo Alto.

As in the case of the Inca empire of South America, the Ancestral Pueblo societies from Chaco Canyon and other areas constructed an extensive road system without knowledge of wheel or draft animal.

Buildings and other structures were constructed alongside the roads. First and foremost, are the *herraduras*, low (usually up to one meter) C-shaped, circular, or horseshoe-shaped stone structures with a diameter of about five to seven meters (sometimes larger, up to twelve meters). Usually situated on elevated areas with the entrance usually facing east, *herraduras* allowed large sections of roads to be monitored quite effectively (e.g., Vivian 1997a:21–22). Roads sometimes narrowed near the *herraduras* and had more clearly marked edges in the form of higher walls or embankments; there are also small clusters of ceramics that can be interpreted as places of sacrifice (the most popular theory) or as the remains of meals. Other structures and even groupings of buildings found along Chacoan-type roads are so-called *zambullidas* (single or groups of small spaces with a circular or horseshoe layout, without kiva buildings), *avanzadas* (similar to *herraduras*, with single, or groups of, rooms, but built with a rectangular layout) as well as earth mounds and platforms (the latter mostly associated with steps and ramps carved into the rocky slopes) (Nials et al. 1987; Roney 1983; Vivian 1997a).

The function of these roads has most often been interpreted as simple routes by which the Pueblo people could transport wood for construction as well as other materials (e.g., Windes and Ford 1996)—although it seems that this would not have required such wide roads—or perhaps they carried water and functioned as a type of irrigation canal. Another theory claims that they were pilgrimage routes for people going to Chaco Canyon for ceremonies and celebrations (e.g., Judge 1989; Van Dyke 2007). Another interpretation examines both the symbolic and physical role of roads as links in the political and cultural system associated with the Chaco Canyon centers (Vivian 1997b). Yet another proposes that the roads may have served not only as links between settlements (as some do not connect them at all) and Great Kivas, but as routes to landforms such as mountains, springs, and lakes (e.g., Sofaer et al. 1989). This is supported by the interpretation of their symbolic, or rather religious purpose (Kantner 1997; Sofaer et al. 1989; Stein and Lekson 1992), and aligns with the oral tradition of contemporary Puebloans for whom such roads or corridors are, among others, in the Tewa Pueblo language, "channels of the life-giving breath," and two parallel paths are a synonym for the relationship between the living and the dead (e.g., Friedman et al. 2017; Ortiz 1969; Van Dyke 2007, see there for further literature).

The Rise and Fall of the Greatest "Metropolis" of the Pre-Hispanic Southwest

Chaco Canyon and the settlements within and beyond is one of the most studied cultural phenomena to have emerged in the pre-Hispanic North American Southwest for over a hundred years. All of Chaco Canyon was included in the World Heritage List in 1987 and is under the patronage of UNESCO. The UNESCO Committee urged the United States government to bring sites including outliers related to Chaco under the same protection, which has resulted in the inclusion of Aztec Ruins, Pierre's Site, Halfway House, Twin Angels, Salmon Ruins, Kin Nizhoni and Casamero.

Despite so many efforts to understand its character and the role it played in the Ancestral Pueblo world, Chaco Canyon is one of the least understood and perhaps the most underestimated or overestimated areas in terms of the scale of influence and internal organization. Many views clash here, often represented by leading researchers, both those working in the field of Chaco and those who analyze it from the perspective of studies on other areas of the Southwest. Some disputes center on whether Chaco was on the verge of creating proto-state or state structures and perhaps even succeeding, or was only maintaining a chiefdom. Controversy also rages over the theory of whether or not a hierarchical society capable of preserving and passing on inherited power existed. However, most or nearly all Chaco scholars do agree that "rituality" played a key role in integrating the Chacoan system (e.g., Mills 2002, 2018), including Great Houses from the Chaco Canyon itself and outliers.

The communities (and possible elites) of Chaco Canyon were certainly able to create numerous unparalleled gigantic residential and religious architectural complexes. Chaco probably became a hub for the collection and perhaps redistribution of valuable goods—turquoise, ceramics, shells, jade—and a major trade center for exotic goods such as copper bells, parrots and cacao from Mexico and Mesoamerica. The Chaco Great Houses were also probably political and/or religious (cf. the concentration of artifacts and ceremonial buildings) and pilgrimage centers whose influence extended over a vast area of the Southwest. Finally, on the basis of burials, architecture and other data, great social diversity and the presence of elites likely flourished.

One fascinating and as yet unresolved issue is that, since the environmental conditions were not the most favorable (there were many more other places within Ancestral Pueblo world with much better access to water and agricultural land) and huge amounts of objects and raw materials were not produced locally but imported from areas far away from the canyon, why did the largest town-settlements of the Pueblo culture develop in this region? The end of the main phase of occupation in the canyon was most likely brought about by environmental and climatic changes, including a long-lasting drought that hit the region between 1130 and 1180 AD (e.g., Cordell 1997). This drought is well preserved and legible today in the rings of trees used in the construction of the Great Houses in Chaco.

The Mesa Verde Region: The Development, Conflict, and the Migration from the Northern Part of the Colorado Plateau in the Twelfth and Thirteenth Centuries AD

After the collapse of the great Chaco Canyon centers, Pueblo communities likely moved from Chaco to the Mesa Verde region on the border of modern New Mexico, Utah, and Colorado. From about 600 AD to 1280 AD, the Pueblo in this area underwent a fascinating time in human history. From living in small settlements on mesas, they moved to the famous cliff dwellings in the sides of steep canyons now protected within Mesa Verde National Park and Canyons of the Ancients National Monument. During this period, Puebloans experienced great fluctuations in climate and environmental factors, social and economic changes, population growth, and conflicts with other native groups and among their own communities. A convergence of environmental changes, social factors, and warfare ultimately precipitated the complete depopulation of Mesa Verde by the Ancestral Puebloans in 1270s and 1280s AD. Precisely what role each of these influences played has been a subject of research and debate for many years, but researchers and modern Puebloans continue to piece the past together with the rich sources we are fortunate to have available.

Starting around 600 AD and over the course of almost three centuries, the climate gradually warmed while also being reasonably wet, allowing the expansion of the Pueblo community into environmental niches and leading to a steady increase in population. Then, at the end of this period, as shown by the analyses of tree rings and pollen samples, the climate cooled for almost a century, leading to a drastic decline in population. This decline, starting around AD 980, was followed by rather stable population growth until the 1270s and '80s (although fluctuations in cooling and quite dry periods along with a regression in corn crops can be noticed along the way.) Undoubtedly, the largest population growth for this region was recorded in the mid-thirteenth century AD, two or three decades before the collapse of Pueblo occupation of the Mesa Verde region and the mass migration of all Pueblo groups to the south and southeast (e.g., Glowacki 2015; Lipe 1995). Archaeologists from Crow Canyon Archaeological Center, Cortez, Washington State University, Pullman, and researchers involved in the Village Ecodynamic Project (VEP, http://veparchaeology. org/) study climate related demographic changes for the period 600–1760 AD in relation to the intensification or decrease in conflicts.

Correlating population fluctuations are noted in the Mesa Verde region, for example the population increased from the twelfth century AD, but the dynamic demographic and sociocultural development in the Mesa Verde region (e.g., Lipe and Varien 1999; Varien 1999) began earlier— starting at the end of the Basketmaker III period around 600 AD. Fluctuations in the Mesa Verde population over the centuries have been associated with various factors, notably changes in climate that oscillated between periods of reasonable rainfall and dry spells from around 500 BC until 600 AD. These changes drove the first farmers in the area to employ favorable environmental niches (e.g., Kohler 2000; Varien 2000) to successfully develop an agricultural economy. The geological structure of the Mesa Verde region allows for diverse use of the natural environment including periodic and seasonal movement between lower and upper areas. Mesa Verde lies at quite a high altitude—from about 1,550 meters above sea level up to about 2,500, and even over 3,400 meters in some places, although the permanent settlement of the Ancestral Puebloans was concentrated up to a limit of about 2,500 meters above sea level which correlates to the upper limit of altitude where corn can be successfully cultivated (e.g., Adams and Petersen 1999).

Timothy Kohler et al. (2009, 2014) have studied the relationship between changing demographics and conflicts. Their findings were somewhat surprising. In the first section of the studied period (600–900 AD) they didn't find archaeological material showing any drastic increase of the number of conflicts and violence (although some traces of such struggles are known to have occurred at this time); this coincided with a simultaneous increase in the number of people. On the other hand, the period from 1020–1180 AD witnessed a large increase in conflicts visible in the sudden increase in the number of settlements surrounded by palisades, with evidence of such conflicts observable in skeletons, which chronologically preceded the population increase and not the other way round, as might be expected.

The beginning of the thirteenth century brought a return to balance between population and conflict. By the turn of the thirteenth century AD (Pueblo III period), especially in the period between 1260 and 1280 AD, the Mesa Verde region had witnessed significant population growth combined with a centralization of settlements, with most of the population beginning to move to large settlements called community centers. Clusters of a dozen or several dozen smaller satellite villages formed around these community centers (Lipe and Varien 1999; Palonka 2011, 2013; Varien et al. 1996), thus creating settlement complexes, within which individual sites closely cooperated. In periods of climatic instability and conflicts, these centers were particularly relevant for the survival of smaller communities spread over a large area and located up to approximately four or five kilometers from the settlement center (Varien 1999). In the thirteenth century AD in the Central Mesa Verde region there were around sixty such communities, and the total Pueblo population probably ranged from 30–45,000, however these estimates varied greatly among researchers (Lipe 2002; Lipe et al. 1999:303–10; Wilshusen 2002).

The simultaneous growth of population and warfare during the last two or three decades preceded the complete and rapid depopulation of the Ancestral Pueblo societies from the Mesa Verde region. Dendrochronological dating clearly shows that all the settlements in the region were deserted within just a few years (perhaps even three or four years), around 1280 AD.

All told, this abrupt mass migration was precipitated by the intersection of various stressors including environmental and climate change, drought, and a likely shrinkage of available arable land combined with social pressures and societal changes (Cameron 2006; Dean and Van West 2002; Kohler et al. 2008, 2010; Lipe 1995; Lipe and Varien 1999; Palonka 2011; Schwindt et al. 2016; Varien et al. 1996).

Changes in Settlement Location and Architecture

At beginning of the thirteenth century AD, Ancestral Pueblo settlements began to move from flat, open areas on mesa tops to the edges and steep slopes of canyons (*canyon-head settlements*) with layouts often resembling the letter D, similar to sites from Chaco Canyon and to the natural shelters and rock niches and large alcoves on canyons slopes (*cliff dwellings*—figure 4.11). Characteristic site location and architecture of this period indicate their defensive function. In the Mesa Verde region, specific features considered elements of defensive architecture (table 4.3) include: the settlement location, access to water, village-enclosing walls, towers, and

Figure 4.11. Long House, a cliff settlement in Mesa Verde National Park, Colorado, as shown on several levels, with a small plaza and the system of communication between levels via ladders. Photos by Radosław Palonka.

Table 4.3. Characteristic features of the Ancestral Pueblo defensive architecture in the Mesa Verde region in the thirteenth century AD

Settlement location	– Most Pueblo settlements from the thirteenth century AD are situated in defensible locations, difficult to access and easy to defend. Often just one or two paths led to such places. Some of the trails could only be traveled with the use of ladders, ropes, or hand and foot holds cut into the rock – Access between levels of multistory buildings was via ladders and, in the event of a threat, the ladders would be pulled up to the higher floors – Very often such sites featured a water source, usually a small stream or a seep, or reservoirs – The characteristic location of settlements from this period is cited as one of the most visible examples of the defensive nature of Ancestral Pueblo architecture (e.g., Kuckelman 2002; LeBlanc 1999; Palonka 2011)
Village-enclosing walls	– Settlements that were more easily accessible, located on the heads of canyons, were often surrounded by rather high stone walls, seemingly at least 2–3 m high; sometimes adjoined by towers (e.g., Kenzle 1997) – The walls in Pueblo villages stood as a defense against attackers are mentioned later by conquistadors entering today's Arizona and New Mexico in the 16th century, as well as by later Spanish records – Other walls were built along rock niches and defended access to them (especially seen is smaller or "medium-sized" sites); some sites could have functioned as refuges (e.g., sites in Canyons of the Ancients National Monument) – Village-enclosing walls and sometimes featured small rectangular openings (loopholes), which were probably used to observe the paths leading to the site, the area outside, as well as individual buildings inside settlement (although, as some archaeologists suggest, some loopholes could have served as vents)
Towers	– Stone towers were built in a circular, rectangular, square, or D-shaped layout, their height is sometimes difficult to estimate, but it is assumed that they were most often one- or two-story buildings (3–8 m high) – The highest known surviving towers in this region are 6–8 m high, e.g. at the Square Tower House site in Mesa Verde National Park and in Hovenweep National Monument (Utah) as well as some unrecorded on private lands – There were often several rooms within the towers and accompanying buildings (kivas, sometimes connected with the towers via tunnels and others) – In canyon-head settlements, towers were "integrated" with the line of walls surrounding the housing group, as well as inside the settlements; it is also common to find towers standing alone at the edge of a site or at a certain point away from the settlement, from 50 to 200 m – Towers probably had various functions: defensive, observation, communication points (information through smoke, fire, and mirror signals), ceremonial, and astronomical indicators (see more below)
Underground tunnels	– Tunnels connecting individual buildings (mainly towers and kivas) within a site are relatively rare compared to other elements considered to be typically defensive – Most often they are located at the extremities of large sites where the entrance was located and from where, in case of danger, they could provide other escape routes deeper inside the site – Tunnels also exist at small sites located in open spaces (e.g. tower-kiva complexes), where there were no other means of defense

underground tunnels connecting selected buildings in the settlements (e.g., Lightfoot and Kuckelman 2001; Kuckelman 2002; LeBlanc 1999; Palonka 2011, 2019b). Settlements were built very close to water sources and there may have even been water access inside the settlement to ensure greater independence.

Direct traces of conflicts and warfare from the second half of the thirteenth century AD are revealed in archaeological findings; some sites were completely destroyed, and buildings often burned down as were skeletal remains of people without formal burials. The remains of at least forty-one people without burials and traces of injuries caused by axes or arrows were discovered at the Castle Rock Pueblo site in southwestern Colorado (Kuckelman 2000, 2002; Lightfoot and Kuckelman 2001). Similar finds were made at the large Sand Canyon Pueblo site eleven kilometers north of Castle Rock Pueblo where the attack and destruction probably occurred after most of the population had already migrated (Kuckelman 2010, 2017), and possibly at the nearby Goodman Point Pueblo (e.g., Coffey and Kuckelman 2006; Palonka and Kuckelman 2009). Rock art of this period presents conflicts in the form of warriors fighting with bows, arrows, shields, and kinds of wooden clubs or "swords." In the Kayenta region in northeastern Arizona, rock art depictions include shield paintings and ascribed protective magic to their bearers (Cole 2009; Palonka 2019a:241–42, Fig. 4; Schaafsma 2000).

The reconstruction of settlements and defensive architecture is far easier in Pueblo culture than in many others ancient cultures because Ancestral Pueblo settlements have remained fairly well preserved due to the building materials used, their location in rock shelters and other protected areas, and the hot, dry climate. Adding to this well-preserved physical evidence are written Spanish sources from this historic period that describe the defensive nature of the historic pueblos, for example the hard-to-reach location, which took the conquistadors more than one attempt to conquer (as in the case of the Zuni and Acoma settlements), and detailed information on how to defend against and fight the Puebloans of that time, including details of their tactics (e.g., Bandelier 1890; Hammond and Rey 1940). Oral traditions of historic and modern Pueblo people also contain a wealth of information.

The Athapascans (mainly Apache) whose first traces in the fringes of the Southwest can be dated back to the thirteenth century AD are often mentioned as potential enemies of the Pueblo population in the Mesa Verde region (Ives et al. 2014; Seymour 2012; Wilcox and Haas 1994; see also chapter 9), but certainly they were still small groups that probably could not seriously threaten the numerous and well-organized Pueblo communities. Also relevant are Numic speakers, for example the ancestors of today's Utes. Conflicts with other groups such as the Utes are mentioned indirectly by the Hopi tradition recorded in the second half of the nineteenth century, even before professional ethnographic and archaeological research (e.g., Jackson and Holmes 1981; Lightfoot and Kuckelman 2001). Recently, however, most evidence points toward intra-group fighting—that is, conflict and fighting within the Pueblo culture itself, between various settlements or entire communities over shrinking farmland and water sources.

In addition, other studies devoted to the intensifying conflicts of this period (Kohler and Turner 2006) have yielded some interesting analyses of women's burials in the Central Mesa Verde region on the border of southwest Colorado and southeastern Utah. Here there are far fewer burials of women than in the adjacent region of Totah/Eastern Mesa Verde in northwestern New Mexico. In the latter site lie the bodies of women whose bones bear traces indicating physical injuries were often not buried in accordance with the prevailing rites, with no grave furnishings or only a small number of offerings. This is interpreted by these researchers as evidence of the kidnapping of women from the Central Mesa Verde region by Pueblo groups from the adjacent Totah area (Kohler and Turner 2006).

A ritual prevailed in Pueblo culture, practically throughout all phases and periods of its development, regarding burial position—supine, or possibly in a fetal position. The graves were located under the floors of abandoned houses, as well as in separate spaces outside but close to the settlements. These were usually earth pits with graves most likely marked on the surface with some type of individual marking such as sticks with feathers, and stones (e.g., Cattanach 1980). Sometimes burials were under stones or boulders and on the northern slopes of canyons where it was more shaded. In the case of cliff dwellings, graves were usually established under the floors of houses and in rock shelters on the slopes below. Grave goods include pottery, woven baskets and other items from organic materials, bone and flint and stone tools (needles, scrapers, projectile points, *mano* stones and others). Sometimes the bodies were wrapped in blankets of sorts, or mats woven from plant fibers.

Of course, not all settlements from the second half of the thirteenth century AD were destroyed; many bear no sign of an attack, apart from the existence of typically defensive architecture (see table 4.3). Descriptions of the first nineteenth-century explorations and research of many cliff settlements in the area of modern Mesa Verde National Park in Colorado

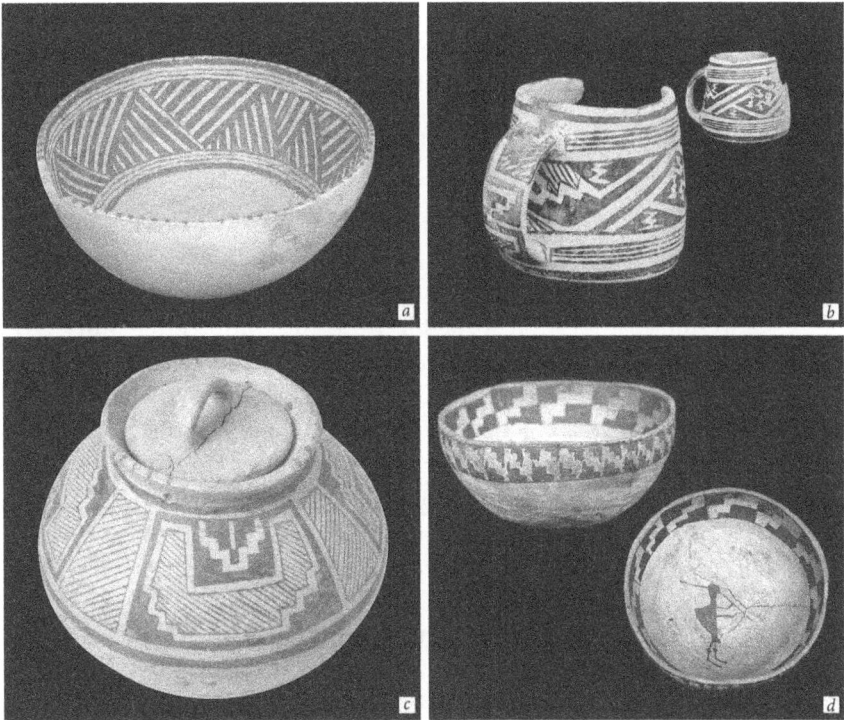

Figure 4.12. Typical forms of Pueblo II–III pottery from the Mesa Verde region: (a) a bowl; (b) a cup; (c) a jar; and (d) a bowl with geometric and anthropomorphic designs. Photos by Katarzyna Ciomek.

(e.g., Nordenskiöld 1990) even state that many everyday objects, including pottery and other items, lay intact, and the buildings had only been disturbed by the passage of time. According to these descriptions, it was as if the inhabitants had left everything and had gone somewhere with the intention of a quick return.

CASTLE ROCK PUEBLO AND FINAL PHASE OF PUEBLOAN OCCU-PATION OF THE MESA VERDE REGION The Castle Rock settlement cluster (Castle Rock Community) was located in three canyons: lower and middle parts of Sand Canyon, East Fork of Rock Creek Canyon, and Graveyard Canyon and occupied primarily in the years 1225–1280 AD—the late Pueblo III period. This complex was comprised of over forty-one small settlements comprised of a few to fifteen to twenty buildings per site. Settlements such as these were concentrated around a large community center. Castle Rock Pueblo (Site 5MT1825), which contained at least sixty to eighty buildings, was the community center of the complex. Features of defensive nature are clearly visible in this cluster of sites around Castle Rock Pueblo (Lightfoot and Kuckelman 2001; Kuckelman 2002; Ortman 2008; Palonka 2011, 2013, 2015, 2019b, Palonka et al. 2020, 2021; Varien 1999).

Of the forty-one documented small settlements, as many as thirty-one were located in difficult-to-access rock shelters, with some buildings located on the slopes below (Palonka 2013, 2019b). Castle Rock Pueblo itself was built around and on top of a twenty-meter rock formation, a butte (quite unusual location for a site from the thirteenth century AD, not following the "rule" of canyon-head or cliff dwelling pattern, but also with strong elements of a defensive location and architecture). Outer walls with loopholes, either wholly or partially preserved, have been recorded in at least six sites in the community; as a rule, these kinds of walls were built along the alcove edges with only one entrance leading inside the site. Some sites had refuges—places that were not permanently inhabited but offered protection in case of danger. At least three such shelters have been found in the Castle Rock Community.

The most important element of the defensive system were the stone towers, both round and rectangular, several meters high, sometimes single-room, but sometimes consisting of several rooms and levels. There were nine such towers at Castle Rock Pueblo itself (Kuckelman 2000) and at least seven to nine towers (or tower-like structures) in the small sites within the community (e.g., Palonka 2011, 2019b). The towers were built in the settlements themselves, very close by or at some distance away, usually 30/40–200 m; it is assumed that the latter were part of the settlement nearest to them. These towers were built in places that were perfectly visible from at least four to six or more other dwellings and other towers (figure 4.13). The strategic location of towers could facilitate rapid communication among allies. Eye-contact or intervisibility between towers was likely used to convey signals and information in case of danger or calling for ceremonies by using fire at night, and smoke or mirrors made of polished pyrite during the day.

Visual contact and communications between sites and towers were probably one of the key—if not the most essential—elements in the survival of such a community in the changing cultural and environmental landscape of the thirteenth century AD Mesa Verde region. Such intervisibility and its significance during times of danger has been documented in different areas of the Southwest, including Perry Mesa (central Arizona), in the Kayenta region (northeastern Arizona), in the Chaco World, and

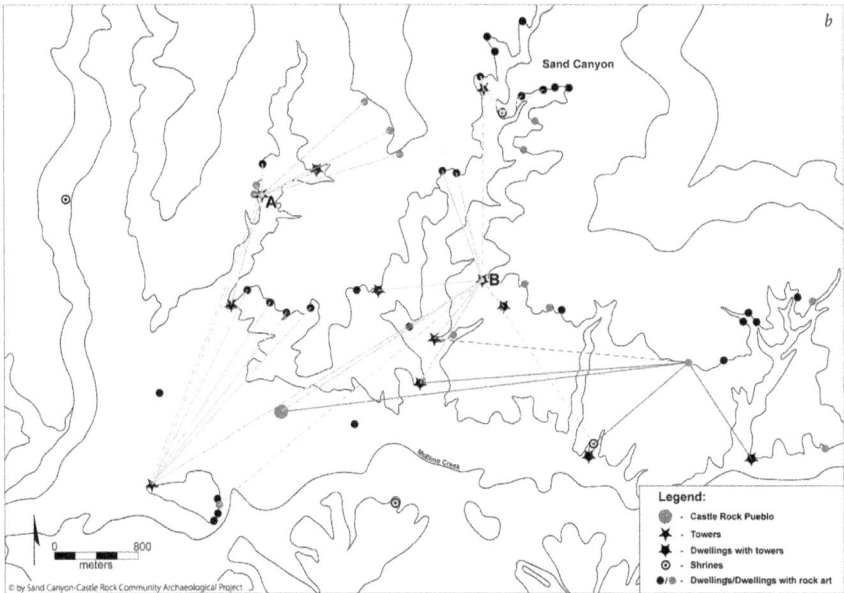

Figure 4.13. Mad Dog Tower from Sand Canyon as an example of a defensive or lookout structure (a) and (b) reconstruction of intervisibility/eye-contact between sites in the Castle Rock community. Compiled by Radosław Palonka and drawing by Michał Znamirowski.

in experimental studies of intervisibility between Navajo *pueblitos* of the Dinétah region in northwestern New Mexico (e.g., Bryan 2009; Haas and Creamer 1993; Wilcox and Haas 1994; Kantner and Hobgood 2016). As is often suggested, towers could have also served other purposes, such as observing the surrounding area for game, storing food, and in some cases, making astronomical observations of the sky to define a calendar and establish days for certain rites and rituals related to agriculture (Johnson 2003; Lipe et al. 1999; Palonka 2019b; Thompson 2004; Van Dyke 2008; Wilcox 2005). Such forms of communication and the transmission of messages over long distances are known from other regions of the world, including medieval Europe, which is confirmed by both archaeological data and written sources about early medieval strongholds, or later, castles, for instance, but it's also confirmed by written Spanish sources from the seventeenth and nineteenth centuries from the Southwest.

Individual settlements with intervisible towers were able to forge an allied community which, thanks to mutual assistance, had a better chance of surviving in the event of an attack or even a crop failure. Such alliances (Spielmann 1994:51-52; Upham et al. 1994), were probably very important for survival in face of the steadily deteriorating living conditions in the region Mesa Verde in the thirteenth century AD. These conditions included changes in the natural environment, increasing social pressures, and intra-group fighting. Quick communication was probably of particular importance for communities and settlements dispersed over a fairly large area such as the Castle Rock community.

Obviously, such a system would have been effective as long as the individual towers and sites were synchronous (functioning in the same period) so determining the mutual chronology of individual settlements in such community is a critical research question. So far, dendrochronological samples have been taken from more than ten sites in the cluster studied; some very precise annual dates were obtained for few sites, ranging from 1254 to 1271 AD, the latter date is taken from the site Sunny Alcove (5MT135). This is one of the latest Pueblo dates for the entire Mesa Verde region, at least for the small sites in the area (Palonka et al. 2020). In turn, the latest dates for the Castle Rock Pueblo site were obtained in the 1990s thanks to research conducted by the Crow Canyon Archaeological Center; these dates align around the year 1274 AD (Kuckelman 2000).

Despite its complexity, this system of mutual relations and defense was not enough to survive the escalation of the entire cycle of changes and unfavorable conditions that occurred mainly in the last three decades of the thirteenth century AD, and consequently led to the abandonment of the entire area by the population of the Castle Rock settlement complex and other communities. Although the complex survived up to a certain point, when it was exposed to such adverse factors, environment stress, or a single massive attack, it failed to withstand them.

In the late 1270s and early 1280s AD, the settlement cluster around Castle Rock Pueblo and the entire Mesa Verde region were completely depopulated. Ancestral Puebloans migrated south and southeast, into northern and central Arizona and New Mexico. There they reached other Pueblo groups that had occupied those regions for hundreds of years; their descendants still live in Arizona (the Hopi) and nineteen pueblos in New Mexico (including Zuni, Acoma, Jemez). Pueblo societies never returned to the Mesa Verde area, with the Navajos and Utes arriving later. The Ute Mountain Ute Tribe and Southern Ute have two reservations in southern Colorado today, the first only a few kilometers away from the Castle Rock Community.

It is evident that, in the second half of the thirteenth century when environmental and climate changes including climatic cooling intensified the amount of rainfall and groundwater level decreased; in addition, the environment was degraded by the Ancestral Puebloans themselves by depletion of resources like wood (e.g., Dean and Van West 2002; Kohler 2000; Van West and Dean 2000) while conflicts and struggles raged, possibly due to these environmental causes. The so-called Great Drought fell during the years 1276–1299 AD probably as a culmination of these unfavorable changes, traces of which are perfectly preserved in the rings of trees used in the construction of Ancestral Pueblo houses. These adverse environmental and climatic changes seem to have occurred far beyond the boundary of today's southern parts of Utah and Colorado, and extended to much larger areas of the Southwest, throughout the whole of North America (e.g., Benson and Berry 2009; Hegmon et al. 2013), and even the entire northern hemisphere. It was the beginning of the so-called Little Ice Age and the cooling was felt in various places in America, Asia, and Europe in the Northern Hemisphere, although it is not certain if this period was "present" in the thirteenth century AD in the American Southwest (e.g., Matthews and Briffa 2005).

Notably however, the above-mentioned environmental and climatic reasons do not fully explain the reasons for migration, in part because this region had experienced much more severe conditions in previous times, and without leading to a complete depopulation (e.g., Van West and Dean 2000). Rather it seems a series of events cascaded into the depopulation. Environmental and climate changes led to competition for available arable land fomenting alongside a disturbance in established social relations and some form of social pressure, related in turn with the increasing intensification of conflicts and warfare.

Reasons for the Ancestral Pueblo culture's abandonment of the Mesa Verde region are also attributed to other factors, such as the attraction of new cults (e.g. the *kachina* cult—see below) and influences from the south that could have been alluring to potential emigrants, especially as Mesa Verde's economic and social systems were collapsing. Notably the Rio Grande basin was, at the time, sparsely populated compared to the Mesa Verde region and had more favorable environmental and climatic conditions that had not changed as dramatically as those in the Mesa Verde region (e.g., Cordell 1997:374–92). In other words, people now had a more attractive alternative than in their current home. This multiplicity of factors was likely to have snowballed to such an extent that it resulted in a complete migration of the surviving Pueblo people from the Mesa Verde region in the late thirteenth century AD.

Rock Art in the Pueblo Period

The transition from the end of the Basketmaker II–III period to the beginning of the Pueblo period appears to have been driven by changes of a religious nature, as indicated by the appearance of kiva-type buildings in settlement sites along with other major shifts in the economy, social structure and material and spiritual culture. Rock art of the Pueblo period reflects these major transitions in the lives of the Ancestral Pueblo societies (e.g., Schaafsma 1980). Most noticeable is the reduction in the size of the anthropomorphic representations so characteristic of the San Juan Anthropomorphic style, as well as the emergence of more complex depictions with a host of motifs and symbols. The majority of these newer images have been found in the San Juan River basin, but there are other regional styles as well.

In the Pueblo II and III periods, rock art reached its furthest geographic extent with a notable diversity of imagery; however, one has to remember that some regions were depopulated and migrations and hiatuses in local settlement appeared, as in parts of the western regions of Virgin Kayenta and Kayenta (Schaafsma 1980:135). This was a period in which huge settlements emerged in Chaco Canyon and beyond, including in the Mesa Verde region, leading to settlement reorganization and social and religious changes. The development of architecture and the construction of large settlements, as well as the production of a rich material culture and the emergence of extensive trade routes, went hand in hand with the growth and enrichment of the motifs and content of rock art from that period.

The richness and diversity of rock art and murals on building walls produced until 1300 AD is extraordinary. Notable features of the art include carving petroglyphs on exposed canyon walls and individual boulders. Paintings are prevalent in shelters and rock niches where settlements were also often established, particularly in the late phase of the Pueblo III period. Unlike the very large anthropomorphic representations of the Basketmaker period, human figures were of a size comparable to other motifs. So-called stick figures—thin and schematically depicted humans—were also fairly common. These are shown with both hands down and raised resembling the orans gesture—which is one of the most common motifs in the rock art of this period. Human hands were also frequently depicted many times using various techniques and there are also engraved representations of human feet and sandals, sometimes finely decorated with geometric motifs including sandals woven from plant fibers.

The geometric motifs are repeated in iconography in painted ceramics, decorated baskets, and in murals in houses and kivas; there is a clear tendency toward the widespread use and repetition of such motifs, including stepped elements, meanders, spirals, and concentric circles and others (Cole 2009; Schaafsma 1980).

Compared to earlier periods, the diligence and precision in the execution of these representations is noticeable, particularly in petroglyphs, as is the rich use of individual elements enhancing their aesthetic appeal. Animals were often depicted, with realistic representations of their anatomy and details such as antlers (in deer or bighorn sheep depictions). Ears and mouths are often included in images of four-legged animals and feathers and beaks of birds were also marked, sometimes with detail that has enabled the identification of particular species. Particular rock art panels with depictions of spirals, concentric circles, and other geometric patterns may have been connected with astronomical observations.

The so-called lizard-man, a variant of stick-figure anthropomorphic representations is one of the more frequent motifs. It is even sometimes difficult to distinguish between representations of human figures and lizard-human hybrids. Rare lizard man figurines have been found, and a lizard-woman was discovered in a kiva at the Salmon Ruin in northern New Mexico (Schaafsma 1980:136). Another variant of anthropomorphic representation is the so-called fluteplayer (Kokopelli) motif which probably evolved from earlier periods. Kokopelli is a human figure playing the flute, often shown with a hump, sometimes with a phallus, and has marked feathers or more lines resembling insect heads. The fluteplayer is sometimes shown lying down or in a scene playing the flute and dancing.

Kokopelli was extremely widespread in the Southwest and is one of the most prevalent images in the rock art of this region, so much so that today it is often used as a logo for shops, motels, restaurants, and objects and has become an element of pop culture. The proposed anthropological explanations of the function and meaning of the fluteplayer motif boil down to its interpretation as a religious leader or "priest" evoking clouds and rain with sounds, which is based among other things on Hopi beliefs in the influence of flute music over water bodies or streams and thus invoking rain—sometimes gourds with water are attached to the flute during such ceremonies—Schaafsma 1980:140).

Other interpretations assume a role related to hunting such as the representations of the fluteplayer with a bow, sheep horns, and game at the Fire Temple in the Mesa Verde National Park. Today the motif is present in the *kachina* cult; *Kachina* Kokopelli is considered responsible for the growth, abundance, and fertility of the land. In his hump Kokopelli carries children, blankets, and corn which he hands out to girls. His role is also associated with the mythical origins of people and their transition from the underworld to the one that exists today. In a broader sense, he may be a trickster archetype sometimes credited with immoral and sexual behavior but also as a shaman summoning rain and assisting in hunting and bringing a certain order in the world (Schaafsma 1980:141, further literature there).

In periods of increased conflict, including those mentioned in the Mesa Verde region during the thirteenth century, one can often see an intensification of fighting scenes including figures of warriors with shields, bows and arrows, and types of clubs or sticks. Characters with these weapons are shown standing or in action, and the battles themselves are sometimes represented. The most well-known rock art panel from Castle Rock Pueblo depicts three fighting warriors (Kuckelman 2000, 2002; Palonka 2019a): two figures hold bows and arrows and are positioned back-to-back. This composition may suggest mutual defense or a jointly conducted attack; a third figure holds an object, probably a shield, and faces one of the figures with a bow (figure 4.14). Similar representations of warriors and fighting scenes may be found in the southeastern part of Utah (Cole 1990; Crotty 2001; Schaafsma 1980, 2000) and northeastern Arizona in the Kayenta region (e.g., Forton 2020; Schaafsma 2000). In the latter area, many representations of painted shields can be interpreted as symbols of group identity, protective magic or of defense and therefore associated with warfare.

Murals are also notable in this period. These colorful wall paintings have been preserved until today in some buildings, generally on internal walls, and images are sometimes etched or carved on clay plaster. Typical

Figure 4.14.   Rock art panel at Castle Rock Pueblo, showing three fighting warriors. Photograph by Michał Znamirowski.

residential rooms (often the first floors if the ground floor was intended for storage), as well as of the kiva type rooms were decorated in this way. The motifs are dominated by geometric representations—triangles, dots, disks, and other geometric motifs—often arranged as a decorative band, as well as animals (deer and mountain sheep) and birds (turkeys, possibly parrots). It is possible that the internal areas of nonresidential buildings were also painted. Sometimes external areas of facades were also decorated.

Pueblo Societies in the Late Pre-Hispanic and Historic Periods: Selected Aspects

The second half and the end of the thirteenth century AD was a time of reorganization and great migrations of Ancestral Pueblo groups from the northern part of the Southwest to the southern and southeastern parts of the Colorado Plateau. Cultural, economic, and social crises must have driven emigration away from the Four Corners region. The population shifted to northern Arizona and west-central New Mexico, the areas of today's Hopi and Zuni reservations and the Little Colorado River and most of all in the Rio Grande Valley. From the beginning of the fourteenth century AD, along with new settlements and social and religious patterns, completely

Table. 4.4. The Most Important Styles in Rock Art in the Basketmaker III to–Pueblo II Period

Rock Painting Style	Characteristic Features and Occurrence
Chinle	– The most famous from Canyon de Chelly (northeastern Arizona)
	– Sometimes referred to as a modified style from the Basketmaker and Pueblo periods; a continuation of some previous representations, but also many new elements
	– Small representations, often monochrome paintings, with the outline of the figure made in another color or figures painted with two colors with a vertical division into two parts
	– Torsos of figures tend to be triangular as opposed to the earlier trapezoidal ones; often characters are shown in rows with their hands down; usually small, rather thin figures (so-called stick-figures) and usually engaged in some type of activity or movement such as running, walking, sitting. Often such figures sit in pairs
	– These stick-figures may be the predecessors of the famous fluteplayer motif, but at this earlier time, they lack the characteristic hump and phallus.
	– Presumably the presence of plumes in the form of lines with dots above their heads or two "horns" (probably a depiction of two feathers)
	– Frequent depictions of birds including turkeys, ducks, herons appear, sometimes sitting on a human's head, perhaps depictions of shamans; birds are sometimes shown in flight with legs pointing backward and at an angle, without wings
	– Other animals were presented less frequently at that time, but sometimes include schematic mountain sheep
	– Other motifs show bows or rainbows painted in two colors over people's heads, spears with feathers, various types of handprints, abstract elements like zigzag lines
Hidden Valley	– Animas River Valley (southwestern Colorado), mainly from the Hidden Valley
	– Very small representations (7–25 cm high), predominantly black, white, green, yellow, and red
	– Paintings of human figures include stick figures and flute players; animals, mainly ducks are shown in groups of 2–20; zigzag lines and circles were painted in rock shelters and caves
	– Representations of small masks in groups from 1–9 are painted red with no facial contours, just the eyes, noses, and lips visible and possibly a feather on top of the head

Rosa
- Upper San Juan River Basin (northwestern New Mexico), and along the Los Pinos River and the Largo Canyon, the southeastern part of the Mesa Verde region
- Depictions, mainly petroglyphs, were dark in color (patina) and were quite exposed
- Anthropomorphic figures prevail. These range from trapezoidal to triangular representations of the torso, sometimes rectangular with elongated necks and small heads, legs, and arms, usually thin and short. Feet and hands are rarely shown, single or two feathers and sometimes necklaces (in the representations of larger figures) as decorations for the head and upper body parts; very often the figures hold hands and are shown in rows without birds on their heads
- Co-occurrence, similar to the Chinle style, of triangular figures and stick-figures (the latter being poorly executed and shown in motion, hands down, also depictions of musicians playing the flute and hunters hunting with a bow)
- Rarely depicted animals include deer, mountain sheep, perhaps sometimes types of traps or pens and corrals as hunting elements; birds also rarely shown (most often wading, with long legs), no representations of ducks
- Geometric and abstract motifs, including wavy lines and small spirals appear
- Depictions of triangular figures, often with arches or curved sticks (perhaps ceremonial) and birds on their heads, as well as occasional four-legged animals that are difficult to identify are found in the north and west including Mancos Canyon in southwestern Colorado and the Central Mesa Verde region

Cave Valley
- Colorado River Basin, from the Central Virgin Kayenta Region to the southwest parts of Utah and adjacent parts of Arizona
- Mainly in rock shelters; images painted in black, red, yellow, green, pink, and white
- Mostly anthropomorphic figures with trapezoidal and triangular torsos and wide heads, short arms, and legs
- Sometimes stick figures and humpback flute players; some hard to identify species of four-legged animals and birds

After Cole 2009 and Schaafsma 1980:121–34.

different murals and rock art began to emerge although some symbolism was continued, including the fluteplayer motif—see figure 4.15).

The last two centuries before the arrival of Europeans in the Southwest in the fourteenth and fifteenth centuries AD (the so-called late pre-Hispanic/pre-Contact or protohistoric period) was a time of the emergence of a new settlement and cultural model. In 1530s and '40s, the Spaniards were the first Europeans to find already well-organized Puebloan communities in the Southwest. In many respects, the Puebloan culture survived throughout the sixteenth century, due to the fact that permanent Spanish settlement in this area only occurred at the end of the sixteenth century. It therefore makes sense to consider roughly the period from 1300 to 1600 AD as a complete unit (as previously defined by Alfred Kidder in 1927 as the Pueblo IV period). Despite the interference of European and American culture, his cultural and settlement model is still largely evident in many aspects today.

Some of the pueblos which were founded in the thirteenth and fourteenth century AD are still functioning today; these include, for example, at least four of twelve Hopi villages from the Antelope, First, Second, and Third Mesas (Bernardini 2005:8) settlements which were established after migrations from other areas including the Mesa Verde region. Later the main migratory sources were the Homol'ovi and Anderson Mesa of north-central Arizona (e.g., Adams 1996, 2002; Adams and Duff 2004; Bernardini 2005; Spielmann 1998). The second area of large Ancestral Puebloan societies which in large part migrated from other areas, are those in the Rio Grande River valley and west-central New Mexico (e.g., Adams and Duff 2004). The dramatic revision in the interpretations by contemporary American anthropology and archaeology describing the period after 1300 AD is extremely interesting in the context of the dynamics and scale of development of the Pueblo culture (e.g., Fowles 2012). Previously a handful of researchers referred to the period before the extensive settlements and culture in Chaco Canyon and Mesa Verde as the Developmental Pueblo period. They viewed the settlement heyday in these two regions (850–1300 AD) as the Great Pueblo period—a time of great creativity and accomplishments—which was followed by a period of regression and a decline called the Regressive Pueblo period. The latter was also associated with a narrowing of the territory which they occupied. Today however, a new perspective on a lack of evidence about the later period of Chaco development suggests a rejection of this path of social development (at least by some) and may explain the egalitarianism of the historic Pueblo peoples and the relative autonomy and independence of individual pueblos/vil-

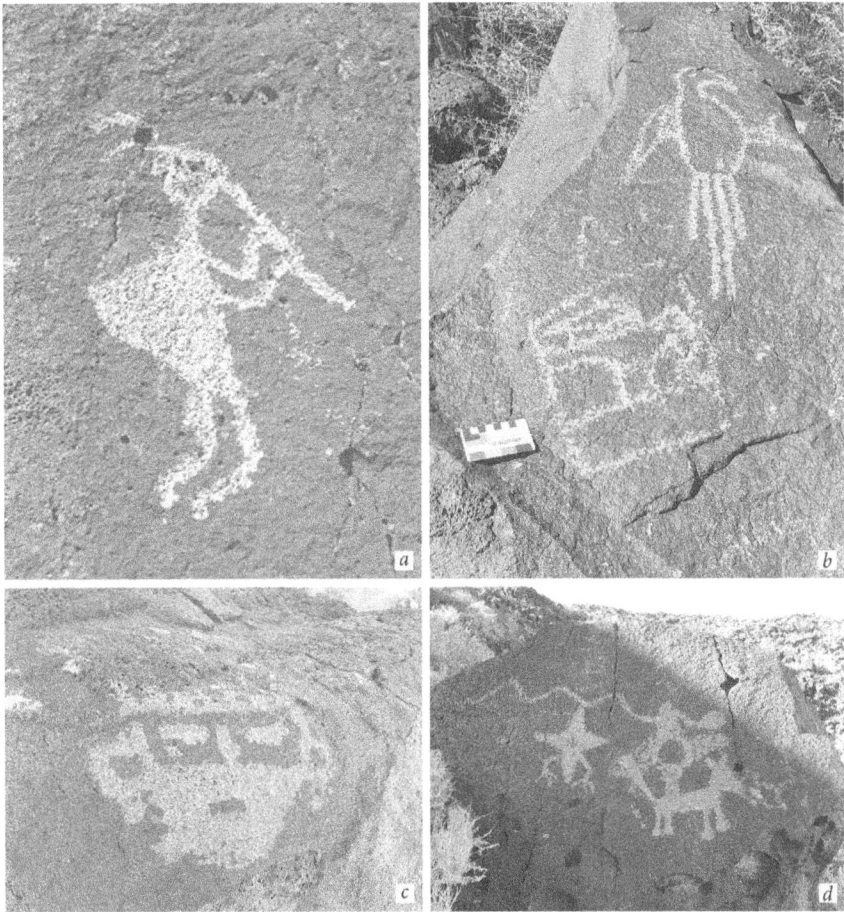

Figure 4.15.   Examples of rock art (petroglyphs): (a) fluteplayer (Kokopelli), Sand Island Petroglyph Panel, Utah as the example of continuation of some motifs to Pueblo IV period and beyond; (b–d) petroglyphs of Rio Grande style (Pueblo IV), Petroglyph National Monument, located north of Albuquerque, New Mexico. Photographs by Radosław Palonka.

lages. In this interpretation, Chaco appears not as the apogee of Pueblo's cultural development, but as the oppressive domination of the people by the elite (Fowles 2012). This is also a very interesting explanation of certain cultural processes in the Southwest.

The period of the fourteenth–sixteenth centuries in the development of Pueblo culture can be treated as a time of reorganization or "reformation," as proposed, among others, by Severin Fowles (Fowles 2012). In the fourteenth century AD, at the sites established, for example, on the Rio

Grande in New Mexico, there tends to be no observable continuation of material culture and architecture that could have potentially been brought by migrants from the Mesa Verde region at the end of the thirteenth century AD (e.g., Lipe 2006). This period is also characterized by migrations and the formation of very large settlements, with the number of rooms and housing units reaching several hundred and the number of inhabitants ranging from several hundred to over a thousand (this also continues in the historic period). The formation of with many hundreds and sometimes up to between 1,000 and 3,000 rooms, vastly exceeded in size any large pueblo villages seen before in the Puebloan world. These large towns indicate a new social order and the presence of integrating organizations that cross-cut lineage affiliation that is apparent for example in the interiors of such settlements which featured plazas for ceremonies as well as kivas, albeit with far fewer such buildings in each village than in previous periods.

When it comes to the scale of these settlement foundations, there is no regression in relation to Chaco, although individual houses were crafted using much simpler techniques, without involving so many resources and labor; nor was there any major distinction among the houses, the whole construction making an impression of standardization and greater egalitarianism.

Some researchers claim that this architecture indicates a lack of significant stratification of society, while others suggest the existence of political and religious stratification was defined by access to certain resources by specific groups of people. The latter theory is supported by other features such as the scale of settlements, the formation of regional groupings such as confederations and alliances often involving at least several thousand people (e.g., Spielmann 1994), the defensive location of many sites in hard-to-reach parts of mesas, and a renewed increase in trade. Trade routes survived until the historic period and were later used by the conquistadors for expeditions from Mexico. A degree of hierarchy is confirmed by ethnographic literature, mainly from nineteenth century research.

Notably this period is marked by the appearance and expansion of the Kachina (also Katsina, Katcina or Katchina) cult which is characterized by a belief in supernatural beings who mediate between human and extraterrestrial worlds, and are associated with bringing rain and well-being to the people (e.g., Schaafsma and Schaafsma 1974:535). Though there is great debate about its exact origins, the Kachina cult arose and flourished at a time of turbulent social change in the Southwest, likely originating among the Pueblo at the turn of the thirteenth and fourteenth centuries (e.g., Adams 1991; Schaafsma 2000; Schaafsma and Schaafsma 1974.). The cult and related religious practices spread throughout the north-central part of the Southwest during the fourteenth century, unifying migrants who came from the north in the Mesa Verde region with the earlier inhabitants of the areas above the Rio Grande, Little Colorado, and adjacent to them parts of Arizona and New Mexico. The wider "belief" system was part of a cosmology related to rain and ancestors with multiple metaphors and symbols shared with Mesoamerica (e.g., Schaafsma and Taube 2006).

Thousands of kachina images can be found in the iconography of pottery, kiva murals, and rock art of this period, including depictions of masks, masked dancers, clouds, and lightning. It is also impossible to separate its early manifestations from the symbolism of war and the intensification of conflict in the Southwest. The close connection between the emergence of this cult and the increase in influences from Mesoamerican areas is also underscored by at some researchers (e.g., Anderson 1955; Schaafsma 1992; 2000; Schaafsma and Schaafsma 1974). Interestingly, kachina cult is practiced today by many Pueblo groups; moreover, it is a vital part of beliefs of the Hopi, Zuni, Acoma, and Laguna, as well as many Pueblo groups in New Mexico such as the Pueblo Keresans (figure 4.16). It is believed that the Kachinas visit the Hopi villages during the first half of the year and so this is the time when many kachina dances are performed. Outside observers are not permitted at all of these ceremonies.

Just as importantly, modern day kachina dancers from the Hopi and Zuni tribes have contributed extraordinary knowledge about their ancestors through the performances and interpretations of ceremonies and dances they do today. Different dances at different times of the year are done to evoke rain and spirits. Images of dancers on murals that date to the 14th century capture many of the same positions and ceremonial clothing, notably elaborate headdresses, as dances that are performed today. The artwork and the participation by Hopi kachina dancers vividly demonstrate the continuity of culture lasting 800 years, and inform our knowledge of spiritual beliefs and ceremonies as a major factor in migration to the Rio Grande area.

Changes in the religious system among the Pueblo communities were universal and unifying. This is manifested by the reduction in the number of ceremonial buildings (kivas.) In in the fourteenth to fifteenth centuries and later, only a few such large structures are found for an entire settlement, which together with centrally located plazas, may indicate ceremonies of a more integrative character that gathered the entire community. The kachina cult itself was most likely only part of a wider belief system that existed in the Pueblo world at the time (e.g., Fowles 2012). This is

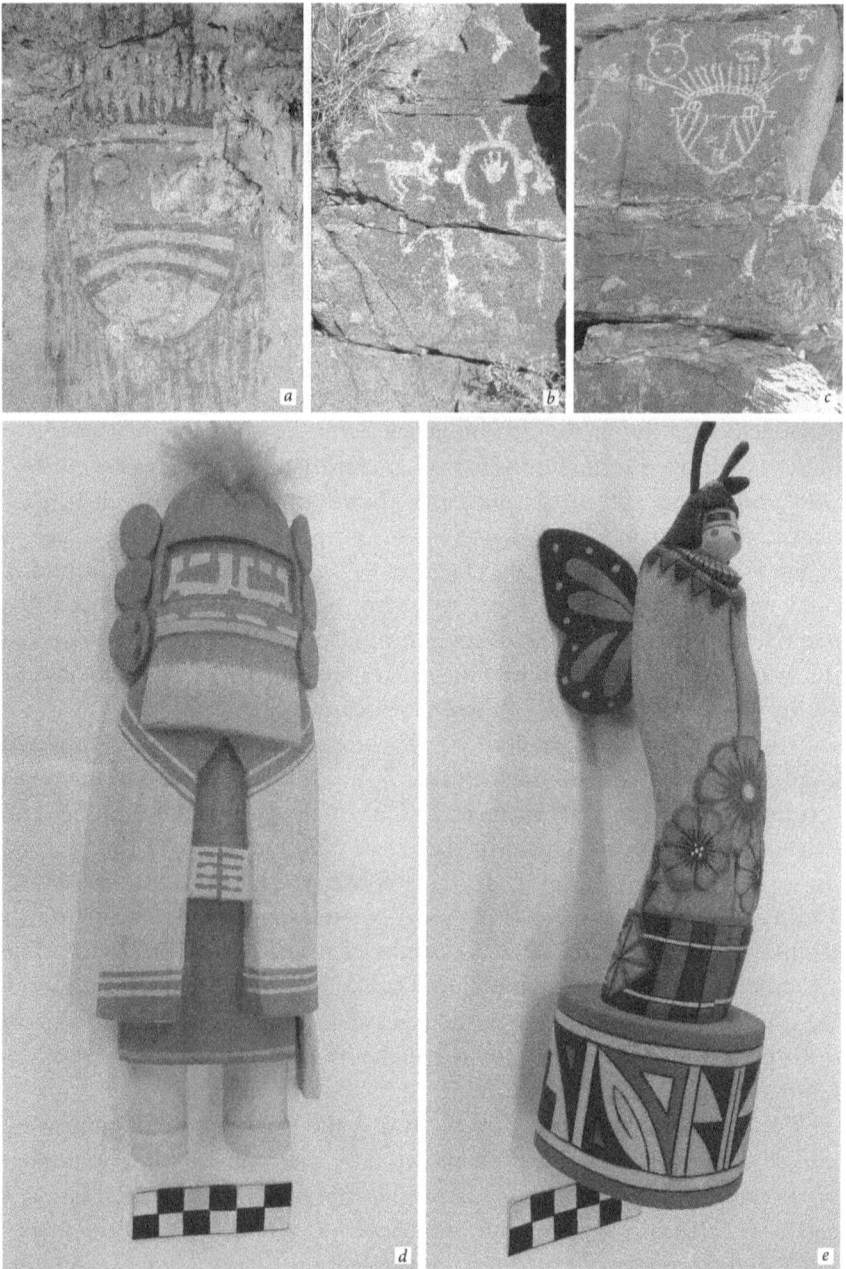

Figure 4.16. Examples of depictions of kachinas from the Rio Grande valley and dated roughly to the period between ca. 1340 to 1680 AD (a–c) and modern Hopi kachina dolls (figurines): Hemis Kachina-mana (b) and Butterfly Maiden kachina (d–e); photos by Polly Schaafsma (a–c) and Radosław Palonka (d–e).

especially noticeable when we take into account the specificity of local differences even within one culture, in the Southwest related to, among other things, the diverse natural environment and landscape.

Significant changes in art and architecture from the fourteenth century AD reflect the societal transformations in the Pueblo culture and offer insight into the influence of religious cults and migration patterns as the Pueblo abandoned their settlements in and around Mesa Verde and moved south to areas where their descendants still live today. The Rio Grande style that became predominant in this period was likely influenced by religious trends. The style encompasses a new quality in the designs and appearance of glazed ceramics. Petroglyphs likewise prevailed over paintings. Iconography from earlier Pueblo periods—largely influenced by the rock art of the Mogollon culture called the Jornada style (e.g., Schaafsma 1992; Schaafsma and Schaafsma 1974; Slifer 1998) feature new types of anthropomorphic representations including masked kachina figures and zoomorphic, plant, geometric, and stepped motifs. The northern part of the Rio Grande valley is dominated by petroglyphs set on dark boulders of volcanic origin. A concentration of these can be seen in the West Mesa and the Petroglyph National Monument near Albuquerque, New Mexico.

The number of murals covering internal and external walls increases, as shown by data obtained through archaeological research and descriptions written by the first conquistadors in this area (e.g., Schaafsma 1980). Well-known sites with murals from the Pueblo IV period include the Awatovi and Kawaika-a pueblos near today's Hopi villages in Arizona, and the Pottery Mound, Picuris, and Kuaua sites in the Rio Grande valley (e.g., Crotty 1995, 1999; Schaafsma 1980, 2007, 2009; Smith 1952) (figure 4.17).

Today many descendants of the Ancestral Puebloans who inhabited Mesa Verde and Chaco Canyon live in twenty reservations in Arizona and in New Mexico. The Western Pueblos, or Hopi tribe, inhabit the semiarid areas of Arizona, and the Zuni, Acoma and Laguna occupy the western parts of New Mexico. The Eastern Pueblos include the remaining sixteen pueblos and reservations in the Rio Grande valley in New Mexico—for example Taos, Jemez (Walatowa), San Juan (Ohkay Owingeh), Santa Ana, and Santa Clara. A large number of modern Pueblo communities—the Hopi Oraibi and Walpi villages and Acoma Pueblo—have continuously occupied settlements that were founded in the thirteenth and fourteenth centuries AD, making them the oldest settlements still inhabited in the United States today (see also chapter 1, figure 1.6).

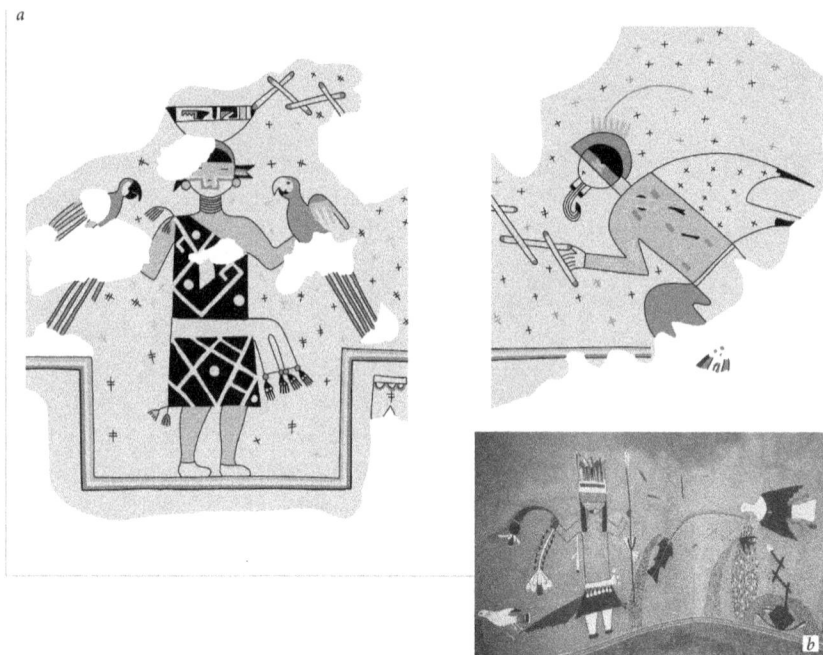

Figure 4.17. Kiva murals from sites in New Mexico from the fourteenth–fifteenth centuries: (a) Pottery Mound; (b) Kuaua Pueblo. Drawing by Magdalena Lewandowska after various sources and photo by Radosław Palonka.

To this day, as they have for generations, Pueblo communities continue to pass down oral histories and traditional customs and beliefs, providing extraordinary continuity and keeping the past alive. Over the past two or three decades, Pueblo people and other Native American communities are increasingly open to collaborating with researchers, and some have become archeologists themselves. These cooperative efforts have greatly advanced research, museology, and exhibit design.

Notes

1. The word *pueblo* in Spanish means "village," "town," or "people." However, the term *pueblo* is used in at least three meanings—as a term for the culture (people), as well as to denote a certain stage (period) of its development and as the name of Ancestral Pueblo settlements built of sandstone or sun-dried bricks (*adobe*). The name was first used by the Spaniards in the sixteenth and seventeenth centuries for the many farming communities in the Rio Grande Valley and northern Arizona and to distinguish them from the mobile hunter-gatherer communities of the Apache, Navajo, or Ute.

2. The forms *katchina* and *katsina/k'atsina* (always pronounced ka-*chee*-na) are also used. There are many representations of these intermediaries in rock art and ceramics of both the pre-Hispanic and historic periods, and many are also known from numerous museums and collections of wooden or richly decorated kachina figurines (often wrongly called dolls). At this point, the Hopi tribe alone distinguish about two hundred different *kachinas*, and even more than five hundred in all Pueblo groups.

3. In particular, the ratio of strontium 86 to strontium 87 and other elements partially illustrates the chemical composition of the water and soil where the plant was grown.

4. Much of the data from these projects and others on the Chaco Canyon itself are available digitally at the Chaco Research Archive: http://www.chacoar chive.org/cra/outlier-database/ (the Chaco Canyon Outlier Database was built by John Kantner and is still being updated) and on the National Park Service website: (a) https://www.nps.gov/chcu/learn/historyculture/chaco-project-publications .htm, (b) https://www.nps.gov/chcu/learn/historyculture/archives.htm, and (c) https://www.nps.gov/museum/exhibits/chcu/.

Civilizations in the Arizona Desert   **5**
The Hohokam and Salado Cultures

⊞

The Hohokam Culture

THE HOHOKAM COMMUNITIES developed south of the Ancestral Pueblo culture in southern and central Arizona, and in the northern part of the Mexican state of Sonora starting in 450 AD and lasting until about 1500 AD, immediately before the arrival of the Spaniards. To the north, the Hohokam culture spread to the Agua Fria River and the central Verde River basin in Arizona almost as far as today's Flagstaff. From the northeast, their extent was limited by the Mogollon Rim mountain range. The Mogollon culture which is distinct from the Ancestral Pueblo and the Hohokam, developed further to the east, and to the southeast of the Dragoon Mountains, with the Growler Mountains to the west (figure 5.1). The main regions where we find evidence of the largest population centers of the Hohokam culture include the Phoenix and Tucson basins and Papaguería (southwestern Arizona and the northwestern state of Sonora), as well as Tonto region in central-eastern Arizona.

The natural environment of the area occupied by the Hohokam is characterized by scarce rainfall, a hot, dry climate, and considerable environmental diversity offering the possibility of exploiting semiarid areas, upland and mountain areas, and their environmental resources, along with the opportunity to harvest at least some cultivated plants twice a year. Settlements were concentrated mainly on the larger rivers, including the Salt, Gila, Santa Cruz, Verde, and San Pedro, and their tributaries.

The Hohokam also built irrigation canals and settled in these areas. The tradition of irrigation canals in this area dates to the Late Archaic/Early Agricultural period (see chapter 3). The earliest corn cultivation occurs

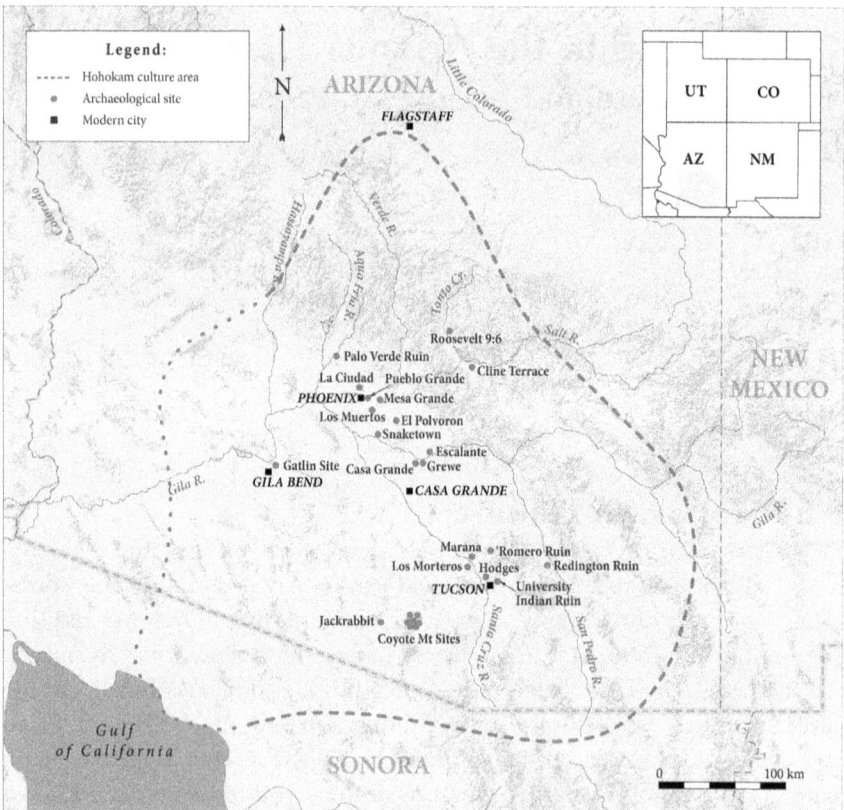

Figure 5.1. Map of the Hohokam culture area indicating larger and well-known sites. Compiled by the author (after Fish and Fish 2007 and other sources) and drawing by Michał Znamirowski.

around 2000/2100 BC in the Tucson Basin region and the first irrigation canals appeared here. In the first centuries AD, however, the economic model and the prevalence of agriculture completely changed, and with it emerged the beginnings of a cultural unification of this area and the development of the Hohokam culture.

Adolph F. Bandelier and Frank Hamilton Cushing first studied the Hohokam culture in the second half of the nineteenth century. With the initiation of extensive analyses and the work of Alfred V. Kidder and Harold S. Gladwin, research greatly progressed in the 1920s and 1930s. In 1931, at the Gila Pueblo conference and the Santa Fe Pecos conference, archaeologists formally distinguished the Hohokam as a distinct cultural entity. Crucial research on the Hohokam culture was done by Julian Hayden and perhaps its most famous researcher, Emil Haury, who had been conducting research since the 1920s as a teenager, participating in archaeological investigations in Arizona until the beginning of the 1990s. Haury later served as the director of the Arizona State Museum and Department of Anthropology at the University of Arizona, Tucson.

Until the 1970s, the Hohokam culture was dated mainly on the basis of research done at the Snaketown site in central-southern Arizona. Since then, a surge in data has led to the refinement of the chronology of the Hohokam culture. Continued headway in publications on the Hohokam culture has been made since the mid-1980s and early 1990s (e.g., Clark and Abbott 2017; Fish and Fish 2007:10). By posing new questions, setting research goals, and conducting studies related to road and urban investments, Contemporary Cultural Resource Management has helped clarify issues regarding the chronology, genesis, and social structure of various Hohokam groups, and the culture's origin was brought forward (e.g., Wallace 2007b).

The origin of the Hohokam culture has always raised doubts and evoked discussion, boiling down to a clash of two main theories: local development versus the emergence of the Hohokam as a result of influence from the Mesoamerican area (McGuire et al. 1994:245–46; McGuire and Villalpando 2007a; Toll 1991:77–80). While the theory of Mesoamerican influences (backed by Haury, among others) prevailed from the 1930s, from the 1960s it was argued that the Pioneer period (the first stage of the Hohokam culture's development) was local, and any more significant cultural influences from Mesoamerica can be observed from the beginning of the Preclassic period (from the eighth century AD). Today the dominant theory is that the Hohokam culture developed locally, but with some influences from Mesoamerica. Numerous cultural connections may be observed in the form of specific architecture (ballcourts, platform mounds with houses built on top), as well as material and spiritual culture.

Today researchers generally agree that the Hohokam culture began around 450 AD and developed until the second half of the fifteenth century, which is sometimes referred to as the millennium of the Hohokam culture's development. For the most part, the culture disappeared only a few decades before the arrival of the first Europeans, so the first written sources by the Spanish do not refer strictly to the Hohokam communities.

Though much evidence suggests that Hohokam communities were egalitarian, they appear to have been hierarchical, at least during some periods (Fish and Fish 2007:5). For centuries they managed to build and maintain an impressive network of irrigation canals extending up to twenty and thirty kilometers from the main rivers to supply water to farmlands. The irrigation canal system is the largest known in pre-Hispanic America north of Peru (Fish and Fish 2007). The construction and maintenance of irrigation canals, ballcourts, and platform mounds during the Preclassic and Classic periods required the manpower and engagement of many people, meaning they must have relied on some type of power structure to organize and control the labor required to achieve such accomplishments.

Unlike the Ancestral Puebloans, the Hohokam culture has not survived to this day, but some scholars (e.g., Bahr 2007:123-24, 127) argue that certain aspects of the Hohokam heritage were adopted by the historic and contemporary Akimel O'odham and the Tohono O'odham groups currently living in the Sonoran Desert in southern Arizona and in northern Mexico. Whether or not they are descendants is unclear (see also recent studies by Hill 2019). The Akimel O'odham are more likely than not to claim that when their ancestors arrived in these areas, they only found the ruins of ancient settlements left by people whom they called *Huhukam* (*Huhugam*), which we can translate as "those who were before" (Fish and Fish 2007).

Traces of Hohokam culture after the arrival of the Spanish include written sources from Marcos de Niza's expedition in the early sixteenth century. The Akimel still lived in permanent settlements. It is assumed that these were large Hohokam sites like Casa Grande located south of Phoenix (Bayman 2001:293; Ezell 1963). There is no clear evidence that the Hohokam culture continued to develop in the form of the historic and contemporary Akimel O'odham groups (but again see Hill 2019 for developed discussion on this topic of "continuity question"). Other aspects of cultural similarities include settlement type, the use of polychrome ceramics (the Gila type), the use of bronze and Red-on-Buff ceramics, similar forms of weaving, analogies in types of burials, and a similar economy, including ways of obtaining food through foraging and agriculture with the construction and extensive use of irrigation canals.

The chronology of the Hohokam culture (table 5.1) is based mainly on ^{14}C dating and archaeomagnetic dates. Many artifacts and sites are dated in relation to the typology and designs of pottery and comparison to the artifacts of other cultures, including Pueblo, found at the Hohokam sites. Due to the smaller quantity of wood from the remains of buildings and other constructions, dendrochronological methods are more limited than dating the Pueblo culture (Bayman 2001:263–65). A general chronology has been proposed for the whole culture, with subregions—Tucson, Phoe-

Table 5.1. General periodization of the Hohokam culture and the most important features of individual periods and phases

Period/Phase	Dating (AD)	Characteristic Features
Contemporary Akimel and Tohono O'odham (descendants of the Hohokam?)	1500/1700–today	Settlement hiatus, later arrival of O'odham peoples (Tohono O'odham—Papago and Akimel O'odham—Pima); a probable lack of cultural ties between these peoples with the Hohokam culture
Classic period — Late Classic Period (Civano phase)	1300–1450/1500	More "residential" platform mounds, "monumental" architecture made of adobe, concentration of settlements in several areas, migrants from the Pueblo culture appear; new ceramic styles (polychrome styles of the Salado culture); around 1500 AD, the region was completely depopulated; sometimes the period between 1350 and 1450 AD is referred to as the Polvoron phase
Early Classic Period (Soho phase)	1150–1300	Reduction in the number of ball courts, reorganization of the settlement, platform mounds as places to build public architecture and dwellings
Preclassic period — Sedentary period	900–1150	Increase in the number of irrigation canals, the development of trade, the first platform mounds for ceremonies and dancing
Colonial period	650/700–900	Settlement expansion to other areas; similar organization of settlements, Red-on-Buff ceramics (present until the end of the Hohokam culture's development), ball courts appear
Pioneer period	450/500–650/700	Pithouses around small courtyards, settlements organized around central plazas; large-scale artificial irrigation in the Phoenix Basin; first ceramics, palettes for grinding dyes and incense censers (with religious significance), first clay figurines

After Cordell 1997:200–202 and Fish and Fish 2007.

nix, Papaguería, and Tonto basins—having specific chronologies because cultural processes took place at different times.

Three Main Periods of the Hohokam Culture

Hohokam culture is divided into three main periods (e.g., Cordell 1997:200–202; Fish and Fish 2007; see also table 5.1). The Pioneer period (450/500–650/700 AD) is characterized by settlements concentrated mainly in the Salt and Gila river basins, with agriculture concentrated alongside rivers and major streams; arable fields were most often established on river floodplains. In this period, the first pottery, palettes for grinding paints, incense censers with religious significance, and clay figurines appeared. At the end of the Pioneer period, large-scale irrigation canal systems occur near today's city of Phoenix and in the Phoenix Basin.

The architecture and layout of the settlements during this period involved pithouses constructed from beams and branches, covered with a layer of clay and mud and slightly recessed into the ground. Houses were combined in two to four complexes with entrances facing each other and, at the same time, facing small courtyards or plazas. Building complexes throughout the settlement were usually grouped around a central plaza. Alongside the pithouses were functional structures called *ramada*. Similar to a gazebo, pergola, or lean-to, ramadas were formed by two covered poles leaning on the wall of a house or freestanding on four poles; ramadas provided shade and protection from the sun, while allowing work or rest.

There were small cemeteries, workshops, and middens (garbage dumps) covered with clay and *caliche* earth—a soil rich in calcium that hardens after drying—and converted into platforms. Up to a hundred people inhabited a settlement. The most important sites from the Pioneer period include Hardy, Valencia Vieja, Pueblo Grande, and Snaketown in central Arizona. Snaketown, being the largest of these sites, has three large structures, including two ballcourts that are examples of public architecture characteristic of later periods of Hohokam culture (e.g., Cordell 1997).

The Preclassic period (ca. 650/700–1150 AD), divided into Colonial (650/700–900 AD) and Sedentary (900–1150 AD) periods brings expansion of settlements beyond the Salt and Gila basins. Red-on-Buff pottery was first produced and continued to be made until the end of the Hohokam culture. The Hohokam culture achieved their greatest influence in the Sedentary period when their largest sites—Snaketown, Pueblo Grande, Hardy, and Casa Grande reached their peak in terms of physical and demographic size, engineering achievements, and culture. The development of trade and the number of irrigation canals surged, as did the emergence and expansion of public architecture, most notably ballcourts which began to appear at the end of the Pioneer period. Yet another type of public architecture—platform mounds which most likely served as places for ceremonies and dances—appeared in the late Preclassic period or at the beginning of the Classic period. Most structures on these sites were pithouses modeled on the previous period with several such houses grouped together around courtyards. The fact that these groups of buildings were enclosed within walls was an unprecedented phenomenon.

The Classic period (1150–1450/1500 AD is subdivided into the Early Classic Period/Soho phase: 1150–1300 AD and Late Classic Period/ Civano phase: 1300–1450 AD, which heralded major changes in architecture and probably in social structure. Large settlements included single and sometimes multistory homesteads built on the tops of platform mounds. Though some houses were still semi-dugout, buildings constructed entirely aboveground with walls made of wooden beams and adobe or *caliche* earth were more common. Groups of buildings entered onto an inner courtyard and, as in an earlier period, were surrounded by high walls made of adobe brick or *caliche*. Some of the most important sites from this period are Pueblo Grande, Casa Grande, Los Muertos, and Marana. The only surviving three-story Hohokam building is at the Casa Grande site, located south of today's Phoenix, but it is suspected that even at the end of the nineteenth century, remains of Hohokam houses that were higher than ground-floor still existed at the sites of Los Muertos and Mesa Grande, areas that today are mostly covered by the modern city of Phoenix.

Interestingly, some sites from an earlier period were abandoned, including the largest, Snaketown in south-central Arizona. Other sites moved slightly and still others relocated to nearby areas. For example during the Classic Period, the Grewe site was followed by the construction of the Casa Grande site directly adjacent; a reduction in the number of ballcourts also occurred. These changes were manifestations of the social changes and wider transformations that affected the Hohokam community. Undoubtedly, it was also a period of population growth particularly in the first part of the Classic period; the Phoenix basin area itself may have been inhabited by thirty thousand to sixty thousand people at a time (e.g., Plog 1997:136), and it is clearly visible that while some areas were abandoned, people were concentrated and centralized in smaller numbers, yet in large sites.

The end of the early phase of the Classic period and its subsequent Civano phase witnessed many changes in Hohokam culture visible in the architecture and settlement layout as demonstrated by the construction of residential buildings, ballcourts, and platform mounds likely related to the rituals. It was the apogee of an extensive networks of irrigation canals and a trade network. In the thirteenth century AD, immigrants from the world of the Pueblo culture arrived in the northern parts of Hohokam territory; elements of architecture, ceramics, and other features intertwined, starting in the northern parts of the Hohokam world. Many traces of ceramics imported from the Mogollon/Mimbres area around the border of Arizona and New Mexico have also been found. These ceramics influenced a new decorated, polychromatic style called the Salado style, from which the Salado culture takes its name. During this time, the Salado style spread throughout almost the entire Southwest, replacing also the earlier Ho-hokam style of Red-on-Buff pottery.

The Hohokam economy was based primarily on intensive agriculture which, thanks to artificial irrigation and the construction and maintenance of a canal irrigation network, could be scaled up and applied in the semi-arid and desert areas of central and southern Arizona (mostly the Sonoran Desert). Agriculture was based primarily on the cultivation of corn, as well as squash and beans, agave, cotton and amaranth, tobacco, and wild pota-toes, as well as a type of barley (*Hordeum pusillum*) independently domesti-cated by the Hohokam societies. Additional nutrition came from foraging for wild plants including the fruits and flowers of the Saguaro cactus, other cacti and opuntia, mesquite, cholla plants, and other fruits and nuts from shrubs and small trees, as well as hunting hares, deer, and mountain sheep (e.g., Bayman 2001; Fish and Fish 2007). In addition to botanical remains, traces of foraging were left by products made of shoots, stems, and plant fibers, as well as characteristic knives used for cutting agave and yucca and numerous underground ovens for baking agave hearts, similar to those in the Casas Grandes cultural tradition further south.

Foraging for wild plants in addition to agriculture, was an important source of food and was made possible by the growing seasons in the So-noran Desert. Compared to other deserts of the region such as the Mojave Desert and Chihuahua Desert, the Sonoran Desert has two rainy seasons—mild rains in winter and violent storms in summer, which bring the most rainfall—and they promote the growth and survival of vegetation. These two rainy seasons also are beneficial to agriculture, providing more pre-cipitation as compared to the Mojave and Chihuahua. The temperature in this region is high, around 40 °C or higher for at least three months of the year (Fish and Fish 2007:8).

Fishing was another important dietary supplement, as evidenced by the settlement model alongside rivers. While hunting was likely an important part of the Hohokam economy, surprisingly few wild animal bones were found at this culture's sites; game may have been butchered away from settlements or at the hunting ground, with only some parts of the carcass brought into the village. Another explanation is that bones may have been dispersed by dogs and coyotes and then poorly preserved in the soil of this region. This latter theory is supported by ethnographic analogies to the historic inhabitants of the Tohono O'odham societies in these areas, who mention that about twelve to fifteen deer and a much larger number of rabbits and smaller game would be hunted in one year by the members of those villages (Cordell 1997:277).

As early as the Late Archaic period (3000–1000 BC), the first irrigation canals appeared in the Tucson Basin region, primarily in the Santa Cruz Basin and its main tributaries; these canals were one to two kilometers long (Fish and Fish 2012). About 1,500 years later, in the Pioneer period at the beginning of the Hohokam culture, they were often five or seven kilometers in length, mainly grouped in the Salt and Gila basins and in the Phoenix Basin. These canals were dated in part by examining pottery shards found in them.

In the periods that followed, this irrigation system expanded through the creation of a huge network of canals running from rivers. These were in turn divided into second- and third-rank canals (figure 5.2). Water flow was regulated by small dams that blocked the water or allowed it to flow into further sections of the canals or agricultural plots. A row of pitholes was discovered at this type of dam at the Snaketown site, suggesting that wooden stakes driven vertically into the bottom of the canal were part of the dam structure. Similar structures were used by Akimel O'odham up until recently and were renovated every year. The plots may have been surrounded by low earth embankments that functioned like dikes or levees to properly regulate and retain water (Doolittle 1991).

To date, about six hundred kilometers of canals have been found in the region of present-day Phoenix alone (Cordell 1997:269–71). During the peak time of their construction and development in the Preclassic and Classic periods, the longest canals ran up to thirty kilometers, were two meters deep and up to about three meters wide in the upper part, and irrigated 20,000–40,000 hectares (Fish and Fish 2012). Classic canals were U-shaped or V-shaped in their cross-section and most often covered with clay. Near the Phoenix metropolis alone, about five hundred canals built by the Hohokam culture have been found; the scale of their range and domination of the landscape of the central and southern Arizona river valleys is evidenced by their usage by the first European and American settlers

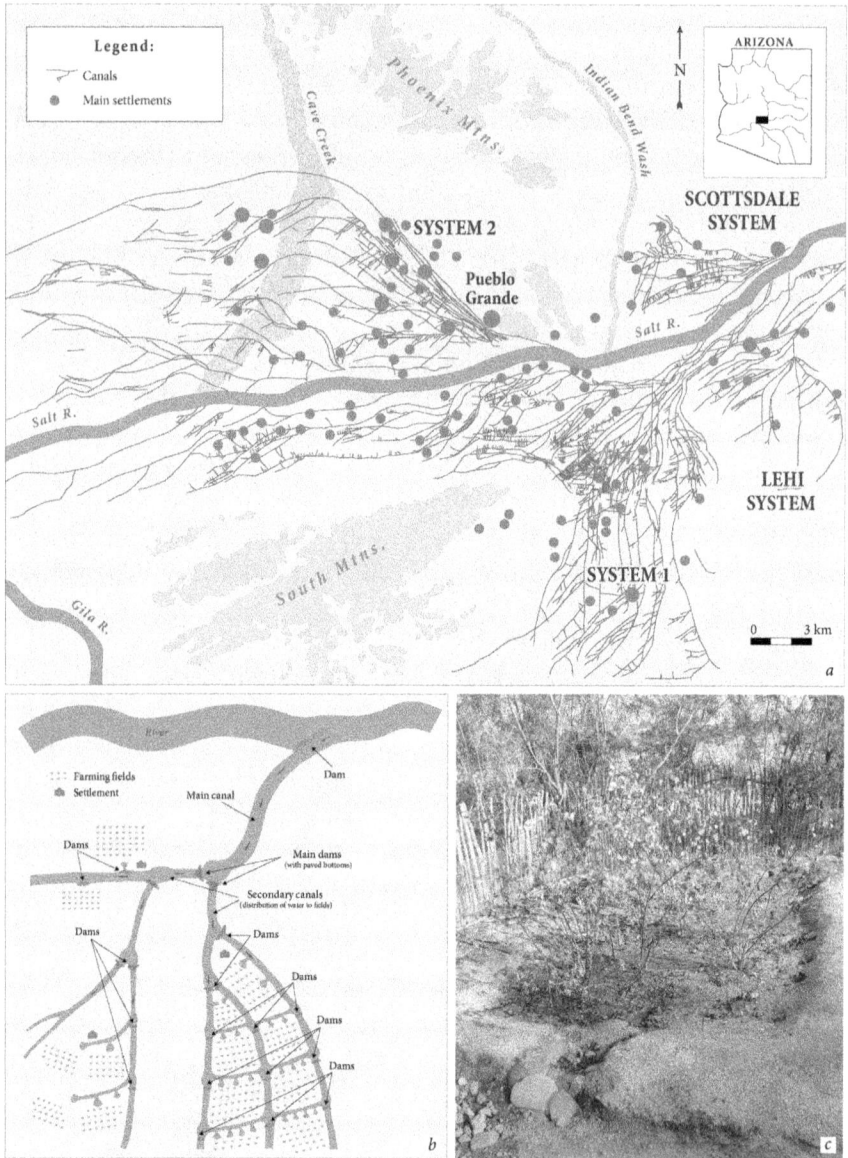

Figure 5.2. The main Hohokam canal systems running from the Salt River (a); (b) reconstruction of water distribution to cultivated plots by a system of first-, second-, and third-rank canals (after Doyel 2007: Figure 10.2 and other sources); and (c) fragments of experimental farming fields with cotton established *in situ* at the Pueblo Grande. Drawings by Michał Znamirowski (after various sources); photo by Radosław Palonka.

in this area; some canals were even incorporated into the modern water and sewage system of the city of Phoenix in the early twentieth century. Their remains were admired by the first settlers in southern Arizona—Spaniards and Mexicans, and later Americans.

It had been assumed that comparable or larger artificial irrigation systems in the New World were only developed in South America, but we know that the Hohokam people designed, constructed, administered, and maintained an extensive network of irrigation canals for over a thousand years. In the Classic period, fifteen or sixteen extensive irrigation canal systems lay in the lower part of the Salt River basin alone (e.g., the Lehi System, Systems 1 and 2, and the Scottsdale System (see figure 5.2a). Large settlements grew around these canals, with the number of inhabitants often reaching several hundred or even a thousand in some cases. Individual sections of the canals could be controlled and managed by a community of at least several thousand people, even three to ten thousand people, depending on the size of the canal system and settlements (Doyel 2007; Fish and Fish 2007). In addition, as was found nearby, previously separated and unconnected canals could be connected into one irrigation system, which may indicate that some leadership groups or social elites exercised control over these systems and thus over more territory.

David E. Doyel (2007) suggests, with agreement from researchers, that the Hohokam communities were run by chiefs according to the neo-evolutionist approach, which would have been simple in the Preclassic period, but later became more complex as the culture expanded geographically and demographically. Doyel believes that some of the canals and the bodies of water that fed them were controlled by the inhabitants of the small villages along the canals, but others were a kind of tribute or tax paid to the chiefs. This also assumes the possibility that a group of warriors could, at the behest of the chief, enforce the collection of tithes.

Agriculture based on artificial irrigation in an arid region required significant risk and enormous expenditure of effort. Too little water in the river resulted in dry canals while floods could destroy the entire dam system. It also clearly required engineering knowledge and skills, such as the design and construction of dams and the creation of slopes and ground level differences to allow water to run off, and the construction of terraces using stones. The system also required regular maintenance including cleaning the canals which was most probably carried out in spring (Fish and Fish 2007:8).

The unpredictability of rivers and fluctuations in water levels has been recorded since the historic period and exists today; this may explain why wild plants were so prevalent in the diet of the Hohokam people (e.g., Cordell 1997:272). The Salt and Gila Rivers, which originate in the mountains of central and eastern Arizona generally only reach high water levels twice a year, in late spring and late summer.

The Akimel O'odham, who used artificial irrigation in the historic period and still do to this day, can harvest crops twice a year. In drier years with less water in the rivers, they focus on foraging edible and wild plants. If the first harvest in June is not successful, then the flowers and fruits of the Saguaro cactus are gathered *en masse* in July when it begins to bloom (Cordell 1997). The second sowing is carried out at the end of July and the beginning of August. However, if there is insufficient rain in the summer, with little chance of a good second harvest, then in September the Akimel O'odham harvest mesquite (*Prosopis*), among others wild plants. In years of prosperity, good environmental conditions, and sufficient water, they cultivate the soil and forage wild plants. In the first half of the twentieth century, two out of every five years had a very poor harvest due to the instability of the water level, but the Akimel O'odham compensated by harvesting wild plants that made up about 60 percent of their diet. Similarly, alternating methods of obtaining plant food could have characterized the economy of the Hohokam culture, supplemented by game, for example hunting rabbits that probably came close to farmland.

Hohokam Public Architecture—Ballcourts and Platform Mounds

BALLCOURTS Ballcourts are one of the most characteristic elements of Hohokam architecture, and we now know of over 200 from at least 160 sites throughout the Hohokam area. In this section we will explore theories drawn from material evidence from sites, historic documents written by the Spaniards, and ethnographic studies and oral traditions on the purpose and function of these fairly common public structures. These theories range from the use of ballcourts for religious ceremonies and festivals, engaging in ballgames, and as meeting or trading places.

According to many researchers, Hohokam ballcourts are an indicator of direct cultural interactions with Mesoamerica. Although this is the most logical hypothesis, structurally Hohokam courts are significantly different from those in Mesoamerica or even those from the Paquimé site and the Casas Grandes tradition. In contrast to the I-shaped typical Mesoamerican courts, most Hohokam ballcourts were shaped in an elongated oval (figure 5.3a) and surrounded by earth and stone embankments where spectators

Figure 5.3. An oval ballcourt from the Pueblo Grande in today's city of Phoenix (a) and (b) ballcourt model with players from the Nayarit state in Mexico. Photos by Radosław Palonka (a) and Wikimedia Commons (b).

could gather. Their dimensions ranged from 15 × 25 meters to 30 × 60 meters; they were dug to a depth of about 2.5–2.7 meters at maximum. Hohokam ballcourts lacked the characteristic stone rings of Mesoamerican courts and the surface of the lower central area was sometimes smoothed clay, which was often slightly inclined toward the interior. Three stone markers were sometimes placed in the middle and ends of the ballcourts, and similar markers also denoted the upward leading entry and exit points from the court.

Ballcourts were located within large Hohokam sites that were usually settlement centers for microregions. The northernmost courts associated with the Hohokam culture lie in the upper part of the Verde River valley, about 200 kilometers north of today's city of Phoenix (Elson 2007).

The orientation of the ballcourts varies widely and is difficult to characterize according to a regular scheme, although David Wilcox (Wilcox 1991) has suggested that this orientation could have been related to astronomical observations, rituals, and religious cycles in the annual calendar of celebrations; participants in such festivities and ceremonies could have celebrated on different courts at certain times of the year. At times, large ballcourts were situated on a north-south and east-west axis, although this pattern was not always repeated (Wilcox 1991:118).

Sometimes there were two courts (one large and one smaller) or more in a given site, often accommodating up a few hundred people, with 700 in the largest (Elson 2007:51). These people could have included dancers and spectators who would have stood on embankments (types of stands) around the perimeters.

As their name suggests, ballcourts may have been used for some version of a ball game from west Mexico or/and Mesoamerica, although without necessarily replicating the exact game and beliefs related to it. The relatively small number of rubber balls found in Mesoamerica contradicts information known from ethno-historic Spanish sources regarding the shipment of 16,000 rubber balls from a place in the Mexican West Coast as a tribute to the Aztecs (Cordell 1997:269; Elson 2007:52). A fair number of stone balls have been discovered at Hohokam culture sites and only a few non-stone (made of rubber, resin, or other "organic" materials). In the sixteenth century, Spaniards recorded observations about similarities between ballcourts at Hohokam sites in Arizona and those in Mesoamerica. They also documented ball games played in the historic period among the Akimel O'odham on the border of Arizona and Mexican Sonora, and a similar game in western Mexico that is still played to this day. Played on a flat surface specially prepared and defined (but without the stone rings known from the Mayan or Aztec ballcourts), this game was a large competition between individual players and entire villages. Rituals and feasts lasting several days were an important part of such matches and competitions.

The theory that the Hohokam used these structures as ballcourts is supported by finds of models of such ballcourts populated by figures of players with a ball and spectators sitting in banks or ridges above the surface of the court. Although these were discovered in Mexico in the state of Nayarit (see figure 5.3b) and other parts of central-western and northern Mexico, some Hohokam ceramic figures, especially from the Early Pioneer period, are also interpreted as representing ball players (e.g., Wilcox 1991:104–5). David Wilcox even claims that the idea of playing ball games could have emerged much earlier than the courts themselves in southern Arizona, and these courts in the Pioneer period were probably a kind of invention independent of Mesoamerica. Not all Hohokam culture sites had ballcourts, so it should be assumed that, apart from social stratification, there existed some sort of settlement hierarchy which is especially visible in the Classic period.

Other interpretations suggest these structures may been used for ritual ceremonies and dances, based on, among others, similarities to historically known designated dance places called *wiikita*, among the Tohono O'odham. Wilcox proposes that they also functioned as marketplaces for trading, possibly with Aztec merchants/spies called *pochteca* (e.g., Wilcox 1991; Wilcox and Sternberg 1983) and, less likely, with Mayan traders called *ppolom*. These long-distance traders made their fortune, among other ways, by importing various exotic products and raw materials from beyond the territory of their own areas (e.g., Fish and Fish 2007). A theory that ballcourts were used as water reservoirs has been rejected based on recent excavations showing a lack of silt and sediment associated with water.

The Hohokam culture began to establish ballcourts in the Early Preclassic period (Colonial period) or even in the Late Pioneer period, around 700 AD. However, most courts were created after 900 AD in the Sedentary period (the late Preclassic period). No new courts were built and older ones were probably abandoned during the Classic period and even earlier, between 1050 and 1100 AD, or certainly until the end of the thirteenth century. Archaeological data show that only a few were still used in the Phoenix basin and in the basin of the Verde River after that date. The abandonment of the creation and use of ballcourts coincides with other changes in this culture, including in social structure, religion, and with a decline in trade and Hohokam influence beyond the Phoenix Basin (e.g., Elson 2007; Wilcox 1991).

In the central-northern part of Arizona near the present-day town of Flagstaff, there are several ballcourts associated with the local Sinagua and Cohonina cultures (Elson 2007:50). They appear to be from a later development than the Hohokam ballcourts and were built after the Hohokam societies had abandoned the concept. Any possible ties between the Hohokam communities with the Sinagua and Cohonina people and the establishment of ballcourts are quite difficult to reconstruct at this stage.

PLATFORM MOUNDS Regardless of their function, ballcourts are an example of public architecture. Platform mounds were another public structure, at least partially related to religious beliefs and rituals. It should be noted that the ballcourts came first chronologically and were most likely not under construction when the large platform mounds began to be erected, suggesting that the change in structure type may be related to the transformations that took place in the social structure and beliefs of the Hohokam people. The extent of sites featuring mounds is smaller than the area where ballcourts were built.

In the early phase of the Colonial period, the Hohokam people constructed smallish round platform mounds, not exceeding ten or so meters in diameter and just over one meter in height. Such mounds are known from large sites such as Snaketown and Gatlin. Sometimes these mounds were accompanied by palisades or types of wooden fences and places for burning the bodies of the dead. Some low platforms were built on garbage sites that were later covered with clay such as in Snaketown. Around 1200 AD, in the Early Classic period, larger-scale platform mounds—sometimes as high as five or six meters, often with several terraced levels—were erected in the Phoenix Basin. It seems that between 1250 and 1350 AD, the practice of building mounds began to spread to other Hohokam areas, with the largest mounds still visible in the area of today's Phoenix (the Casa Grande, figure 5.4, and Grewe sites). Currently about 120 large platform mounds have been recorded from nearly 100 sites (Elson 2007:52–53).

Houses ranging from one to as many as thirty in number were built on top of the mounds in the Classic period and differed in size and probably in function. Buildings on platform mounds were established inside spaces limited by walls built of adobe or *caliche*, where there were also other buildings at ground level or just slightly above.

Spaces inside the walls are visibly divided into sectors, while sometimes there were buildings adjacent to the mounds themselves that are interpreted as types of watchtowers guarding the entrance to the platform mound (Elson 2007:52). This in turn suggests that only some people, prob-

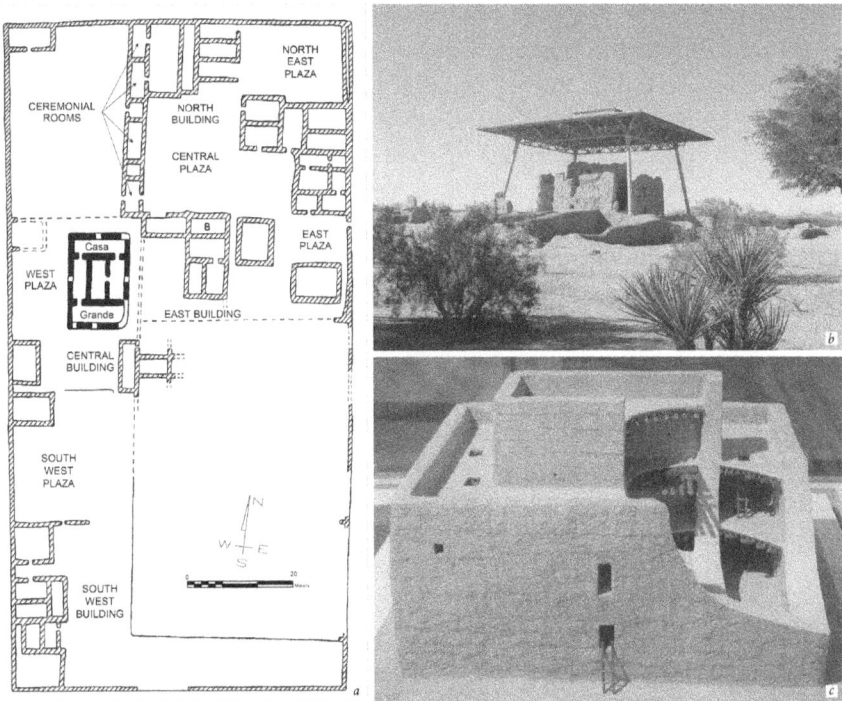

Figure 5.4.   Plan of Compound A at the Casa Grande site (a); the tallest surviving building of the Hohokam culture at Casa Grande (b); and (c) model of the building from Casa Grande Museum. Drawing by Bolesław Zych (after Abbott 2003 and other sources) and photos by Radosław Palonka.

ably the elite, had access to inside the platform mounds. These mounds and distinct buildings mark a big difference from the chronologically earlier courts that could probably be accessed by most, if not all, of the community. Based on our knowledge of changes in Hohokam public architecture, it seems that around 1200 AD, major changes of a sociocultural nature and considerable inequalities emerged, transformations that are reflected by the changes in architecture (even with the establishment of a social and settlement hierarchy). The notion of increased social hierarchy and the formation of an elite class is further supported by the development of an increasingly complex system of irrigation canals as well as the emergence of significant differences in burials. Evidence in the form of artifacts and building complexes also suggests that the higher the mounds, the higher the status of the people living there.

The role of the platform mounds is still being analyzed, although it seems that the central buildings on top were inhabited by either secular or religious elite. It is still not clear if they were used to perform rituals and ceremonies that could be seen by most of the public below. The mounds may have been centers of trade and redistribution of goods, and possibly even water management control in the form of irrigation canals. Unfortunately, no information has been found in Spanish sources that such structures were used in the Southwest in the historic period. Very few of these mounds have been archaeologically examined by excavation, hindering data collection; exceptions include the famous Pueblo Grande, located today in the center of the city of Phoenix, Casa Grande (e.g., Abbott 2003), and Marana Mound located northwest of today's city of Tucson. Sometimes burials are found on platform mounds, including some richly equipped graves of adults and children.

Inhumation burials—burying the dead as opposed to cremation followed by burial—are prevalent in Hohokam funeral rites in the Pioneer period. However at the end of this period, evidence of bi-ritualism (that is the practice of both skeletal burials and cremation at the same time) occurs. Cremation became more commonplace in the periods after 700 AD, but in some sites, skeletal burials were prevalent even in the Classic period; differences in ways of burying the dead may indicate a constant clash of two "currents" in the religious beliefs of the Hohokam people, or burial rituals may have differed along class, ethnic, or cultural lines (e.g., Bayman 2001); the Hohokam culture did not necessarily function as a homogeneous ethnos from the very outset. In certain periods and regions (e.g., in the Classic period in the Tonto Basin region) mass burials of up ten or so people with a maximum of eighteen have been found (e.g., Bayman 2001).

Burials at the Pueblo Grande site from the end or at least the second part of the Preclassic period have been very well researched (Mitchell 1994, 2003). Excavations revealed 836 burials, including 647 skeletal and 189 cremation burials confirming that cremation did not prevail in all sites after the Pioneer period. All these burials were grouped in seventeen known cemetery areas, and among buildings and on platform mounds. Skeletal burials were generally placed in rectangular earthen pits, often with small embankments on their sides, suggesting that some type of roof covered the burials; the supine (on the back) position was dominant, although some skeletons have been found in a sitting position or dismembered; 35 burials consisted of two or more people in one grave.

More often than not, skeletal graves at the Pueblo Grande site were oriented east-west with the head facing east (80 percent) and 10 percent with heads facing west (Mitchell 2003:108). Most cremation burials were in burial pits in separate cemeteries; cremated remains were placed in ceramic vessels and covered with ceramic bowls. Sometimes a vessel with human remains would be turned upside down with the remains lying on the ground. In these cases, burnt grave goods from the cremation stacks were placed in adjacent shallow pits; the mortuary items are fundamentally different those placed with the dead in skeletal burials. Cremation burials were usually oriented along the east-west axis.

In the Pioneer period, a differentiation in grave goods already emerged suggesting the existence of many social groups. Burial goods for inhumated graves included ceramics, shell jewelry, flint, and stone tools such as obsidian, and chert points. These artifacts changed over time and later included conch shell trumpets that were highly characteristic of rich, predominantly male burials, especially in the Preclassic period. Cremation burials, including from the Preclassic period, often featured small stone vessels, clay figurines, stone pallets, and stylized arrowheads (Bayman 2002:279).

In the Classic period, burials were sometimes located near or on platform mounds. Their location, ages of the people buried, and grave goods have led some researchers to believe that these may offer clues to indicate social stratification among this culture's population. At sites such as Pueblo Grande from the Classic period, the burials of infants or children are the most opulently furnished (Bayman 2002; Mitchell 1994). Burials also show that women in the Hohokam community had a relatively high status as evidenced, for example, by their burials in the highest positions on the platform mounds, which may have related to their marriages, their participation in the specialized production of some objects of material culture, and their active participation in religious life as shamans (Crown and Fish 1996). Most people were buried outside the mounds, in separate cemeteries or among groups of buildings.

Some burials are interpreted as the graves of shamans—at least two such graves (No. 1006 and 1048) were also found at the Pueblo Grande site (Mitchell 2003:117–21). Shamanic burials in Pueblo Grande were separated from a larger group of twenty-nine burials, with an unprecedented quantity and variety of grave goods. Burial 1006, a cremation grave in a separate cemetery (BG 5), was equipped with burned artifacts in the form of a stone pallet, arrowhead, several hundred beads made of stone, a few shell beads and eleven obsidian cores, a dozen or so quartz crystals, other minerals and stones, lizard-shaped shell pendants, bird-shaped stone figurines, several fragmentarily preserved bracelets and three pointed stones.

Another shamanic burial at the site is that of a skeleton of a young man in one of the central cemeteries. This grave contained an even richer set of relics in the form of three decorated bowls, a jug, a scoop, beads, and pendants made of shells including some lizard-shaped specimens, shell needles, bone pins, an obsidian arrowhead, and quartz and hematite crystals, the latter of which were located on the legs of the deceased and next to the body. Additionally, at the man's feet lay four golden eagle feathers arranged in pairs and two raven wings. Other burial monuments outside Pueblo Grande also considered to be related to shamans contained bird feathers, quartz crystals, stone pallets, turtle-shell rattles, bones and wood scored with specific motifs, and unique items such as a hawk bone necklace (Mitchell 2003:120–21). Bird motifs also appear in the iconography of Hohokam pottery including birds attacking or eating a snake, and are also found on pendants and other jewelry made of shells.

Hohokam Pottery; Its Iconography and Stylistic Changes

Pottery is a major marker of the Early Pioneer and later periods of Hohokam material culture. Early pottery was gray, brown, or covered with a red slip. At about 500 AD, ceramics painted red also appeared, at first on a gray and then a buff background. This Red-on-Buff was the most important, long-lasting ceramic style in the culture, although new research shows that at the end of the eleventh century AD (Late Preclassic period) the number of pieces made in this style decreased dramatically (Wallace 2007a). During the Late Preclassic, numerous clay figurines, pallets, small stone vessels (bowls for food preparation and eating), and stone vessels for grinding paints were produced.

Red-on-Buff pottery (red on a buff, brown or sometimes gray background) were used at least for a time in parallel with Red-on-Brown pottery. This style included fired clay figurines and effigy—zoomorphic and anthropomorphic—pottery. The Hohokam societies like those later of the later Mogollon culture, produced unpainted brown, brownish, or gray ceramics—so-called brown wares—which, according to some, may prove that both cultures or at least their ceramic traditions) branched from the same source (Bayman 2001:269). Unpainted ceramics had a slightly different technological design and had a rougher surface compared to painted ceramics.

The iconography of Red-on-Buff ceramics (table 5.2) at the beginning of the Preclassic period often included naturalistic motifs such as plants, especially flowers, animals, and birds, sometimes in flight in the form of a stylized letter "z" grouped in a decorative band. This iconography also appears later with some additional new elements such as geometric motifs, including straight and wavy lines, spirals, triangles, and more free-form patterns, often reflecting the decoration of woven baskets. Hohokam bowls, jars, and other forms were often decorated on the outside and around the edges; in this way all or most of the entire surface of the vessel was decorated (Fish and Fish 2007). Other variants serve to categorize painted decorations: a surface divided into four parts touching each other or separated into sectors and those without a clear pattern or order.

Anthropomorphic representations are characteristic iconography found on Red-on-Buff pottery. Motifs include groups of dancers holding hands and a highly characteristic motif of a man with a basket on his back held by a headband and holding a cane (a kind of "crosier") in one hand (figure 5.5a); this character is very often identified with the *pochteca* (Aztec long-distance traveling merchants). Hohokam pottery designs feature other ref-

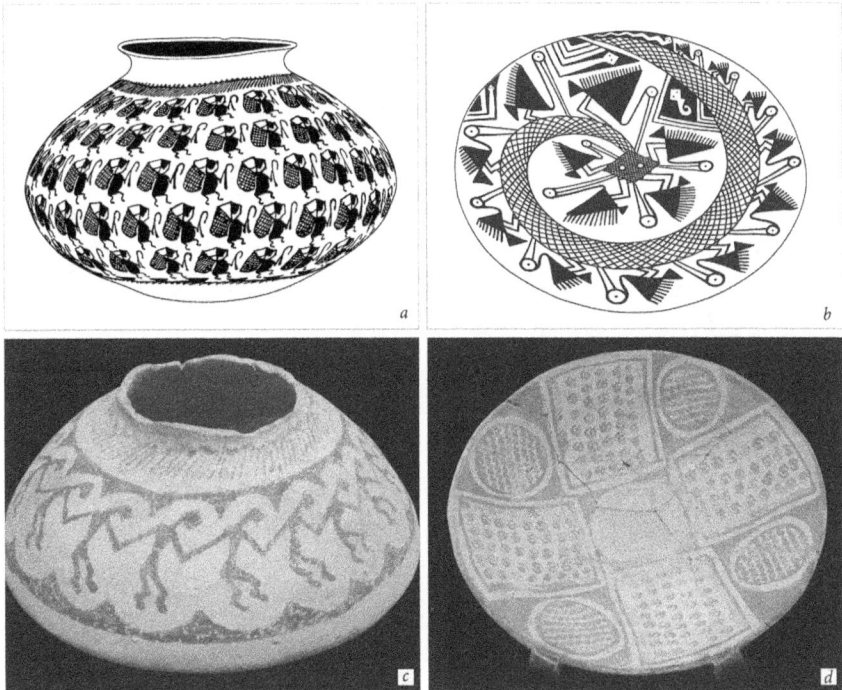

Figure 5.5.   Examples of Hohokam pottery iconography: (a) possibly *pochteca* (Aztec merchant) motif; (b) depictions of birds tearing apart a snake; (c) dancing/ceremonial scene; (d) Sacaton Red-on-Buff pottery with ornamentation divided into four symmetrical parts as an examples of interactions and contact with Mexican areas. Drawings by Michał Znamirowski and photographs by Radosław Palonka.

Table 5.2. The most important types of painted ceramics from the Hohokam and Salado cultures with the main characteristics traits

Type (Style of Ornamentation)	Dating (AD)	Characteristic Features
Polychrome Salado also known as Roosevelt Red Ware or Salado Red Ware style	1280–1450	– Mainly related to the Salado culture; polychrome types: Cliff, Dinwiddie, Gila, Nine Mile, Los Muertos, Phoenix, Pinto, Tonto, and types; Cliff White-on-red, Salado Red, Salado White-on-red – Range of occurrence includes southern, central and midwestern and eastern Arizona; these ceramics are also found far beyond the Hohokam territory, in Texas and Chihuahua in Mexico – Bowls, jars, pottery in non-standard shapes or forms – Red or white vessel surface, black, red, or white designs
Casa Grande Red-on-Buff	1150–1300/1375	– Mainly the Gila River basin – The last type of ceramics painted on buff ware – Jars and jugs with a long, straight neck, rarely bowls – Designs often on the neck of the vessel, two decorative bands on pots, decoration of bowls on the exterior
Sacaton Red-on-Buff	950–1150	– Produced in the central part of the Gila River Valley, but found throughout Hohokam territory – Characteristic forms include pots with a wide bottom, sometimes straight (rather than rounded) sides, and bowls with a rounded rim; mica visible on the pottery surface – Rim designs are separate from the decoration on the body in the case of bowls; mainly geometric motifs; thick lines with workmanship slightly inferior to the previous Santa Cruz type
Santa Cruz Red-on-Buff	850–950	– Produced in the middle Gila River Valley, but found throughout and beyond Hohokam territory and into Northern Mexico, Colorado River Basin, New Mexico – Thin-walled vessels with visible mica particles on the surface – Designs consisting of relatively thin lines even as small as 2 mm, a cross-hatch motif, straight and wavy lines, zoomorphic and anthropomorphic motifs

Type	Date	Description
Gila Butte Red-on-Buff	750/775–850	– Mainly the central part of the Gila River Valley and the Salt River Valley, reaching the Tonto Basin in the north and the Tucson Basin in the south – Various forms of vessels, distinctive bowls, and jars with recurved rims, often bowls with a flat bottom – Geometric and figural designs, often figural motifs with a kind of cross-hatch pattern, shallow engraving
Snaketown Red-on-Buff	650–750	– The central part of the Gila River valley and Queen Creek, gradually extending south to the Tucson area where the local variant Snaketown Red-on-brown appears – Mainly bowls (sometimes with recurved rims, jars, a type of incense censer, scoops, and figural (effigy) pottery appear – Decorative cross-hatching, up to 10% of the designs in the early phase, and then constituting the whole ornamentation in the late phase; quite thin lines less than 2.5 mm, vessels often gray in color, without a slip (slips would appear later on), notching/scoring parallel to the rim
Sweetwater Red-on-Gray	600–650	– The central part of the Gila and Queen Creek valleys, gradually extending south to the Tucson area) – Bowls, jars, censers, scoops, effigy pottery – Gray or brown surfaces, "clouds" from firing, slightly smoothed with visible mica particles, cross-hatching fills the ornamentation (the thickness of the lines of the cross-hatching is similar to the thickness of the lines of the designs, rather thick decorative lines of about 4 mm.

After Lyons 2012; Wallace 2001, 2014; swvirtualmuseum.nau.edu/ and other sources.

erences to relations with Mesoamerica, the most vivid being the Sacaton Red-on-Buff type, particularly bowls with decoration painted inside the vessel and its division into four equal and symmetrical parts (figure 5.5d). A similar arrangement of painted sectors of the vessel and the iconography itself are found on bowls in western Mexico at the sites of Alta Vista in the Zacatecas state and Chupícuaro in Guanajuato. Images on other types of Hohokam ceramics also evoke contacts with Mesoamerica, including the motif of a bird pecking or devouring a snake-figure 5.5b (e.g., McGuire and Villalpando 2007a; Whittlesey 2007). Small bowls set on three legs and decorated in the Red-on-Buff style constitute another intriguing and exotic style that possibly originated in Mesoamerica in Teotihuacan and the Maya culture.

Dating the Hohokam culture on the basis of pottery alone is quite difficult due in part to the multitude of ceramic types, and because at least two large production centers can be pinpointed along with related stylistic and chronological changes: the Gila River basin, home to the Middle Gila Buff Ware tradition and the Tucson basin associated mainly with the production of brown ware (Craig and Woodson 2017). In 2001, Henry D. Wallace (2001) presented a new concept of how to divide Hohokam ceramics, assuming among other things, a distinction between two main decorative styles of pottery, primarily for the areas of central and partly southern Arizona—that is, the Gilla Butte style (mainly the Preclassic Colonial period) and the Sacaton style (the second part of the Preclassic Sedentary period), with a further division into individual sequences within them.

Researchers have correlated phases and styles of ceramic decoration with the evolution of iconography of rock art and the decoration of textiles and other artifacts including shells and stone pallets for grinding paints and other objects (figure 5.6) and distinguished three styles (Craig et al. 2012; Craig and Woodson 2017; Wallace 2014:Fig. 11.5). Style 1 is still associated with the Pioneer period with some occurrences at the beginning of the Preclassic period. Style 2 is associated with the appearance of ballcourts and the widespread distribution of Red-on-Buff decorated vessels. Style 3 appears around 1000 AD, around the middle of the Preclassic Sedentary period.

In recent decades, data from petrographic analyses of the composition of the admixture and ceramic masses has enriched our understanding of style changes in the Hohokam culture. Examples from La Villa in the Phoenix Basin and Honey Bee Village near Tucson (Ownby et al. 2015) show that decorated ceramics were initially produced mainly in the central part of the Gila River basin, and to a much lesser extent in a few other

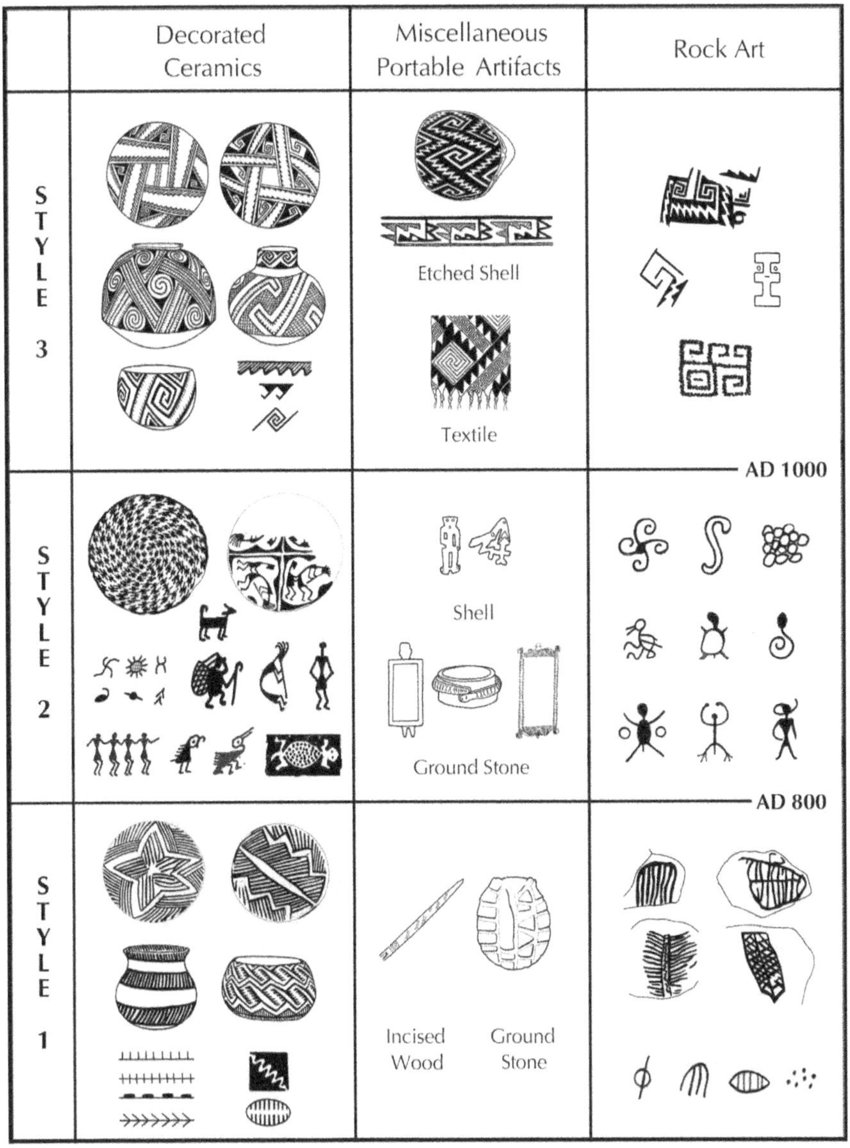

	Decorated Ceramics	Miscellaneous Portable Artifacts	Rock Art
STYLE 3		Etched Shell Textile	
			AD 1000
STYLE 2		Shell Ground Stone	
			AD 800
STYLE 1		Incised Wood Ground Stone	

Figure 5.6. Correlation of stylistics changes in the iconography as shown in ceramics, rock art, and stone and wooden decorated artifacts, textiles, and other artifacts in the Hohokam culture (after Wallace 2014:Fig. 1.15). Courtesy of the author.

locations and exported to the Phoenix and Tucson Basins. In the Preclassic and Classic periods, pottery production expanded in local centers, although the potters of the Gila River valley continued to dominate the ceramics industry.

In an analysis of the production and distribution of pottery during the Sedentary period (i.e., the Late Preclassic period in the Salt and Gila basins, David Abbott and colleagues (e.g., Abbott 2003) showed that essentially all of the pottery production (bowls, jars, and *ollas*) in the center of the Hohokam world took place in five pottery manufacturing and production centers: three in the lower Salt Valley (on both sides of the this river) and two in the central part of the Gila River valley. This challenged earlier, long-standing theories that pottery was produced locally in virtually every household.

Located on the right bank of the Salt River and its tributary Cave Creek, the first of these five production centers, Las Colinas, produced unpainted pots of medium and large sizes and, to a lesser extent, undecorated bowls. This pottery was made from local clays, and clays that appear to have been transported and distributed via or along two main systems of irrigation canals, so-called System 2, and System Scottsdale (Abbott 2003:203). On the other side of the Gila River on the outskirts of the South Mountains, two more centers produced large thick *ollas* (vessels for storing water) which were distributed to the Salt River Valley. Two centers in the central part of the Gila River were discovered on its right bank near the Snaketown site. One of these centers also produced undecorated bowls and pottery dishes, while the other, closer to Snaketown, produced Red-on-Buff painted pottery. The latter was the main center of painted pottery production in the region with some work produced by local potters and artists who maintained certain standards of pottery decoration.

The transportation and mass distribution of ceramics from these five production centers required the existence of a market system of exchange, which must have had a tremendous impact on the local economy, possibly leading to the enrichment of individual settlement units, groups, and microregions. It is also assumed that in the Preclassic period, the system of organizing the production and distribution of ceramics in this large central region of Arizona may have functioned as a model to produce and exchange other goods, such as agricultural products, decorated shells, *mano* and *metate* stones, axes and knives, obsidian blades and arrowheads, and stone pallets, along with minerals and other resources, such as argillite, steatite, and serpentine (Abbott 2003:206–7).

Hohokam societies participated in the entire system of contact between Southwestern cultural traditions and Mesoamerica, and seems to have played a significant and active role therein. References to highly developed Mesoamerican and western and central-northern Mexican cultures are visible in the examples of architecture and site layout, such as locating buildings around central courtyards and plazas, which resemble Mesoamerican groups of buildings around plazas and patios, sometimes enclosed by an outer wall, and ballcourts and platform mounds. Connections to Mesoamerica are further evidenced by material culture beyond pottery iconography such as imported copper bells made using the lost wax method, pyrite mirrors, and long obsidian blades (e.g., McGuire and Villalpando 2007a). These relations were also manifested in the migration of religious ideas and beliefs and in the trade of various products of material culture with other areas.

It appears that material culture including pottery and stone vessels, clay figurines, pallets for grinding paints—which may have been mirrors or surfaces on which hallucinogenic substances were sprinkled or poured—and shell and turquoise jewelry, reached its zenith and peak of expression in the Preclassic period. Perhaps some of the characteristic shell jewelry (mainly bracelets or armlets) may have been a kind of symbolic identification sign of belonging to a specific social group (Bayman 2002:79–82).

Jewelry made by the Hohokam people primarily consisted of bracelets (possibly armlets), necklaces, pendants, and rings made of shells mainly from the *Glycymeris* family, which were obtained off the coast of the Gulf of California, especially its northern area Sea of Cortez, and to a lesser extent in the western part of California on the Pacific Ocean. Characteristic shell jewelry, mainly bracelets or armlets, may have been a kind of sign of belonging to a specific social group (Bayman 2002:79–82). The full range of jewelry made from shells encompasses at least forty-three types and sixty-two species of seashells (Bayman 2002:79). Shell jewelry was made by drilling a small hole in the center of a shell, enlarging this hole by cutting it, and then polishing its surface. The thickest part of the shell was usually decorated with engraving or incising as well as appliqués like turquoise or other minerals, sometimes formed into mosaics; more often than not, the images were of birds, lizards, snakes, and other animals and sometimes the whole pendant or bracelet was formed in the shape of a given animal. Bracelets have been discovered in various contexts, from graves (figure 5.7) to houses and loose finds.

The largest known group of shell bracelets are the simple hooped and unembellished variety. It is believed that most of these simple bracelets

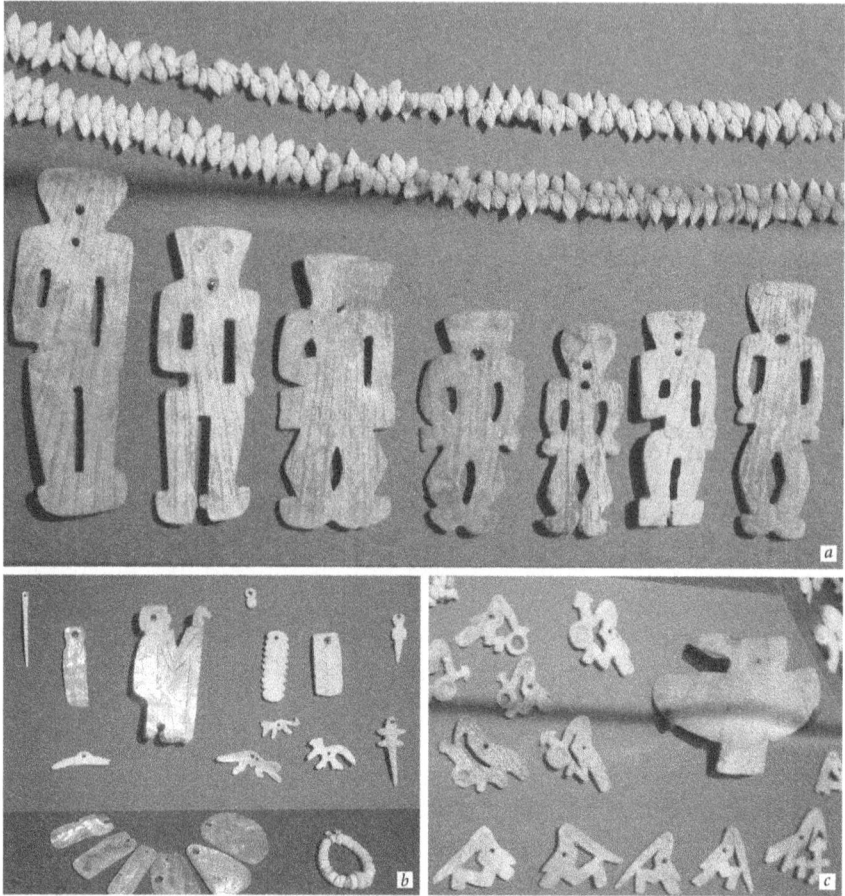

Figure 5.7.   Burnt jewelry made of shells: beads, anthropomorphic and zoomorphic pendants, and other types. Photographs by Radosław Palonka.

were created between 500 and 1150 AD, mainly in the westernmost areas near the coast of the Gulf of California and in the Papaguería region, from where they were most likely transported as finished products to other Hohokam areas. Two known shell-processing sites include Shelltown and Hind Site in southwestern Arizona (Marmaduke and Martynec 1993). Shell mounds near the Gulf of California in the area of Puerto Peñasco and in Sonora in northern Mexico are likely remnants of Hohokam trade and Patayan culture expeditions for shells (e.g., Mitchell and Foster 2000).

Bells made from the shells of *Conus* sea snails were another popular product and were clearly used to make sounds; they were perhaps used during ceremonies and dances. These bells were probably sewn as appliqués on clothes; some such examples are known from the historic Pueblo, including the Hopi and Zuni groups (Bayman 2002). Beads and pendants made from the shells of sea snails (*Olivella*), ranged from simple discoidal to tubular forms to those in the shape of animals and sometimes human figures. These were most often found in tomb contexts from the Preclassic and Classic periods and were also found on platform mounds (Bayman 2002:Fig. 3). Musical instruments, mainly trumpets, were also made of various types of shells including *Strombus galeatus*, *Strombus glacilior*, *Melongena patula*, *Muricanthus*, and *Olivella incrassate*. According to James Bayman (2002), these may have been symbols of prestige and perhaps even power. Among the historic Hopi and Zuni, similar "trumpet" shells were used by priests during religious ceremonies to imitate the "water snake" (Mills and Ferguson 2008). Trumpets are very often found in the context of male burials from the Preclassic period and later, although in the Classic period there are far fewer of them and they do not appear in the burial context, but instead tend to be found on platform mounds.

Large pendants made of whole shells of edible cockles, mussels of the *Laevicardium elatum* species, were decorated with etched geometric motifs and representations of animals using something like the European "Aquaforte" technique, though this was discovered in the Old World much later. Pendants decorated in this way were created from around 850 to 1200 AD and were a rather rare type of jewelry. Before the etching process, the shell was most likely soaked in a kind of plant sap, resin, and possibly some insect secretions to protect it from the consequences of the subsequent etching process, then the image was scratched into it. Then fermented Saguaro cactus juice was likely applied to the image to complete the etching process. The fermented juice stuck to the scratched representations and the longer the shell was exposed, the deeper the image was recessed. These etched images were sometimes painted.

The second phase of the Preclassic period witnessed a standardization in the production of pottery, shell products (bracelets, necklaces), flint, and obsidian blades and other artifacts, which may suggest their production by some groups of craftsmen (e.g., Cordell 1997; Crown 1983, 2007). At the end of the Preclassic period, the scope of the Hohokam culture's development began to retract somewhat, and the later Classic period would see a reconcentration of settlements in their original center of development, mainly in the Phoenix Basin.

Obtaining seashells is just one sign of long-distance trade. Apart from the acquisition of shells, the Gulf of California was probably visited for salt (Bayman 2002:81). The Hohokam culture's network of contacts with other areas was impressive and encompassed the coasts of the Gulf of California and Mesoamerica, the Pueblo, Mogollon/Mimbres cultures, and the Great Plains area. Ceramics were exchanged locally and over long distances with other southwestern cultures, especially during certain periods (e.g., Classic). While many raw materials were obtained locally, flint, stone, and obsidian blades were sought over long distances, especially obsidian, which was obtained in many locations throughout the so-called Grand Southwest, in Arizona, New Mexico, and the present-day states of Sonora and Chihuahua in Mexico (Bayman 2001). Petrographic analyses have revealed that the Hohokam people imported obsidian from the Colorado Plateau and the Mogollon Mountains, engaging in some interactions and forming relations with the Pueblo and Mogollon communities inhabiting these regions. Other data indicates that obsidian was obtained from deposits in the Sauceda area of central Arizona, and this, along with other evidence, demonstrates that much of the obsidian—along with copper bells and salt imported from western Mexico— may have been distributed by the Gatlin site in midwestern Arizona (Bayman 2001:278; Mitchell and Shackley 1995.

On the other hand, research by Douglas Mitchell and Steven Shackley on a sample of nine Hohokam sites using X-ray analyses as well as fluorescence (XRF) and X-ray diffraction methods suggests that most of the obsidian was in fact obtained locally, from the nearest sources and outcrops. These findings were presented in 1995 in the *Journal of Field Archaeology* (Mitchell and Shackley 1995). Regional differences in obsidian have also been discovered, for example at Tucson Basin sites and in the Phoenix Basin, researchers discovered blades from several local outcrops; five of nine sites had at least five different deposits, and two sites featured at least eight different places where obsidian was obtained.

Analysis of flint and obsidian points and blades at the Snaketown site demonstrates clear traces of standardization. As in the case of the ceramics mentioned earlier, this may prove that they were produced by groups of specialized craftsmen and then distributed. Obsidian blades are found in settlement contexts and among skeletal and cremation grave goods; at Snaketown, an accumulation of hundreds of obsidian points was associated with just a few cremation burials. A host of loose finds of undamaged blades and points (especially from the Classic period) from clusters of buildings and platform mounds suggest their use for ritual purposes, perhaps as part of religious offerings, as is known from the Southwest in the historic period and until the present day. These finds include a large number of arrowheads from the Preclassic and Classic periods with side-notched blades with a fairly wide base and shaped in the form of a slender, elongated triangle along with tools such as are classic piercers and drills.

Hohokam Rock Art

Systematic research on Hohokam rock art only began relatively late. The first regular studies and inventories were carried out in the 1960s and 1970s, including in the South Mountains south of what is now the city of Phoenix (Snyder 1966). More research followed, culminating in one of the last major rock art documentation and inventory endeavors—the South Mountain Rock Art Project (SMRAP), organized and run by Arizona State University and the City of Phoenix Parks and Recreation Department. Polly Schaafsma (1980) and Todd Bostwick (2002) have published the most comprehensive reviews on the rock art of Hohokam culture, along with illustrated examples. Based on the number and nature of the rock art representations in this region, Bostwick suggests the South Mountains were a sacred place for the Hohokam people visited mainly for religious reasons.

Research from the 1960s and 1970s shows Hohokam rock art panels tend to occur on boulders and mountain rock walls, very often close to settlements, farmlands, and irrigation canals, both in valleys and on individual *mesas* (plateaus) (see also Schaafsma 1980:96–97). These placements suggest that this rock art marks individual areas and their ownership or use by specific groups or a possible religious relationship with agriculture, including farming, rituals, etc. (Schaafsma 1980 after Kearns 1973).

Rock art observably connects with the landscape. Some panels are situated by water reservoirs, streams, and rivers and the so-called *tinajas* (natural rock pools where rainwater collects) and other places where water is permanently or periodically present. Other studies (e.g., Wallace 1989; Wallace and Holmlund 1986) identify a recurring relationship between the location of rock art and certain landforms—sites such as places where raw minerals were extracted and accessed by mountain trails and which were also important for both economy and rituals.

In the area with the highest concentration of rock art panels in the South Mountains, individual panels were located very close to two large irrigation systems and accompanying settlements as established by research by SMRAP projects and archaeologist Aaron M. Wright. In addition, these investigations uncovered numerous mounds and stone circles identified today as shrines, or sites of worship and sacrifice for historic Native

American groups, who perhaps felt themselves to be the heirs of the pre-Hispanic Hohokam culture as Wright (Wright 2016:4) seems to suggest.

The tradition in which the Hohokam culture made their petroglyphs is often referred to as the Gila petroglyph style (Schaafsma 1980:81-103). Some stylistic differentiations occur based on the technique used to make it (e.g., Wright and Bostwick 2009). By attempting to make similar works of art with the same raw materials and appropriate tools—an approach called experimental archeology—researchers have managed to differentiate the Hohokam Scratched Style that relies on delicate engraving and creating individual images by scratching or scraping. These techniques do not make a dominant impression on the rock surface and petroglyphs created in the Hohokam Scratched Style are often much less visible than other petroglyphs in strong sunlight. Works in these two styles could have had different functions in the community, indicating the probable simultaneity of their creation and function. Because the research sample is quite limited, it is not clear whether this distinction can be applied to the entire Hohokam culture and the rock art.

In northern areas, petroglyphs are largely geometric and feature abstract motifs such as wavy lines, zigzags, spirals, circles, rhombuses and rectangles, concentric circles, and possible representations of solar disks. Spirals are particularly popular, probably the most statistically numerous of all the other cultures of the Southwest (Schaafsma 1980:90) and circles appear in various forms individually as well as in groups (figure 5.8). There are also many anthropomorphic and zoomorphic images—turtles, dogs, lizards, snakes, birds, and insects, and hunting scenes with mountain sheep. The noses, mouths, and ears (which resembles the letter V) of four-legged animals are elongated and some animals are presented with large bellies suggesting that they are images of pregnant females.

Anthropomorphic characters are schematically treated human figures. Dancers, probably ritual (see figure 5.8c), are similar in style to the those on Hohokam ceramics (see figure 5.5.c). In hunting scenes, human figures are usually shown with bows and arrows; depictions of just bows are grouped mainly in the area of present-day Tucson in southern Arizona (Schaafsma 1980:83). There are regional differences in Hohokam rock art as shown by the prevalence of certain representations over others in certain areas. For example, in the Tucson Basin, there are more geometric and abstract representations, and human figures are more schematically represented than in the Phoenix Basin and at the confluence of the Salt and Gila Rivers (Schaafsma 1980). The latter region is dominated by geometrical

Figure 5.8. Examples of Hohokam petroglyphs: (a) from the Hieroglyphic Canyon; (b) concentric circles and zoomorphic figures, site AZ T:339(ASM); (c) dancing scene (?), site AZ T:12:8(ASM). Photograph and drawing by Aaron M. Wright.

representations of people and animals appearing individually and in groups, accompanied by other geometric elements.

Some representations were highly schematic and not very elaborated, while other panels were made with extreme precision. Rock walls or individual boulders for these detailed petroglyphs were carefully selected, with the rock surface intentionally prepared. Sometimes petroglyphs were purposely placed in specific places on the rocks to emphasize their crevices, edges, or even tones produced by rocks (so-called bell rocks), which in turn shows that the rocks themselves were important to the overall composition. A reading of the rock art in its entirety should take into account various factors, including the location of individual panels within the terrain and the surface of the rock on which they were placed (e.g., Hernbrode and Boyle 2016; Rozwadowski 2017; Wright 2014).

Most representations of Hohokam rock art that we see today are petroglyphs. Ethnohistoric sources including an account written by the Jesuit Jacobo Sedelmayer from 1749 and later records from the end of the nineteenth century suggest that at least some of the petroglyphs were painted, specifically at sites in today's Painted Rocks State Park (Schaafsma 1980:96 after Wasley and Johnson 1965). It is puzzling that these paints were visible in the nineteenth century. According to some researchers (e.g., Schaafsma 1980; Aaron M. Wright, personal communication, 2022), this may be due to the fact that by that time, they had been repainted successively by the O'odham groups in the historic period. The ongoing restoration of paint is confirmed in archaeological and ethnographic sources, at least for the Akimel O'odham, who worshiped these ancient rock art images and perhaps even incorporated them into their beliefs (e.g., Fewkes 1912:148–49). Evidence that petroglyphs were once painted can be found in small cupules carved in the rock panels that were perhaps used for grinding the minerals and staining paints. Cupules and longitudinal marks typically made after grinding or mashing plants or minerals can be found at Painted Rocks Park and at the Picture Rocks and Tumamoc Hill sites.

Paintings on their own are quite rare in the rock art of the Hohokam culture and tend to be concentrated in the southern area. These are mainly geometric and figural representations found in caves and rock shelters or small niches, and sometimes on boulders in open spaces. Red, black, and white paints made of minerals were used (Wright and Bostwick 2009:75); currently there is no evidence of paintings in the Phoenix Basin area.

Dating Hohokam rock art presents difficulties, as the task involves dealing with petroglyphs, which are hard to date absolutely because they lack organic materials. It is sometimes possible to point out chronological differences in terms of different degree of patina on individual petroglyphs, but these differences only translate into relative rather than absolute/calendar dating. Recent studies (Wright 2016) comparing the motifs of rock art to the iconography of ceramics offer us some hope of assigning some representations to specific periods, suggesting that most Hohokam rock art from the South Mountains can be dated to the Preclassic period.

The meaning of rock art is also difficult to decipher, although some representations may be influenced by Mesoamerican religions and ideologies (e.g., Schaafsma 1980:90-91, 102-3) from the Mexican states of Sinaloa and Nayarit, where similar representations are found. This theory is supported by similarities in the iconography of animal and human figures from the early pottery and rock art of the Hohokam culture and the Chupícuaro and Chalchihuites pottery from central and northwestern Mexico.

The Salado: New Cultural and Stylistic Trends in the Southwest

Based on results of research from the Gila Pueblo site near the present-day town of Globe and other sites in south-central Arizona, the appearance of the Salado Culture was initially interpreted as a transition from the Preclassic period to the Classic Hohokam culture. According to the first theories proposed in 1935 (the term *Salado culture* was proposed by Harold and Winifred Gladwins), the Salado people migrated to Hohokam territory and replaced, or assimilated with them. Based on subsequent research, the most often considered regional variant of Hohokam culture during the Classic period was first present in the Tonto Basin and region around Globe. Salado ceramics serve as an example of a more expansive production of polychrome ceramics in various regions of the Southwest in the Classic period, and thus reflect major changes of a socioreligious nature rippling through almost the entire region.

The Salado culture developed between the end of the thirteenth century AD until around 1450 AD. Its beginnings and development were likely related to an influx of immigrants at the end of the thirteenth century from the Kayenta region of northern Arizona, or as far as Monument Valley from the Ancestral Pueblo world to the Tonto Basin and Safford Valley in eastern Arizona, and the central Salt River Basin and the San Pedro River Valley in southern Arizona (e.g., Cordell 1997; Clark and Huntley 2012; Clark and Abbott 2017:362–63; Huntley 2012; Lyons 2012). Interestingly, the groups of migrants were probably not numerically large, but they were well-organized socially, economically, and culturally.

Trademarks of the Pueblo people from the Kayenta region in southern Arizona include architectural elements related to the organization of space and the central parts of the house and hearths. These characteristic features occurred until the end of the thirteenth century AD in the Kayenta region, and only later in central-southern Arizona. Notable pottery included plates perforated with holes around the rim, and Maverick Mountain pottery in central-southern Arizona which is technologically and decoratively copied from northern Arizona styles (for example Tsegi Orange type). There were noticeably fewer influences from Tusayan ceramics, which are related to the ancestors of the Hopi tride (e.g., Lyons 2012). Additionally, the local population continued to make pottery in the Red-on-Brown style and the

Middle Gila Buff Ware type which emerged in a slightly different form than the earlier types of Hohokam pottery.

Salado pottery (figure 5.9), also known as Salado Polychrome, evolved from Maverick Mountain and Middle Gil Buff Ware. Salado pottery is noted for its polychrome decorations with exterior and interior parts of the vessel. Decorations are painted with rather thick lines in black, red, or white, with the surface of the vessel most often in red or white. Iconography is dominated by geometric motifs, but there are also figural representations, masks, and Mesoamerican influences that symbolize rain and soil fertility—the feathered serpent, lightning, and clouds (stepped motifs). Snakes with feathers or horns on their heads are interpreted as emanations of Quetzalcoatl or Kukulkan (Crown 1994; Clark and Abbott 2017; Nelson et al. 2017). To this day, the Feather Serpent is identified among Pueblo groups of the Southwest such as the Hopi and Zuni with rain, abundance, and the fertility of the earth. Perhaps this symbolism was part of a new ideology and belief system that helped unite various groups.

While iconographic motifs and the use of plant-based paints characterized ceramics in the Kayenta and Tusayan regions in northeastern Arizona and Mesa Verde in southwestern Colorado, Salado ceramics featured more

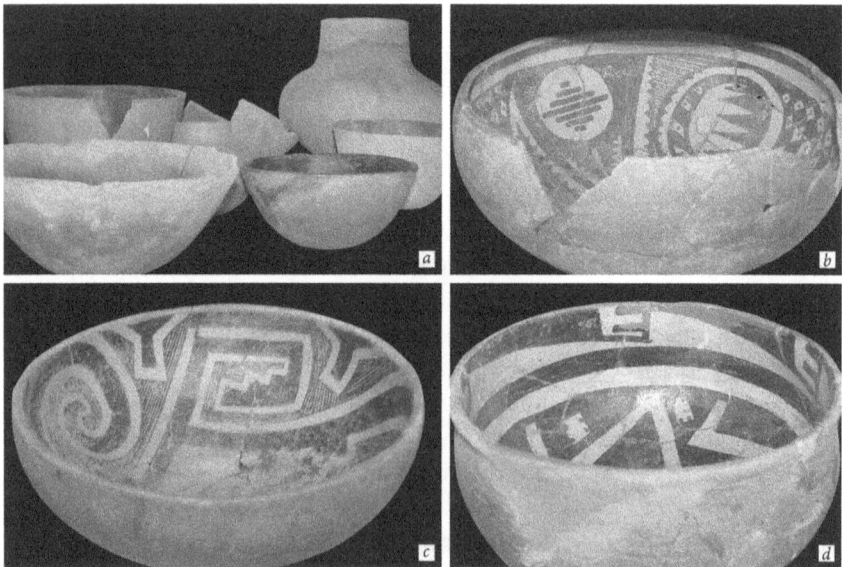

Figure 5.9.   Some undecorated Salado ceramics, Roosevelt Red Ware and Salt Red (a) and (b–d) selected Salado pottery decorated in the Gila and Tonto Polychrome styles. Photos by Radosław Palonka.

distinct influences of Pueblo and Mogollon ceramic production (e.g., Clark and Abbott 2017 after Crown 1994). This in turn led to the theory that the continuity of ceramics production was preserved among the Pueblo community possibly by women (but see e.g., Kantner et al. 2019 for an alternate theory of labor division) who created ceramics. Continuity in ceramics and of many other elements of culture testified to strong ties with the areas in the north that had been abandoned by migration. Thus the Kayenta and other Ancestral Pueblo communities in Hohokam territory may be considered as a kind of diaspora.

In addition to pottery, it was important to acquire and trade other goods, including obsidian, just as it had been in the "classical"/earlier Hohokam culture. The Kayenta/Salado population in Mule Creek in New Mexico operated a large obsidian outcrop. Here Kayenta migrants joined an existing settlement, as they had in other regions (e.g., Clark and Huntley 2012). The trade and exchange of obsidian appear to be related to the spread of a new ideology and culture.

Demographically, the northern Pueblo migrants constituted a minority in relation to the local Hohokam culture. But it was new arrivals who, within a fairly short time, imposed a certain rhythm of cultural changes, and thus, most likely ideological and religious shifts, which soon encompassed almost the entire territory occupied by Hohokam communities. It is also clear that the migrants retained much of their own culture for at least two generations and even, as some researchers claim, for nearly a century (e.g., Clark and Abbott 2017:364). Individual Hohokam settlements began to adapt this new style of ceramics and other aspects of the Salado culture, changes that likely occurred until the mid-fourteenth century AD in the major site of Casa Grande and other centers such as Las Colinas and Los Muertos at the lower part of the Salt River Valley.

It seems that the influx of immigrants from the north was not always peaceful and, at least in some of the northern areas of the Hohokam culture, led to conflicts and fighting with the local population (e.g., Wallace and Doelle 2001). Archaeological data show that some enclaves of the northern arrivals from the Kayenta region inhabited hills and cliff edges that offered natural defense, with elements of architecture that can be interpreted as defensive. Then the local population began migrating from smaller, scattered settlements and villages to larger settlements that were surrounded by walls. Platform mounds were built inside these large settlements and played a similar role as those in the Preclassic and Classic period of Hohokam culture. During the period of domination and development of the Salado culture and style, the platform mounds could have had special significance for the local population, a style distinct from that of the immigrants from the north (Clark and Abbott 2017).

The period during which the Salado culture flourished marks the final stage in the development of the great Hohokam cultural tradition. The depopulation of Hohokam territories began as early as the Classic period, in the fourteenth century AD, but the process extended over time and continued throughout the fifteenth century; while some microregions and settlements continued to develop, others fell into decline or gradually depopulated. Attempts to integrate and perhaps redevelop some centers by gathering the population into individual settlements along the irrigation canals did not result in any greater cultural revival in the long term.

It is not known what caused the decline and depopulation of this area. The most common theory revolves around a series of catastrophic floods that were supposed to have hit central and southern Arizona around 1350 AD as well as other adverse environmental and climate changes. On the other hand, the oral tradition of the O'odham groups often mentions conflicts and fighting that were thought to have caused migration and the abandonment of these areas. During the period between 1450 and 1650 AD, the southern area and to some extent, central Arizona area was visibly inhabited by a relatively small number of people which is manifested by the limited amount of archaeological data from that era. It must be admitted however, that some Spanish sources from the sixteenth century do record some permanent native settlements, including those on the Salt and Gila Rivers.

Communities on the Fringes of Great Traditions: The Sinagua and Patayan Cultures

Some sites in the vicinity of today's Flagstaff in northern Arizona are defined as the Sinagua culture or tradition. These feature architecture and Black-on-White pottery that relates-to both the Pueblo and Mogollon cultures and other cultures of the Southwest region. These include the Hohokam ballcourts from the vicinity of Flagstaff, which resemble those from central and southern Arizona. Major phases in the development of this cultural tradition occurred from around 500 AD until around 1400/1425 AD with Cindar Park, Sunset, and Rio de Flag phases lasting until 1064 and the Padre, Angell, Winona, Elden, Turkey Hill, and Clear Creek phases starting in from 1070 AD.

Deposits of volcanic ash, especially from the eruption of Sunset Crater north of Flagstaff, may have ultimately attracted groups of people to the Flagstaff area. This eruption began around 1064 AD followed by major eruptions in 1064–1065 and 1066–1067. These probably continued intermittently for another 200 years (Cordell 1997:174–75). Though the volcanic ash was devastating to the immediate area, some researchers believe that in the long run it fertilized the soil in the surrounding areas. In turn, the rich soil attracted different migrant groups from regions inhabited by the Pueblo, Hohokam, and Mogollon people. Other scholars have rejected the theory that the soils were significantly enriched by the volcanic ash, but two centuries after the main eruption, the soil was so depleted that the Sinagua people moved to other areas (some probably to Hopi mesas).

The agricultural economy of the Sinagua culture was based on rainfall and periodic flooding, but small irrigation canals and dams are known to have existed; some Sinagua groups practiced hunting and gathering on a large scale, depending on environmental conditions and location. They seem to have traded with many different regions, possibly including Mesoamerica, as is evidenced in the presence of ballcourts, imported copper bells, and parrots and shells from the California coast.

The Sinagua culture represented complexity where the characteristics of several southwestern agricultural cultures met and mixed together; it also created features that distinguished it from neighboring cultures, including pithouses with stone architecture and a characteristic site layout, as well as brown ceramics with an admixture of crushed stone. Initially, from around 600/800 AD until 1125 AD, the most visible influences are those of the Hohokam culture, a period that is a major research priority today. In later periods, the main ties were clearly with the western groups of the Ancestral Pueblo culture, most probably ancestors of historic Hopis (e.g., Cordell 1997; Bostwick 2014).

Montezuma Castle is one of the most famous Sinagua sites. It represents a trend that began around the twelfth century AD and is characterized by the location of settlements in rock shelters, the cliff dwellings at Walnut Canyon National Monument, and the Palatki and Honanki settlements near Sedona. Large sites on open, flat terrain or hilltops include Elden Pueblo, the site complex at Wupatki National Monument (Wupatki, Wukoki, Citadel, Nalakihu, Box Canyon, and Lomaki), the Tuzigoot settlement, and the V-Bar-V Heritage Site with numerous intriguing examples of rock art that may be of an astronomical nature and connected with solar calendars.

The Patayan (Hakataya) culture was another tradition greatly influenced by the Hohokam people. The Patayan culture flourished in western Arizona, southern California, and the California Peninsula as well as southern Nevada, mostly in the Lower Colorado River and some of its tributaries. The term *Patayan* (*pah-tah-yáhn*) is an Anglicized form of the word *pataya*, which comes from a Native American language in the Pai group (Hualapai, Havasupai, Yavapai, and Paipai) belonging to the Yuman-Cochimí language family; roughly translated, it means "old people" or ancestors. The Patayan tradition remains one of the least studied Native American communities of the pre-Hispanic and early-historic Southwest as the borderland between western Arizona and southeastern California has not been well studied.

Pottery-making technology and forms in the Patayan differed from those of the Pueblo, Hohokam, and Mogollon cultures. The culture is also distinguished by its complex designs in petroglyphs and paintings, as well as the creation of geoglyphs—large figures and patterns made with the use of dark stones of volcanic origin or the removal of parts of the earth to create a pattern. Geoglyphs which could be observed from distant places were often created on terraces along the Gila River. These are best seen from a bird's eye view, similar to the famous Nasca geoglyphs in Peru.

The development of Patayan culture is often divided into three main phases (e.g., Cordell 1997): Patayan I (700–1050 AD), which that is associated with the emergence of farming communities and knowledge of ceramics mainly along the lower Colorado River; Patayan II (1050–1500 AD), when the cultural tradition spread to southern Nevada, western Arizona, and the area around the Salton Sea lake in southern California; and Patayan III (1500–1900 AD), which is associated with historic Yuman communities such as the Piipaash groups, Opa, and Cocomaricopa. The latter phase is also marked by the formation of large settlements at the confluence of the Gila and Colorado Rivers, the movement of the Patayan community upstream of the Gila River to the Gila Basin and Phoenix Basin (to their earlier migration territory occupied by the Hohokam people), as well as in interactions with local communities, including trade as well as conflicts and fighting, which is visible in the iconography of the rock art, especially after 1100 AD (e.g., Doelle et al. 2011).

Patayan settlements feature pithouses, wooden and earthen structures on a plaza and rectangular plan with entrances in the shorter side, as well as stone buildings consisting of small, rectangular rooms. The pottery of the Patayan tradition was rarely painted, and after firing it was mainly buff, red-brown, and gray in color. The material culture of the pre-Hispanic Patayan tradition clearly overlaps with the extent of historic Yuman-speaking tribes, and it is often claimed that Patayan societies were their ancestors.

Economically, upstream groups were highly mobile. Like the historic Pai Indians in this region, they moved seasonally depending on food avail-

Figure 5.10.   Examples of Patayan rock art from the lower Gila River valley, with large-scale panels on basalt rocks with a stylized representation of a hunter (right) hunting an animal (left) (note the dramatic placement of the motifs on the two boulders). Photo by Henry D. Wallace.

ability; their settlements were rather short-term, featuring only a small quantity of products of material culture with a predominance of items made from organic materials. On the other hand, the Patayan communities inhabiting the Gila and Colorado river valleys grew crops on the floodplains and inhabited populous settlements of up to several hundred inhabitants. Although these settlements existed for a long time, there are no confirmed traces of public architecture and larger establishments of a religious nature. These riverside settlements revealed numerous traces of damage to houses caused by floods. When the Europeans arrived, the peoples historically known as Kohuana, Halyikwamai, Xalychidom, Cocopah, Quechan, Mojave, and Piipaash tribes lived there, among others.

Pottery and Settlements in the Highlands 6
The Mogollon and Mimbres Cultures

Mogollon Cultural Development

THE NAME OF THE MOGOLLON CULTURE comes from the mountains of the same name, the Mogollon Rim, on the border of Arizona and New Mexico, which is named after Don Juan Ignacio Flores Mogollón, a governor of New Mexico in the eighteenth century. The name of the mountains corresponds with the area they inhabited, mainly uplands and mountainous areas with small valleys, as well as lower-lying semiarid areas, from central-eastern Arizona and central-western and southern New Mexico in the Little Colorado River basin to northwest Texas and the northern parts of the Mexican states of Sonora and Chihuahua (Cordell 1997) (figure 6.1). In 1931 Emil Haury was the first to distinguish the culture from others of the Southwest (Cordell 1997:171).

A territory as huge as this is highly diverse in terms of geography, environment, and topography. The Mogollon Mountains rise over 3,300 meters ASL and feature alpine meadows, while the semiarid and desert areas are located at a much lower altitude, below 900 meters ASL. In the semiarid areas, cacti and a few grassy plants and shrubs prevail, with juniper trees, piñon pine, and ponderosa pine growing in slightly higher areas. These large variations in elevation and the north-south mountain ranges made east-west travel very difficult during the pre-Hispanic period, as it remains today. Several indigenous groups, sometimes also referred to as cultures, are distinguished in this diverse environment: Mimbres, Jornada, San Simon, Forestdale, Reserve, and Point of Pines; the latter three are sometimes called the "Mogollon Mountain" groups (Anyon and Gilman 2017; Cordell 1997).

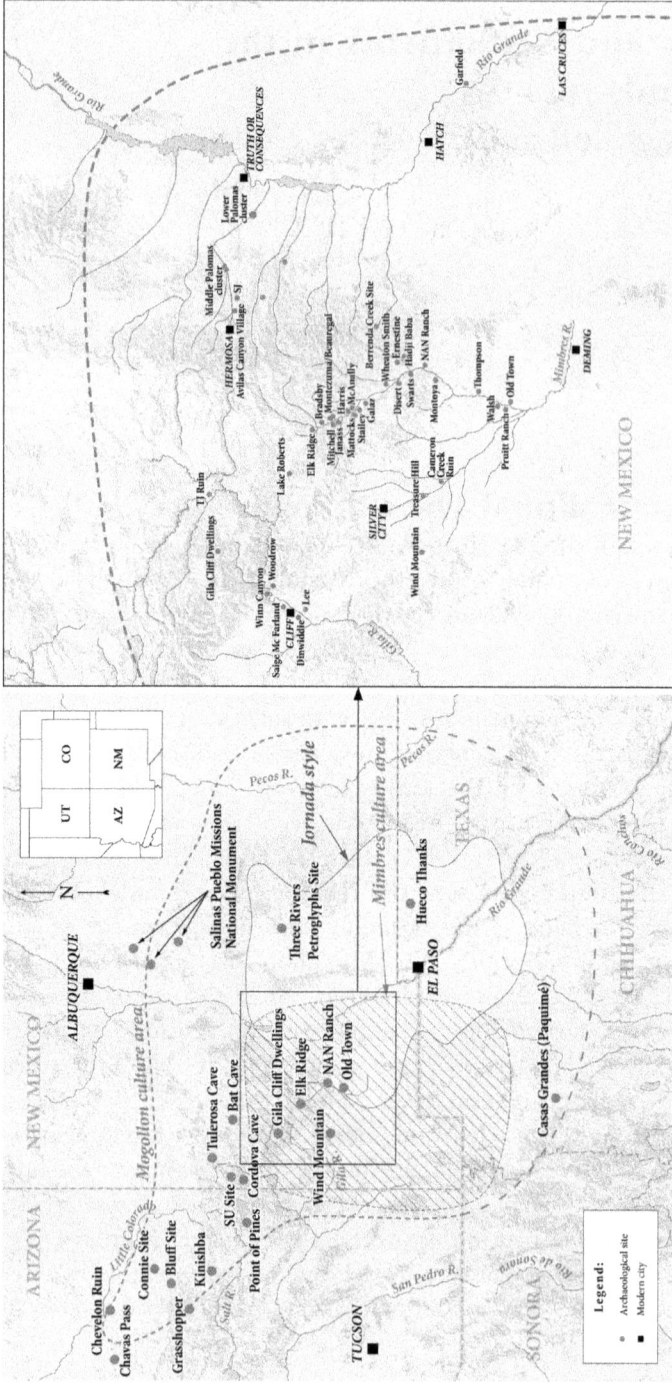

Figure 6.1. The extent of the Mogollon and Mimbres cultures along with their most important sites. Compiled by Radosław Palonka on the basis of various sources and drawing by Michał Znamirowski.

The Mogollon culture appears to have evolved from the Cochise culture of the so-called the Archaic Desert. Mogollon developed around 200 to 1400/1450 AD (Anyon et al. 1981; Cordell 1997) a time period that is largely correlated with the rhythm of cultural and chronological changes in other Southwestern cultures. Mogollon chronological sequences cover three phases or periods: the Early Pithouse period (ca. 200–550 AD), the Late Pithouse period (550–1000 AD), and the Mogollon Pueblo period (1000–1400/1450 AD) with the latter including the Classic Mimbres dating from 1000 to 1130/1150 AD.

In the Early Pithouse period, the Mogollon people lived mainly in upland areas in settlements characterized by a small number of houses (some no more than ten to twenty). Settlements were located in fertile areas and in hard-to-reach places on plateaus, slopes, and isolated hills, often with stone barricades along the trails or roads leading in, suggesting that they were chosen for defensive reasons from the outset. They lived in pithouses dug about 0.5–1.5 meters into the ground, built in a circular or oval layout with a diameter of 3 to 5 meters, and an entrance on one side of the house. Round roofs were supported by a central post and earthen walls, or on several poles that also were parts of the walls. Roofs were constructed with thick wooden beams upon which branches were laid and then covered with a layer of earth and mud. Hearths can be distinguished in some houses, although not all buildings had them, and these have been interpreted as houses inhabited outside the winter season. There are also traces of cave dwellings, which were probably occupied in the winter months (Cordell 1997:204); as indicated by fragments of clothing made of rabbit fur, woven baskets, grass bedding, bird feather blankets, and *mano* and *metate* stones for grinding corn.

The pottery used during this period consists mainly of brown or brown-red vessels, sometimes covered with red slip. Clays came mostly from alluvial soils and thus did not require any additional admixture. Like most pottery in the Southwest, the pottery of the Mogollon culture was made by hand-molding and clay rollers and later smoothed. Typical vessels include pots, sometimes with a long or well-defined neck, bowls, and smaller vessels with narrow openings, mainly used for storing corn or other grains.

The Mogollon economy was based primarily on agriculture, although hunting and gathering likely played an important role in obtaining food, particularly by those living in upland areas surrounded by forests inhabited by wild animals and deer. Not all Mogollon groups immediately adopted large-scale agriculture, in part because the short growing season and greater

Table 6.1. Chronology of the Mogollon and Mimbres Cultures Along with the Sequence of These Cultures' Pottery Styles

Period	Phase	Calendar Dates and Area of Occurrence	Main Ceramic Styles
Postclassic Period	Cliff	1300–1450+ AD The western Mimbres culture and Southern Arizona (Upper Gila Basin and Mimbres River Valley)	Pottery of the Salado culture – Gila Polychrome style
	Black Mountain	1200–1300/1400 AD The southern part of the Mimbres River valley and the areas further south	The end of Mimbres pottery; ceramics connected with influences from the south including Casas Grandes: Playas Red Incised, El Paso Polychrome, Chupadero Black-on-White, Ramos Polychrome, Chihuahuan Corrugated
	Mimbres Reorganization	1150–beginning of the 13th century AD Eastern region of the Mimbres culture	Coexistence of pottery from the Classic Mimbres and styles from other cultures including Playas Red Incised, El Paso Polychrome, Tularosa Black-on-White, Tularosa Patterned Corrugated, St. John's Polychrome
	Final phase of the Classic Mimbres	1130–end of the 12th century AD The central and southern part of the Mimbres River Valley	Coexistence of pottery from the Classic Mimbres and pottery from other cultures including; El Paso Polychrome, Playas Red Incised, Chupadero Black-on-White, Tularosa Patterned Corrugated, Chihuahuan Corrugated
Classic period (Mogollon Pueblo)	Classic	1000–1130/1150 AD The extent of the Mimbres culture	Style III: Black-on-White pottery
Late Pithouse period	Tree Circle	750–1000 AD The extent of the Mimbres culture	Styles I and II: Black-on-White and Three Circle Red-on-White
	San Francisco	650–750 AD The extent of the Mimbres culture	Mogollon Red-on-Brown, (painted pottery appears for the first time in the Mimbres area)
	Georgetown	550–650 AD The extent of the Mimbres culture	San Francisco Red
Early Pithouse period	Cumbre	200–550 AD The extent of the Mimbres culture	Brown, unpainted ceramics including the Alma Plain type

After Anyon et al. (1981); Hegmon (2002:Table I, 312–14); Trask (2016), with modifications from the author.

variability of precipitation at high altitudes hampered these efforts so that some settlements resembled hunter-gatherer communities.

Around 550 AD the Mogollon moved their settlements to lower-lying areas, mainly the lowest terraces above the river floodplains. This change was the most important determinant of the next period of this culture's development, known as the Late Pithouse period (550–1000 AD) leading to the establishment of a stable settlement systems lasting several centuries. The move was associated with a greater dependence on agriculture and the cultivation of squash and beans, although hunting and gathering still played a major role. The appearance of a slightly different type of pottery iconography, mainly the San Francisco Red type, was another indicator of cultural changes. These were highly smoothed vessels featuring red slip. Over time (from around 650 AD in the southern Mogollon territory) ceramics began to be decorated with red paint on a brown background called Red-on-Brown pottery. Then decorative motifs evolved toward painting with white paint on a red background, White-on-Red, and then Black-on-White (black on a white background).

Around 600 AD Mogollon houses evolved from circular and D-shaped constructions to rectangular buildings (figure 6.2). The structures of the walls and roofs of typical houses were similar to those of the previous period, but the roof was supported by at least three or more poles. A centrally located hearth and often one or several large storage pits became integral parts of these houses. As the Mogollon culture developed, storage pits were apparently replaced functionally by large ceramic storage vessels. Settlements were still not very large, with a maximum of a few to a dozen or so houses, although there were larger ones with up to fifty buildings in one settlement, in the last part of the Late Pithouse period, also called Tree Circle. Researchers have calculated that four to six homesteads could have been inhabited by a population of about thirty (Cordell 1997:205). Such small groups comprised of large families must have met at certain times of the year with other similar groups for hunting, holidays and ceremonies, access to various types of food, mutual trade, support in times of environmental instability or climate fluctuations, and even to marry. For these social and economic reasons, they were likely not entirely self-sufficient.

During the Late Pithouse period, some pithouses were up to four times larger than previously, with unusual elements such as *sipapu* openings (floor holes/openings commonly found in the kivas of the Pueblo culture) and oblong, rectangular openings in the floors that were similar to vaults, and were present in Great Kivas.

Figure 6.2. Cross-sections of pithouses from the first periods of the Mogollon culture (a); (b) Classic and Postclassic typical houses with marked burials under the floors divided into three worlds according to the cosmogony of different cultures from the historic period in the Southwest; (c) South Diamond Creek Pueblo (Classic Period) in Gila National Forest, located in the northern part of Mimbres/Mogollon territory. Drawings by Michał Znamirowski based on the various sources and photo by Fumi Arakawa.

In Mogollon settlements, three types of organization, building type, and number of buildings can be distinguished (Cordell 1997:205–6). The first group is notable for the appearance of large kiva-type buildings with innovative architectural features such as roof types or shades around the entrances to buildings and *sipapu* and vaults known from kivas. Such sites could have grouped tens of buildings in one settlement. The second settlement type, located mainly in the uplands and mountains in the central and western part of Mogollon territory, consisted of only two or three separate households with a centrally located Great Kiva. Located farthest to the north and northwest of Mogollon territory, the third group consists of communities that included small sites with one to five houses as well as a central settlement with fifty to two hundred rooms, some with Great Kivas. These probably also served as centers for people from the surrounding small settlements, as well as for entire settlement microregions. However, with the possible exception of the third group, this period was basically characterized by settlements/sites that were inhabited by only one or at most a few families that used large pithouses. Toward the end of the period, proportions flipped as more and more people lived in one site, but in smaller houses than before.

The move to lower lands brought major transformations to the entire culture. The period between 950/1000 and 1150 AD marks the Classic period of the Mogollon culture, also known as the Mogollon Pueblo period. This phase marks the development of one of the most interesting social and cultural phenomena in the Southwest in the pre-Hispanic period, the rise of the Mimbres culture, which lasted less than 150 years. Architecturally, the Mogollon communities abandoned pithouses and shifted entirely to aboveground pueblo-type masonry consisting of many interconnected stone rooms between groups of buildings, just the Pueblo culture had done several centuries earlier. The creation of large settlements was associated with a population increase and expansion into new areas using less fertile land for agriculture. Also notable is a period of great artistic expression and the evolution of technology and decoration of ceramics, which involved the replacement of brown and red ceramics with black and sometimes red paints on white, gray, or brown slip.

The beginnings of pueblo-type construction and stylistic references to Black-on-White pottery have led some modern archaeological theories to consider the Mogollon culture from this period as part of the western or southern world of Pueblo culture (e.g., Haury 1988). Theories have even suggested that the Pueblo dominated (possibly militarily) the previously scattered Mogollon communities. However, this notion has not been fully confirmed throughout all Mogollon culture and is not widely accepted. At many sites, such as the famous Mimbres NAN Ranch Ruin, local development is confirmed along with the transition to a new type of construction and decoration of ceramics, with no obvious influences or outside interference (LeBlanc 1989; Shafer 2003).

Mimbres Culture

Sometimes referred to as the Mimbres phase of the Mogollon culture, the Mimbres was indeed a peculiar phenomenon in the development of the Mogollon cultural tradition. Named after the Mimbres River in southwestern New Mexico where most sites have been found, the name in Spanish means "little willow" and may also refer to the poplar tree. "Mimbres" also refers to the singularly characteristic ceramics produced by this culture, richly decorated with painting in naturalistic and abstract styles. The Mimbres culture developed in its classical form in a relatively short period from 1000 to about 1130/1150 AD, and the whole of this cultural phenomenon falls within a maximum time frame running between 750 and 1200 AD (Anyon and Gilman 2017; Hegmon and Nelson 2003). Ceramics technologically identical to Mimbres pottery appear even before 1000 AD but were not yet as decorated as those the Classic Mimbres style.

For over one hundred years, research on this culture has been one of the most important areas in the archaeology of the Southwest. The Mimbres culture developed mainly in the southwestern part of New Mexico and some adjacent areas bordering a small section of Arizona in the upper Gila River Basin, and to a greater extent in the northern part of the state of Chihuahua in northern Mexico (see figure 6.1). This vast area was the center of the Mogollon cultural world. As with the rest of the Mogollon culture, agriculture formed the basis for the existence of the communities, with the most important crops being corn, squash, and beans. The cultivation of cotton was also important for the economy. Their diet was supplemented with the meat of wild animals, mainly antelopes, deer, rabbits, birds, and sometimes fish (Cordell 1997). Numerous seeds and nuts of wild plants have also been discovered at Mimbres sites, including juniper, cactus, and mesquite. Importantly, like the Hohokam and to some extent the Pueblo societies, the Mimbres people used artificial irrigation through water-supply canals.

Mimbres settlements were characterized by a considerable number of homesteads in one village. Buildings were most often constructed from river cobbles held together with clay. In terms of area and number of buildings, the Mimbres sites often exceeded even Pueblo settlements, but did not survive as well as the Ancestral Pueblo settlements, which were built with sandstone; only in the final period of their culture were Mimbres settlements built of adobe and sandstone. Despite the creation of very large settlements, it is not apparent that Mimbres communities elaborated any system of significant settlement or social hierarchy (Cordell 1997:348–49).

Richly decorated pottery is one of the most distinctive features of the Mimbres culture. Production of Mimbres pottery peaked in the Classic period of Mimbres/Mogollon cultural development. Mimbres pottery was decorated with geometric and figural designs in the so-called Mimbres Black-on-White style. The ceramics were made of red clay and covered with white slip, upon which red or black decorations were painted. Bowls comprise the vast majority of Mimbres pottery. Geometric designs account for approximately half of the representations painted on Mimbres pottery (Brody 2004), recent research (Hegmon et al. 2021:26) shows that geometric representational ratio is about 65:35 (see also table 6.2—transitional style II).

Three main styles of Mimbres pottery may be discerned by their decorations (Anyon et al. 1981; Hegmon 2002; Shafer and Brewington 1995) (table 6.2). The basic forms are hemispherical bowls, pots, *ollas* (water containers) and zoomorphic vessels, all richly decorated. It's possible that after 1130/1150 AD, the production of characteristic pottery continued for some time, mainly in the southern part of the former territory of the Mimbres culture (Hegmon 2002), up to the Black Mountain phase, when ceramics resembling those from the Paquimé (Casas Grandes) site in the state of Chihuahua in Mexico begin to appear (table 6.2, see also table 6.1); but generally in the late 1100s the Mimbres pottery it's not being made any more.

The most important stylistic determinants of individual Mimbres ceramic styles I–III are indicated in table 6.2. Although these bowls were extremely valuable for the Mimbres community as evidenced by the craftsmanship applied in decorating and by the fact that they were placed in graves along with the dead, they are very rarely found outside the Mimbres cultural area (Hegmon et al. 2021; Moulard 1984), as if they were only rarely, or even never, traded but were assigned to special functions (other than their utilitarian role) in this culture's communities.

As shown by detailed studies conducted since the 1980s and 1990s, some of which involve chemical analyses (petrography and neutron activation analysis, NAA and INAA), Mimbres ceramics were produced at various sites and by many potters. There were more than just a few special-

Table 6.2.   Examples of the Mimbres Pottery Styles I–III Decorative Motifs

Style I (750–950 AD)	Style II (Transitional style) (880/1020 AD–950/1000 AD)	Style III (Classic style) (1000/1010–1130/1150+ AD)

Compiled by Radosław Palonka and drawings by Katarzyna Ciomek (also consultations with Michelle Hegmon.

ized production centers for ceramics (Creel et al. 2002; Hegmon 2002), although a careful stylistic analysis suggests that the most complex designs could be the work of one or just a few artisans.

Taking into account the total number of sites and the chronology of the development of the Classic period, estimates suggest that if a few potters produced fifty to one hundred bowls per year, this would have been sufficient to produce the total amount of Black-on-White Mimbres ceramics known to us today (see summary at Hegmon 2002). Currently we are aware of just over ten thousand such vessels (data from the Mimbres Pottery Images Digital Database—MimPIDD—https://core.tdar.org/collection/22070/mimbres-ceramic-database), although it is not fully known how many more bowl and other pottery types might be dispersed in private collections and museums worldwide (see also the end of this chapter).

Some data suggest that potters were women; for example, a woman from the NAN Ranch Ruin site was buried with tools for making and smoothing pottery and a scene painted on a bowl depicting a woman making a ceramic vessel. But researchers are not unanimous as to whether it was only men or only women who were involved in producing and decorating pottery. The depiction of many scenes related to rituals that were possibly only accessible to men, and the depiction of exotic items such as fish and ocean mammals suggests that at least some of the vessels were decorated by men who had access to these animals and certain ceremonies. That there were male potters may also be supported by the fact that childbirth depictions (not correctly presented) and some other scenes were decorated by men who were completely unfamiliar with the process (Hegmon and Trevathan 1996) but some researchers (e.g., Espenshade 1997) are skeptical of such an inference. They claim that although Mimbres pottery art can be read in naturalistic terms, scenes depicted are not always realistic in the portrayal of various processes, therefore one should be careful about accepting these reconstructions (LeBlanc 1997). Finally, there are suggestions that at certain times of increased demand for Mimbres ceramics and economic pressure, both women and men could have produced and decorated them (e.g., Mills 1995).

Many Mimbres bowls have been found in graves. Bowls would be placed next to the head, or more often used to cover the heads or faces of the deceased. A hole called a *kill hole* was often made in the center of the vessel/bowl. The deliberate piercing of the bowls and their placement upon the head or face may have been intended to entice the soul of the deceased to leave the body and travel to the afterlife, or to summon the "soul" of the bowl itself, which would travel with the deceased. According to the beliefs of the Hopi, the soul of the deceased, or the deceased himself, could remain on earth for up to four days after the burial, and later traveled to the Maski/Land of the Dead (Ferguson et al. 2001:12).

Mimbres ceramics were often decorated with geometric representations with abstract and highly complex patterns and designs. The dominant motifs are circles, spirals, squares, diamonds, sometimes forming checkerboards, as well as triangles, wavy lines and straight or zigzag lines perhaps running parallel, often creating a *hachure* motif. Variants of the *hachure* motif on black-on-white ceramics may also be, as some researchers claim (e.g., Russell et al. 2008), schematic representations of green and blue (turquoise or water, the sun and the sky, and the male element as in Pueblo mythology) or yellow (the female element and the symbol of corn, the earth, and the moon).

About one-third of known Mimbres bowls have representational designs that depict animals and sometimes humans (see MimPIDD database). Single figures make up about half of all figural representations—and extensive scenes involving people and animals or combined human and animal figures (hybrids) such as the bird-man also appear. About 15 percent of such representations are narrative scenes like hunting (figure 6.3), pictures of everyday life—weaving, activities related to farming, trapping birds and other animals, and rare scenes like a woman with a pot (maybe painting the pottery). Scenes and ritualistic images, such as dances with accessories like rattles and prayer sticks with feathers accurately portray ceremonies and rituals that have analogies in such practices to this day in Southwestern communities. There are also images of single warriors in regalia and weapons in the form of bows and arrows, as well as rare scenes of decapitation and scalping. The motif of head cutting is familiar from at least a few Classic Mimbres vessels (only three or four known examples) and is likely

Figure 6.3.   Depictions of hunting scenes, most likely for bears, on Mimbres bowls (a); mountain sheep (d); including the transport of hunted antelopes or deer (e); and images of warriors with shield/armor and weapons (c); as well as probably a ritual (war?) dance scene (b). Compiled by Radosław Palonka and drawings by Katarzyna Ciomek.

related to the influence of beliefs from Mesoamerica (e.g., Gilman et al. 2014; Fewkes 1916:538–39; Shafer 1995).

Human figures and zoomorphic motifs sometimes appear in the central part of the bowl or on opposite sides of the bowl's wall. Sometimes figures formed narrative scenes and complex compositions with different designs around the inside of the vessel. Anthropomorphic characters were usually painted with a thick layer of paint filling large spaces while faces often remain white and unpainted. The most frequently and precisely treated elements are the head and face decorations and loincloths or aprons, which are different for men and women. Some anthropomorphic images may be associated with representations of masked dancers related to the *kachina* ceremonies, present in the Pueblo culture from at least the turn of the fourteenth century AD until today (see figure 6.4b).

Many anthropomorphic figures are depicted with sexual features, such as breasts in women, and so one may at least partially try to reconstruct certain social roles and functions dependent on gender (e.g., Brody 2004; Munson 2000). Men seem to have been featured more often than women, though it is often difficult to determine gender unambiguously (Brody 1977; 2004); men were generally shown performing a variety of activities such as hunting large animals and fishing or performing ceremonies—scenes of a dynamic nature. Women are presented more often in static positions, with children or burden baskets for carrying items, and with various types of jewelry. Women are sometimes shown with parrots, which were undoubtedly brought from distant areas and probably bred in Mimbres communities for ritual purposes. This indicates a clear connection of some women (perhaps from certain families) with female roles in ceremonialism and religion.

Animals, mainly species of mammals found in the territory are another popular motif in Mimbres pottery. These include deer, antelopes, mountain sheep, rabbits, bears, and bats; as well as birds—hawks, quails, turkeys, herons, ducks—and reptiles, notably turtles; amphibians; fish; and insects (grasshoppers, butterflies). As with anthropomorphic figures, single representations of animals were positioned in the center of the bowl or symmetrically on opposite sides of each other, in pairs of two or four animals on the walls and partially on the bottom. There are also numerous, highly stylized geometric representations of animals, sometimes made up of several species; sometimes the images of animals and geometric motifs combined to form anthropomorphic figures. Body parts of animals, such as eyes, ears, legs, antlers, and feathers, are shown quite realistically to the extent that it is possible to identify not only the species but also the sex of the animal.

Of particular interest are the negative paintings of animals, for example rabbits, which appear to have been composed with white paint on a black background but were in fact created by applying the black background and leaving only a white rabbit-shaped slip. Pottery decorated with this rare technique may have been largely the work of the same potter/artist (Hegmon and Russell 2013). It is also worth noting that representations of animals precede the appearance of anthropomorphic motifs in Mimbres ceramics (Hegmon and Kulow 2005:326).

Represented animal species were important not only from an economic point of view, but also in relation to mythology and beliefs. The purely aesthetic aspect of some representations cannot be ruled out, and animals could be symbolically associated with cardinal directions, underground worlds, or with ancestral (clan) symbolism and totemism (e.g., Moulard 1984, but see Hegmon et al. 2018 for other interpretations). There are some depictions of exotic animals, such as types of parrots from Mexico (figure 6.4a,c), ocean fish, as well as fantastical or mythological animals, representations that combine several different animal motifs or human-animal hybrids. Parrots occur frequently, including the large green military macaw (*Ara militaris*), with a body length of up to 70 centimeters and bright green-blue plumage, and the Mexican thick-billed parrot (*Rhynchopsitta pachyrhyncha*) found in the states of Sonora and Chihuahua in northern and central Mexico, relatively close to the Southwest and the area where the Mimbres culture developed. Other parrot species found in the Southwest such as the scarlet macaw (*Ara macao*) only occur naturally very far to the south—from the Huasteca region in the state of Tamaulipas on the Gulf of Mexico in southeastern Mexico, and even farther away in southern Central America and in South America (Creel and McKusick 1994; Gilman et al. 2014; Wyckoff 2009). The scarlet macaw can be recognized in the iconography of Mimbres ceramics due to its white beak (its upper part).

Parrot burials have been found at several large Mimbres sites including Cameron Creek, Galaz Ruin, Eby, Mattocks, Old Town, and Wind Mountain; parrots were often placed in buildings distinguished for their size and other features. This evidence, together with traces of parrots being offered up for sacrifice (probably in the spring, perhaps during the spring equinox as the spring season is indicated by fully developed tail feathers), demonstrates that these birds played a special ceremonial and ritual role, most likely associated with their extremely colorful plumage. This is confirmed in other Southwestern cultures like Pueblo and Hohokam. Most ritually sacrificed parrots appear to have been between 11 and 13 months of age, which is broadly in line with data from other sites in the Southwest

Figure 6.4.   Depictions of transport and training of parrots with special hoops and sticks (a); a masked dancer, perhaps participating in a ceremony connected with the *kachina* cult (b); image of a species of parrot (possibly scarlet macaw) (c); and scenes probably from Mesoamerican mythology: representations of twin brothers (d–e), where drawings *d* may symbolize the brothers swallowed by a fish. Compiled by Radosław Palonka and drawings by Katarzyna Ciomek.

(Creel and McKusick 1994:517–18; Crown 2016). Ceramics depict both young specimens from the seventh week to the fourth month of life to those slightly more than one year old. Birds that were transported from the south appear to have been at least seven weeks old (Bullock 2007; McKusick 2007).

The presence of these exotic birds in the Mimbres cultural area is a reflection of the wider phenomenon of their import and probably subsequent breeding in the Southwest during the years 750–1450 AD, which is confirmed in numerous Ancestral Pueblo sites, including Pueblo Bonito (Chaco Canyon) in New Mexico and Wupatki in Arizona, and above all in Casas Grandes (Paquimé) in northern Mexico (see next chapter). The green macaw, one of the most popular parrot species in the Mimbres culture, appears to have been imported mainly after 1000 AD (Gilman et al. 2014), although skeletons of other parrot species occur earlier in the Mogollon/Mimbres culture. Pottery iconography of parrots being carried in baskets by both women and men may be testimony to their import to the Southwest. The role played by women in the transport and training of these birds using hoops and poles is also depicted on ceramics and in a woman's burial with a parrot skull at the Galaz Ruin site (Creel and McKusick 1994:518, 521).

Parrots brought to the Southwest from Mesoamerica and depictions of human decapitation are just some examples of contact with and influence from Mesoamerican civilizations. Around 1000 AD, versions of images that are likely associated with Mayan myths appear, including that from the Mayan K'iche book Popol Vuh about heroic Twin Brothers, which can be found on Mimbres bowls (figure 6.4e,d) (e.g., Brody 1977; Gilman et al. 2014; Thompson et al. 2014, but see also Schwartz et al. 2022).

Southwestern archaeologists interpret these representations slightly differently than Mesoamerican researchers do, although there is a canon of similar representations related to religion that occur in both areas. Some researchers associate the images of Mayan myths with the simultaneous intensification in the import of parrots and other goods such as copper bells from northern, central, and southern Mexico (e.g., Gilman et al. 2014; Thompson et al. 2014). Along with imported goods, elements of Mesoamerican beliefs and cults may have also been transported to the Southwest, as is also clearly visible at the turn of the fourteenth century when the kachina cult emerged in the Pueblo culture; these religious elements are represented both in iconography of pottery and rock art of Mimbres/Mogollon cultural tradition and in the so-called Jornada style (e.g., Schaafsma 1980; Schaafsma and Schaafsma 1974).

Fish Iconography on Mimbres Pottery

Images of fish comprise about 11 percent of all known animal representations on Mimbres ceramics (MimPIDD Database). These aquatic creatures comprise a fascinating and relatively numerous exotic image, which testifies to the Mimbres' long-distance trade relations (figure 6.5). In addition to ocean fish, some species of freshwater fish (Jett and Moyle 1986) originating from the Colorado, Mimbres, Yaqui, and Rio Grande rivers have even been identified. These include the Longnose Gar (*Lepisosteidae*, *Lepisosteus osseus*) and the white sucker fish (*Catostomus commersonii*) as well as fish from mountain streams and rivers in the region where the Mimbres culture developed—types of salmon and *cyprinids*, most likely roach and catfish (*Ictaluridae*); the latter being quite common in many rivers of North America, from Alaska to Central America (Guatemala). Most astonish-

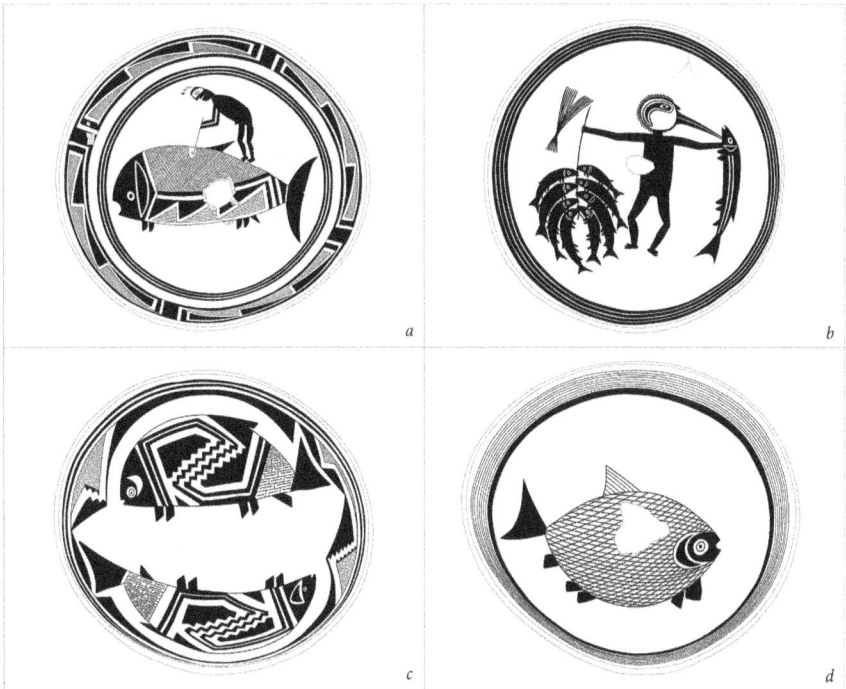

Figure 6.5.   A hunting scene with a harpoon for fish or sea mammals (a) and drawings of selected representations of fish, most likely oceanic (from the Pacific Ocean) (b–d). Compiled by Radosław Palonka; drawings by Katarzyna Ciomek and Michał Znamirowski.

ing are realistic depictions of fish that are marine and oceanic, with many anatomical details marked which could only have been noticed while observing them directly in their natural environment (Jett and Moyle 1986).

Realistic depictions of "exotic" ocean fish, fishing scenes and accessories such as baskets and ropes or nets may indirectly testify to the possibility that some potters traveled quite large distances and observed these animals in their natural habitat (Jett and Moyle 1986:714-15). There are characteristic depictions of fish living near the seabed as well as those inhabiting the open ocean from beyond the Gulf of California including silversides (*Atherinidae*), flying fish (*Exocoetidae*) and other predatory fish (*Atherinidae*), for example swordfish. Several bowls may depict whales, including scenes in which these marine mammals are being hunted (Jett and Moyle 1986).

The most likely habitats of these ocean fish species are the shores of the Gulf of California, at least some 500–700 kilometers away from the Mimbres sites as the crow flies with the open section of the Pacific Ocean an additional 300–400 kilometers away. The region around the present-day city of Guaymas in Sonora, Mexico, is often mentioned as a potential area where Mimbres people traveled, mainly due to the presence of many species of fish depicted on Mimbres pottery. These expeditions could have taken place simply to obtain seashells including *abalone* that were used by the Mimbres people and many other Southwestern cultures to make jewelry. Some shells were clearly obtained from the Gulf of Mexico, located even farther from Mimbres sites—over 1,500 kilometers away. Although rarer, representations of fish are also found in the Mimbres rock art (e.g., Schaafsma 1980). Mythological images—fish people or people with bird heads carrying fish—are all the more astounding for communities that lived among the mountains and deserts of the Southwest.

It is also worth noting that while most fish presented on Mimbres bowls are edible—species that are commonly considered tasty even today—some are unfit for consumption and were probably presented purely for aesthetic reasons as they are colorful and simply delightful in appearance. Historic data shows that the diet of most of the Southwestern communities and adjacent parts of the Great Plains was absent of fish, but archaeological sites such as Kartchner, Galaz, and others in the Mimbres valley have yielded fishbones indicating that fish were sometimes eaten. Traces of fish consumption are also known from some Ancestral Pueblo sites in Arizona and New Mexico: Rio Grande, Chaco Canyon, Aztec Ruins, Grasshopper Pueblo, and sites in the Bandelier National Monument and at Casas Grandes and other sites related to this tradition, although fish-eating was never common in the Southwest.

Challenges interpreting the meaning of the iconography on Mimbres/Mogollon ceramics and rock art are similar to those faced by researchers of most cultures that have left no written record. In analyzing the iconography of Mimbres, analogies to the historic Pueblo communities—mainly the Western Pueblos—that is, the Hopi, Zuni, and Acoma groups (e.g., Moulard 1984)—may seem to be justified based on the iconography of their ceramics that have been well deciphered thanks to ethnographic research conducted since the nineteenth century. This ethnographic knowledge also applies an understanding of historic and contemporary Pueblo myths and legends. Many studies have shown these stories function in the same or similar form for many centuries, therefore Mimbres iconography may well be consistent with the religion and beliefs of the Ancestral Pueblo and Mimbres cultures (Moulard 1984:xviii), but others don't agree with this interpretation. Contextual analysis of ceramics at Mimbres sites and coinciding phases of the Ancestral Pueblo culture is extremely important.

Rock Art of The Mogollon Culture—The Jornada Style

Four main styles of rock art may be distinguished for Mogollon culture (e.g., Bostwick 2001; Schaafsma 1980):

- the red pictographic style (ca. 500–1250 AD), which was probably an evolution and continuation of the styles of hunter-gatherer communities from the Archaic period,
- the Chevelon Polychrome style (1100–1350 AD) from central-eastern Arizona,
- the Jornada style (ca. 1000 AD or earlier until 1450 AD)—found throughout much of the Rio Grande Valley, Tularosa Basin, and the Mimbres territory of New Mexico and reaching as far as southeast Arizona, northwest Texas, and northern Mexico (the state of Chihuahua where the Casas Grandes tradition developed),
- the Reserve style, present after 1000 AD mainly in the San Francisco and Tularosa River Basin in New Mexico, evidence of the Pueblo culture's influence on the Mogollon culture.

The Jornada style (figure 6.6) by far the most famous and widespread, includes both petroglyphs and paintings. The motifs are familiar from the iconography of artifacts from the Casas Grandes tradition, and may be a blend of hunting motifs on Mogollon/Mimbres ceramic iconography with elements of Mesoamerican agricultural symbolism (Bostwick 2001:424). Jornada rock art images include animals—mountain lions, jaguars (?), mountain sheep, snakes, fish, tadpoles, insects, birds (including parrots, thrushes, cuckoos, and eagles), and anthropomorphic figures with bodies richly decorated with step motifs, perhaps symbolizing clouds, zigzags, lines, and masks. There are numerous motifs of paw prints, claws of various animals, and human footprints. As a rule, zoomorphic figures are presented statically, with attributes such as antlers and feathers clearly marked, and bodies decorated with geometric motifs; snakes feature attributes of other animals, such as feathers and horns resembling some Mesoamerican deities.

The most spectacular representations of the Jornada style are anthropomorphic figures associated with certain Mesoamerican deities. These include rectangular or trapezoidal figures with large round eyes and a dot in the center, which are often interpreted as the personification of the rain god Tlaloc, and horned or feathered serpents associated with Quetzalcoatl. Representations related to water and clouds in the Mimbres valley may

Figure 6.6.   Iconography of Mogollon/Mimbres rock art from New Mexico and Texas featuring probable depictions of Mesoamerican deities: (a) snake motif with horns, a "horned serpent", a possible representation of one of the local images of Quetzalcoatl; (b–d) probable representations of the rain-god Tlaloc. Drawings by Magdalena Lewandowska.

have been an attempt to ensure rainfall in the event of adverse environmental changes and may also have marked out special places inhabited by deities or related to specific myths, or may have been associated with demarcating the territorial boundaries of individual communities and their properties, such as water sources. The entirety of this iconography, which includes masks as well as anthropomorphic and zoomorphic figures with the attributes of Mesoamerican deities, has a highly symbolic and most likely a religious overtone possibly associated with the *kachina* cult, which can be observed among late pre-Hispanic, historic and contemporary Pueblo societies (e.g., Schaafsma and Taube 2006; Thompson et al. 2014).

Looting and Protection of Mimbres Sites

The extraordinary iconography of Mimbres pottery has attracted treasure hunters who have been destroying many Mimbres sites for over a hundred years and plundering these richly decorated ceramics. From the late 1960s and early 1970s, the looting of Mimbres sites was systematic, often carried out with the use of bulldozers and other heavy equipment. At the time, individual Mimbres bowls fetched dizzying prices on the global black market which still tempts robbers to this day. The looting of Native American graves is unfortunately still practiced in many parts of the Southwest, though perhaps on a smaller scale. It is assumed that many of the beautifully decorated vessels of the Mimbres culture have been dispersed throughout private collections and are more numerous than those in official museum collections. As mentioned before, the number of Mimbres vessels known to be held in museums and private collections is now estimated at over 10,000 (Cordell 1997; Mimbres Pottery Images Digital Database—MimPIDD).

As with many cultures in the Southwest and throughout the United States, preserving Mimbres heritage and culture is challenging. Although many archaeological sites are protected in the United States by the 1906 Antiquities Act law and other regulations, these laws apply primarily to state or federal lands, with little or no reference to private land. However, some Mimbres pottery are protected as mortuary items under the protection of the 1990 Native American Graves and Repatriation Act (see chapter 1 for more detailed discussion on this topic).

In the 1960s and 1970s, the archaeological community began to address the extraordinary destruction caused by looters (often commissioned by private collectors). The Mimbres Foundation was established and led by Steven LeBlanc in the 1970s to protect sites and recover Mimbres cultural heritage. Later, the foundation sort of morphed into the Archaeological Conservancy and conducted protection plundered Mimbres sites to identify and document, to the extent possible, the archaeological context. The foundation also educates landowners about the need to protect cultural heritage, encourages cooperation with scientists, and raises funds from private and state sources for the purchase of Mimbres archaeological sites. Together with other organizations, the Mimbres Foundation has also begun purchasing important archaeological sites in other parts of the United States.

These efforts have aligned with significant changes in regulations to protect graves and cemeteries on private lands. Actions undertaken in recent decades also play a major role, consisting in the protection of Mimbres sites. In 2011 Archaeology Southwest, a nonprofit organization in Tucson, Arizona, protected three Mimbres sites—Mattocks, Janss, and Wheaton-Smith—and organized education for public and private sector institutions regarding the need to protect other Mimbres sites that are still endangered.

Expanding access to artifacts beyond museums walls opens knowledge to scientists around the world and to the general public. The Digital Archaeological Record (tDAR) is a repository of digital archaeological resources primarily from North America and other parts of the world featuring artifacts such as ceramics, GIS, and other data that has been collected from these sites. Michelle Hegmon of Arizona State University in Phoenix-Tempe and Steven LeBlanc of the Peabody Museum at Harvard University have created a database of 10,000 Mimbres ceramic vessels (Mimbres Pottery Images Digital Database—MimPIDD: https://core.tdar.org/collection/22070/mimbres-ceramic-database), with a version for general interest and one for professional use that is coded to guard against black-market access to artifacts.

The Border between Mesoamerica   7
and the Southwest
Casas Grandes and the Cultural Traditions of
Northern Mexico

⊞

S INCE THE ARCHAIC PERIOD and the beginning of agriculture, rich
traditions and cultures developed in the Mexican states of Sonora and
Chihuahua; human traces from the Paleoindian period may also be
found there (see chapter 3). In terms of the social structures, researchers
worldwide consider Casas Grandes (Paquimé) in the state of Chihuahua in
northern Mexico to be the largest and most complex site of the pre-Hispanic and protohistoric period in the Southwest. Unfortunately, these sites'
and cultures' location on the present-day border between Mexico and the
United States, has resulted in a dearth of knowledge about the peoples who
once lived here. As a vivid illustration of this research gap, more than one
hundred thousand sites have been documented and recorded in Arizona
(an area of 114,000 square miles) while just under two thousand have been
documented in the Mexican state of Sonora (an area of 184,000 square
miles) (Villalpando and McGuire 2017:381).

Historically, American archaeologists rarely conducted work in this
area due to, language barriers and other obstacles (e.g., Minnis and Whalen 2003; Whalen and Minnis 2017; Villalpando and McGuire 2017).
Meanwhile Mexican archaeologists have focused their research on traces
of the great Mesoamerican cultures and civilizations in central and southern Mexico. Such archeological neglect may often be the fate of regions
on the fringes of administrative and political borders, despite cultural and
civilizational changes that took place there.

Despite the sparse archeological data from this area of northern Mexico,
there is an abundance of ethnohistoric sources from the sixteenth and seventeenth centuries, starting with the journeys of Cabeza de Vaca, Francisco
Vásquez de Coronado (primarily by his chronicler Juan Jaramillo), and

Francisco de Ibarra, as chronicled by Baltasar de Obregón (e.g., Flint and Flint 2005; Hammond and Rey 1940). These records speak of numerous thriving communities in the region marked by extensive settlement systems located equidistant from each other in an organized network.

Apart from the cultural tradition of Casas Grandes with its main center, the Paquimé site, the archaeological sources do not confirm the complexity and social advancements suggested by Spanish sources (Doolittle 1988:2-4; Villalpando and McGuire 2017). The Spaniards may have, for example, "exaggerated" their reports for use as a propaganda tool, to encourage preparations for further expansion of this area by the Spanish Crown.

Cultural and social processes that took place in this region are interpreted differently by Southwestern archaeologists and by Mesoamerican researchers: the former perceive this area as part of the Southwest, while the latter look upon it from a central Mexican perspective as part of an area that was on the outskirts of great Mesoamerican civilizations but still within their orbit of influence (e.g., Cordell 2015; Spence 2000; Villalpando and McGuire 2017) and within the Gran Chichimeca region (Di Peso 1974).

Only since the beginning of the twenty-first century have researchers brought new interpretations of a more complex cultural picture of this area that was under the strong influence of other civilizational circles with its own rhythm of cultural changes. These more comprehensive and nuanced interpretations are based on collaborations that began in the 1980s between researchers from Mexico and the United States with the establishment of two branches of the National Institute of Anthropology and History (Instituto Nacional de Antropología e Historia—INAH), one based in Hermosillo, Sonora, and another in Chihuahua (Villalpando and McGuire 2017).

The spectacular architecture of Paquimé and its unique role in the cultural development of this part of North America led to its inclusion on UNESCO's World Cultural and Natural Heritage List as an Archaeological Zone in 1998. This site also falls under the protection of the State of Mexico and is managed by the National Institute of Anthropology and History in Mexico (Rodriguez Garcia 2003). Museo de las Culturas del Norte, has operated there since 1996.

Paquimé Site and the Casas Grandes Tradition

Scientists have long considered Paquimé to be one of the largest and most significant centers in the cultural development of the entire Southwest. The Casas Grandes tradition (Spanish for "Great Houses") with the eponymous site of Casas Grandes (Paquimé)[1] in the state of Chihuahua, Mexico, near the present-day border with the United States (figure 7.1) is often thought to have been a kind of trading post that mediated pre-Hispanic trade between the Southwest and Mesoamerica. Although located within the modern borders of Mexico, Casas Grandes seems to be more geographically and culturally related to the Southwest, albeit with strong

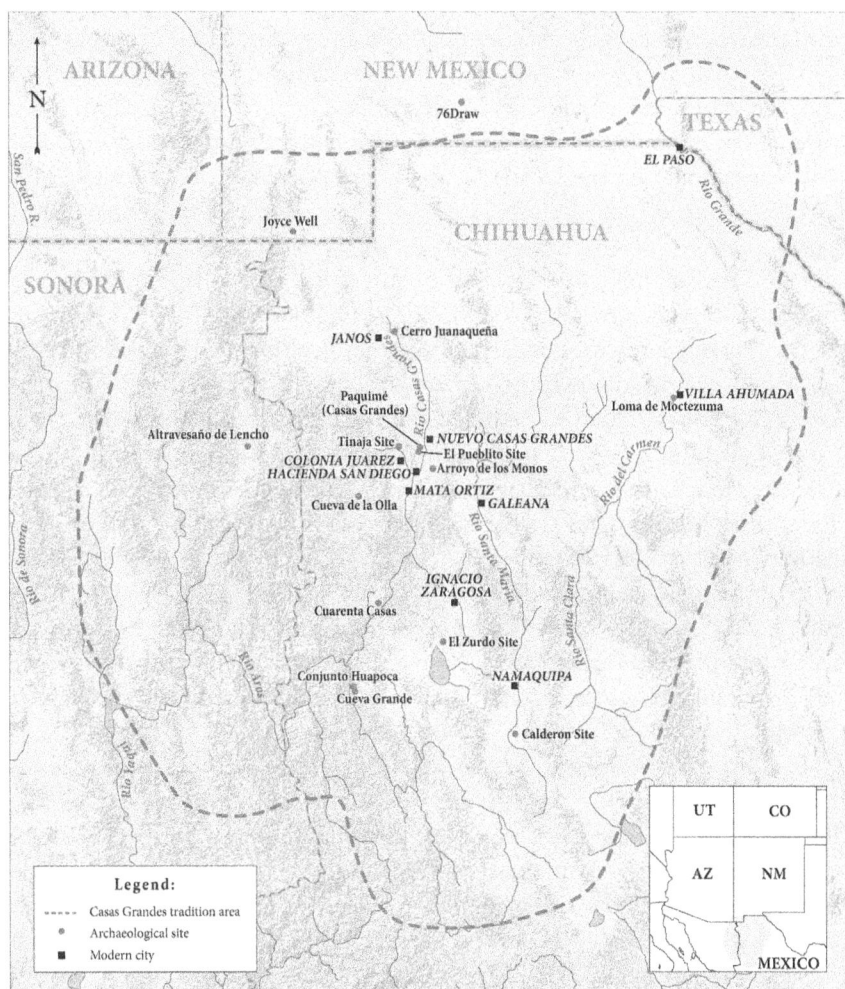

Figure 7.1.   Map showing the extent of the Casas Grandes cultural tradition with Paquimé site (after Minnis and Whalen 2003:2 and Villalpando and McGuire 2017). Compiled by Radosław Palonka and drawing by Michał Znamirowski.

Mesoamerican influences visible in the religious architecture and material culture (e.g., Di Peso 1974; Di Peso et. al 1974; Kelley 2000).

The impact of central Mexico on Paquimé is the most significant of any sites in the Southwest, including Ancestral Puebloan Great Houses in Chaco Canyon and the Hohokam and Mimbres societies. This influence is manifested in the architecture—site layout, platform mounds, ballcourts, colonnades in front of buildings, siting of buildings in relation to astronomical observations, and water management systems. Likewise these influences are also apparent in material culture, including imported metal objects such as bells made mainly of copper, clay spindle whorls (discs used to weight a spindle when spinning yarn), the breeding of parrots imported from the south, and ceramic and rock art iconography (e.g., Kelley 2000). Most of these similarities are linked to the central and northwestern areas of Mexico including the La Quemada, Zape, Alta Vista, and possibly Tula sites (e.g., Ericson and Baugh 1993; McGuire et al. 1994; Nelson 2002, 2006).

Paquimé became a Southwestern center after the collapse of the great centers of the Ancestral Pueblo, Mimbres/Mogollon and, to some extent, the Hohokam cultures. Researcher Stephen Lekson (e.g., Lekson 1999) sees Paquimé as a destination where Ancestral Puebloan elites from the Aztec and Salmon Ruins migrated after a previous move from Chaco Canyon. Paquimé, which lies at the intersection of trade routes, might have developed due to earlier interests of the Southwestern people, including the Mimbres/Mogollon societies, whose pottery is found in large quantities at the Casas Grandes site before its heyday (e.g., Kelley 2000). Without negating the relationship of this site with Mesoamerican civilizations and interactions and influx from the north (mainly from the world of the Pueblo culture), somewhat newer theories perceive its emergence and development as a manifestation of local evolution (e.g., Villalpando and McGuire 2017).

Paquimé was described as early as 1584 by Baltasar de Obregón, who may have been one of the first Europeans to visit and write about the site. His invaluable account describes a center that had been abandoned several decades before his visit. Paquimé made a great impression on de Obregón, who noted that the buildings were multistory (up to six stories high!), with numerous towers, and generally looked like a defensive town (Whalen and Minnis 2001a:27). Obregón (1584) devotes a great deal of attention to the architecture, describing walls of buildings made of adobe, stones, and wood, painted in various colors and patterns. He also mentions pointed columns supporting structures made of large wooden beams

Table 7.1. Chronology and Development of the Paquimé Site and Casas Grandes Tradition

Period	Phase	Traditional Dating	Alternative Dating (Newer)	Characteristic Features
Españoles	(no name) San Antonio	1660–1821 AD		– Western part of the Mimbres territory and Southern Arizona (Upper Gila Basin and Mimbres Valley) – Further cultural transformations and population migrations – Abandonment of the center and the subsequent influx of other communities
Late period (Tardío)	Period of contact with Spaniards Robles	1340–1660 AD	1450–1600(?) AD	– Similarities to the protohistoric cultures of southern Arizona and New Mexico – Cultural transformations and population migrations
Middle period (Medio)	Diablo Paquimé Buena Fe	1060–1340 AD	1200/1250–1450 AD	– The heyday of the Paquimé center and other sites in the region (extensive settlement network) – Public architecture shows influences from Mesoamerica and domestic architecture (Pueblo and Mogollon cultures) – Thriving trade – Probably conflicts and warfare
Early period (Viejo)	Perros Bravos Pilon Convento	700–1060 AD	700–1200/1250 AD	– Pithouses in a circular layout; at the end of the period, overground *jacal* structures appeared – Small, independent settlements, limited exchange and trade, no regional and supra-regional settlement structures

After Dean and Ravesloot 1993; Di Peso 1974; Whalen and Minnis 2001a, 2001b.

that were likely brought over considerable distances, as they had been in Chaco. Over the next century of sustained Spanish presence in the area, little more attention was paid to Paquimé.

Only pioneering archaeological and ethnographic research conducted mainly by Americans in the final decades of the nineteenth and early twentieth centuries yielded further descriptions of Paquimé, which had, in the meantime, suffered from the ravages of time and human interference. Of these American works, research by Adolph Bandelier at the end of the nineteenth century comes to the fore. Bandelier described segments of the site, divided the layout in terms of functions, and identified its role in long-distance trade based on finds of shells and copper artifacts and the high quality of the ceramics made there, which he compared to the Pueblo communities he had studied ethnographically. He made a field survey beyond the site itself, placing the Casas Grandes/Paquimé site at the center of a wider settlement network that dominated a fairly large area. Archaeological investigations (mainly surveys) were conducted in the 1930s involving excavations in other Casas Grandes culture sites, including those from Sierra Madre Occidental (Minnis and Whalen 2015).

Much of Bandelier's theory has since been confirmed by later research and significant studies conducted by the Joint Casas Grandes Project (JCGP) between 1958 and 1961 at Paquimé, and studies at nearby sites by Charles Di Peso from the American Amerind Foundation and Eduard Contreras Sánchez from the National Institute of Anthropology and History in Mexico (Di Peso 1974; Di Peso et al. 1974; Minnis and Whalen 2003). Thanks to excavations led by the Joint Casas Grandes Project, about one-third of the Paquimé, mostly focused on its western part where there is a large concentration of public architecture, has been examined. Since 1989, the Casas Grandes Regional Survey Project run by Michael Whalen and Paul Minnis has concentrated on the regional surroundings of Paquimé (e.g., Minnis and Whalen 2003, 2015; Whalen and Minnis 2017).

Charles Di Peso's excavations from the 1960s and 1970s still form the basis for studies conducted at Paquimé, but research carried out in recent years has slightly modified earlier interpretations. For example, estimates put the number of housing units at one thousand instead of Di Peso's proposed two thousand, which immediately translates as a reconstruction of the potential demography down from five thousand to one thousand inhabitants (Whalen and Minnis 2017). Newer theories also suggest that Casas Grandes was not just a center for trade, but as an important religious center, which is why so many exotic items and raw materials were accumulated there (Whalen and Minnis 2017:402-3).

Casas Grandes (Paquimé) (figure 7.2) is situated at the foot of the Sierra Madre Occidental and close to the headwaters of the Rio Casas Grandes (Casas Grandes River) and the town of the same name. Compared to other parts of the Southwest, the site is well irrigated and has very fertile soils.

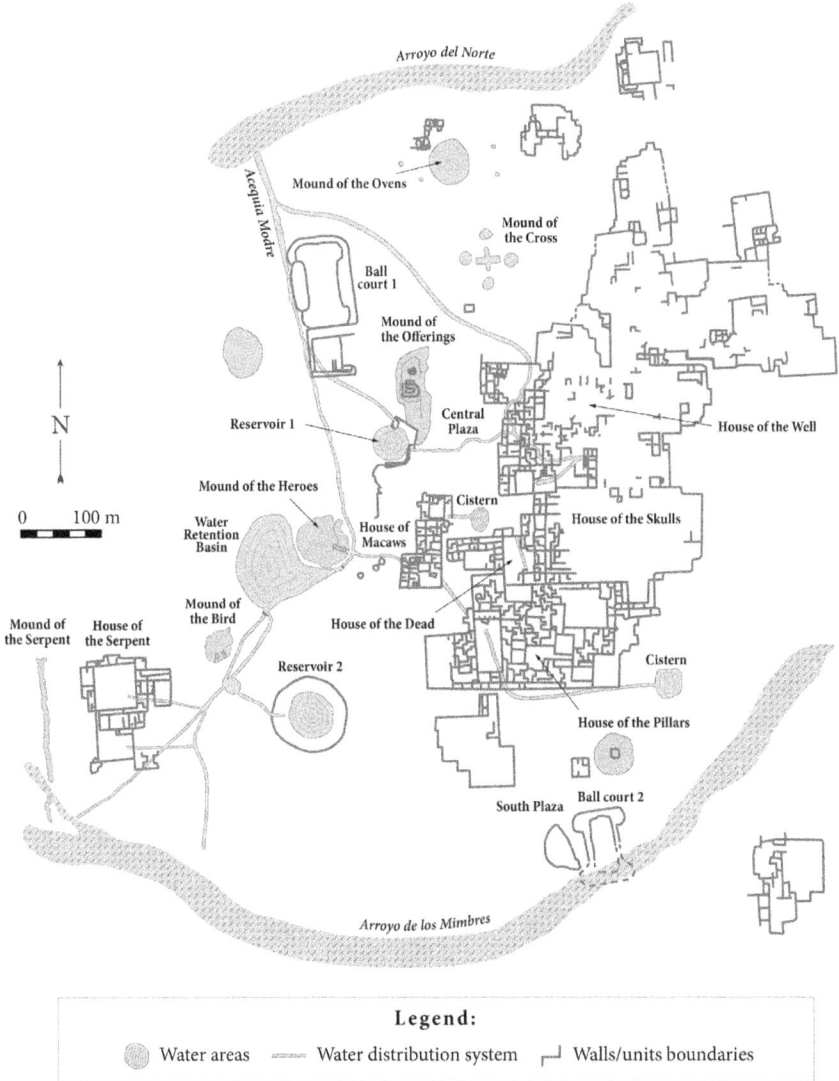

Figure 7.2.   Plan of the Casas Grandes (Paquimé) including the excavated part and the most important structures on the site (after Bradley 2000:Fig. 13.2). Compiled by Radosław Palonka and drawing by Michał Znamirowski.

It was not only these attributes that determined the center's blossoming; most of all its development was driven by specialization in the production and import of certain products—shells and copper in particular—as well as ceramics and parrot breeding and its mediation in wide-ranging trade, which is especially visible in the middle (Medio) period of Casas Grandes cultural development.

The site covers an area of thirty-six hectares and consists of more than two thousand residential, storage, and ceremonial facilities (though new estimates place this number closer to one thousand as mentioned above) which refer architecturally to the Pueblo and Mogollon cultures of the Southwest. Its complex system of water supply and irrigation, earthen mounds, plazas, and ritual ballcourts are typical of Mesoamerican cultures (Di Peso 1974; Di Peso et al. 1974; Kantner 2004; Whalen and Minnis 2017). Even today, the surviving ruins of buildings rise to a height of two and three floors (up to ten meters in height). At its apogee, the influence of Casas Grandes was felt in areas far removed from Paquimé itself— from northern Mexico to western Texas and southern Arizona and New Mexico.

The water distribution system included a five-kilometer canal that carried water from the permanent large stream of Ojo Varaleño (and later from the Rio Casas Grandes) and other streams to at least two reservoirs created by the residents of Paquimé (Minnis and Whalen 2015) (see figure 7.2). The water was then distributed through small canals to individual groups of buildings. One reservoir appears have been in operation when the system was slightly adapted, and a second reservoir was built. Other canals were created to drain rainwater from individual building groups. In Reservoir 2, one of two large reservoirs, a ceramic vessel (Playas Red type) containing a necklace made of turquoise beads and shells was found hidden in a rock bend; next to it were other necklaces and a bison or mountain sheep horn (Minnis and Whalen 2015:63, 80). This cache may have represented a foundation offering that was made after the reservoir was built and before it was put to use. A dozen or so shells of small Sonora mud turtles (*Kinosternon sonoriense* and *Kinosternon sp.*) were found in the water supply canals, and several others in the living quarters too. These turtles were probably brought from Sonora in Arizona, where they occur in their natural environment.

Though Hohokam irrigation canals were engineered in a similar way, they were mainly used to supply water to agricultural land, not to residential areas. The transportation of water to and from residential and ceremonial zones and farmland was unique to Paquimé and has no analogues

Figure 7.3.   Part of the Paquimé/Casas Grandes site. Photo by Wikimedia Commons.

in other cultures of the Southwest. In conjunction with monumental and public architecture, this water management system is evidence of a well-planned and well-maintained center that functioned for centuries.

The House of the Walk-In Well (Unit 8) in the center of the site and situated in one of the largest and highest clusters of buildings is a unique example of water management at Paquimé. Its location indicates that a limited group of people had access to it, most likely members of the political and religious elite. Under the building floor was a water source—a kind of well—that was undoubtedly associated with the rituals that were performed there. The upper part of a human skull was intentionally placed in the floor at the entrance of the building. On the steps or stairs leading down this "well" (nineteen steps in all), numerous items made of turquoise, shells, copper bells and small stone figurines were found (Di Peso 1974:2:356; Di Peso et al. 1974:4:377; Waller et al. 2018). Other artifacts include animal bones such as bison, lynx, antelope, and hawk, as well as several human bones; these may have been deposited there as offerings thrown into water (VanPool 2003:702). In several rooms within this grouping of buildings, huge quantities of jewelry made of shells and turquoise were uncovered, as well as other spectacular artifacts including some richly decorated ceramic vessels ("headless" anthropomorphic vessels), clay pipes and others.

The symbolism and significance of water was probably extremely important to Paquimé in terms of daily life as well as a deeper religious aspect likely including elements of the cult of Tlaloc, the Mesoamerican god of water and rain, often personifying a mountain of gushing water, and perhaps Quetzalcoatl (Di Peso 1974; Miller and Taube 1993; Schaafsma and Taube 2006). The elites probably supervised the construction of the system of irrigation canals to arable fields as well as water supplies, and distribution to the site itself.

Many examples of public and ceremonial architecture with references to Mesoamerica have been found in Paquimé and other sites of the Casas Grandes tradition. Three ballcourts similar to those typical of Mesoamerica including two I-shaped (figure 7.3b) and one T-shaped were discovered in Casas Grandes itself. All three ballcourts featured openings in the center, each covered with a stone, which may recall and symbolize the *axis mundi* from Mesoamerica (a symbolic passage from the underworld or a link between different worlds), and *sipapu* holes familiar from the Puebloan kivas. The latter symbolize the place of emergence of the Pueblo ancestors from the underworld. Three female burials were found below the surface of the T-shaped court. These appear to have been foundation offerings (possibly similar in function to the deposit under Reservoir 2) or sacrificial victims of a different kind. One of the women sacrificed had her right arm severed, which was later placed on her shoulders and back (VanPool 2003 after Di Peso 1974:414); the second sacrificed woman was pregnant, while the last had her feet removed (Minnis and Whalen 2015). In conjunction with human sacrifice, the ballcourts evoke parallels to cults and religious practices in Mesoamerica.

Ballcourts existed at other Paquimé-related sites in northern Mexico in the states of Chihuahua and Sonora. Also, more than two hundred ballcourts associated with the Hohokam culture of central and southern Arizona have been discovered so far. In relation to shapes, location and accompanying structures (for example mounds), those in the Casas Grandes tradition are the closest to those from the Mesoamerica. Research by Whalen and Minnis (Whalen and Minnis 1996) confirmed the presence of at least twelve ballcourts in the northern part of Chihuahua including at the Tinaja-Site 204. Most are located within thirty kilometers of Paquimé, and there are four courts at sites related to the Casas Grandes tradition in Sonora (Tinaja de Zorillo, El Ranchito, Son K: 4:24 OU and Son K: 4:72 OU), and two in New Mexico (Joyce Well and Timberlake Ruin). Ballcourts were usually located within the settlements, but they tend to be in their own separate space at least 50-70 meters apart from the groups of buildings. One exception is an I-shaped ballcourt located on the plaza inside a cluster of buildings at Paquimé which gives the impression that it functioned only for a group of people living in this complex of buildings and was not publicly accessible (Minnis and Whalen 2015; Whalen and Minnis 1996).

The most common type of ballcourt in the Casas Grandes tradition was the I-shaped ballcourt (figure 7.3b) sunk more than 1.3-1.6 meters. These were dug partially around to form a profile and small earthen and stone embankments. The letter I was either completely closed off or had empty spaces at the four corners. T-shaped courts, which were also fully closed off or only open in the corners, are much shallower, sometimes recessed only 15–21 centimeters into the ground. A third type of ballcourt was marked by two parallel lines formed by embankments or earthen-clay or stone mounds delineating their rectangular outline. The last type of ballcourt (not unanimously recognized as such by all researchers) is a rectangular or plaza structure made of piled stones, somewhat reminiscent of a historic animal corral. The area of the ballcourts in Paquimé and those related to this site varies from 244 to more than 1,000 square meters, with the largest I-shaped ballcourt in Paquimé measuring 19 × 50 meters. The dating of the courts places their construction and operation more or less in the Medio period—1200–1450 AD (Whalen and Minnis 1996:737–38).

The practice of establishing ballcourts undoubtedly arrived along with a whole "package" of influences from Mesoamerica. Given the lack of written sources, it is challenging to determine the function of these structures within the Casas Grandes communities. As in the case of the Hohokam ballcourts, it is not known whether they were used for ritual ball games, as they had been in Mesoamerica, or if their shapes were "imported" and their functions differed (e.g., Minnis and Whalen 1993, 2015; Whalen and Minnis 1996). In addition to ball games, they may have served as places of trade, meetings, and ceremonies as in theories proposed for the Hohokam ballcourts. Much more is known about the functions of Mesoamerican ballcourts due to Spanish sources, Mayan glyphs, and the discovery of rubber balls at several ball courts (although a small number of rubber balls have also been found at Casas Grandes).

Some ballcourts were adjoined by clay and stone platform mounds. The mound adjacent to the southern part of the largest I-shaped ballcourt in Paquimé features a stone-covered layer and at least one more mound on the long west side. There are eighteen mounds in Paquimé itself, including platform and figural mounds. One unusual grouping is comprised of five platform mounds alongside each other, one in the shape of an isosceles cross (Mound of the Cross), with four mounds in a circular layout at the extension of each arm of the cross, at a certain distance from them. This complex may have been associated with solstices and equinoxes, astronomical observations, and ceremonies and rituals connected with them (Minnis and Whalen 2015).

Additionally, two effigy mounds have been discovered—one 17 × 24 meters in the shape of a headless bird (Bird Mound) and the other 115 meters long, in the shape of a feathered and horned serpent (Snake Mound). A building was located on one platform mound in the southern part of the site, a somewhat uncommon practice in Paquimé (buildings on mounds). Another large mound measuring 55 × 40 meters (Mound of the Heroes), was located in the immediate vicinity of a huge pit used for baking agave hearts, which could highlight its role for the preparation of large amounts of food related to ceremonies and feasts for the general public.

Most examples of monumental, public, and ceremonial architecture (including the ballcourts, platform and effigy mounds) are located in the central and western parts of the site, while the "ordinary" residential and storage architecture is concentrated in the eastern part. Most structures in Casas Grandes are built from sun-dried adobe; stone was used, but mainly as a cladding for brick structures, similar to techniques used in central Mexico. Toward the end of Paquimé development, construction techniques became far poorer; often unprocessed or partially processed stones were used and fixed with clay or adobe mortar. Walls of buildings were about fifty-five to eighty-five centimeters thick with thicker walls in multistory and ceremonial buildings close to the central part of the site—(Di Peso et al. 1974). In addition to adobe, wooden beams were widely used in construction. Two types of residential architecture can be distinguished (Di Peso et al. 1974:4:198–202; Whalen and Minnis 2001b): one-story buildings forming groupings with entrances facing an internal courtyard, and multistory buildings creating larger architectural complexes facing inner and outer courtyards and plazas. Buildings were arranged in a plaza or rectangular layout and varied in size, ranging from a few to more than a hundred square meters, with most of the buildings surveyed being less than thirty square meters. Some buildings were erected according to an L-shaped plan or in irregular shapes in the form of polygons, the largest even having twelve sides.

Entrances and the doors between rooms were rectangular in shape, or—as in many Puebloan sites—T-shaped. Many buildings also had "standardized" architectural features, such as wall niches and types of platforms made of adobe set mainly in the corners. These seem to have been used for storing utensils and food rather than for sleeping (Whalen and Minnis 2001b:655). Hearths also varied in size and manner of execution, from simple round ones set in the floors of houses to larger, clayed fireplaces, and more elaborate hearths placed on small specially prepared adobe platforms.

Monumental and public architecture, a complex water distribution system that clearly illustrates the well-planned and coordinated construction of the site as a whole, and opulent burial furnishings indicate the presence of elites in Paquimé (e.g., Minnis and Whalen 1993; Waller et al. 2018). Skeleton burials at Casas Grandes are located under the floors of houses and in urns. Three examples of richly equipped burials may be found in sizeable urns located in the Mound of the Offerings and in a group of buildings in the northwest of this site, where the dead were placed in clay vessels in special burial chambers (sometimes several people in one chamber) with burial goods made of exotic raw materials including four million—weighing over two tons!—products from sea shells. An adjoining room contains a kind of T-shaped stone altar; this room led onto the ceremonial plaza, which was additionally surrounded by several open-air buildings. A carefully curated store of *metate* stones and deposits of items made of turquoise, shells, and other materials were also discovered in several houses, suggesting that such items were amassed, probably in the hands of a small group of people, for further distribution. This may indicate that Casas Grandes elites maintained control over local and long-distance trade with areas hundreds and thousands of kilometers away from this city-settlement.

Another opulently furnished burial (or, rather, burials) is Tomb 44-13 (Waller et al. 2018), consisting of two levels, where at least twelve people were buried. Seven people of high social status were buried on the lower level. Bioarchaeological analyses have revealed that they were very well nourished. The burials were equipped with many goods including richly decorated ceramics and objects made of exotic materials. Four stratigraphic layers related to these burials can be distinguished. In the first, two adult women were buried in a sitting position. In the second lay a man, probably the leader of the community, whose burial seems to be the most distinctive, and with him lay an adult woman with her head near the man's pelvis and her pelvis next to the male's skull. The next burial contained a woman lying on her right side, and the last of this layer is once again the burial of a man and a woman, where the man was additionally bestowed with goods rarely found elsewhere—objects that were likely ceramic drums, fragments of minerals, a sacrificed turkey and a type of pottery associated with the cult of the dead (the Black Ramos type), the woman's skull, along with numerous stone and shell beads, rests beside the man's arms (Waller et al. 2018:411–13).

On the upper level of Tomb 44-13, the dismembered remains of at least five people, mostly children or adolescents, were deposited along with numerous gifts, including shell jewelry and damaged hand drums. These people probably had a completely different status, and were, first and foremost, noticeably less well nourished, as indicated by bone analysis. The treatment of the bodies of these five people may indicate that they were sacrificed, while the marks on parts of the bones also perhaps points toward cannibalism, which, along with human sacrifice, may have been a part of the funeral rituals. It may have also been due to reinterment, as remains were sometimes disinterred and replaced. A myth that has survived in the oral tradition of the Tohono O'odham living today on the border between Arizona and Mexican Sonora refers to child sacrifice. The story speaks of a great flood that hit the earth. To thwart this disaster, a sacrifice of two boys and two girls chosen from each group of this tribe was made; according to these beliefs, they live in the underground world and therefore they should be remembered and commemorated (McIntyre 2008:18).

Construction of the grave described above included an earthen bench with a wooden structure, which indicates that it was possible to access after the dead had been placed there, probably in order to add further burials or to remove the remains of people buried there so that they might "participate" in religious ceremonies. Information on these and other richly endowed burials and human sacrifices in Paquimé the presence of monumental architecture, and other data suggest that Casas Grandes society was extremely hierarchical, and power could have been passed down from one generation to another, rather than acquired new leaders.

Agriculture formed the basis of the Casas Grandes economy, with the cultivation of corn, beans, squash, agave, cotton, and other crops. Paquimé lies in a well-watered valley, with a microclimate that allowed for a slightly longer growing season than elsewhere. Artificial irrigation that supplied farmlands with water from canals was of key importance for this agricultural economy. Two types of farming fields may be distinguished according to where they are located: in river valleys or in higher areas (Minnis and Whalen 2015); the former was most likely the basic type of arable land for the whole culture and Paquimé itself, but some groups of plants were cultivated together according to altitude; and so corn, beans, and cotton were grown together in the lower parts of the valley, while corn and agave were cultivated in higher locations. A very interesting fact is the fact that in several sites, about two kilometers from Paquimé itself, chili (*Capsicum annuum*) is confirmed to have been cultivated—most likely the only such example in the Southwest. Additionally, Casas Grandes tradition together with Hohokam culture are the only known pre-Hispanic southwestern cultures to grow barley (*Hordeum pusillum*).

The second type of agriculture involved the establishment of farmlands on terraces and small water supply canals on the slopes of hills and in the Sierra Madre Occidental itself, a technique that was common in other cultural traditions of today's Chihuahua. Agave was among the crops grown; the size of the farmland in the higher areas is about 0.8 hectares, while several very large farmlands with an area of about 10 hectares each have been confirmed to have existed, suggesting that some fields belonged to chiefs or group leaders (Minnis and Whalen 2015). The Paquimé people's diet of corn, agave and other plants was supplemented by food obtained from foraging wild plants and hunting animals—mainly deer, antelopes and even bison and, to a lesser extent, smaller animals such as rabbits, evidence of which are more often found at smaller sites.

Paquimé and the Casas Grandes Culture Settlement System

Paquimé was by far the largest and most complex site in the pre-Hispanic and protohistoric period in northern Mexico, and one of the largest in the Southwest. In addition to its trade dimension, this site had an extremely important ceremonial and religious significance. It was part of a wider Casas Grandes cultural tradition whose sites created a settlement network around Paquimé. To this day, disputes persist among researchers as to the actual role of Casas Grandes/Paquimé site and the potential extent of its influence (e.g., Minnis and Whalen 2015; VanPool 2003:701; Minnis and Whalen 2003). The domination or direct "sovereignty" of Paquimé is said to have extended within a radius of thirty kilometers, along with a much larger area of indirect influence, as far as what is now southern Arizona, New Mexico, and western Texas.

The people of the Casas Grandes tradition built many structures, possibly of a religious nature on Cerro Moctezuma hill five kilometers west of Paquimé. These included a spiral stone construction and a circular structure (*atalaya*) that could have been a ritual building or a signaling station. The hill is visible at least twenty kilometers away from three different valleys, and some researchers estimate that similar structures on other hills would have allowed signals to be transmitted for distances of at least seventy-five kilometers (Pailes 2017 after Swanson 2003). Data from other sites supports the theory of a long-range signaling system in this part of the present-day Chihuahua.

Cerro Moctezuma contains a cave, a possible water reservoir, a large agave oven, cultivated terraces and numerous trails leading to the summit where the settlement of El Pueblito, is located. El Pueblito consists of several dozen adobe and stone buildings (stone as a building material is rather unusual for this region), fragments of free-standing walls and what is perhaps a defensive wall on the eastern side of the site. According to Todd Pitezel (Minnis and Whalen 2015; Pitezel 2003, 2007), this entire site was hugely important for the ceremonies and rituals of Paquimé residents (and perhaps surrounding settlements) and possibly for transmitting signals from the top of the hill and communicating with other sites. It seems likely that El Pueblito was a pilgrimage destination from the surrounding settlements.

So far, several hundred smaller sites have been identified in the area within seventy to a hundred kilometers from the Paquimé (Minnis and Whalen 2003). These sites are generally small and located near watercourses and fertile areas. They were once inhabited by farming communities that cultivated corn, agave (its fibers also used for weaving), and other crops using a variety of techniques including artificial irrigation. No public or monumental architecture has been discovered at most of these sites, although some had ballcourts. Larger settlements were the Galeana site to the east of Paquimé, in Santa Maria valley, and the Tinaja site (Site 204), fifteen kilometers to the west at the foot of the Sierra Madre mountains, where about two hundred houses, a large ballcourt, and several agave ovens were found. Radiocarbon dates indicate that it operated between around 1270–1430 AD (Minnis and Whalen 2015).

Research by Paul Minnis and Michael Whalen (e.g., Minnis and Whalen 2015) shows that apart from Cerro Moctezuma, there are no sites with public or monumental architecture, traces of parrot breeding, or large agave pits within a radius of ten to fifteen kilometers of Paquimé. Such sites only occur around fifteen to thirty kilometers from Casas Grandes, but without signs of hierarchical settlement organization that was the case in Paquimé. According to Minnis and Whalen, this demonstrates that the immediate sovereignty or supremacy of Paquimé extended up to thirty kilometers, the distance of a day-long round trip from Paquimé, though limited influences may have extended further afield. The exception is Tinaja, where there is a large and carefully constructed ballcourt and the only platform mound, apart from Paquimé, in the entire Casas Grandes tradition.

Although the vast majority of the Casas Grandes community lived on the plains and in river valleys, there are some settlements in the spectacular rock shelters and caves in the Sierra Madre Occidental. These settlements used the nearby, lower river valleys for agriculture and fishing, and built

Figure 7.4.   Cliff dwelling of Cueva de la Olla located roughly fifty kilometers southwest of Paquimé. Photographs by Paul Minnis and Michael Whalen.

terraces for crops on the slopes of hills and mountains. Pine and other woods were obtained from the surrounding mountains and used for constructing buildings.

Some settlements feature one and two-story buildings in rock shelters, similar to those built by the Ancestral Puebloans in the Mesa Verde region on the border of Utah and Colorado. Like most buildings in the Casas Grandes tradition, these were made of adobe. Large storage buildings shaped like ollas or mushrooms, which may be compared to modern-day silos, were characteristic of these cliff settlements. Some storages were very large, at times taller than the surrounding buildings. The houses often had T-shaped doors, a direct reference to Paquimé and the Pueblo culture. Examples of such sites include Cuarenta Casas (Forty Rooms) approximately ninety kilometers southwest of Casas Grandes, the settlement of Cueva de la Olla (Olla Cave) fifty kilometers from Paquimé, and the sites of Madeira Conjunto Huapoca and Cueva Grande. A ballcourt has been found at least one such site (Gamboa and Pío 2003).

The Casas Grandes cultural tradition associated with Paquimé also spread throughout the state of Sonora in the Bavispe, Bacerac and Huachinera basins, on the western side of the Sierra Madre Occidental. Shifts in Casas Grandes architecture and settlement models on the western side of Sierra Madre at the turn of the tenth century AD went hand in hand with changes in material culture including the appearance of Red-on-Brown ceramics in the Carretas Polychrome style. It is worth noting that some theories claim that Carretas pottery spread from Sonora to Chihuahua and not the other way around. This may be evidence that some of the Sonoran part of the Casas Grandes tradition arose as a separate variant within this cultural tradition or split quickly from its main section on the eastern side of Sierra Madre in Chihuahua (Villalpando and McGuire 2017).

One of the main determinants of Paquimé's development was long-distance trade and exchange. The two most important exotic items traded were parrots imported from northern Mexico and possibly the tropical forests of southern Mexico and the border between Mexico and Guatemala, and shells obtained mainly from the Gulf of California. During excavations, researchers have uncovered four million beads and semi-finished shells in just two rooms at Casas Grandes. Other trade items include copper bells and other copper products, turquoise, and turkeys mass-bred in Paquimé; products characteristic of the Great Plains, including bison skins, have also been found. Like turkeys, parrots were most likely obtained for ritual purposes because of their rich plumage. In Paquimé, parrots appear in large numbers in the iconography of ceramics (as in the Mimbres culture); in Casas Grandes and related sites, a fairly large group of parrot-shaped zoomorphic vessels or with some attributes of this bird (usually head and beak) were discovered, usually decorated in the so-called Ramos Polychrome style. Paquimé is known to have had numerous cages or pens made of clay having characteristic stone hoops with an entrance hole in the center and pivots that blocked these entrances. They were located within building groups in fairly large inner courtyards. Such pens existed in other sites in the Southwest including in Pueblo Bonito in Chaco Canyon.

The number of turkey skeletons found at Paquimé is almost equal to the number of parrots, showing that their role was similar, although their population varied depending on the period (McKusick 2007); for example, 175 parrot skeletons and only 16 turkey skeletons were discovered for the period of the twelfth and the turn of the thirteenth century AD, after which a hiatus in parrot imports is recorded. From around 1200 to 1275 AD there are practically no known parrot skeletons throughout the Southwest—only 5 skeletons at Paquimé compared to 174 turkeys from that time. Then at the turn of and during the fourteenth century, over 300 parrot skeletons were found at Paquimé in comparison to 100 turkey skeletons.

In the Pueblo culture of Chaco Canyon and the Mimbres culture in the tenth, eleventh, and the early twelfth century AD, we find the largest number of parrot skeletons and representations on ceramics; the latter in Mimbres pottery (e.g., McKusick 2007). Another wave of interest in parrots occurred in the twelfth century AD at the Wupatki site in Arizona. A third wave came during the development of Pueblo settlements on the Rio Grande in New Mexico and the Casas Grandes site in Chihuahua at the turn of the fourteenth century AD and in the fourteenth century itself.

A total of five hundred parrot skeletons were found at Paquimé, which is equal to all or even more than all other parrots found at hundreds of Pueblo and Mogollon/Mimbres sites (Crown 2016; McKusick 2007; Minnis and Whalen 1993). Although conducted on a small sample, DNA tests on several parrot skeletons from Grasshopper Pueblo in Arizona, Cameron Creek in the Mimbres valley and Salmon Ruins in northern New Mexico indicated that the skeletons were red macaws, also known as the Scarlet macaw (*Ara Macao*), whose natural habitats are in the Huasteca region of Tamaulipas on the Gulf of Mexico, in southeastern Mexico, and further south at the Mexico-Guatemala border (Bullock 2007).

The scarlet macaw sporadically appeared in the Southwest before the Casas Grandes flourished and may have become a popular import commodity for this area. Notably all these birds passed through the Casas Grandes center (McKusick 2007) which controlled their distribution to other Southwest areas. This coincides with other data that only about 20 percent of the parrots imported into Casas Grandes were military macaws (*Ara militaris*) from northern Mexico and therefore much closer to the Southwest or even within its boundary, the rest being mostly scarlet macaws from much farther south of Mexico; the proportions from Paquimé correlate to data from other Southwestern sites.

Ramos Polychrome Style and the Ceramic and Rock Art Traditions of Northern Mexico

Ceramics from the Viejo period (700–1060/1200 AD) were characterized by their brown surface and sometimes cream, red, and black, depending on the firing technique and the degree of exposure to smoke. They were both undecorated and decorated, and sometimes carved, engraved, polished, smoothed or left with a rough clay surface (VanPool et al. 2008:60–64). Vessels were decorated with painted geometric designs of the Black-on-Red type, and in Red-on-Brown. Decoration consisted of straight lines, spirals and triangles forming certain motifs, often triangular fields that repeat around the vessel. There are several types of Red-on-Brown ceramics (Rakita and Raymond 2003; VanPool et al. 2008:63–64), such as Madeira, Anchondo, Leal, Pilon, Fernando, and Mata. Additionally, more types of unpainted ceramics that are not diagnostic for chronology and remain relatively unchanged over time may be distinguished both for the Early (Viejo) and the Middle (Medio) period.

The most characteristic polychrome pottery, often referred to as the Casas Grandes or Chihuahua polychrome styles, originates from the Medio period (1200–1450 AD). There are many types distinguished, including the most famous and recognizable Ramos Polychrome style. These vessels were decorated with black or red designs on a cream or brown-reddish background. The designs include geometric decorations including complex combinations of lines, step motifs, and spirals (figure 7.5) as well as anthropomorphic and zoomorphic motifs including parrots and owls, dogs, rabbits, badgers, frogs, snakes, lizards, and fish, as well as larger animals like mountain sheep. There are also numerous representations of human/animals, for example, the bird-man motif; this hybrid may be identified with a shaman guided to the afterlife by a bird (e.g., Powell 2006). The ceramic admixture contains sand, finely crushed rocks, and mica particles. The vessels typical of the Medio period usually have painted decorations running in bands around the body of the vessel; these bands are cut in two or four places to form two or four horizontal decorative parts. There are also numerous effigy pottery (figure 7.5), and miniature vessels.

While the pottery forms, production technology, and the iconography appearing on them were quite "standardized" (e.g., Woosley 2001:172), the interpretation of the representations of this iconography presents nu-

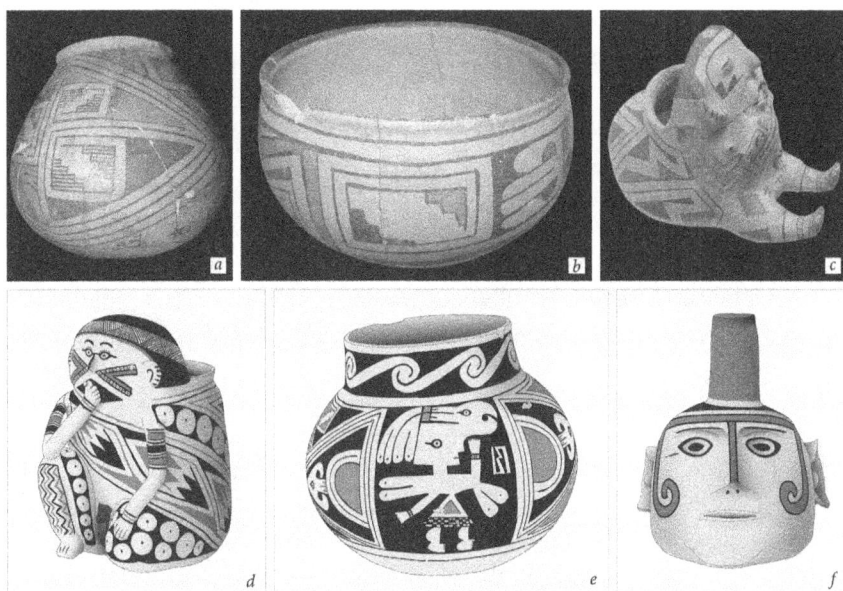

Figure 7.5.   Ramos Polychrome pottery with geometric iconography (a–b) and effigy (anthropomorphic) pottery and pottery with anthropomorphic motifs (c–f). Photographs by Radosław Palonka and drawings by Katarzyna Ciomek.

merous challenges. The most common decorative motifs include geometric representations such as lines, zigzags, triangles, circles, squares, checkerboards, and spirals, as well as S-shaped and V-shaped motifs. Some symbols may form more complex motifs, for example checkboards (white and black squares) around the wrist to create bracelets, but individual motifs can also form entire human and animal figures. It seems that some geometric motifs on pottery are similar or the same as the designs on fabrics, and some can be the representations of clouds and rain ("stepped" motifs and triangles) or lightning (zigzags), which is interpreted in a similar way when it comes to the symbolism of the Pueblo and other Southwestern cultures.

One curious motif is a white square with a black outline and a black dot inside either in a single representation or in groups and grids of such connected representations. This is interpreted as a motif symbolic of corn or blue and green stones; and can also be interpreted as related to serpents, clouds, rain, lightning, and the fertility of the earth (Webster et al. 2006).

Another motif likely directly related to Mesoamerican iconography and mythology is the depiction of snakes with various attributes: feathers, horns, squares with dots. Researchers often associate the depiction of a feathered serpent with Quetzalcoatl, one of the most important deities in the Mesoamerican pantheon (e.g., Schaafsma 1980; Woosley 2001:173–74). In many communities of the Southwest and Mesoamerica, the serpent was a symbol of the fertility of the earth, the underworld, death, as well as rebirth. In addition, depictions of "feathered snakes" may also bear corn symbolism (e.g., Taube 2000; Schaafsma 1980; Webster 2007)

Some Casas Grandes pottery forms are typical only in this tradition. This applies to figural vessels with a hooded effigy or double bowls. Although typical of the Casas Grandes tradition, these vessels are found far beyond their territory in the Sierra Madre Occidental on the Sonoran side, in southern Arizona, mid-southern New Mexico, and western Texas, where they had been transported (e.g., Kelley 2000). It is sometimes assumed that the beginning of the production of polychrome vessels in the Casas Grandes tradition may be associated with influences from the north, from the Mimbres societies (although there are still many chronological doubts related to the state of research on this topic on the Mexican side). However, it is possible that these communities had similar perceptions of many phenomena and shared similar belief systems and rituals, which translated directly into the similarities in their iconography.

Some figural motifs on Casas Grandes ceramics may be associated with images of shamans and with a belief system related to shamanism. This would align the religion and beliefs of the people of this cultural tradition more with Mesoamerican belief systems beginning with the Olmecs than with the cults and beliefs existing in the pre-Hispanic period in the Southwest (VanPool 2003); shamanism was also present in South America. Of course, shamanism also occurred in some form in the Southwest as evidenced by the iconography of the Mimbres culture and the rock art of the region, including Archaic Barrier Canyon anthropomorphic style, but shamanism has been insufficiently researched. Shamans could have been the leaders of a given community, but their main role was to mediate contact with the supernatural world (possibly when the shaman went into a trance), heal the sick, predict the future when it came to planning hunting and wars, forecast (and, in a way, "steer") the weather, and explain past events. In an article published in *American Antiquity*, Christine S. VanPool (VanPool 2003) even suggests that the shamanistic system was so developed in the Casas Grandes community that shamans were priests in an anthropological sense, exercising actual power, along with secular leaders, over society. The manifestation of the presence and dominant influence of shamans/priests on the functioning and perhaps the emergence of this culture is visible in the rich iconography of its ceramics.

Representations on Casas Grandes ceramics that may be associated with shamanism include painted iconography depicting dancing or "flying" anthropomorphic characters and bird-man figures, as well as effigy pottery in the shape of kneeling men smoking short clay pipes (see figure 7.5d). Dancing figures (perhaps in a trance) often wear distinctive headgear in the shape of birds or snakes with horns (the horned rattlesnake motif). This iconography includes characteristic body decoration such as small white circles with a black dot in the middle, and a checkered motif with or without a dot in the middle—both motifs are most often found on the legs and chest—and "patches" on clothes, along with stepped motifs, triangles, and others. Pipe representations indicate ritual smoking, which was practiced by many pre-Hispanic native communities in the Southwest, including in the historic period. Today it is still practiced—for example, by Pueblo people—as an element of ceremonies and rituals. These images may show phases of transformation and the so-called shaman's flight to the other world (VanPool 2003:697–99) to bring back with him the answers and solutions for important issues (mentioned above). The bird accompanying the shaman (often a parrot in the case of Casas Grandes) would guide the shaman's journey between the earthly and the supernatural world; at some point, the shaman loses his human form and himself becomes someone from the supernatural world.

The particular phases of shamanistic transformation and journey to the world beyond in the iconography of the Ramos pottery may include (e.g., VanPool 2003 and other sources): (a) the beginning of the trance depicted, for example as a seated shaman smoking tobacco, datura (a hallucinogenic in the nightshade family), or peyote (a hallucinogenic cactus) in the earthly world; (b) the second stage shows the Shaman's slow "exit" from the earthly world represented by shedding elements of clothes and face decorations and sometimes with arms/wings prepared to flap; (c) the shaman slowly transforms into a supernatural form, a bird, or horned figure; (d) and finally the shaman as a man with a bird's head, in this case a parrot, completing the transformation such that he completely loses his human form and turns into a supernatural being.

The iconography of pottery from Paquimé and sites related to the Casas Grandes tradition provides us with a host of information about the appearance and clothes of people at that time. Elements of clothing can be distinguished which, apart from the anatomical features that are sometimes shown, determine gender (VanPool et al. 2017). Representations of intricately arranged headbands and sandals were typical for men, who seem to be presented in more "sophisticated" types of clothing, although this may be due to the fact that a large proportion of these images showed them during certain rituals that required special "costumes" and regalia. Women were depicted with belts or aprons arranged horizontally on their hips, relatively in the company of birds, and with symbolism representing clouds and the fertility of the earth.

Some of the depictions of jewelry such as armlets or jewelry worn on the arms, hands and ears were appropriate for men and women, although some differences in the way they are displayed can be distinguished. Anthropomorphic vessels representing men usually show figures seated with knees tucked under the chin or reaching to the shoulders or one leg tucked up. Women are seated with straightened legs and sometimes holding a child or a bowl belly-high or on the head.

Anthropomorphic vessels most likely present people from the Casas Grandes community who played important roles, such as shamans. Women and men often have painted faces—usually lines or dots arranged in patterns made with black paint for women, and black and red for men—interpreted as tattoos or paintings. These and other decorations may indirectly testify to a certain hierarchy, rank, and position in society. This iconography refers to decorations and similar clothes and motifs occurring both in the cultures of the Southwest (Mimbres culture) and in northern Mexico (e.g., in the Tarahumara/Rarámuri communities), and applies not only to the pre-Hispanic period, but also to the continuation of a similar "fashion" in the historic period (VanPool et al. 2017; Woosley 2001).

Located several kilometers south of Casas Grandes, Arroyo de los Monos is an example of a rock art site created by the Casas Grandes people and is probably the most well-known rock art site in the Chihuahua state. It includes anthropomorphic and geometric petroglyphs placed into rocks and free-standing boulders, and representations of the horned serpent, also known from several other sites of the Casas Grandes tradition (O'Connor and Parks 2012). Another exemplary site is the cliff dwelling of Cueva de la Olla with paintings and sites in Valle de las Cuevas (Cave Valley), featuring geometric and anthropomorphic paintings. The state of research on rock art in this region and, in some cases its degree of preservation (especially paintings in overhangs and rock shelters), remains sparse. At least two clusters of petroglyphs near Paquimé have been found on the road leading to the Cerro Moctezuma summit. Images include concentric circles, other geometric motifs, and depictions of parrots.

Other Cultures and Traditions of Sonora and Chihuahua

Paquimé and the entire Casas Grandes tradition is a manifestation of one of the traditions of the northern areas of Mexico (the states of Sonora and Chihuahua) that developed since the end of the Archaic period. The size of Casas Grandes with Paquimé at its center, and its role were special, but other communities emerged in the territory of what is now northern Mexico, and shared the cultural features of the Southwest and Mesoamerica while participating in and mediating the complex trade system between the two large areas.

In the first centuries AD, most communities inhabiting today's states of Sonoran and Chihuahua fully embraced agriculture—farming of corn, squash, beans, and agave that is characteristic of this region—and settlements were concentrated on rivers and streams. For this period and until the arrival of the Spanish, six major cultural traditions have been distinguished in this area: Casas Grandes as described previously, Costa Central (Middle Coast), Trincheras, Río Sonora, Huatabampo, and Serrana (Pailes 2017; Villalpando 2000; Villalpando and McGuire 2017) (figure 7.6).

Río Sonora Tradition

The majority of northeastern Sonora was dominated by the Río Sonora tradition that developed between the Sierra Madre Occidental and the San Miguel and Yaqui Rivers and the border between Mexico and the United States (Arizona) (figure 7.6). In the period between 200 and 1000 AD, areas in the basin of much of the Sonora River witnessed a hiatus and settlement void (Doolittle 1988; Villalpando and McGuire 2017:391). Later came the Temprana phase (1000–1200 AD) with characteristic pithouses and brown ceramics decorated with imprints from textiles and engravings. The Transitional phase (1200–1350 AD) was characterized by aboveground constructions whereby the buildings were usually constructed of adobe and featured stone foundations, most often made of river pebbles, in a plaza layout. The last phase (Tardía phase: 1350–1550 AD) saw an increase in settlements and the presence of public architecture including plazas.

In the historic period, the area of the Rio Sonora tradition was still inhabited by numerous Opata communities. Estimated to have numbered about seventy thousand in population in the sixteenth/seventeenth century, these communities occupied large settlements/towns and were connected by a network of irrigation canals spread over a dozen Sonora rivers. Various theories identify the Opata as most possible direct heirs of the

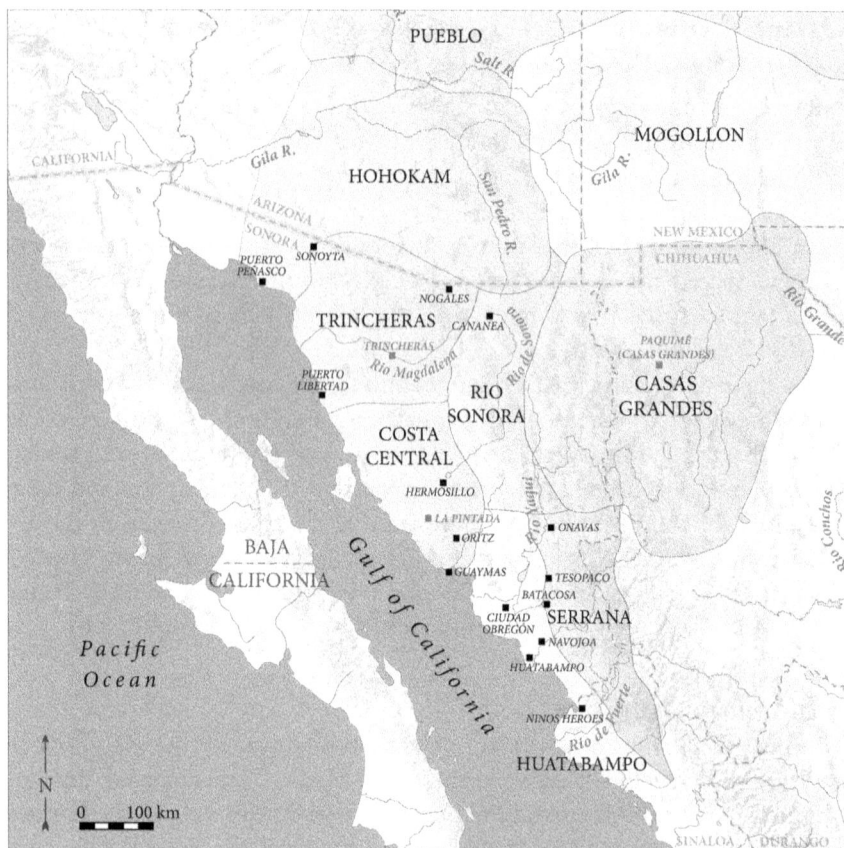

Figure 7.6.   Cultural traditions of Sonora and Chihuahua during the development of agriculture and before the arrival of the Europeans (after Pailes 2017:Fig. 3; Villalpando 2000:Fig. 14.1; Villalpando and McGuire 2017:Fig. 18.1). Compiled by Radosław Palonka and drawing by Michał Znamirowski.

Casas Grandes tradition who are thought to have moved farther west after the fall of this tradition, or as a cultural mix of the Casas Grandes and Rio Sonora traditions (Villalpando and McGuire 2017:391). These communities were decimated by the Spaniards in numerous wars.

Trincheras Tradition

From around five hundred AD, the Trincheras cultural tradition incorporated communities in the basin of the Altar, Magdalena, and Concepción Rivers, and seasonally on the Pacific coast. The purpose of the coastal strip centered on the acquisition of seashells from which jewelry was made and which were later traded. During this period, funeral rituals gradually changed, and cremation was practiced more frequently than skeletal burials, a similar process that can be observed further north in the Hohokam culture. The two successive periods in the development of this culture are the Atil phase (700–1000 AD) and the Altar phase (1000–1300 AD) (Villalpando and McGuire 2017). The pottery became more sophisticated in the Atil phase—red slip and purple decorative motifs obtained from hematite among others, were applied to the brown vessels typical of earlier times. In addition to agriculture, turkeys and dogs were domesticated.

In the Atil phase, the Trincheras people began building types of stone corral pens on the tops of volcanic hills for herding animals. In the Altar phase, settlements were located on the peaks, slopes, and terraces of these hills, hence the name of this type of site, *cerros de trincheras* (closed trench), which is characteristic of the landscape of the Arizona and Sonora border and also occurred in the Hohokam culture and the Rio Sonora and Casas Grandes traditions; Fish et al. 2007; Villalpando and McGuire 2017). Examples of such sites that are at least partially studied sites include Cerro de Trincheras, Tío Benino and La Hormiga.

Archaeologists have distinguished a settlement model consisting of *cerros de trincheras* sites located on isolated hills equidistant from each other and communities consisting of pithouses located in river valleys in the middle Magdalena River basin and the lower reaches of the Altar River. Suzanne and Paul Fish (Fish et al. 2007) claim that perhaps the inhabitants of these river valley settlements only used the *cerros de trincheras* sites on the hills seasonally and ritually. Other theories claim that the terraced structures of the hills served a defensive function and provided shelter for people from settlements in the river valleys (Villalpando and McGuire 2017).

The next phase of the Trincheras tradition was the Cerros phase dated from 1300–1450 AD, which produced the largest known and best-studied *cerros de trincheras* site of the same name. Archaeological research was carried out there by researchers from INAH in Sonora in 1991, 1995-1996 and 2007-2012; today it is probably the only archaeological site in the state of Sonora with a museum and an educational trail open to tourists. Covering an area of about a square kilometer, the Cerro de Trincheras site is comprised of nearly 900 terraces which were able to accommodate from 1,000 to 2,000 people (Fish et al. 2007; Villalpando and McGuire 2017). It would appear that this concentration of people in one place may have been a manifestation of the migration of the Trincheras tradition under pressure from the Hohokam culture to the north.

Alternately the move may have been the result of some of the society becoming wealthier and the emergence of a social elite, a theory that is confirmed by evidence. Three-quarters of the terraces at the Cerro de Trincheras site were used for buildings, with the highest terraces (those closest to the heavens) inhabited by the elite. Many raw materials and exotic items found in these houses include parrot skeletons, polychrome-decorated pottery and clay pipes likely imported from Paquimé. Plants including large crops of agave were grown below the residential terraces at the very bottom of the hill. The lowest terraces above the cultivated plots served as a ceremonial plaza—La Cancha, as it is called. Terraces above La Cancha were inhabited by weavers and craftsmen who made tools and objects from stones and flints; higher still were terraces for craftspeople who specialized in manufacturing shells. The uppermost part of the hill was walled with only three entrances; inside this limited space were housing facilities and buildings of a storage and ceremonial character; the highest spiral-shaped ceremonial structure is called El Caracol. At the highest point of the hill are two V-shaped structures formed of naturally lying stones that were erected, undoubtedly for astronomical observations; one was related to the summer, and the other to the winter, solstice (Villalpando and McGuire 2017).

These traces indicate that the settlement of Cerro de Trincheras traded mainly with the Casas Grandes center that thrived east of the Trincheras tradition, but there are no major signs that they also engaged in trade with the Hohokam culture. The existence of extensive trading may also be proved by the burials. Cremation prevailed as a funeral rite at the Cerro de Trincheras, and many artifacts have been found in the urns where the remains of the deceased were kept, including items made of shells, turquoise, stone, and bone pendants, and even a few copper bells.

Osteological studies clearly show that one urn could contain the remains of more than one person. As a result of rescue research conducted between 2007–2012, 144 urns with ashes and remains were discovered along with a crematorium zone about half a kilometer away, where human corpses were burned. These encompass forty-three different spots in this area (Villalpando and McGuire 2017). The urns were placed in shallow tombs that sometimes contained older urns, suggesting that the tombs were marked on the surface or that the urns themselves protruded partially above the ground to mark the site. The cemetery in Cerro de Trincheras is located at the foot of the hill outside the residential area but situated so as to be clearly visible to the residents, as was the entire process of cremation and burial which seems to suggest a strong relationship between the living and the dead that was reflected in their burial practices.

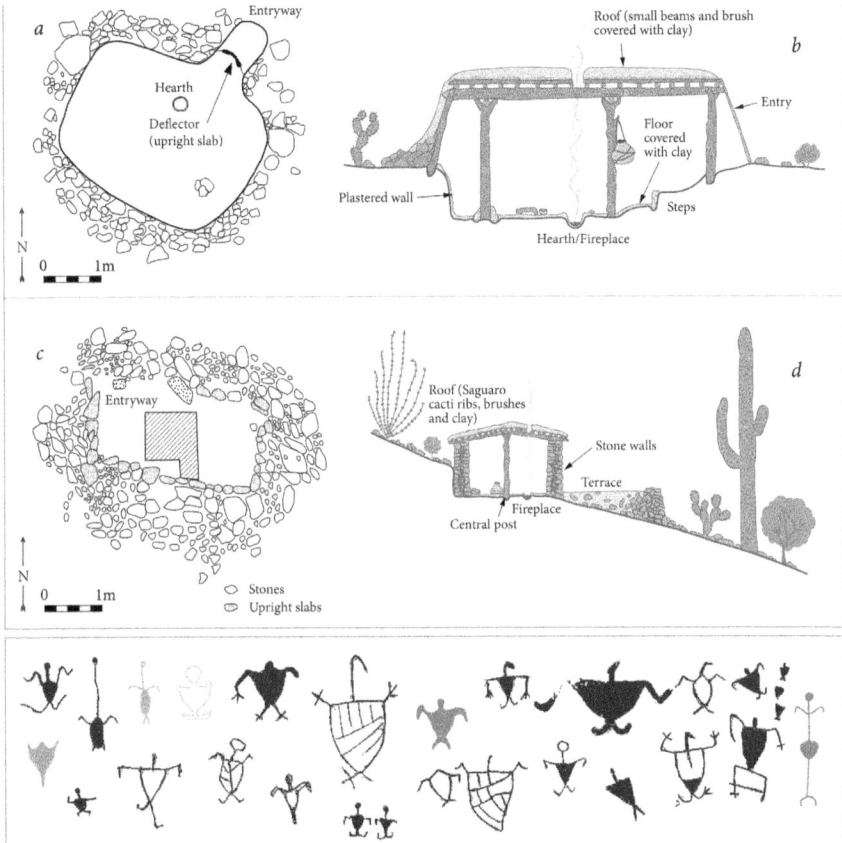

Figure 7.7. Plan and reconstruction of houses from *trincheras* sites in southern Arizona: (a, b) Linda Vista Hill site; (c, d) Cerro Prieto site (after Downum 2007:4.3 and other sources) and below: examples of rock art from the Sierra Libre mountains in northeastern Sonora with anthropomorphic and zoomorphic depictions including images of sea turtles (after Vigliani 2019:Figuras 3–6). Compiled by Radosław Palonka and drawings by Michał Znamirowski and Bolesław Zych.

Costa Central Tradition

The Costa Central tradition occupied part of the central coastal section of Sonora, with traces also found on the islands of Tiburón and San Esteban on the Gulf of California coast. These areas are very dry and this tradition—the ancestors of the historic and modern Comca'ac and Seri peoples—was the only one that did not embrace agriculture, even to a small extent. These were hunter-gatherer communities without permanent settlements who relied largely on food from the Gulf of California. The people of Costa Central practiced seasonal movements (transhumance) to gather food, balancing a diet of food from the sea and desert. Many sites of this tradition are under threat today, notably by the shrimp industry. Much of archaeological work is classified as rescue excavations, which have revealed traces of trade with farming communities who exchanged mollusks and corn, a trade pattern that was still practiced in the nineteenth century.

La Pintada in the Sierra Libre mountains is one of the most important sites of the Costa Central tradition (figure 7.7). La Pintada features rock art, typically paintings of animals, birds (probably condors) as well as people (anthropomorphic figures), including the characteristic large depiction of a rider on an animal that may be a horse. Images are usually painted in red, black, and white. At the rock art site, traces of a multiphase human presence have been found. These include evidence of a ritualistic nature (possibly connected with rock art panels) as well as flint workshops and places for weaving baskets and preparing food, including pits where agave were stored or roasted. Similar roasting techniques are used even today in Sonora and Arizona. Numerous stone blades, scrapers, piercers, stones for grinding seeds, stone pestles, and jewelry made of seashells were also found at this site. In historic times, the Seri took refuge from Spanish attacks in the Sierra Libre Mountains.

Huatabampo Tradition

The Huatabampo tradition began in the first centuries AD when Archaic communities adopted a more sedentary lifestyle and began farming. Mainly corn, other crops, and cotton were grown there, but the economy of the groups belonging to this tradition was also largely based on food obtained from the sea. The Huatabampo tradition developed mainly in the Mayo River basin as far as the Mocorito River in the State of Sinaloa. The archaeology of the Huatabampo is quite challenging because the present-day city of Huatabampo has been constructed on top of many of the sites. This urban development is driven by the expansion of agriculture and the shrimping industry.

Huatabampo pottery was intensely red in color and smoothed from the inside. Forms included anthropomorphic vessels similar to the Hohokam effigy pottery from Arizona and the pottery of the Chamelta Mesoamerican communities from the Aztatlan tradition in the state of Sinaloa (Villalpando and McGuire 2017:392). Mesoamerican connections (mainly with western Mexico) are visible in obsidian blades and other items, and ties with middle/northern parts of the Southwest are manifested in turquoise artifacts. In the late pre-Hispanic period, the Huatabampo traditions merged with the Gusave people who were arriving from western Mexico to the south. The immediate descendants of Huatabampo groups are the indigenous groups living in the southern part of Sonora today—the Yoreme (Mayo) and Yoeme (Yaqui) (e.g., Sheridan and Parezo 1996).

Serrana Tradition

The Serrana tradition arose in the southern part of Sonora and the northeastern part of the State of Sinaloa from the Yaqui River to Tacuichamona. The Serrana shared some cultural traits with that of the Huatabampo and may have been different groups that sprang from the same cultural tradition. Serrana settlements consisted of a small number of houses situated on rivers or larger streams. Material culture was typified by brown ceramics (Venadito Brown type) decorated with imprints of rope, fabrics, and engravings that formed geometric patterns. Narrow *metate* stones and *mano* grinding stones with protruding ends have been found. Archaeological data also confirm that the Serrana participated in the trade that had developed between the Casas Grandes tradition and western Mexico. Today's descendants of the Serrana tradition possibly include historic Cáhita groups, including the Sinaloas and Tehuecas people from present-day Alamos in Sonora. After the Spanish conquest some of this population joined the Yoreme (Mayo) groups.

Descendants of Pre-Hispanic Traditions Today

As in the area of the Southwest within US borders, the descendants of the pre-Hispanic native societies of Sonora and Chihuahua still live in the areas occupied by their ancestors, though their territories are much reduced (Sheridan and Parezo 1996; Villalpando and McGuire 2017). The Seri and Comca'ac live in the very dry areas of the central coast of Sonora and, along with the Cocopah groups from the lower Colorado River, speak a language belonging to the Yuman family.

Other indigenous groups from Sonora live in thriving agricultural communities and speak Uto-Aztec languages. These groups include the Cáhita who used to live from northern Sinaloa to southern Sonora, the Yoreme (Mayo) and Yoeme (Yaqui) on the Mayo and Yaqui Rivers, and the Guarijio societies in the Sierra Madre Occidental. The Akimel O'odham live in two areas stretching from the Sierra Madre mountains nearby the Opata who were almost completely annihilated by the Spaniards. The indigenous populations from this area were often engaged in devastating warfare with Spanish/Mexican armies with the most recent war between the Yaqui and the Mexican army occurring in the 1920s (Villalpando and McGuire 2017:383). Today, unlike many Native American cultures in the American Southwest, most of these indigenous groups still speak their native languages.

The historic and contemporary Native American communities of this desert and semiarid region of northern Mexico bordering Arizona, California, and some of New Mexico constitute an unusually rich and diverse world of many cultural traditions and tribes. Archeology has captured only a glimpse of these cultures due to the state of the fieldwork. In the absence of more extensive archeological data, we possess many other types of sources that teach us about the cultures of this area, including written accounts from the conquest period and permanent Spanish settlement, and ongoing studies of ethnographic material conducted from the end of the nineteenth century until today.

Note

1. The term Casas Grandes has at least three uses: (a) Casas Grandes as the name of place/site used interchangeably with the site name of Paquimé); (b) Casas Grandes as the name of cultural tradition; and (c) Casas Grandes as a discrete territory.

Farmers and Hunter-Gatherers from Utah
The Fremont Culture

8

T HE FREMONT CULTURE arose in the northern part of the Southwest, the Colorado Plateau and part of the Great Basin area. This long-lasting culture developed from as early as the turn of the era until around 1300 AD (possibly even later in some subregions) (Janetski and Talbot 2014; Madsen and Simms 1998; Simms 2010). The Fremont culture was first defined in 1931 by Harvard University student Noel Morrs while studying sites in the Fremont River Valley in central-southern Utah.

Fremont culture is characterized by semi-agricultural or hunter-gatherer societies in terms of their economy (depending on the territory), architecture, material culture, and rock art. The Fremont societies developed in what is now Utah mainly north of the Colorado River, and in adjacent western parts of Colorado, eastern Nevada, and southern parts of Idaho and Wyoming. To the south and east, the Fremont culture was bordered by the agricultural Ancestral Pueblo and the Patayan (Hakataya) cultures, and hunter-gatherer communities from the Great Basin to the west and the Great Plains to the northeast. Fremont societies are strikingly different from other southwestern cultural traditions.

Five or six regional Fremont groups have been distinguished based on similarities and differences in the technology and iconography of pottery, architecture and settlement structure, economy, and types of clay figurines and iconography of rock art (figure 8.1). The Great Salt Lake/Utah Valley group may be dated to approximately 400–1300/1350 AD, Uinta: ?–950 AD, San Rafael: 700–1260 AD, Sevier: 780–1260 AD, and Parowan: 900–1300 AD (e.g., Cordell 1997).

Based on ethno-archaeological research on tribal communities from other parts of the world, archeologists Joel Janetski and Richard Talbot

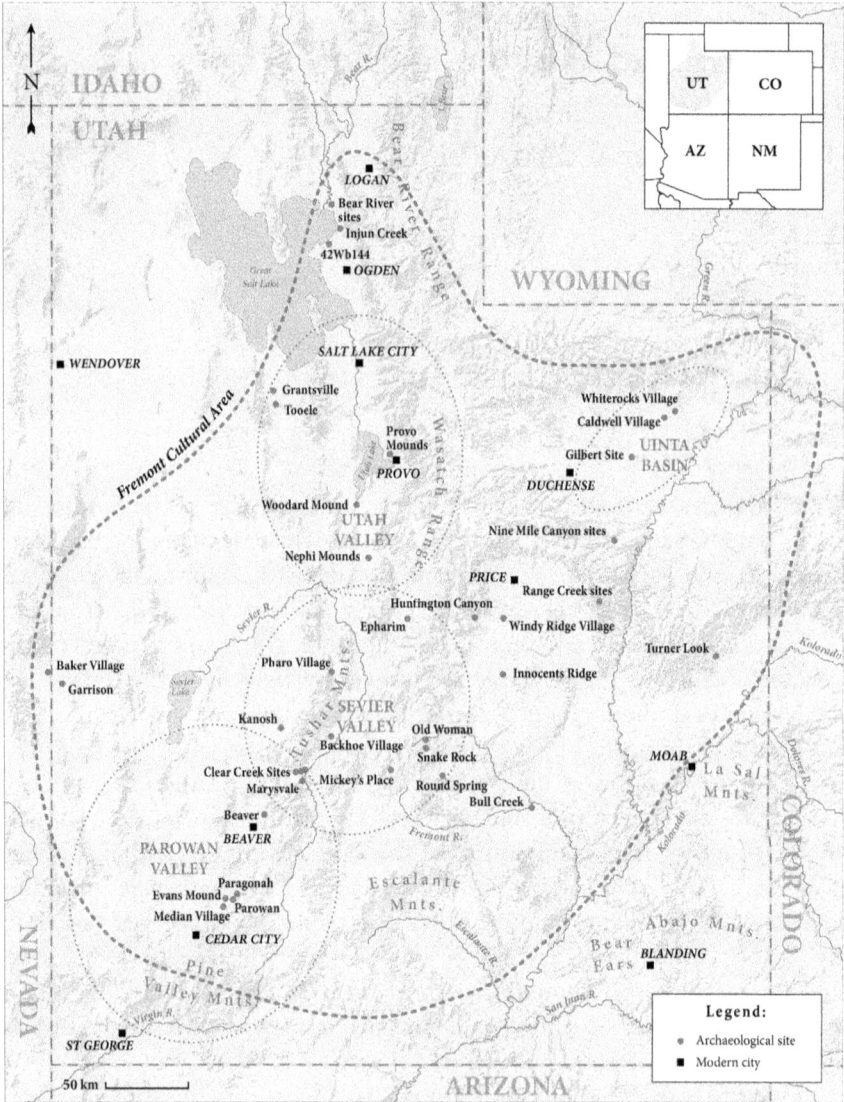

Figure 8.1.   The territory of the Fremont culture with important groups and sites (after Janetski and Talbot 2014:Figure 10.1; Johansson et al. 2014:Figure 1; Schaafsma 1994:Figure 2 and other sources). Compiled by Radosław Palonka and drawing by Michał Znamirowski.

consider the Fremont culture to be a large tribe encompassing many communities (Janetski and Talbot 2014). These communities can be divided into smaller subgroups (more just individual villages) that are linked in various ways—for example, in the form of material culture such as ceramic figurines and grinding stones and the iconography of the rock art.

Fremont Material Culture and Society

Elements that connect Fremont groups include baskets and containers woven from plant shoots and fibers with relatively simple weaving techniques; unpainted gray pottery (though painted in the Pueblo and Mogollon style by some groups in certain periods); types of arrowheads; large *metate* stones for grinding corn, seeds, and grains into flour; leather moccasins; and richly decorated figurines from unfired clay; along with paintings and petroglyphs—that is, rock art (figure 8.2) (e.g., Allison 2015; Cordell 1997). These artifacts very rarely co-occurred at the same archaeological sites; even today, not all scientists agree that the term "Fremont culture" may be legitimately used for all the groups and communities that compose it.

It is difficult to state the fate of the Fremont communities after the thirteenth/fourteenth century AD, so we do not know their direct descendants (Janetski and Talbot 2014). Genetic data suggest that their descendants might be found among the historic and modern Ute and Shoshone tribes (Noble 2000:33), but the issue has not been sufficiently well researched. Certainly, the Fremont cultural communities had not survived

Figure 8.2.   Examples of the Fremont rock art: petroglyphs from the Capitol Reef, Utah, including visible traces of vandalism. Sadly, rock art panels in the Southwest are often used for target practice. Photos by Wikimedia Commons.

as one cultural entity before the arrival of the Europeans, so there are no written sources upon which to base a reconstruction; the most important findings are yielded by archaeology and field research.

The territory that was inhabited by the Fremont communities is located within two great geographic areas—the Colorado Plateau and the Great Basin. An area this large is characterized by a varied natural environment and climate that encompasses arid and semiarid areas with deep canyons refreshed by occasional spring and summer rainstorms, valleys with wetlands, and mountainous areas with alpine vegetation and valleys abundant in game. This diversity of the natural environment translated into a diverse economy and cultural features. Archaeologists faced considerable challenges in defining this cultural unit because its features differed so greatly from neighboring cultures—the agricultural Pueblo culture and the hunting-gathering communities of the Great Plains and the Great Basin.

Stephen H. Lekson (2014) hypothesizes that the cultural development of the Fremont communities from the ninth/tenth century AD (when aboveground sandstone pueblo-type architecture appears in the Fremont area) was strongly influenced by the Pueblo world, mainly by the Great Houses of Chaco Canyon. According to Lekson, Chaco Canyon dominated the cultural and political development of the Southwest for several centuries and had a similar effect on the Mimbres culture of Arizona and New Mexico. These influences coincided with a period when the fluctuating climate of the Southwest again became milder and wetter (a period lasting several centuries), and therefore more favorable for agriculture. Research on some Fremont skeletons (Parr et al. 1996) indicates significant genetic differences between the Fremont and Pueblo people, which would confirm the thesis that the interactions were more cultural and ideological than biological.

Influences from different cultures manifested in the great diversity within the Fremont culture itself are visible in its economy and settlement patterns. The Fremont economy which was influenced by the Pueblo culture was partly based on cultivating varieties of corn (the Fremont Dent type) and squash and beans. This agriculture is especially evident in the eastern part of the Fremont in the Colorado Plateau. Fremont Dent corn was also directly related to certain varieties from Mexico that differed genetically from other types of corn from the Southwest including that grown by the Ancestral Pueblo people. Fremont Dent grains were more concave with slimmer, denser cobs than typical Pueblo corn. Perhaps this strain of corn was cultivated as a response to the shorter growing seasons in Fremont territory (Cordell 1997:213).

These were mainly garden crops grown in small plots, often near canyon walls, and with artificial irrigation in the form of small canals. This economy was, to a much greater extent than the Pueblo, supplemented with hunting (mountain sheep, deer, and bison) and gathering. In some groups and during certain periods, this hunter-gatherer economy prevailed, while agriculture was treated marginally or was nonexistent.

The practice of agriculture dawned slowly upon the world of hunters and gatherers, starting on a larger scale about 500 AD. As time passed, some groups abandoned agriculture in favor of hunting and gathering, depending on the changing climate and environmental conditions. Some Fremont groups, mainly those in the Great Basin area in the west, never adopted agriculture, perhaps because natural resources in the region were sufficient for a comfortable existence, and the investment of energy and resources in agriculture would not have yielded a greater food supplies. In other words, the Fremont communities may not have perceived farming as something that would make their livelihood more secure (Barlow 2002; Madsen and Simms 1998).

Cultural influences within the Fremont communities (e.g., Janetski and Talbot 2014; Simms 1999) also are visible in their architecture and building types. These include pithouses and aboveground masonry pueblo-type buildings, as well as lodge-like structures known as *wikiups* (a round frame covered in branches and brush) among the historic tribes of the Paiutes, the Shoshones, and later the Apache, and constructions similar to teepees. Typical Fremont settlements consisted of several or a dozen pithouses. Pithouses built in a circular plan were found more frequently in the eastern part of Fremont world and those laid out in a square or rectangular plan were found more often in the western part. Circular layouts tend to be chronologically older than rectangular ones. Pithouse walls were constructed with wooden beams filled with wickerwork and covered with clay and a roof that was usually supported by four poles. As with Pueblo pithouses, the entrance was located in an opening in the roof, and the homesteads often had adjoining storage rooms. The central part of these houses contained a hearth made of clay, and an underground ventilation tunnel in one of the walls that circulated fresh air. Next to the hearth were storage pits, with walls faced with sandstone slabs, as in Puebloan structures. Aboveground adobe or stone buildings alongside residential buildings were used for storage or food production such as grinding.

From around 900 AD, aboveground construction prevailed in the form of several adjacent rooms divided by walls. These structures were built of adobe and sandstone using *jacal* and *wattle and daub* construction—thin beams filled with branches and sticks tied together and covered with clay and mud. Because these structures were not particularly durable, there is less evidence of them today. Fremont settlements were reminiscent of Pueblo settlements, except that there were no underground kivas and masonry construction was not as advanced as that of their southern neighbors. This period is associated with increases in settlement size as the lifestyle of their inhabitants became more sedentary and with the expansion of agriculture. Small storage structures built from stone and clay mortar were often located high up in hard-to-reach places like rock crevices on canyon walls; they looked somewhat like huge beehives.

According to some researchers, pithouses and aboveground buildings could have had multiple uses such as accommodation for shorter or longer periods; food storage; work rooms for grinding corn and grains into flour; and meetings, ceremonies, and rituals for the entire community (e.g., Johansson et al. 2014:46–47). Public architecture at Fremont sites includes central buildings, structures much larger than other pithouses and storage buildings, and plazas between groups of buildings in a manner similar to the Pueblo.

These types of buildings can be found, among others, at the Wolf Village site (42UT273), which was studied in 2009–2013 within the scope of Brigham Young University's Archaeological Field School (e.g., Johansson et al. 2014). Wolf Village was inhabited for several decades in the late eleventh or early twelfth century AD, as shown by radiocarbon dating. Located in the southern part of the Utah Valley south of Lake Utah, Wolf Village represents a Fremont settlement with diverse residential and storage architecture in terms of construction (pithouses and aboveground buildings), building materials, and technologies used, as well as the size of individual buildings ranging from twenty to seventy square meters or even larger. Construction and maintenance of these buildings likely required the cooperation of many members of the community. In addition to their size, these structures' uniqueness is evidenced by the artifacts that were not found in other buildings, including richly decorated figurines or objects made of turquoise and *olivellas* shells. Interestingly, based on the data available so far, it seems that these buildings served not only religious purposes, but may also have been used for social gatherings and ceremonies.

Plazas are another interesting element in the architecture and layout of these settlements. Plazas situated as the most important places may testify to the existence of ceremonialism and an extensive religious and social life encompassing the entire settlement and perhaps people from the surrounding areas. Plazas are known to have existed at the sites of Big Mound at

Paragonah, Beaver, Five Finger Ridge, Turner Look, and Old Woman (see figure 8.1). Plazas were usually located in the central parts of the settlements close to the largest buildings, which may additionally demonstrate the connection and relationship between plazas and large buildings in Fremont settlements. Recently, increasing numbers of researchers have pointed out the similarities between public structures and buildings and thus social organization, in the Fremont and Pueblo societies, and others in the Southwest.

Defensive sites associated with intensifying conflicts and fighting, probably of an intra-cultural nature, are a separate and relatively poorly studied group of settlements. One such site in Range Creek Canyon in eastern Utah was purchased from private owners by the state of Utah in 2001 and is now being extensively explored; previously only some sites in this canyon were known, including the spectacular deposit of eleven figures (see below). Range Creek Canyon has been studied as a defensive settlement for several years by Duncan Metcalfe of the University of Utah in Salt Lake City within the scope of the Range Creek Research Project (Kloor 2007). Metcalfe has located and cataloged many sites in hard-to-reach rock niches, as well as on hilltops. These studies include mostly residential sites, and buildings or lone-standing storage rooms located in hard-to-reach places and sometimes effectively masked from the sight of strangers.

Fremont funeral rites mainly involved skeletal burials in pits, often under the floors of houses. The deceased were interred with bent knees or in an extreme fetal position. Grave goods from sites in the Great Salt Lake region in northern Utah (Simms 1999) show that the deceased were relatively poorly endowed with burial goods, which mainly included pottery, bone needles, small tools made of deer antlers and bison horns, jewelry made of bones and shells, and grinding *metate* stones (Utah type) or other stones often placed in the vicinity of the pelvis of the deceased. Most of these items were additionally covered with red ochre. Some burials may have been symbolic for a person who died far from the settlement. In these cases which were common, a part of the body was brought back for burial. At times, the deceased were added to pre-existing graves, for example a child placed on top of a cremated adult (Simms 1999:29).

There were also animal graves, and dogs seem to have been quite lovingly treated. Dogs sometimes accompanied humans, which, taken together with rock art representations of these animals (possibly shown as hunting assistants), may suggest their special status in the Fremont culture (possibly it was similar in other Southwest cultures, see for example *Archaeology Southwest* 22(3), 2008 and Monagle and Jones 2020).

Isotope studies of human bones also show that a large number of sites related to the more agricultural Fremont communities, such as Backhoe Village, Evans Mound, and Caldwell Village, were based on a corn-rich diet (e.g., Barlow 2002:68). On the other hand, DNA analyses reveal genetic differences between the Fremont and Pueblo populations and the Athapaskans (proto-Apache and Navajo) coming from the north: the Fremont people lack or have only a small amount of haplogroup A, one of the most typical haplogroups for North American native communities, while a high percentage have haplogroup B and a high percentage of 9 bp deletion (a type of mutation or change in genetic material), which is characteristic of many Asian populations, and some Native Americans and Polynesians (Parr et al. 1996:512–14).

Fremont pottery was mostly gray with an admixture of sand and crushed rock. Bowls, jars, and pot-shaped vessels decorated with artistic elements such as knobs, engravings, and carvings prevail; these decorative motifs are often found at the top of the vessel. In later stages, pottery—for example, bowls, jars, and *ollas*—were painted with geometric designs (e.g., Richards 2015) in black-on-white and black-on-gray, where the color of the white and gray ceramics differs due to the firing process and technique. The influence of the Pueblo culture is clear in these designs. The motifs and the red paint that is sometimes used also refer to the Mogollon culture from the border of southern Arizona and New Mexico, which is a surprising considering the distances between the two cultures. Large amounts of pottery with analogies to the Mogollon culture have been found, including in Parowan Valley in the central-southern part of Utah (figure 8.3) (e.g., Lekson 2014; Richards 2015).

Large numbers of blades, arrowheads, flint knives, drills, and huge *mano* and *metate* stones have also been found at Fremont sites; quern-stones on which grains were ground (*metate*) represent the Utah type. *Metate* stones of this type were much larger than those in the Pueblo culture and usually had two grinding platforms with a smaller, shallower one in the upper part of the stone. This type of *metate* stone alludes to similar, earlier artifacts of this type from the Mogollon culture, just as similarities in Fremont and Mogollon pottery relate.

A very large number of artifacts found at Fremont sites are made of organic materials such as baskets, mats, or items of clothing produced from willow or other plants. Weaving techniques characteristic of the Fremont culture included simple weaving and the one-rod-and-bundle. Sometimes artifacts made of perishable materials are spectacular finds, such as a plume of 370 woodpecker feathers from sixty-one birds that were subspecies of

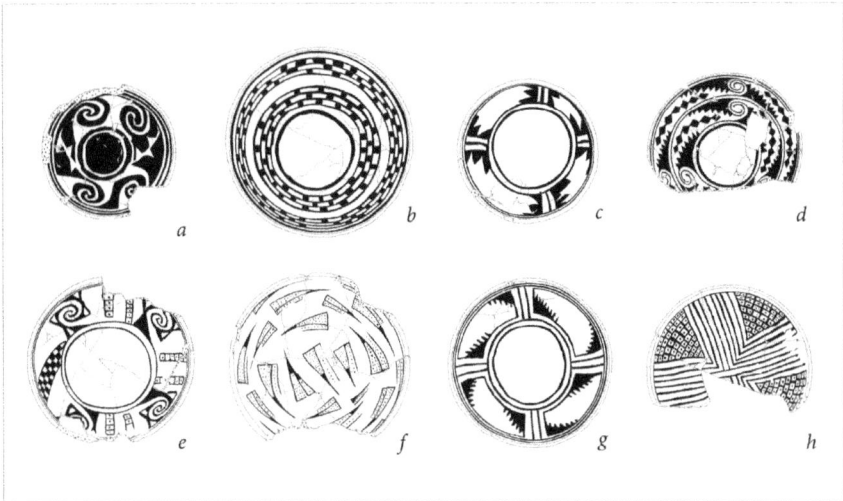

Figure 8.3.   Examples of black-on-white painted ceramics from the Parowan site with decorative motifs referring to the iconography of Mogollon and Pueblo pottery (after Richards 2015). Drawing by Katarzyna Ciomek.

woodpeckers endemic on eastern and western sides of the Rocky Mountains. The feathers were precisely trimmed at the top and embedded in deer skin and what is most likely weasel fur. Radiocarbon dating (AMS) of this plume suggests that it was made sometime between 996 and 1190 AD (Simms 2010:18). The plume was carefully wrapped in deer hide and placed in a shallow cavity in Mantle's Cave in the present-day Dinosaur National Monument in Colorado and is now curated at the University of Colorado Museum of Natural History in Boulder. In addition to this artifact, many other items made of exotic materials were discovered there, probably at least some of them of a ceremonial nature.

Such unique artifacts also include a miniature baby cradleboard or carrier that was found at a cave site in Capitol Reef National Park in Utah. The cradleboard was made of willow twigs, shoots and fibers of the *Asteraceae* family plant, and animal skin, and an anthropomorphic painted figurine from unfired clay was discovered in the cradleboard. Leather moccasins are quite common in the inventory of items made of perishable/organic materials. Moccasins were often produced by joining three sections of leather onto a sole made from the skin of the hind legs (mainly the knee area) of animals such as deer or mountain sheep. Such footwear distinguished the Fremont people from the Pueblo communities, who wore mostly plant-woven (yucca) sandals. Other elements of surviving attire include entire plumes and fragments of plumes as well as other parts of head-decorative motifs. This clothing closely resembles that featured in Fremont rock art, which helps to date it indirectly. Many artifacts made of organic raw materials are preserved at museum and university collections in the Southwest and beyond.

Fremont Clay Figurines and Rock Art

Anthropomorphic figurines made of unfired clay (e.g., Janetski and Talbot 2014; Yoder 2015) and richly decorated with artistic elements and painting (figures 8.4a,b, 8.5) are important artifacts that may help reconstruct the chronology, social structure, and the appearance of the Fremont people. The figurines occurred more frequently in the eastern part of Fremont territory. Figure shapes and their body decorations bear close comparison with depictions in Fremont rock art. So far, between four hundred and six hundred figurines have been discovered (Pitblado et al. 2013; Yoder 2015), but they are still unique when it comes to artistic and three-dimensional art in the cultures of the Southwest (similar numbers of figurines have only been found in the Pueblo and Hohokam cultures). Fremont figurines have been found at sites located in Nine Mile Canyon, Wolf Village, and Old Woman sites in Utah. Most have been uncovered in residential buildings and middens. Figures differ in size and shape. Rectangular forms prevail, but there are also trapezoidal and cylindrical figures. Production techniques and decoration differ from one site to another (Morss 1954; Pitblado et al. 2013; Potts 2011; Yoder 2015). Stylistically, many figurines are associated with the Barrier Canyon–style rock art of the Archaic period (see also chapter 3). Similarities are expressed in the lack of arms, hands, and legs, and human shapes that are trapezoidal and rectangular tapering downward and slightly resembling "mummies." Faces and bodies are covered with painted decorations of dots, lines, and zigzags (figure 8.4).

Fremont figurines are known from excavations and accidental and amateur finds. They can be fairly well dated stratigraphically, and some examples of Fremont rock art may be dated indirectly by analogy (e.g., Potts 2011; Yoder 2015). It has been difficult to establish a chronological distinction between different styles of producing and decorating because figurines made in different styles can be found in one archaeological layer. Some researchers argue that these figurines may have been passed down from generation to generation, although their exact nature and function in different Fremont groups is not fully understood. Nevertheless, like rock art, these figurines provide us with a vast trove of information about how

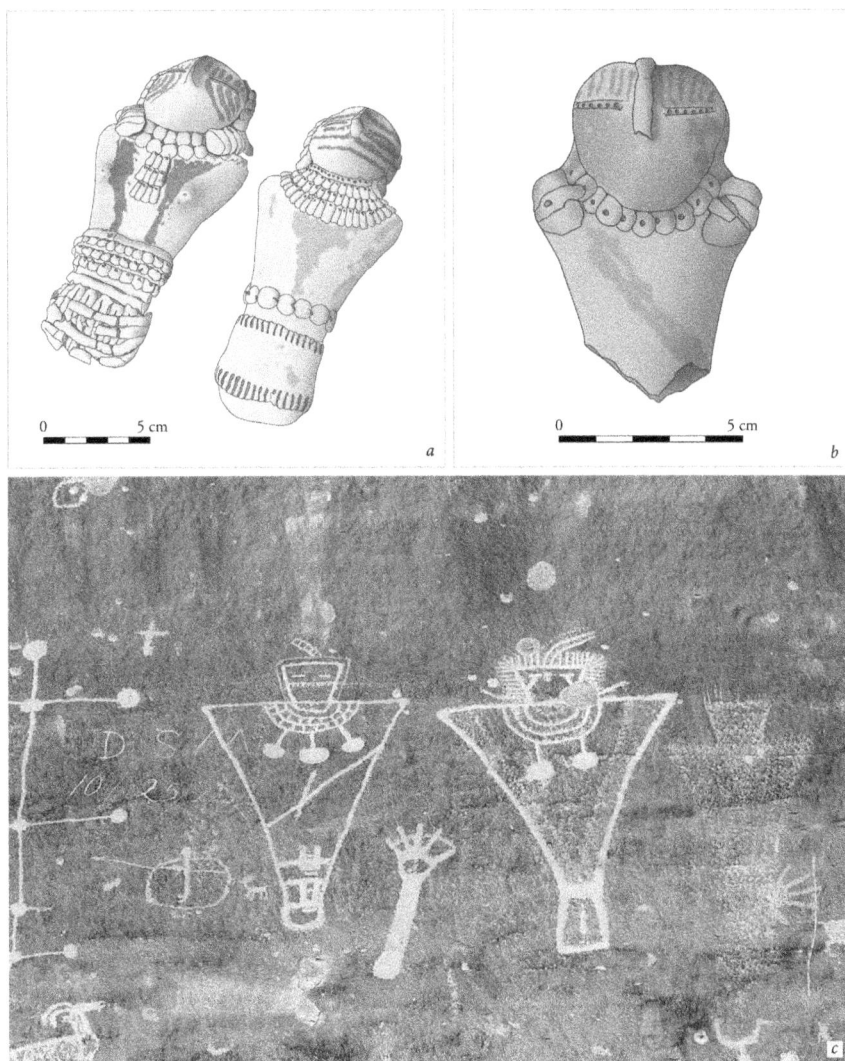

Figure 8.4.   Two Fremont figurines from cache from Range Creek Canyon (a); (b) anthropomorphic figure from a site in the Nine Mile Canyon; (c) Fremont rock art from Sego Canyon (Thompson Wash), Utah; Fremont petroglyphs overlap earlier paintings in the red paint of the Archaic Barrier Canyon style. Drawings by Katarzyna Ciomek (based on Pitblado et al. 2013:Fig. 3 and other sources) and photo by Radosław Palonka.

people dressed, the way they styled their hair, and the jewelry they wore especially on the upper part of body and head (e.g., Schaafsma 1994; Yoder 2015).

The Pilling Collection: A Spectacular Find

The most spectacular find of figurines from the Range Creek Canyon is the so-called Pilling Collection, due to the rather excellent condition of these artifacts as compared to those found in other Fremont areas.

The Pilling Collection consists of eleven unfired clay figurines (figure 8.5) that were discovered by accident in Range Creek Canyon in eastern Utah in 1950 by ranchers from the Pilling family: Clarence, Art, and Woodrow, who were accompanied by Tony Finn and Dusty Pruit. The figures were found in a rock shelter on the slope of a steep canyon. The shelter also contained at least one building with an oval layout measuring approximately 10 × 6 meters. The wood used for the construction of this building was dendrochronologically dated to around 995–1005 AD, thus giving an indirect estimate of the figurines' age (Pitblado et al. 2013:4). Also discovered there was a fragment of gray ceramics typical of the Fremont culture, *metates* and, in a niche in the cliff, a white-painted image of a trapezoidal human figure about 8 centimeters high.

The height of the figurines ranges from 8.5 to 13.4 centimeters; six represent women and five represent men. The gender can be identified by anatomical features and clothing such as clearly marked breasts and wide hips and a type of skirt or apron worn by women, sashes for the men, as well as by hairstyles depicted quite lovingly and with finesse in each figure. Like most other Fremont figurines, these were made of unfired clay and painted in red, buff, and sometimes black and blue. Many elements of clothes and jewelry (necklaces) are made of glued clay. The women's hair is tied up in two kinds of heavy bobs bound with cord and falling on the shoulders; necklaces and straps are made of clay rings which were probably supposed to imitate beads. Dots and lines painted in red are found below and above the eyes that were represented with horizontal cuts or dotted indentations.

Noel Morss (1954), who first studied these figurines stated that they had been made by the same artist, most likely in pairs. The eleventh female figurine was either created as a separate element or her companion has been destroyed or lost. It is unlikely that all were made at the same time, as indicated by distinctive differences in the clothes and body decorations (Morss 1954:6). The figurines were intended to be viewed only from the

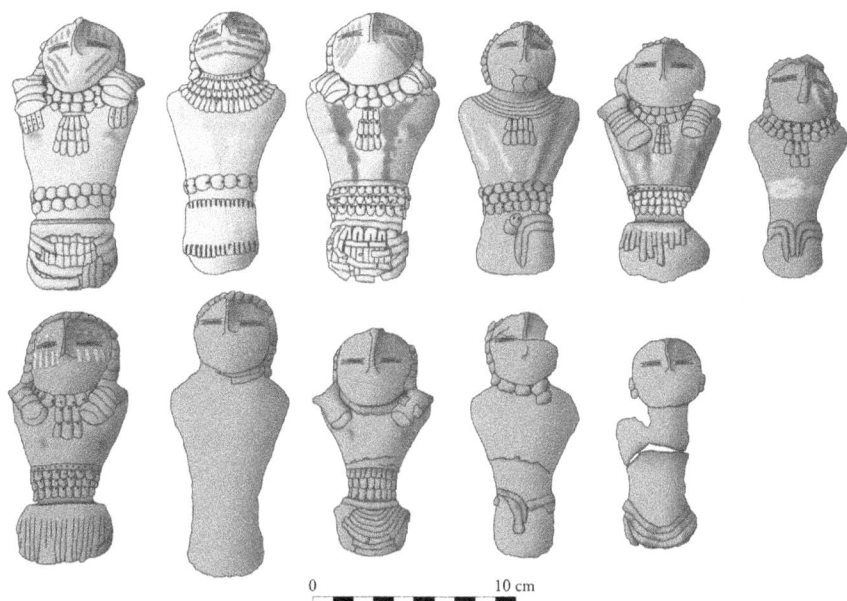

Figure 8.5. Drawing of anthropomorphic Fremont figurines from the so-called Pilling Collection (drawing by Katarzyna Ciomek).

front as they have virtually no intentional decoration on the rear. Morss interpreted these figurines as elements of a fertility cult, possibly related to agriculture.

Soon after its discovery, the collection was displayed in at least a dozen locations in Utah—banks, public buildings, and hotels—and it finally found its way to the College of Eastern Utah (now Utah State University Eastern). In the mid-1970s, one of the male figures (the most richly decorated and the best preserved) disappeared under mysterious circumstances from the university collection. Then in 2011, more than thirty years later, an anonymous donor sent the missing figurine to archaeologist Bonnie Pitblado, director of the Museum of Anthropology at Utah State University, who together with an interdisciplinary team, began researching its authenticity (Pitblado et al. 2013).

To that end, the research team examined the ten figurines from the Eastern Prehistoric Museum at Utah State University and another, from the Museum of Peoples and Cultures at Brigham Young University in Utah which had been discovered at Nine Mile Canyon in eastern Utah. Three methods were used to establish the authenticity of the returned figurine (Pitblado et al. 2013): (a) analysis of comparisons of prints made by the woven baskets on which the figures lay while the clay was still wet (b) scanning electron microscopy (SEM) studies of traces of a preservative used by Morrs to join chipped-off fragments of figurines during his research in the 1950s, and (c) tests conducted with portable fluorescence spectroscopy (XRF) which examined the clay composition of the Pilling collection figures and the Nine Mile Canyon figures. All three methods confirmed the authenticity of the returned Pilling collection figurine.

The Fremont style along with styles from other areas and periods—the Archaic Barrier Canyon anthropomorphic style, Glen Canyon Linear style (GCLS), San Juan Basketmaker II–III comprise a long rock art tradition featuring large anthropomorphic figures. Each style features its own distinctive elements such as jewelry. Some researchers think that Fremont rock art derives from the earlier Archaic style. Apart from depictions of anthropomorphic forms, potential continuation of Archaic rock art depictions can be observed in the use of the same paint combination of red and white and just red at rock art sites in the Nine Mile Canyon and Utah Bookcliffs area such as in Sego Canyon (see figure 8.4c) (Cole 2004; 2009). Many Fremont sites featuring rock art are located where the Archaic style occurred. Due to chronological and geographic discrepancies in the two styles, many researchers view Fremont rock art as more aligned with the San Juan Basketmaker II and III style of the Ancestral Pueblo culture. This suggests common ground for the development of at least some groups belonging to these cultures (Cole 2009; Schaafsma 1994:139–41; Simms 2010:74–84).

Fremont rock art is primarily represented by petroglyphs, although there are also paintings. The most common subjects are anthropomorphic figures with animals, people as single figures or in groups, and people in narrative scenes such as hunting (e.g., Cole 2004; 2009; Schaafsma 1980; Scotter 2015) (figures 8.2, 8.4c, 8.6). Local variants have been distinguished that correlate with various local Fremont groups. Rock art panels were located at relatively high altitudes, even about two to three thousand meters above sea level, but sometimes higher than three thousand meters above sea level. Depending on the region in which they occur, the main styles of Fremont rock art are classic Vernal, northern San Rafael, southern San Rafael, painted from Utah, Sevier A, and Barrier Canyon (e.g., Cole 2004; Schaafsma 1980:163–79; 1994).

Characteristics of Fremont rock art are:

- trapezoidal shapes, most often frontal representations of figures with broad shoulders lowered downward at some distance from the body, in large and even life-sized images

- figures often appearing in pairs or groups, sometimes in rows, some images overlapping older ones (such rock art "stratigraphy" is the basis for dividing individual representations into relative chronology), sexual characteristics sometimes shown;
- round or trapezoidal heads or heads in the shape of "helmets," realistically depicted body parts (eyes, arms, legs, sometimes visible muscles), hands disproportionately large, legs and feet often pointing outward;
- some figures without arms and legs, with very broad shoulders and a strongly tapered torso, with a kind of waist belt;
- extensive head decorative motifs (plumes, horns, caps, individual feathers, etc.), sometimes mask-like heads;
- designs on the upper body, necklaces, bracelets, and head designs on faces, often painted or with engraved dots and lines;
- figures holding shields often covering the entire torso, as well as discs and spirals, weapons, baskets, severed human heads;
- sometimes arcs or rainbows above the heads of the human figures.

Animals in Fremont rock art that prevail are listed in their order of occurrence: mountain sheep, deer (including large species), bison, and birds, less frequently snakes and insects too (Schaafsma 1994). Parts of animals were sometimes represented symbolically, for example a stylized and schematic bear or badger paw. In addition to game animals, dogs were illustrated (probably as assistants in the hunting mountain sheep). Animals and hunters themselves were shown with corrals or pens made of branches and stones for rounding up the game (e.g., Schaafsma 1980, 1994). Sometimes geometric designs accompany people and animals. These include zigzag lines or arcs and often multiple arcs that recall the rainbow, which is widespread today among many cultures of the Southwest, including the Navajo and Pueblo, though it is difficult to identify or assign specific functions and meanings.

Data from individual panels showing young specimens of various animals with adults indicate that hunting was carried out at different times of the year, mainly in summer, but also in autumn and winter. Attempts have been made to reconstruct hunting strategies from individual rock art panels and by using ethnographic analogies from other Southwest cultures and archaeological records.

The Cottonwood Panel (also known as The Great Hunt) from Nine Mile Canyon, Utah, is one of the most famous Fremont rock art panels. This dramatic hunting scene depicts mountain sheep at different ages including lambs, suggesting that the hunting took place in late autumn or

Figure 8.6.   An example of the location of Fremont rock art panels above the ground in the Colorado River Canyon in Utah; (b) an enlarged fragment of the panel. Photo by Radosław Palonka.

winter when lambs would be present in the herd (Matheny et al. 2004; Simms 2010). All the animals' heads are turned to the right, perhaps indicating their migration from high-altitude meadows and pastures to valleys for the winter. Also depicted are hunters with weapons including bows and arrows, poised as if lurking for game. An anthropomorphic figure with horns on his head in the center of the highest line of animals is often interpreted as a shaman (e.g., Cole 2004); these reconstructions come mainly from analysis of ethnographic data.

Sometimes it is also possible to date rock art, especially in the case of paintings. Two examples are the Horned Men Alcove and Ceremonial Cave sites from Utah, where the AMS method of dating paint was success-fully applied. The analysis indicated 675 ± 55 BP, which in calibrated dates translates to around 1272-1379 AD or 1250–1400 AD (Geib and Fairley 1992). Both absolute dating and indirect dating of artifacts were applied at Dios Blancos (Geib and Fairley 1992). In the case of Dios Blancos, ^{14}C dating resulted in 1200 ± 80 BP, which calibrates to 660–1000 AD.

The end of the Fremont culture's development is still the subject of scientific debate, but some researchers suggest its collapse may have been caused by the adverse environmental and climate changes that affected the entire Southwest in the thirteenth century AD, especially its northern part. These environmental changes also drove migration and transformations within much more economically and socially developed cultures such as the Pueblo and Hohokam. These environmental changes may have begun to affect the Fremont communities even 100/150 years earlier than the Hohokam and Pueblo, as shown by recent studies, for example at sites in Range Creek Canyon (Kloor 2007). The tremendous local variations in the Southwest in terms of the scale and timing affected the ways that differ-ent communities responded to these changes. Conflicts (with outsiders, or more likely among different Fremont groups) over shrinking arable lands and unfavorable changes in the natural environment may have accelerated migration and cultural dissolution, as it had in the Ancestral Pueblo culture of the Mesa Verde and Kayenta regions.

Hunter-Gatherers in the Pre-Hispanic and Early Historic Period in the Southwest

The Apache, Navajo, and Ute

9

⌗

HE NORTH AMERICAN SOUTHWEST is one of the few areas of the continent where developed farming communities prevailed in the pre-Hispanic period at the same time as Native American hunter-gatherer communities who also played a major role in the cultural and social traditions of this region up through the first centuries of Spanish presence. The importance of hunter-gatherers and their influence on the shape of the Southwest appears to have waxed and waned, increasing during certain periods, mainly in times of instability and changes in the climate and environment. Climatic fluctuations and sociocultural changes occurred in many Southwest communities, notably at the turn of the thirteenth and fourteenth centuries AD, when deteriorating environmental conditions contributed to a reduction in the ecumene (permanently inhabited lands, as opposed to areas that are occupied only temporarily) of agricultural peoples to enclaves in northern, central, and southern Arizona and the Rio Grande Valley in New Mexico, and in northern Mexico. And it was to these areas that had been deserted by the farming communities that the groups of hunter-gatherers gradually came (figure 9.1). The time of their arrival to the Southwest is debated among scholars and evokes strong emotions in the scientific community.

During the last two centuries leading up to the arrival of the Spaniards in the Southwest and after their arrival, two large hunter-gatherer groups played a key role in the cultural transformation of the Southwest. These influences occur in parallel to the agricultural traditions of the Pueblo, Hohokam, Mimbres/Mogollon, and Casas Grandes, as well as the semi-agricultural Fremont culture. From around the thirteenth century AD or a little later, peoples and tribes speaking Numic languages—for example, the

Paiutes and Utes—began to arrive in the Southwest or at its fringes from California and Nevada to the west, while the Athapaskans (Apache and Navajo) migrated from southwestern and central Canada to the north. These newcomers began to dominate many areas close to the Southwest (and later the heart of the Southwest itself), pushing farmers into microregions that had already been whittled down by environmental and climate changes.

Later, especially in the first half of the eighteenth century, other groups of Numic-language speakers—the Shoshone and Comanche—were still flowing into the Southwest or its vicinity; the Comanche in certain areas (mainly Colorado) effectively thwarted the domination of Apache groups, especially in mountain and upland areas like the Rocky Mountains (Brunswig 2012:31). The Comanche along with the Ute also invaded Navajo settlements, but tended to operate in the peripheral areas of the Southwest and these raids did not lead to their permanent presence in this territory.

In the historic period, Spanish and later American sources often record hostile relations between the nomadic Athapaskan groups and the agricultural Ancestral Pueblo societies. The hostility between the "worlds" of the farmers and the hunter-gatherers did not exclude relations of a different nature. At one point, the Navajo adopted many elements of beliefs and material and economic culture from the Pueblo communities, including large-scale agriculture. Mixed marriages between Navajo and Hopi, posed a significant demographic risk for the Hopi. Today about 12,500 Hopi remain, compared to over 300,000 Navajo according to the census of 2010 (US Census Bureau 2013). The number of individual tribes and the territories inhabited by the Hopi in the past are largely reflected in the size of the reservations now occupied by formerly hunter-gatherer societies. The Navajo Nation (*Diné*) reservation, the largest area in the Southwest, lies within the adjacent parts of Arizona, New Mexico, and Utah, while the Apache have large reservations in Arizona and New Mexico.

When it comes to reconstructing the cultural development of Athapaskan and Numic peoples in the Southwest, archaeology provides a limited number of resources, especially from the period of migration and the moment immediately after their arrival in the vicinity of the Southwest. Much of the information we have comes from Spanish and Mexican chronicles. The earliest use of the term *Apache* has been found in Spanish documents from 1598 (e.g., Hammond and Rey 1940), and occurs later in American administrative reports, censuses, and other government documents. Archaeology also uses the results of ethnographic, ethno-archaeological, and linguistic research conducted from the mid-19th century.

Figure 9.1. Map of potential Numic migration routes (from the west of the North American continent, mainly from California) and the Athapaskans from the areas of today's Canada and Alaska (after Matson and Magne 2007:Fig. 66; Seymour 2012; Simms 2008:Fig. 6.4). Compiled by Radosław Palonka and drawing by Michał Znamirowski.

Archaeological research is obstructed by the fact that little remains of these highly mobile nomadic peoples whose material culture was defined by their economic model and way of life; in addition, it is difficult to distinguish specific characteristics between the early Ute and Athapaskan sites because of their comparable adaptations to the environment, similarities in material culture, and the fact that they occupied the same lands consecutively in relatively short intervals of time (e.g., Wilshusen and Towner 1999:353-54). For archaeological research related to Athapascan and Numic groups it is necessary to use the traditional methodology for researching hunter-gatherer societies (e.g., Herr et al. 2009), even those from the Archaic or Paleoindian period.

Archaeological excavations in the second half of the twentieth century and at the beginning of the twenty-first century, including those by Earl Morris, shed new light on the migration of Numic speakers but primarily Athapaskans to the Southwest and have made major breakthroughs in the quest to discover the first traces of their presence in this region. This research brings together archaeological and dendrochronological studies (e.g., Brunswig 2012; Brunswig and Butler 2004; Lewandowska 2019; Matson and Magne 2007; Schaafsma 1996; 2002; Seymour 2012; Thompson and Towner 2017; Towner 1999; 2003).

However, the exact time of the Athapascans' arrival to the interior of the Southwest is a topic of debate among scholars. Many scholars believe Athapascans were in the Southwest (but the questions remain in what number) in the pre-Hispanic period, for example penetrating some areas of the Southwest during the changing thirteenth century social and environmental landscape (e.g., Metcalfe et al. 2021, Seymour 2012). But some theories based on research posit that the Apache and especially Navajo ethnogenesis in the Southwest occurred much later, placing the earliest archaeological evidence of it in the second half of the seventeenth century (ca. 1670, Schaafsma 2002:308) or at least in the sixteenth century AD, just prior to the Spanish entrada.

Research on the Migration of Athapaskans and Numic Speakers

The thorny issue of exactly when the first Athapaskans hunter-gatherer groups arrived in the Southwest generates a lively discussion in American archaeological and anthropological circles, mainly due to recent discoveries, dating, and publication of earlier possessed data from two sites: Promontory Caves in Utah and Franktown Cave in Colorado just beyond the northern "border" of the Southwest region (e.g., Billinger and Ives 2015; Gilmore 2005; Ives 2014; Ives et al. 2014; Metcalfe et al. 2021; Seymour 2012). Stratigraphic levels from these sites are associated with the first groups of nomadic Athapaskans (proto-Apache and proto-Navajo) and date back to the mid-thirteenth century AD. Genetic and linguistic data also testify to a fairly recent chronology for the arrival of Athapaskan tribes to the Southwest, although not before around 1200/1300–1500 AD. However these studies contradict the oral traditions of Apache and the Navajo groups in which their ancestors had always lived in the Southwest "forever since the dawn of time and the moment of their ancestors' creation." Many myths surrounding the creation strongly reference particular mountain ranges, peaks, and other characteristic forms of terrain and landscape, which is curious given that these groups have only lived in this area for a relatively short period. However, it should be added that other myths link the origins of these peoples with the north.

Based on archaeological and other research, it can be concluded that the ancestors of the modern Apache (Ndee) and Navajo—that is, groups speaking Na-Dene or Athapaskan languages, came to the Southwest from the areas of present-day British Columbia, southwestern and central Canada, and Alaska. They were likely one of the last waves of migration from Asia to America. Even after their arrival in the New World, they lived in the far north, mainly in what is now southern and central Alaska and western Canada (including British Columbia). Only around 800–1000 AD did certain groups (possible ancestors of today's Apache and Navajo) break off from the main Athapaskan core in the north and initiate the great southward migration of (e.g., Matson and Magne 2007; Seymour 2012).

It is traditionally assumed that the first Apache and Navajo arrived in the Southwest in the fourteenth or fifteenth century AD at the earliest, possibly several decades before the Spanish conquistadors, although new data confirms theories of earlier arrivals which determine the thirteenth century AD as the first archaeologically tenable moment for the arrival of Athapaskan groups. Some of these migrants settled on the Pacific coast in what is now northern California and Oregon (these are the so-called Pacific Athapaskans and include the contemporary Hupa and others), but the main expansion was toward the Great Plains followed by the Southwest. Perhaps some remained in the Great Plains (possibly the historic Sarcee and Apache-Kiowa groups), but most headed to the Southwest.

The Athapaskan migration from the north was most likely driven by a volcanic eruption in 803 or 804 AD, likely of Mount Churchill, which appears to have been one of the greatest environmental disasters in North America over the past several thousand years, and one that destroyed much of the natural environment (Matson and Magne 2007; Preece et al. 2014). Nearly 340,000 square kilometers of Alaska and northwestern North America appear to have been directly affected by the aftermath of this volcano's eruption. Traces are visible in a volcanic ash deposit called White River Ash that spread over a vast area, likely destroying the possibility of a normal existence and significantly contributing to the deterioration of living conditions in adjacent areas. Studies of lake sediments and peat bogs show that traces of this eruption may have also reached Greenland and probably even farther to the east (Preece et al. 2014:1020).

This environmental devastation may have sparked a chain reaction of population shifts; as one group pressured neighboring groups and tribes, everyone moved southward in search of more attractive areas for living. The decisive factor may have been the positive "pull" from the Great Plains by groups who were successfully hunting bison or farming, making the area highly attractive to migrants from areas affected by a natural disaster.

The presence of Athapascans in the territory of the Southwest has been theorized by researchers who suggest that their raids drove the great migration of Ancestral Puebloans from the Mesa Verde region bordering in Arizona, Colorado, Utah, and New Mexico at the end of the thirteenth century AD. According to these theories, hunter-gatherer Athapaskan groups attacked the "peaceful" farming communities of the Pueblo, forcing them to abandon their homes. But these potential conflicts are by no means proven archaeologically. Only mutual hostility interspersed with alliances between these two indigenous cultural worlds is known in the period after the Spaniards arrived, and it is from Spanish and Mexican sources and correspondence from the seventeenth and eighteenth centuries that we have this knowledge. As noted above, it is also known that the first Apache and Navajo reached the northern fringes of the Southwest on the eve of the great Pueblo migration in the second half of the thirteenth century. For now, the question of the actual impact of the Athapaskans on the migration of Pueblo peoples remains unresolved. There is also a very interesting theory about the possibility of common ancestry of some Navajo (Diné) and Ancestral Puebloan clans, including "common" histories and relations to the same places, such Chaco Canyon, for example (Iverson 2002; Kelley and Francis 2019; Weiner and Kelley 2021).

Linguistics, Genetics, and Rock Art Illuminate the Migration of the Athapaskans

Although they arrived in the Southwest comparatively late, the Apache and Navajo are essential in its history and cultural development. To determine when and how they arrived, researchers are using data from three disciplines—linguistics, genetics, and archeology—to give us the clearest picture of the arrival of the Navajo and Apache in the Southwest that we have ever had. Advances in technology, notably radiocarbon dating, data analysis, bioarcheology, and genomic sequencing now make it possible to analyze DNA in ancient samples. There are also important ethical issues and Native American rights related to obtaining DNA samples (see for example Reich 2018).

The Apache and Navajo belong to the same Athapaskan-Eyak language family, which is an offshoot of the great *Na-Dene* language family (Opler 1983; Rice 2012; Young 1983). The Southern Athapaskan language group (the southernmost representatives of this family), also referred to as Apache languages, include the close dialects of the Navajo, Western Apache (including San Carlos and White Mountain), Chiricahua, Mescalero, Jicarilla, and Lipan. The Kiowa-Apache (Plains Apache) language is often treated as Athapaskan, but it differs in many ways from the others as do the Jicarilla and Lipan dialects.

The northern Athapaskan language group consists of as many as twenty-three languages and dialects of the peoples who today live in western Canada and Alaska, while the western group consists of eight Athapaskan languages that are still used in northern California and Oregon. Linguistic kinships between the Apache and Navajo and between the Athapaskan peoples from Canada and Alaska were proposed as early as 1852 by William W. Turner. Importantly, Turner's studies were conducted before the reservation period and the large-scale intermingling of various Apache groups and their languages. A full documentation of these linguistic connections between the north and the south was completed in 1936 by Edward Sapir (Brugge 2012; Sapir 1936). To this day, the Sapir publication is the basis of all considerations on the linguistic and cultural relationship of the Athapaskans from Canada and the Southwest (Hoijer 1938;1956; Matson and Magne 2013; Young 1983).

Linguistic research including glottochronology—the use of statistics to pinpoint the date of diversion of language from its common source—has been conducted to help determine when the Northern and Southern Athapaskans split. This type of research operates under the assumption that language functions like genes, with alterations and variants occurring at a population level. When populations separate, subsequent genetic or linguistic changes that arise in one group but not the other can help determine the date of the split. These findings from linguistic studies suggest that a split between the Northern and Southern Athapaskans occurred around 950–1000 AD (e.g., Hilpert 1996:66). Indeed, the dates proposed by glottochronology align well with both the archaeological and genetic data, which is important because it is difficult to pinpoint absolute dating using glottochronology alone.

This linguistic research is supported by DNA studies (Malhi 2012; Malhi et al. 2003) that reveal relatively low genetic variation among the Southern Athapaskans, leading to the conclusion that a small group of Apachean societies probably migrated from the north. Direct evidence that the ancestors of the Southern Athapaskans (Apache and Navajo) were the Athapaskans of Canada is demonstrated by the study of mitochondrial DNA (mtDNA), which is transmitted exclusively (or mainly) in the female line from the mother. These DNA samples are found in hundreds and thousands of copies in a single cell, due to the fact that it is relatively easy to obtain from ancient samples. The male Y chromosome is transmitted in the male line from father to son. In studies of the Y chromosome, geneticists examine the non-recombined part of the chromosome which can only be changed by mutation. Notably in the Apache and Navajo groups, the male Y chromosome has an occasional C haplogroup (a group of similar haplotypes)[1] which is almost entirely absent in other pre-Hispanic and historic communities in the Southwest.

Most relevant in the study of Athapaskan migration from the north and their arrival in the Southwest is haplogroup A of mitochondrial DNA which dominates a large proportion of the Athapaskan populations in the Subarctic region in the north. Haplogroup A now occurs in 50 percent of cases among the Navajo and Western Apache (in the past it was probably more), with the remaining 50 percent being a combination of other haplogroups: B, C, D, and X. These various haplogroups may in turn indicate intermingling of indigenous populations that have lived in the Southwest for a many generations, such as the Pueblo and other groups. Haplogroup A is hardly ever found before the arrival of the Apache and Navajo in pre-Hispanic Southwestern communities, including the Pueblo. In addition, the subhaplogroup A2a is extremely relevant because it occurs among almost 100 percent of western Apache, and a very large percentage of all Athapaskans in the Southwest. Subhaplogroup A2a is often found among the Athapaskans in the Subarctic region of Canada including in the Dogrib group, which is also very similar linguistically to the Apache and are thought to be one of the main groups related to the Apache and Navajo in the Southwest (e.g., Malhi 2012); the subhaplogroup A2a was also found in Siberia.

After their arrival in the Southwest, the Athapaskans mixed with the peoples who previously inhabited these areas—for instance, haplogroups B and C (mtDNA) appear among the Apache and Navajo, but haplogroup A does not increase significantly among the Pueblo, indicating a fairly one-way genetic drift and tending to confirm that Pueblo women were abducted by the Apache and Navajo; this is confirmed in written Spanish sources from the colonial period (e.g., Seymour 2009). Apache and Navajo may have also mixed with other tribes and peoples during their migration, which is also indirectly observable in the genetics (Malhi 2012:241). Since their arrival in the Southwest (or perhaps even a little earlier), the genetic "paths" of the Apache and Navajo as well as their languages diverge slightly.

Archaeological data in the form of rock art confirms and enriches reconstruction of the migration routes taken by these two Athapaskan groups between Alaska and Canada and the Southwest. Rock art depictions of warriors in the Garden Shields style found in the valleys of Big Horn and Wind River and the valleys in the northern part of Wyoming are interpreted by Larry Loendorf (e.g., Loendorf 2004) as almost identical to the style typical of the early Navajo in the Southwest—that is, the Gobernador style, which has also been confirmed by other researchers (Greer and Greer 1999:6–8; Matson and Magne 2007:145, 154). Similarities include comparable preparation techniques of the rock surface before creating the art, and the simultaneous occurrence of petroglyphs and paintings. Notably the use of green color in Garden Shield style, rather unusual in the Great Plains, is popular among Navajo rock art in the Southwest. Warriors are depicted with horns on both sides of heads, and details such as multiple triangles, rectangles and diamonds are used to form and fill shields or turtle figures (figure 9.2). Recently, however, reexaminations of Garden Shields–style sites (for example in terms of their chronology) suggest that some of this rock art may have also been made by Fremont people heading north, introducing shield warriors images to the Athabaskans who might have brought it to the Southwest (Larry Loendorf, e-mail personal communication, 2019); the possibility of Fremont origin of these images was suggested earlier by Jim Keyser (1975).

The Rio Grande valley region stretching from southern Colorado to southern New Mexico and northern Mexico is critically important in the

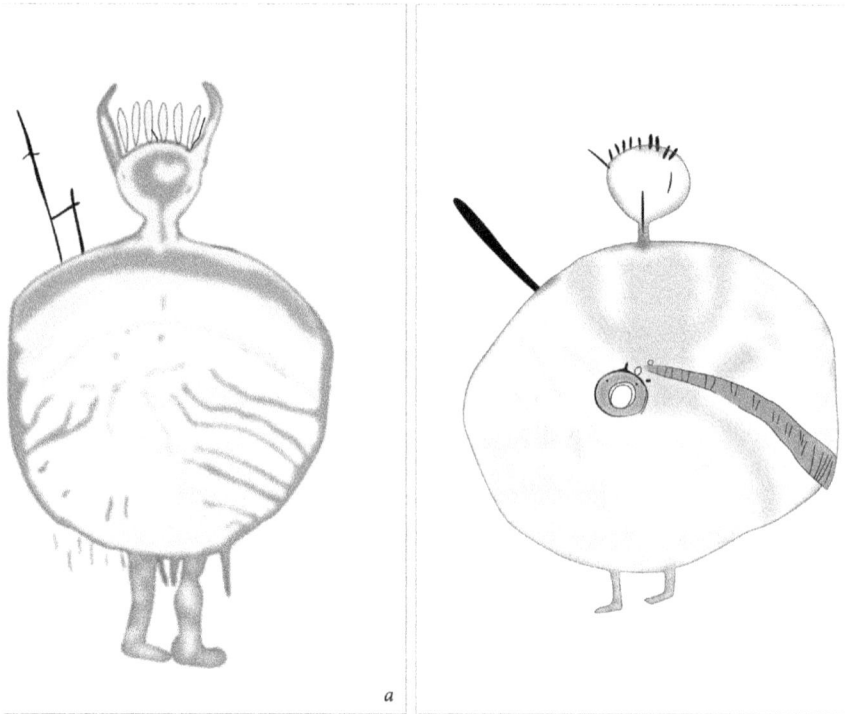

Figure 9.2. Depictions of warriors with shields in the Garden Shields style from the Musselshell site in Montana, interpreted as perhaps being made by the Athabascans along the route of their migration from Canada to the Southwest. Drawings by Katarzyna Ciomek after Palonka 2019:figure 9.5a, original drawings by Larry Loendorf and Sacred Sites Research (https://www.sacredsitesresearch.org/).

study of Athapaskan rock art in the Southwest. At the Rio Grande valley we can trace the intersection of least three major cultural traditions (though not exactly simultaneously)—the Athapaskan, the Pueblo and Mogollon, and the so-called Rio Grande tradition with depictions of anthropomorphic figures with horns, warriors with large, round shields, masks, weapons, and a plethora of animal species. Although analyses of rock art in this area have not revealed dating that could set back the date of the migration of the Athapaskans to the Southwest, they have shed new light on the coexistence of agricultural peoples with incoming hunter-gatherer communities.

Promontory, Franktown, and Dismal River Cultures and the "Problem" with the First Athapascans in the Southwest

The once lively discussion about when the first Athapaskans appeared in the Southwest was revived a few years ago by new discoveries and the verification of older studies on two sites in the northern fringes of the Southwest—the Promontory caves in Utah near the Great Salt Lake and Salt Lake City, and the Franktown Cave on the eastern side of the Rocky Mountains near Denver in central Colorado. These studies may shed new light on when the Athapaskans first appeared farther south, practically in the heart of the Southwest.

The Promontory caves complex was discovered and partially researched in the early 1930s by Julian Steward from the University of Utah. This research was continued by Jack Ives from the University of Alberta from 2011. Both periods of study, mainly from caves number 1 and 2, yielded invaluable information on the first Athapaskans in the Southwest. The analysis and subsequent dating of art found in several caves at the Promontory site became possible with modern technology. Data clearly show that around 850 years ago, in the mid-thirteenth century AD, fairly large groups of people suddenly appeared in this area. Radiocarbon dates (^{14}C and AMS) show that they were inhabited from about 1250 to 1290 AD (Billinger and Ives 2015; Ives 2014; Ives et al. 2014).

A wealth of artifacts mostly made of organic materials have been discovered here, including fragments of woven mats, fishing nets, clothes, parts of musical instruments (drums), woven baskets and bags, ceramics, and flint tools, and bows and arrows (Ives 2014); much of the collection is now at the Utah Museum of Natural History in Salt Lake City. Numerous bones of bison and large species of deer clearly show that most of the food eaten by the inhabitants came from hunting large mammals (including bison); at the same time, there was very little plant food in the diet.

The most interesting information came from an analysis of footwear from excavations conducted in the 1930s as well as new finds from 2011, resulting in the documentation of more than two hundred items of various shoes, mainly leather moccasins. What aroused the interest of researchers and caused a sensation in the scientific world was the fact that leather moccasins, so-called types BSM 2 (Ab) and BSM 2 (Bb) differed from all other moccasins worn by the Southwestern groups of the time, but are almost identical to those produced in the Subarctic region in today's territory of southwest, western, and southern Canada, including the Canadian provinces of British Columbia, Alberta and Saskatchewan, and Alaska, from where the Athapaskans originated (Ives 2014; Ives et al. 2014). Comparative studies even link the discovered moccasins with specific peoples of British Columbia, including the Tsimshian, Tlingit and Tahltan tribes; the oldest known moccasin of this type are dated to around 558–663 AD and are native to the Yukon (Hare et al. 2004). This may prove that some traditions already existed then and were later continued by the proto-Athapaskans, and similar shoes are found in the nineteenth century among the Athapaskans and Algonquians in Canada.

This method of making of leather shoes differed from other groups in the Southwest in that moccasins in both the subarctic region and the Promontory caves were made of one piece of hard leather, most often bison, up to ankle height, while the tongue and uppers were of softer skin from other parts of a bison or deer. The upper often had fur on the inside, and the whole moccasin was decorated with various accessories. Interestingly, as many as 82 percent of moccasins and sandals found in the Promontory caves belonged to children or adolescents up to twelve years of age, while the rest belonged to adults. According to Jacek Ives (e.g., Billinger and Ives 2015), this may indicate that children and adolescents constituted quite a large group within the entire community. Combined with evidence that the inhabitants of the Promontory caves were relatively well-nourished compared with neighboring hunter-gatherer/agricultural Fremont communities and agricultural Pueblo societies of the same period, this evidence suggests that the newcomers adapted well to the new environment and territory to which they had just arrived, and were a thriving community able to later successfully colonize further parts of the Southwest. This is interesting because the thirteenth century AD was a period of climatic and environmental instability, including a long-lasting drought that afflicted practically the entire Southwest, although it seems that the community living in the Promontory caves did not suffer from its effects; on the contrary, they even flourished.

The Promontory site contains other evidence that may speak of potential contact and indirectly testify to migration from the north to the Southwest, which is less known: rock art. Promontory Cave 1 features representations of trapezoidal or triangular anthropomorphic figures with short legs and types of plumes—one of the figures holds objects in his hand. Similar depictions can be found in Fremont art in the Southwest (e.g., Cole 2009; Schaafsma 1980), and identical works comprised of single figures and groups of dancers with a flute-player (similar to the fluteplayer motif from Pueblo rock art) appear in Grotto Canyon in the southwest of Alberta, Canada, which Ives directly associates with relations between the Southwest and the territory of the Northwest and British Columbia in Canada, and with the migration of Athapaskan groups from north to south (e.g., Ives 2004:158 after Magne and Klassen 2002).

Traces of proto-Athapaskans, perhaps the ancestors of the Apache, in the same time frame as those at Promontory, were discovered at Franktown Cave in central Colorado, about forty kilometers south of Denver, on the eastern side of the Rocky Mountains and at the junction of the Great Plains. Like those at Promontory, these discoveries date to the thirteenth century AD (Gilmore 2005; Gilmore et al. 2016). Researchers from the Department of Anthropology at the University of Denver in Colorado have been studying this site since the 1940s. A multiphase settlement stood here at least from the Archaic to the early historic period, from around 8600 BC until 1725 CE, interrupted by numerous hiatuses (e.g., Gilmore 2005; Robert H. Brunswig, personal communication, 2016). AMS radiocarbon dating reveals traces of the presence of Athapaskan people between 1280 and 1400 AD. As with the Promontory caves, the items found are mainly leather moccasins and sandals, as well as some gray ceramics with an admixture of mica, characteristic of the Dismal River culture from the western Great Plains, a culture associated with proto-Apachean migrants from the north.

Interestingly, the populations of the Dismal River/Franktown and Promontory cultures (both cultures were separated by a distance of at least 700–750 km) used obsidian from the same two sources throughout their development—Malad in Idaho and Obsidian Cliff in Wyoming. This may also be proof of the kinship and common lineage from which the Athapaskan people emerged, or at least their strong cultural ties. Moreover Obsidian Cliff is very much embedded in the Apache oral tradition to this day and its name in the Apache language (*Beshtłizhee*) describes the entire area of present-day Yellowstone Park (Carmichael and Farrer 2012).

Most often, the migration of the Athapaskans is studied from the perspective of the Southwest, but several well-researched sites in Canada feature first-class stratigraphy from areas that can be linked with the Athapaskan people, suggesting a starting point for their southern migration. One such site is Eagle Lake in British Columbia (Matson and Magne 2007), where the material culture (mainly flint blades) and other data point to cultural similarities between the Northern and Southern Athapaskans.

The discovery of the Franktown and Promontory sites sheds new light on the arrival of the Athapaskans in the Southwest and tells us a great deal about the potential routes of migration from the north. The main route probably led through present-day Idaho and Wyoming where it may have split into two, with one route running through what is now Utah—a branch associated with the Promontory site (Navajo are known to have lived there later) and the other through the eastern part of the Rocky Mountains through which the proto-Apache may have migrated. (Brunswig 2015; 2020; Gilmore and Larmore 2012; Gordon 2012; Seymour 2012; Wilcox 1981).

Sometimes three different routes from the north to the Southwest are considered for proto-Apache and proto-Navajo, with population movements occurring at different times (Gilmore and Larmore 2012:37–38): (a) the first of these routes may have run along the west of the Rocky Mountains and its ridges, and between the Rocky Mountains, the Cascade Mountains, and the Sierra Madre (the intermountain region) and dates more or less to the second half or the end of the fifteenth century based on data from the Dinétah region of north-central New Mexico); (b) the second route ran through the western part of the Great Plains on the eastern fringe of the Rocky Mountains and is dated slightly later, generally between 1540 and 1680, but probably much earlier (see for example Hill and Trabert 2018) and (c) a "mixed" route using both of the above. It also seems that the ancestors of the modern Navajo may have taken a slightly different route to the Southwest than their Apache brethren, although this split may have taken place just before "entering" the Southwest.

Routes along mountain ridges including the Ute Trail led through the alpine tundra zone of the Rocky Mountains in Colorado and through Rocky Mountain National Park, often at altitudes approaching or exceeding 3,500 meters ASL. The route has been known since the Paleoindian period and was used until relatively late by the Ute, Apache, and Arapaho during the historic period (e.g., Brunswig 2012; Toll 2003:31–34). The accurate determination of the southward migration route taken by Athapaskan tribes is encumbered by the scarcity of archaeological finds. The last few years have improved this picture slightly after the study of proto-Apache sites and the development of archaeology on both sides of the Rocky Mountains in Colorado (e.g., Brunswig 2012; 2020; Gilmore and Larmore 2012; Seymour 2012). The most recent data largely confirm the presence of Athapaskan tribes in this area as early as the fourteenth and fifteenth centuries, and perhaps a little earlier, which corresponds, to the finds from Franktown and Promontory.

From the turn of the fifteenth century, the Apache were undisputedly present in the area of today's Rocky Mountains National Park. For several centuries, the Apache and Utes seem to have taken advantage of the environmental resources of the valleys and mountains during the summer months. The Apache however are thought to have lived in the eastern fringes of the mountains during the winter while the Ute inhabited the western area (e.g., Brunswig 2012; 2020). This coexistence of these two groups of hunter-gatherers continued uninterrupted until 1725 when the Shoshone and Comanche (other Numic speaking groups linguistically related to the Ute) arrived and disrupted the Ute-Apache relationships (figure 9.3).

It is not always fully appreciated how important the oral traditions of the Apache and Navajo are to our understanding of their arrival in this area. Although both groups agree that they have always lived in the Southwest, some of the mythology and naming of places, especially among the Apache, undoubtedly refers to the northern areas. Such is the case for example, with Great Bear Lake in present-day northwestern Canada where, according to the beliefs of the Mescalero Apache, their ancestors

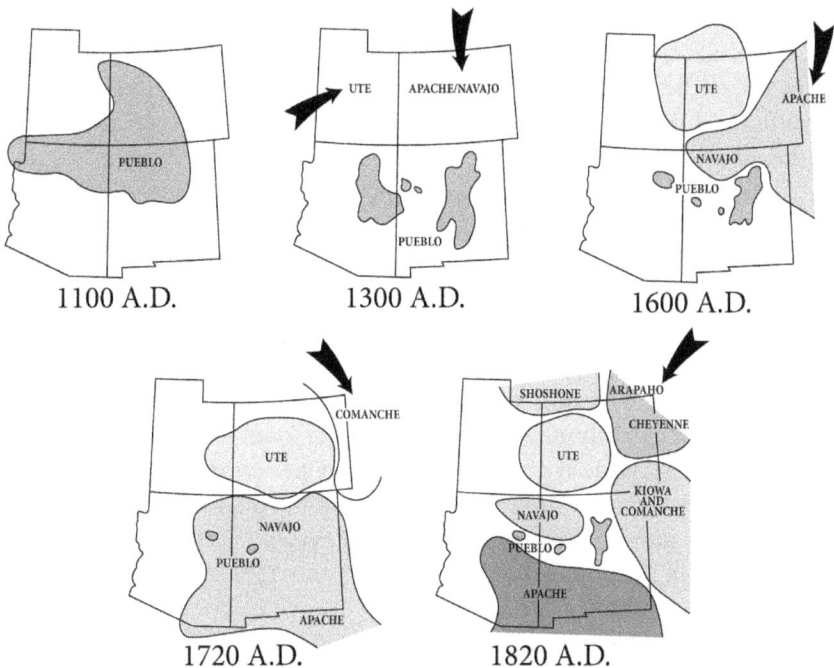

Figure 9.3.   Schematic presentation of changes in the presence of Pueblo culture and selected hunter-gatherer tribes in the Southwest in the late pre-Hispanic and historic period (after Abbott et al. 2013:18; Cassells 1983:Figure 10–12). Compiled by Radosław Palonka and drawing by Michał Znamirowski.

were born—their ancient fathers, the Twin Brothers of War (Carmichael and Farrer 2012; Gordon 2012). The elder brother, the Killer of Enemies, prepared the land for the Mescalero Apache by removing all nuisances, while the younger, Born of Water, created plants and animals for them. These myths and legends also speak of fighting between the ancestors of the Apache and their relatives in the far north, a great catastrophe, and migration to the south. Oral tradition also mentions the names of other places in the north such as Great Slave Lake and Lake Athabasca, and most significantly, the Mescalero Apache claim that their ancestors came from the north from the Land of Ever Winter (Carmichael and Farrer 2012:183) (for Apache place names see also Anschuetz 2002 and Samuels 2001).

The presence of the first Apache on the fringes of the Southwest is associated with the Dismal River Complex (or Dismal River Aspect) that includes sites from eastern Colorado, western Kansas, southeastern Wyoming, and southwestern Nebraska (figure 9.5) (e.g., Cassells 1983:186–87; Gilmore and Larmore 2012). Apache sites are characterized by houses built with a circular layout and with a diameter of about seven to eight meters and either aboveground structures or pithouses often with five main wooden beams constituting the main structural backbone and smaller poles placed between them. Traces of seven structures of this type have been found Cedar Point Village in Colorado in a Dismal River settlement identified with the Apache.

Stones arranged in circles that formed the base of teepee-style residential structures and shelters made of branches distinguish these sites. As shown by radiocarbon studies, such circles may be the remnants of some much older structures, even from the Archaic period (Cassells 1983:189). Researchers are trying to determine the relative chronology of these stone circles and the remains of houses by comparing their diameters. The smaller circles are assumed to have been built before horses were used by Native American communities, and the larger ones after the appearance of horses, which made it possible to transport heavier and larger skins for teepees, and for transporting all their belongings. Examples of sites with Dismal River stone circles are Red Top Ranch and Carizzo Ranches, the latter having been radiocarbon dated to around 1350–1355 AD (Cassells 1983:190).

Dendrochronological dating from preserved wood at the western variants of the Dismal River Complex ranges from 1625 to 1750 AD (Brunswig 1995; Gilmore and Larmore 2012:40). Earlier radiocarbon dates are also available from eastern examples of the Dismal River Complex.

Figure 9.4.   Historic Ute (seventeenth to nineteenth century) rock art at the Strawman Panel Site, Canyons of the Ancients National Monument, southwestern Colorado; the petroglyphs depict anthropomorphic figures, bear paws, and extended scenes that include fighting warriors sometimes on horses and hunting of large animals, mostly deer, bighorn sheep, and bison. Historic inscriptions such as initials, names, and dates (including Spanish and American) are also present. Some of these marks were left by early explorers, settlers, cowboys, and Mexican-American shepherds passing through the canyon at the turn of nineteenth and twentieth century. Photo by Radosław Palonka.

This earlier group is associated with the Apache because their territories and villages are featured in seventeenth-century written sources from the Spanish expeditions to the Great Plains. Despite this dating and traces of material culture, the connection between the Apache and Dismal River is not unequivocally accepted (e.g., Brunswig 2012), although it does seem to be the most logical and plausible theory.

The Tierra Blanca and Cerro Rojo cultural complexes also appear to be associated with the first Athapaskan groups in and around the Southwest (Hughes 2012; Seymour 2004, 2012). The Tierra Blanca complex from northeastern Texas on the Red River and bordering Oklahoma (Texas Panhandle) is dated approximately between thirteenth and sixteenth/seventeenth century AD. Tierra Blanca is characterized by red on gray or black pottery with mica particles, glazed ceramics which have analogies in the Southwest, triangular arrowheads with or without side notches and often made from obsidian, and other types of blades. Settlements were short-term camps with characteristic stone circles and remnants of *wickiups* or teepees and economies based mainly on bison hunting. Cerro Rojo complex in the southern part of the Southwest, mainly southeastern Arizona, southern New Mexico, southwestern Texas, and northern Mexico (the northern parts of Sonora and Chihuahua) is dated to the thirteenth–nineteenth century. Cerro Rojo was defined by Deni J. Seymour mainly on the basis of an inventory of flint and obsidian artifacts and similar types of houses as in the Tierra Blanca complex. Seymour connects this archaeologically distinguished cultural unit with the historically known Chiricahua and Mescalero Apache groups (Seymour 2004, 2012).

Intense research has been devoted in recent years to hunter-gatherer communities in the Southwest. Seymour argues that sites previously unclassified in rock shelters and those constructed as platforms made of branches and stones and filled with grass and yucca leaves were storage facilities for meat and nuts. These can be dated back to the thirteenth/fourteenth century AD (e.g., Powell 2014),

For the Navajo, it often assumed that the earliest ceramics (the Dinétah Gray type) and houses known as *hogans* come from the Dinétah region bordering northern New Mexico and southern Colorado. The oldest confirmed radiocarbon dating associated with the Navajo from this region comes from the LA 55979 site and hovers around 1540/1541 AD. Back then, the Navajo were likely to have been a hunter-gatherer community who were perhaps partially agricultural, growing just corn, squash, and beans.

Information from Spanish missionaries and conquistadors on the Navajo and Apache is quite thin. The Spaniards did not initially distinguish between these two groups, identifying them at the turn of the sixteenth and seventeenth centuries collectively as Querechos or Apache and Cocoyes. Later, the Navajo were distinguished as Apaches del Nabaxu or Apaches de Nabajó—that is "Apache who farm in the valley" (e.g., Opler

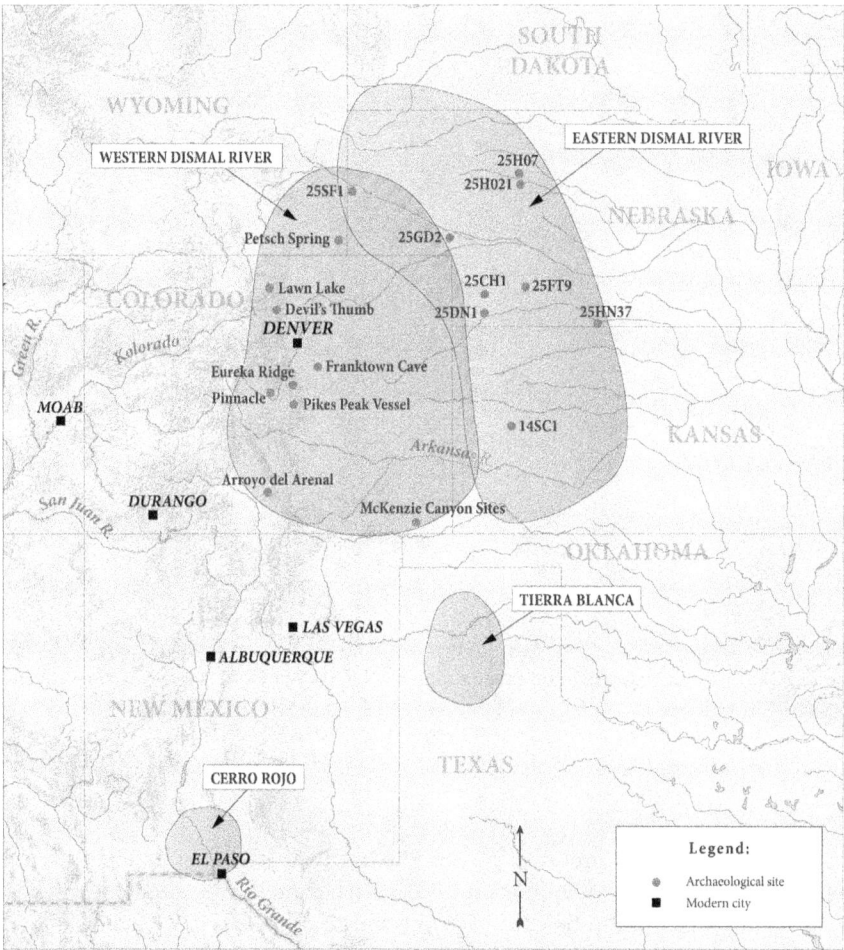

Figure 9.5. The extent of the Dismal River culture (eastern and western variants) and the Tierra Blanca and Cerro Rojo cultural complexes (after various sources). Compiled by Radosław Palonka and drawing by Michał Znamirowski.

1983). Although this geographic division was visible to the Spaniards, they perceived a kinship and strong relationship between the Navajo and Apache. More information about the Athapaskans, in particular the Navajo appears in written sources from the seventeenth century which refer to their conflicts with the Pueblo, Ute, and Spaniards. Recognizing that the Navajos had learned how to breed sheep, goats, horses, and cattle, piqued Spanish curiosity and the Navajo would come to rely more on a pastoral economy, which has to some extent continued until today.

Figure 9.6.   Depiction of Spanish entrada (possibly led by Antonio Narbona in 1805) as the example of historic Navajo rock art; Standing Cow Ruin in Canyon del Muerto, Canyon de Chelly National Monument in northeastern Arizona. Photo by Radosław Palonka.

Note

1. A haplotype is a group of genetic variants that usually occur together and are passed down from only one parent. Haplotypes are shared among individuals in a population, and can be used to define and track their origins, branches, and movement. In the case of mitochondrial DNA (mtDNA) which is inherited only through the maternal side, a haplotype can date ancestral lineage back thousands of years. Unlike most of our DNA which is stored in the cell's nucleus, mitochondrial DNA is found in the mitochondria.

Afterword

S A BOY DREAMING about the American Southwest, I could never have imagined that the reality was so much more fascinating—and that so much of it remained undiscovered. It has been a great joy to pursue a career in archaeology during this time of unprecedented progress. In the last decades, technological advances, growing cultural understanding and relations, expanding public awareness and legislation, and increased funding from government and philanthropic sources have led to remarkable new views of Native American cultures before the arrival of the Europeans, in some cases reversing previous views about various aspects of their history. We have learned how rich and varied the indigenous cultures were and still are, how these cultures responded to their environment, changes in climate, and interactions with other cultures and tribes, much of which is expressed in their architecture, extraordinary artwork, engineering and technology, and their religious practices.

Importantly, today Native American nations and tribes are participants in the scientific study of their past. Collaboration between indigenous communities and archaeologists/anthropologists particularly through native oral traditions and knowledges has provided evidence that has changed the methodology, scientists' perceptions, and our understanding of the past. Native Americans oral histories, passed down from generation to generation in the form of stories, myths, and legends, yield important information about the architecture, the iconography of rock art, and the entire system of social and cultural changes, as well as beliefs. They provide the links between the past and present and the cultural continuity from the pre-Contact/pre-Hispanic period to the present day. Since the second half of the twentieth century, these collaborations have continued to grow and yield invaluable insights.

The North American Southwest is a region rich in environmental and cultural heritage. This book aims to present significant aspects of Native American cultures from the period of first appearance of humans in the Americas until the last centuries or decades before the arrival the Europeans, in particular the first Spanish expeditions. Describing the highly developed farming and cultural traditions from the pre-Hispanic period, including Ancestral Pueblo, Hohokam, Mogollon/Mimbres, or Casas Grandes, I have learned more than I could ever have expected before I started working on it. In this book, I have attempted to share what I have learned about these complex economies, technologies, social structures, and beliefs, as well as artistic (and religious) expressions in the form of decorated pottery, as well as rock art: paintings and petroglyphs on the canyon walls, rocks, and cliff alcoves. Comparing these agricultural societies with the hunter-gatherer and nomad tribes of the period before the introduction of agriculture to the Southwest and later with the historic period was an illuminating and exciting experience. These include pre-Contact Paleoindian, Archaic, and later semi-farming Fremont cultures and the first Athapascans (Apache and Navajo) and Numic speakers (Utes) that actually probably were in or on the fringes of the Southwest before first Spaniards came there. These topics are among the most fascinating emerging explorations in southwestern archaeology and are providing new answers (and new questions).

The future of southwestern archaeology is connected with the future of this branch of science in other parts of the world. Notably, the increasing use of digital methods in archaeological investigations is a key component of noninvasive archaeological protection and conservation of cultural heritage. These methods include laser scanning, photogrammetry, and other advanced digital technics of documentation and subsequent analysis in the virtual environment. Nevertheless, detailed regional studies including excavations and surveys have been and will be essential in discovering the past. With a growing number of regional studies, for example of rock art sites, the documentation and protection of cultural heritage against vandalism, changing weather conditions, and climate unpredictability is and will be one of the most important challenges in the next few decades.

References

Aasen, Diane Katrien. 1984. Pollen, Macrofossil, and Charcoal Analyses of Basketmaker Coprolites from Turkey Pen Ruin, Cedar Mesa, Utah. Unpublished master's thesis, Department of Anthropology, Washington State University, Pullman.

Abbott, Carl, Stephen J. Leonard, and Thomas J. Noel. 2013. *Colorado: A History of the Centennial State.* Boulder: University Press of Colorado.

Abbott, David R. 2003. The Politics of Decline in Canal System 2. In *Centuries of Decline during the Hohokam Classic Period at Pueblo Grande,* edited by D. R. Abbott, pp. 201–27. Tucson: University of Arizona Press.

Abbott, David R., and Michael S. Foster. 2003. Site Structure, Chronology, and Population. In *Centuries of Decline during the Hohokam Classic Period at Pueblo Grande,* edited by D. R. Abbott, pp. 24–47. Tucson: University of Arizona Press.

Adams, E. Charles. 1991. *The Origin and Development of the Pueblo Katsina Cult.* Tucson: University of Arizona Press.

———. 1996. The Pueblo III–Pueblo IV Transition in the Hopi Area. In *The Prehistoric Pueblo World, AD 1150–1350,* edited by M. A. Adler, pp. 48–58. Tucson: University of Arizona Press.

———. 2002. *Homol'ovi: An Ancient Hopi Settlement Cluster.* Tucson: University of Arizona Press.

Adams, E. Charles, and Andrew I. Duff (eds). 2004. *The Protohistoric Pueblo World, AD 1275–1600.* Tucson: University of Arizona Press

Adams, Karen R., and Kenneth L. Petersen. 1999. Environment. In *Colorado Prehistory: A Context for the Southern Colorado River Basin,* edited by W. D. Lipe, M. D. Varien and R. H. Wilshusen, pp. 14–50. Denver: Colorado Council of Professional

Adler, Michael A., Todd Van Pool, and Robert D. Leonard. 1996. Ancestral Pueblo Population Aggregation and Abandonment in the North American Southwest. *Journal of World Prehistory* 3(10): 375–438.

Akins, Nancy J.. 1986. *A Biocultural Approach to Human Burials from Chaco Canyon, New Mexico*. Reports of the Chaco Center No. 9. Santa Fe, NM: Branch of Cultural Research, National Park Service.

Allison, James R. 2015. Introducing the Fremont. *Archaeology Southwest* 29(4):3–5.

Anawalt, Patricia R. 1992. Ancient Cultural Contacts between Ecuador, West Mexico, and the American Southwest: Clothing Similarities. *Latin American Antiquity* 3(2):114–129.

Anderson, Frank G. 1955. The Pueblo Kachina Cult: A Historical Reconstruction. *Southwestern Journal of Anthropology* 11:404–19.

Anschuetz, Kurt F. 2002. A Place of Power at the Edge: Apache Cultural Landscapes and the Petroglyph National Monument. In *"That Place People Talk About": The Petroglyph National Monument Ethnographic Landscape Report,* edited by K. F. Anschuetz, T. J. Ferguson, H. Francis, K. B. Kelley, and C. L. Scheick. Unpublished report prepared by National Park Service, Petroglyph National Monument, Albuquerque, New Mexico.

Anyon, Roger, and Patricia A. Gilman. 2017. Mimbres Preservation, Pithouses, Pueblos, and Pottery. *Archaeology Southwest* 31(1):3–6.

Anyon, Roger, Patricia A. Gilman, and Steven A. LeBlanc. 1981. A Reevaluation of the Mogollon-Mimbres Archaeological Sequence. *Kiva* 46:209–25.

Bahr, Donald M. 2007. O'odham Traditions about the Hohokam. In *The Hohokam Millennium*, edited by P. R. Fish and S. K. Fish, pp. 123–29. Santa Fe, NM: School for Advanced Research Press.

Ballenger, Jesse A.M. 2010. Late Quaternary Archaeology and Paleoenvironments in the San Pedro Basin, Southeastern Arizona, U.S.A. Unpublished PhD dissertation, Department of Anthropology, University of Arizona, Tucson.

Ballenger, Jessen A.M., Vance Holliday, and Guadalupe Sánchez. 2017. The Earliest People in the Southwest. In *The Oxford Handbook of Southwest Archaeology,* edited by B. Mills and S. Fowles, pp. 209–29. New York: Oxford University Press.

Bamforth, Douglas B. 1991. Flintknapping Skill, Communal Hunting, and Paleoindian Projectile Point Technology. *Plains Anthropologist* 137(36):309–23.

Bandelier, Adolf. 1890. *Final Report of Investigation among the Indians of the Southwestern United States, Carried on Mainly in the Years from 1880 to 1885, Part 1.* Papers of the Archaeological Institute of America, American Series No. 3. New York: AMS Press.

Bandi H. G., and Janusz K. Kozłowski. 1981. Le probleme des racines asiatiques du premier peuplement de l' Amerique. *Bulletin de la Société Suisse des Américanistes,* No. 45.

Barlow, K. Renee. 2002. Predicting Maize Agriculture Among the Fremont: An Economic Comparison of Farming and Foraging in the American Southwest. *American Antiquity* 67(1):65–88.

Bayman, James M. 2001. The Hohokam of Southwest North America. *Journal of World Prehistory* 15(3):257–311.

———. 2002. Hohokam Craft Economies and the Materialization of Power. *Journal of Archaeological Method and Theory* 9(1): 69–95.

Bednarik, Robert G. 2014. Pleistocene Palaeoart of the Americas. *Arts* 3:190–206.

Bellwood, Peter. 1997. Prehistoric Cultural Explanations for Widespread Linguistic Families. In *Archaeology and Linguistics: Aboriginal Australia in Global Perspective*, edited by P. McConvell and N. Evans, pp. 123–34. Melbourne: Oxford University Press.

———. 1999. Austronesian Prehistory and Uto-Aztecan Prehistory: Similar Trajectories? University of Arizona Department of Anthropology Lecture Series, Tucson.

Benedict, Ruth. 2006 [1935]. *Patterns of Culture*. New York: Mariner Books.

Bennett, Matthew R., David Bustos, Jeffrey S. Pigati, Kathleen B. Springer, Thomas M. Urban, Vance T. Holliday, Sally C. Reynolds, Marcin Budka, Jeffrey S. Honke, Adam M. Hudson, Brendan Fenerty, Clare Connelly, Patrick J. Martinez, Vincent L. Santucci, Daniel Odess. 2021. Evidence of Humans in North America during the Last Glacial Maximum. *Science* 373(6562):1528–31.

Benson, Larry V., and Michael S. Berry. 2009. Climate Change and Cultural Response in the Prehistoric American Southwest. *Kiva* 75(1):89–119.

Benson, Larry V., E. M. Hattori, J. Southoni, and B. Aleck. 2013. Dating North America's oldest petroglyphs, Winnemucca Lake subbasin, Nevada. *Journal of Archaeological Science* 40:4466–76.

Benson, Larry V., J. P. Smoot, S. P. Lund, S. A. Mensing, F. F. Foit Jr., and R. O. Rye. 2012. Insights from a Synthesis of Old and New Climate-Proxy Data from the Pyramid and Winnemucca Lake Basins for the Period 48–11.5 cal ka. *Quaternary International* 310:62–82.

Bernardini, Wesley. 1999. Reassessing the Scale of Social Action at Pueblo Bonito, Chaco Canyon, New Mexico. *Kiva* 64(4):447–70.

———. 2005. *Hopi Oral Tradition and the Archaeology of Identity*. Tucson: University of Arizona Press.

Billinger, Michael, and John W. Ives. 2015. Inferring Demographic Structure with Moccasin Size Data from the Promontory Caves, Utah. *American Journal of Physical Anthropology* 156:76–89.

Binford, Lewis R. 1962. Archaeology as Anthropology. *American Antiquity* 28(2):217–25.

Boas, Franz. 1928. *Keresan Text*. Publication of the American Ethnological Society no. 8, part 1. New York: American Ethnological Society.

Bostwick, Todd W. 2001. North Native American Agriculturalists. In *Handbook of Rock Art Research*, edited by D. S. Whitley, pp. 414–58. Walnut Creek, CA: Altamira Press.

———. 2002. *Landscape of the Spirits: Hohokam Rock Art at South Mountain Park*. Tucson: University of Arizona Press.

———. 2014. A Good Place to Live for More Than 12,000 Years: Archaeology in Arizona's Verde Valle. *Archaeology Southwest* 28(2):3–5.

Boyd, Carolyn E. 2013. *Rock Art of the Lower Pecos*. Anthropology Series vol. 8. College Station: Texas A&M University Press.

———. 2016. *The White Shaman Mural: An Enduring Creation Narrative in the Rock Art of the Lower Pecos*. Austin: University of Texas Press.

Bradley, Bruce, and Dennis Stanford. 2004. The North Atlantic Ice-Edge Corridor: A Possible Palaeolithic Route to the New World. *World Archaeology* 36(4):459–78.

Bradley, Ronna J. 2000. Recent Advances in Chihuahuan Archaeology. In *Greater Mesoamerica. The Archaeology of West and Northwest Mexico,* edited by M. S. Foster and S. Gorenstein, pp. 221–39. Salt Lake City: University of Utah Press.

Brody, J. J. 1977. *Mimbres Painted Pottery*. Albuquerque: University of New Mexico Press.

———. 2004. *Mimbres Painted Pottery*, revised edtition. Santa Fe: School for Advances Research Press.

Brugge, David M. 2012. Emergence of the Navajo People. In *From the Land of Ever Winter to the American Southwest. Athapaskan Migrations, Mobility, and Ethnogenesis,* edited by D. J. Seymour, pp. 124–49. Salt Lake City: University of Utah Press.

Brunswig, Robert H. 1995. Apachean Ceramics East of Colorado's Continental Divide: Current Data and New Directions. In *Archaeological Pottery of Colorado: Ceramic Clues to the Prehistoric and Protohistoric Lives of the State's Native Peoples,* edited by R. H. Brunswig, B. Bradley and S. M. Chandler, pp. 172–207. Occasional Papers No. 2. Denver: Colorado Council of Professional Archaeologists.

———. 2003. Clovis-Age Artifacts from Rocky Mountain National Park and Vicinity, North Central Colorado. *Current Research in the Pleistocene* 20:7–9.

———. 2007. Paleoindian Cultural Landscapes and Archaeology of North-Central Colorado's Southern Rockies. In *Frontiers in Colorado Paleoindian Archaeology: From the Dent Site to the Rocky Mountains,* edited by R. H. Brunswig and B. L. Pitblado, pp. 261–310. Boulder: University Press of Colorado.

———. 2012. Apachean Archaeology of Rocky Mountains National Park, Colorado, and the Colorado Front Range. In *From the Land of Ever Winter to the American Southwest. Athapaskan Migrations, Mobility, and Ethnogenesis,* edited by D. J. Seymour, pp. 20–36. Salt Lake City: University of Utah Press.

———. 2015. Modeling Eleven Millennia of Seasonal Transhumance and Subsistence in Colorado's Prehistoric Rockies, USA. *Contributions in New World Archaeology* 8:45–104.

———. (ed.). 2020. *Spirit Lands of the Eagle and Bear: Numic Archaeology and Ethnohistory in the Rocky Mountains and Borderlands*. Boulder: University Press of Colorado.

Brunswig, Robert H., and William B. Butler (eds.). 2004. *Ancient and Historic Lifeways in North America's Rocky Mountains. Proceedings of the 2003 Rocky Mountain Anthropological Conference Estes Park, Colorado*. Greeley: Department of Anthropology, University of Northern Colorado and Rocky Mountain National Park, National Park Service.

Bryan, Susan Montoya. 2009. Study Looks at Early Navajo Use of Smoke Signals. Date of use: 8 March 2019. phys.org/news/2009-05-early-navajo.html.

Bullock, Peter Y. 2007. Ancient DNA and Prehistoric Macaws. *Archaeology Southwest* 21(1):6.

Burrillo, R. E. 2019. Where Paleontology and Anthropology Meet. *Archaeology Southwest* 33(1–2):16–17.

Cameron, Catherine M. 2006. Leaving Mesa Verde. In *The Mesa Verde World: Explorations in Ancestral Pueblo Archaeology*, edited by David G. Noble, pp. 139–47. Santa Fe. NM: School of American Research Press.

Cameron, Catherine M., and Jefferey J. Clark. 2018. Stone Materials in the Chaco World. *Archaeology Southwest* 32(2–3):50–51.

Cannon, William J., and Mary J. Ricks. 1986. The Lake County Rock Art Inventory: Implications for Prehistoric Settlement and Land Use Patterns. In *Contributions to the Archaeology of Oregon 1983–1986*, edited by Kenneth M. Ames, pp. 1–23. Association of Oregon Archaeologists Occasional Papers no. 3. Association of Oregon Archaeologists.

Carmichael, David L., and Claire R. Farrer. 2012. We Do Not Forget; We Remember. Mescalero Apache Origins and Migration as Reflected in Place Names. In *From the Land of Ever Winter to the American Southwest. Athapaskan Migrations, Mobility, and Ethnogenesis*, edited by D. J. Seymour, pp. 182–97. Salt Lake City: University of Utah Press.

Carpenter, John P. 1992. The Animas Phase and Paquimé (Casas Grandes): A Perspective and Regional Differentiation and Integration from the Joyce Well Site. Unpublished master's thesis, Department of Anthropology, New Mexico State University, Las Cruces.

Carpenter, John P., Guadalupe Sánchez de Carpenter, and Elisa M. Villalpando. 1999. Preliminary Investigations at La Playa, Sonora, Mexico. *Archaeology Southwest* 13(1):6.

Carpenter, John P., Guadalupe Sánchez, and Elisa M. Villalpando. 2005. The Late Archaic/Early Agricultural Period in Sonora, Mexico. In *The Late Archaic across the Borderlands: From Foraging to Farming*, edited by B. J. Vierra, pp. 13–40. Austin: University of Texas Press.

Cassells, Steve E. 1983. *The Archaeology of Colorado*. Boulder, CO: Johnson Books.

Catacchio, N. N. 1986. Badania archeologiczne jako systematyczny program interdyscyplinarny. In *Teoria i praktyka badań archeologicznych*, vol. 1, edited by W. Hensel, G. Donato, and S. Tabaczyński, pp. 43–54. Wrocław, Poland: PWN.

Cattanach George S. Jr. 1980. *Long House, Mesa Verde National Park, Colorado*. Publications in Archaeology No. 7H. Wetherill Mesa Studies. Washington, DC: National Park Service.

Chapoose, Betsy, Sally Mcbeth, Sally Crum, and Aline Laforge. 2012. Planting A Seed: Ute Ethnobotany. A Collaborative Approach in Applied Anthropology. *The Applied Anthropologist* 32(1):2–11.

Charles, Mona, and Sally J. Cole. 2006. Chronology and Cultural Variation in Basketmaker II. *Kiva* 72(2):167–216.

Childe, Gordon V. 1936. *Man Makes Himself*. London: Watts and Co.

Chisholm Brian, and Richard Ghia Matson. 1994. Carbon and Nitrogen Isotopic Evidence on Basketmaker II Diet at Cedar Mesa, Utah. *Kiva* 60:239–55.

Clark, Jeffery J., and David R. Abbott. 2017. Classic Period Hohokam. In *The Oxford Handbook of Southwest Archaeology*, edited by B. Mills and S. Fowles, pp. 381–96. New York: Oxford University Press.

Clark, Jeffery J., and Deborah L. Huntley. 2012. Who or What Was Salado? *Archaeology Southwest* 26 (3–4):5–6.

Coffey, Grant D., and Kristin A. Kuckelman. 2006. *Report of 2005 Research at Goodman Point Pueblo (Site 5MT604), Montezuma County, Colorado*. Date of use: 10 December 2018. www.crowcanyon.org/goodmanpoint2005.

Cole, Sally J. 2004. Origins, Continuities, and Meaning of Barrier Canyon Style Rock Art. In *New Dimensions in Rock Art Studies*, edited by R. T. Matheny, pp. 7–78. Occasional Paper Series No. 9. Museum of Peoples and Cultures. Provo, UT: Brigham Young University.

———. 2009. *Legacy on Stone: Rock Art of the Colorado Plateau and Four Corners Region* (revised edition). Boulder, CO: Johnson Book.

Cordell, Linda S. 1997. *Archaeology of the Southwest*. San Diego, CA: Academic Press.

———. 2015. Ancient Paquimé. A View from the North. In *Ancient Paquimé and the Casas Grandes World*, edited by P. E. Minnis and M. E. Whalen, pp. 192–208. Amerind Studies in Archaeology. Tucson: University of Arizona Press.

Coulam, Nancy J., and Alan R. Schroedl. 1996. Early Archaic Clay Figurines from Cowboy and Walters Caves in Southeastern Utah. *Kiva* 61(4):401–12.

———. 2004. Late Archaic Totemism in the Greater American Southwest. *American Antiquity* 69(1):41–62.

Craig, Douglas B., and T. Kathleen Henderson. 2007. Houses, Households, and Household Organization. In *Hohokam Millennium*, edited by S. K. Fish and P. R. Fish, pp. 31–37. Santa Fe, NM: School for Advanced Research.

Craig, Douglas B., Henry D. Wallace, and Michael W. Lindeman. 2012. Village Growth and Ritual Transformation in the Southern Southwest. In *Southwestern Pithouse Communities, AD 200–900*, edited by L. C. Young and S. A. Herr, pp. 45–60. Tucson: University of Arizona Press.

Craig, Douglas B., and M. Kyle Woodson. 2017. Preclassic Hohokam. In *The Oxford Handbook of Southwest Archaeology*, edited by B. J. Mills and S. Fowles, pp. 323–52. Oxford: Oxford University Press.

Creel, Darrell, and Charmion McKusick. 1994. Prehistoristoric Macaws and Parrots in the Mimbres Area, New Mexico. *American Antiquity* 59:510–24.

Creel, Darrell, Matthew Williams, Hector Neff, and Michael D. Glascock. 2002. Black Mountain Phase Ceramics and Implications for Manufacture and Exchange Patterns. In *Ceramic Production and Circulation in the Greater Southwest:*

Source Determination by INAA and Complementary Mineralogical Investigations, edited by D. M. Glowacki and H. Neff, pp. 37–46. Los Angeles: Costen Institute of Archaeology, UCLA Press.

Crotty, Helen K. 1995. *Anasazi Mural Art of the Pueblo IV Period, A.D. 1300–1600: Influences, Selective Adaptation, and Cultural Diversity in the Prehistoric Southwest*. Unpublished Ph.D. dissertation, Department of Art, University of California, Los Angeles, University Microfilms, Ann Arbor.

———. 1999 Kiva Murals and Iconography at Picuris Pueblo. In *Picuris Pueblo through Time: Eight Centuries of Change at a Northern Rio Grande Pueblo*, edited by Michael A. Adler and Herbert W. Dick, pp. 149–88. Dallas, TX: William P. Clements Center for Southwest Studies, Southern Methodist University.

———. 2001. Shields, Shield Bearers, and Warfare Imagery in Anasazi Art, 1200–1500. In *Deadly Landscapes: Case Studies in Prehistoric Southwestern Warfare*, edited by Glen Rice and Steven A. LeBlanc, pp. 65–83. Salt Lake City: University of Utah Press.

Crown, Patricia L. 1983. Design Variability on Hohokam Red-on-Buff Ceramics. In *Hohokam Archaeology along the Salt-Gila Aqueduct, Central Arizona Project*, edited by L. S. Teague and P. L. Crown, pp. 205–47. Archaeological Series 8(150). Tucson: Arizona State Museum.

———. 1994. *Ceramics and Ideology: Salado Polychrome Pottery*. Albuquerque: University of New Mexico Press.

———. 2007. Growing Up Hohokam. In *The Hohokam Millennium*, edited by P. R. Fish and S. K. Fish, pp. 23–29. Santa Fe, NM: School for Advanced Research Press.

———. 2016. Just Macaws: A Review for the U.S. Southwest/Mexican Northwest. *Kiva* 82(4):331–63.

Crown, Patricia L., and Susan K. Fish. 1996. Gender and Status in the Hohokam Pre-Classic to Classic Transition. *American Anthropologist* 98: 803–17.

Crown, Patricia L., Jiyan Gu, W. Jeffrey Hurst, Timothy J. Ward, Ardith D. Bravenec, Syed Ali, Laura Kebert, Marlaina Berch, Erin Redman, Patrick D. Lyons, Jamie Merewether, David A. Phillips, Lori S. Reed, and Kyle Woodson. 2015. Ritual Drinks in the Pre-Hispanic US Southwest and Mexican Northwest. *PNAS* 112(37):11436–42.

Crown, Patricia L., and W. Jeffrey Hurst. 2009. Evidence of Cacao Use in the Prehispanic American Southwest. *PNAS* 106(7):2110–13.

Crown, Patricia L., Kerriann Marden, and Hannah V. Mattson. 2016. Foot Notes: The Social Implications of Polydacylia and Foot-Related Imagery at Pueblo Bonito, Chaco Canyon. *American Antiquity* 81:426–48.

Crown, Patricia L., and Wirt Henry Wills III. 2018. The Complex History of Pueblo Bonito and Its Interpretation. *Antiquity* 92: 890–904.

Cushing, Frank Hamilton. 1981. *Zuni: Selected Writings of Frank Hamilton Cushing*. Lincoln: University of Nebraska Press.

———. 1986 [1901]. *Zuni Folk Tales*. Tucson: University of Arizona Press.

Davis, Christopher Sean. 2016. Solar-Aligned Pictographs at the Paleoindian Site of Painel do Pilao along the Lower Amazon River at Monte Alegre, Brazil. *PLoS ONE* 11(12): e0167692.

Davis, Leslie B., Matthew J. Root, Stephen A. Aaberg, and William P. Eckerle. 2009. Paleoarchaic Incised Stones from Barton Gulch, Southwest Montana. *Current Research in the Pleistocene* 26:42–44.

Davis, William E., and Jonathan D. Till. 2014. The Lime Ridge Clovis Site. *Archaeology Southwest* 28(3/4):23–24.

Dean, Jeffrey S., and John C. Ravesloot. 1993. The Chronology of Cultural Interaction in the Gran Chichimeca. In *Culture and Contact, Charles C. Di Peso's Gran Chichimeca*, edited by A. I. Woosley and J. C. Ravesloot, pp. 83–103. Albuquerque: University of New Mexico Press.

Dean, Jeffrey S., and Carla Van West. 2002. Environment-Behavior Relationships in Southwestern Colorado. In *Seeking the Center Place: Archaeology and Ancient Communities in the Mesa Verde Region*, edited by M. D. Varien and R. H. Wilshusen, pp. 81–99. Salt Lake City: University of Utah Press.

Decker, K.W., and L. L. Tieszen. 1989. Isotopic Reconstruction of Mesa Verde Diet from Basketmaker III to Pueblo III. *Kiva* 55:33–47.

Deeringer, Martha. 2012. Folsom Bench Mark. The Lindenmeier Site. *Mammoth Trumpet* 27(4):5–9.

Deloria, Vine Jr. 1997. Conclusion: Anthros, Indians, and Planetary Reality. In *Indians and Anthropologists: Vine Deloria Jr and the Critique of Anthropology*, edited by T. Biolsi and L. Zimmerman, pp. 209–21. Tucson: University of Arizona Press.

Dillehay, Tom D. 2009. Probing Deeper into first American Studies. *PNAS* 106(4):971–78.

Di Peso, Charles C. (ed.). 1974. *Casas Grandes. A Fallen Trading Center of the Gran Chichimeca*, vols. 1–3. Flagstaff–Dragoon, AZ: The Amerind Foundation and Northland Press.

Di Peso, Charles C., John B. Rinaldo, and Gloria J. Fenner. 1974. *Casas Grandes. A Fallen Trading Center of the Gran Chichimeca*, vols. 4–8. Flagstaff–Dragoon, AZ: The Amerind Foundation and Northland Press.

Doelle, William H. 1999. Early Maize in the Greater Southwest. *Archaeology Southwest* 13(1):1.

Doelle, William H., Andy Laurenzi, and Ella Pierpoint. 2011. The Great Bend of the Gila. *Archaeology Southwest* 25(1):1–12.

Dolan, Sean G., Michael E. Whalen, Paul E. Minnis, and M. Steven Shackley. 2017. Obsidian in the Casas Grandes World: Procurement, Exchange, and Interaction in Chihuahua, Mexico, CE 1200–1450. *Journal of Archaeological Science: Reports* 11:555–67.

Dongoske, Kurt E., Michael Yeatts, Roger Anyon, and Thomas J. Ferguson. 1997. Archaeological Cultures and Cultural Affiliation: Hopi and Zuni Perspectives in the American Southwest. *American Antiquity* 62(4):600–608.

Doolittle, William E. 1988. *Pre-Hispanic Occupance in the Valley of Sonora, Mexico: Archaeological Confirmation of Early Spanish Reports*. The Anthropological Papers of the University of Arizona, vol. 48. Tucson: University of Arizona Press.

———. 1991. A Finger on the Hohokam Pulse. In *Prehistoric Irrigation in Arizona: Symposium 1988*, edited by Cory D. Breternitz, pp. 139–54. Soil Systems Publications in Archaeology No. 17. Phoenix, AZ: Soils Systems.

———. 1992. Agriculture in North America on the Eve of Contact: A Reassessment. *Annals of the Association of American Geographers* 82(3):386–401.

Doolittle, William E., and Jonathan B. Mabry. 2006. Environmental Mosaics, Agricultural Diversity, and the Evolutionary Adoption of Maize in the American Southwest. In *Histories of Maize: Multidisciplinary Approaches to the Prehistory, Biogeography, Domestication, and Evolution of Maize*, edited by J. Staller, R. Tykot and B. Benz, pp. 109–121. San Diego: Elsevier.

Doolittle, William E., and James A. Neely (eds.). 2004. A Checkered Landscape. In *The Safford Valley Grids. Prehistoric Cultivation in the Southern Arizona Desert*, edited by W. E. Doolittle, J. A. Neely and K. R. Adams, pp. 1–17. Anthropological Papers of the University of Arizona no. 70. Tucson: University of Arizona Press.

Downer, Alan S. 1997. Archaeologists—Native American Relations. In *Native Americans and Archaeologists: Stepping Stones to Common Ground*, edited by N. Swidler, K. E. Dongoske, R. Anyon and A. S. Downer, pp. 23–34. Walnut Creek, CA: Altamira Press.

Downum, Christian E. 2007. Cerros de Trincheras in Southern Arizona: Review and Current Status of the Debate. In *Trincheras Sites in Time, Space, and Society*, edited by S. K. Fish, P. R. Fish and M. E. Villalpando, pp. 101–36. Tucson: University of Arizona Press.

Downum, Christian E., and Todd W. Bostwick. 2003. The Platform Mound. In *Centuries of Decline during the Hohokam Classic Period at Pueblo Grande*, edited by D. R. Abbott, pp. 166–200. Tucson: University of Arizona Press.

Doyel, David E. 1991. Hohokam Exchange and Interaction. In *Chaco and Hohokam: Prehistoric Regional Systems in the American Southwest*, edited by P. L. Crown and W. J. Judge, pp. 225–52. Santa Fe. NM: School for Advanced Research Press.

———. 2007. Irrigation, Production, and Power in Phoenix Basin Hohokam Society. In *The Hohokam Millennium*, edited by P. R. Fish and S. K. Fish, pp. 82–89. Santa Fe, NM: School for Advanced Research Press.

Driver, Jonathan C. 2002. Faunal Variation and Change in the Northern San Juan Region. In *Seeking the Center Place: Archaeology and Ancient Communities in the Mesa Verde Region*, edited by M. D. Varien and R. H. Wilshusen, pp. 143–160. Salt Lake City: University of Utah Press.

Elias S. A., and J. Brigham-Grette. 2007. Late Pleistocene Events in Beringia. In *Glaciations. Late Pleistocene Events in Beringia*, edited by S. A. Elias, pp. 1057–66. Amsterdam: Elsevier.

Elson, Mark D. 2007. Into the Earth and Up to the Sky: Hohokam Ritual Architecture. In *The Hohokam Millennium*, edited by P. R. Fish and S. K. Fish, pp. 49–55. Santa Fe, NM: School for Advanced Research Press.

Erdman, James A., Charles L. Douglas, and John W. Marr. 1969. *Environment of Mesa Verde, Colorado*. Washington, DC: Wetherill Mesa Studies, National Park Service.

Ericson, Jonathon E., and Timothy G. Baugh (eds.). 1993. *The American Southwest and Mesoamerica: Systems of Prehistoric Exchange*. New York: Plenum Press.

Espenshade, Christopher T. 1997. Mimbres Pottery, Births, and Gender: A Reconsideration. *American Antiquity* 62(4):733–36.

Ezell, Paul H. 1963. Is There A Hohokam-Pima Culture Continuum? *American Antiquity* 29(1):61–66.

Fagan, Brian M. 2000. *Ancient North America. The Archaeology of a Continent*. London: Thames & Hudson.

Farrell, Mary Margaret, and Jeffery Franz Burton. 2006. Rock Art of the Southeastern Arizona Sky Islands: Eighty Sites on the Coronado National Forest. In *1994 IRAC Proceedings, Rock Art-World Heritage*, edited by F. Bock and A. J. Bock, pp. 277–88. Phoenix: American Rock Art Research Association, Phoenix.

Ferguson, Thomas John, Kurt E. Dongoske, and Leigh J. Kuwanwisiwma. 2001. Hopi Perspectives on Southwestern Mortuary Studies. In *Ancient Burial Practices in the American Southwest: Archaeology, Physical Anthropology, and Native American Perspectives*, edited by D. R. Mitchell and J. L. Brunson-Hadley, pp. 9–26. Albuquerque: University of New Mexico Press.

Fewkes, Jesse Walter. 1912. Casa Grande, Arizona. In *Twenty-Eighth Annual Report of the Bureau of American Ethnology*, pp. 25–179. Washington DC: US Government Printing Office.

———. 1916. Animal Figures on Prehistoric Pottery from Mimbres Valley, New Mexico. *American Anthropologist, New Series* 18(4):535–45.

Fiedel, Stuart J. 1992. *Prehistory of the Americas*. Cambridge: Cambridge University Press.

———. 2000. The Peopling of the New World: Present Evidence, New Theories, and Future Directions. *Journal of Archaeological Research* 8(1):39–103.

———. 2005. Man's Best Friend—Mammoth's Worst Enemy? A Speculative Essay on the Role of Dogs in Paleoindian Colonization and Megafaunal Extinction. *World Archaeology* 37(1):11–25.

Firestone, R. B., A. West, J.P. Kennett, L. Becker, T. E. Bunch, Z.S. Revay, P. H. Schultz, T. Belgya, D. J. Kennett, J. M. Erlandson, O. J. Dickenson, A. C. Goopaintar, R. S. Harris, G. A. Howard, J. B. Kloosterman, P. Lechler, P. A. Mayewski, J. Montgomery, R. Poreda, T. Darrah, S. S. Que Hee, A. R. Smith, A. Stich, W. Topping, J. H. Wittke, and W .S. Wolbach. 2007. Evidence for an Extraterrestrial Impact 12,900 Years Ago That Contributed to the Megafaunal Extinctions and the Younger Dryas Cooling. *PNAS* 104(41):16016–21.

Fish, Paul R., and Suzanne K. Fish. 2007. The Hohokam Millennium. In *The Hohokam Millennium*, edited by P. R. Fish and S. K. Fish, pp. 1–11. Santa Fe, NM: School for Advanced Research Press.

———. (eds.). 2007. *The Hohokam Millennium*. Santa Fe, NM: School for Advanced Research Press.

———. 2012. Hohokam Society and Water Management. In *The Oxford Handbook of North American Archaeology*, edited by T. R. Pauketet, pp. 571–84. Oxford: Oxford University Press.

Fish, Paul, Suzanne K. Fish, and John Madsen. 2006. *Prehistory and Early History of the Malpai Borderlands*. General Technical Report No. RMRS-GTR-176. USDA Forest Service. Fort Collins, CO: Rocky Mountain Research Station.

Fish, Suzanne K., Paul R. Fish, and M. Elisa Villalpando (eds.). 2007. *Enduring Borderlands Traditions. Trincheras Sites in Time, Space, and Society*. Tucson: University of Arizona Press.

Flannery, Kent V. 1968. Archaeological Systems Theory and Early Mesoamerica. In *Anthropological Archaeology in the Americas*, edited by B. J. Meggars, pp. 67–87. Washington, DC: Anthropological Society of Washington

Flint, Richard. 2005. What They Never Told You about the Coronado Expedition. *Kiva* 71(2): 203–17.

Flint, Richard. and Shirley Flint. 2005. *Documents of the Coronado Expedition 1539–1542: "They Were Not Familiar with His Majesty, nor Did They Wish to Be His Subjects."* Albuquerque: University of New Mexico Press.

Ford, Richard I. 1981. Gardening and Farming before AD 1000: Pattern of Prehistoric Cultivation North of Mexico. *Journal of Ethnobiology* 1(1):6–27.

———. 1985. Patterns of Prehistoric Food Production in North America. In *Prehistoric Food Production in North America*, edited by R. I. Ford, pp. 341–64. Anthropological Paper no. 75. Ann Arbor: Museum of Anthropology, University of Michigan.

Forton, Maxwell M. 2020. House of Shields: Defensive Imagery at Defensive Sites in Tsegi Canyon. *Kiva* 86(1):108–27.

Fowler, Catherine S. 1988. Paleo-Indian Subsistence and Settlement during the Post-Clovis Times on the Northwestern Plains, the Adjacent Mountain Ranges, and Intermontane Basins. *Ethnology Monographs* 12:83–106.

Fowler, Don D. 1982. Cultural Resources Management. *Advances in Archaeological Method and Theory* 5:1–50.

Fowles, Severin. 2012. The Pueblo Village in and Age of Reformation (AD 1300–1600). In *The Oxford Handbook of North American Archaeology*, edited by T. Pauketat, pp. 631–44. Oxford: Oxford University Press.

Friedman, Richard A., Anna Sofaer, and Robert S. Weiner. 2017. Remote Sensing of Chaco Roads Revisited. Lidar Documentation of the Great North Road, Pueblo Alto Landscape, and Aztec Airport Mesa Road. *Advances in Archaeological Practice* 5(4):1–17.

Frison, George C. 1988. Paleoindian Subsistence and Settlement during Post-Clovis Times on the Northwestern Plains, the Adjacent Mountain Ranges, and Intermontane Basins. In *Americans Before Columbus: Ice-Age Origins*, edited by R. C. Carlisle, pp. 83–106. Ethnology Monographs No. 12. Pittsburgh, PA: University of Pittsburgh.

Gamboa, Carrera, and Eduardo Pío. 2003. Exploring the Mountains of Chihuahua: Proyecto Provincia Serrana de Paquime. *Archaeology Southwest* 17(2):9.

Geib, Phil R., and Helen C. Fairley. 1992. Radiocarbon Dating of Fremont Anthropomorphic Rock Art in Glen Canyon, South-Central Utah. *Journal of Field Archaeology* 19(2):155–68.

Geib, Phil R., and Kimberly Spurr. 2002. The Basketmaker II–III Transition of the Rainbow Plateau. In *Foundation of Anasazi Culture: The Basketmaker-Pueblo Transition*, edited by P. F. Reed, pp. 175–200. Salt Lake City: University of Utah Press.

Gillam, Mary, and Robert G. Bednarik. 2015. *Controversial Mammoth Petroglyph at Sand Island, Utah.* Poster presented at Colorado Archaeological Society Conference, October 10, 2015.

Gilman, Patricia A., Marc Thompson, and Kristina C. Wyckoff. 2014. Ritual Change and the Distant: Mesoamerican Iconography, Scarlet Macaws, and Great Kivas in the Mimbres Region of Southwestern New Mexico. *American Antiquity* 79(1):90–107.

Gilmore, Kevin P. 2005. *National Register Nomination Form Franktown Cave (5DA272), Douglas County, Colorado.* Washington, DC: Office of Archaeology and Historic Preservation; Denver: Colorado Historic Society.

Gilmore, Kevin, Derek Hamilton, and John Ives. 2016. *Promontory Culture on the Plains II: New Data from Franktown Cave and the Context for Proto-Apachean Migration in Eastern Colorado.* Paper presented at Colorado Council of Professional Archaeologists Annual Meeting, Salida, CO.

Gilmore, Kevin P., and Sean Larmore. 2012. Looking for Lovitt in All the Wrong Places. Migration Models and the Athapaskan Diaspora as Viewed from Eastern Colorado. In *From the Land of Ever Winter to the American Southwest: Athapaskan Migrations, Mobility, and Ethnogenesis*, edited by D. J. Seymour, pp. 37–77. Salt Lake City: University of Utah Press.

Glowacki, Donna M. 2015. *Living and leaving: a social history of regional depopulation in thirteenth-century Mesa Verde.* Tucson: University of Arizona Press.

Goebel, Ted, Michael R. Waters, and Dennis H. O'Rourke. 2008. The Late Pleistocene Dispersal of Modern Humans in the Americas. *Science* 319:1497–502.

Gómez-Coutouly, and Charles E. Holmes. 2018. The Microblade Industry from Swan Point Cultural Zone 4b: Technological and Cultural Implications from the Earliest Human Occupation in Alaska. *American Antiquity* 83(4): 735–52.

Gordon, Brian C. 2012. The Ancestral Chipewyan Became Navajo and Apache. New Support for a Northwest Plains-Mountain Route to the American Southwest. In *From the Land of Ever Winter to the American Southwest. Athapaskan*

Migrations, Mobility, and Ethnogenesis, edited by D. J. Seymour, pp. 303–55. Salt Lake City: University of Utah Press.

Grant, Campbell. 1978. *Canyon de Chelly: Its People and Rock Art.* Tucson: University of Arizona Press.

Greer, Mavis, and John Greer. 1999. *Two Rock Art Sites in the Powder River Basin.* Paper presented at 4th Annual Meeting of the Rocky Mountain Anthropological Association, Glenwood Springs, Colorado.

Guernsey, Samuel James. 1931. *Explorations in Northeastern Arizona. Report on the Archaeological Fieldwork of 1920–1923.* Papers of the Peabody Museum of American Archaeology and Ethnology 12(1). Cambridge, MA: Peabody Museum.

Guidon, Niede, and G. Delibrias. 1986. Carbon-14 Dates Point to Man in the Americas 32,000 Years Ago. *Nature* 321:769–71.

Guiterman Christopher H., Thomas W. Swetnam, and Jeffrey S. Dean. 2016. Eleventh-Century Shift in Timber Procurement areas for the Great Houses of Chaco Canyon. *PNAS* 113(5):1186–90.

Haas, Jonathan, and Winifred Creamer. 1993. Stress and Warfare among the Kayenta Anasazi of the Thirteenth Century A.D. *Fieldiana Anthropology*, New Series, No. 21, Publication 1450. Chicago: Field Museum of Natural History.

Hammond, George P., and Agapito Rey. 1940. *Narratives of the Coronado Expedition, 1540–1542.* Albuquerque: University of New Mexico Press.–

Hard, Robert J., and John R. Roney. 2005. The Transition to Farming on the Rio Casas Grandes and in the Southern Jornada Mogollon Region. In *The Late Archaic across the Borderlands: From Foraging to Farming*, edited by B. J. Vierra, pp. 141–86. Austin: University of Texas Press.

Hare, P. Gregory, Sheila Greer, Ruth Gotthardt, Richard Farnell, Vandy Bowyer, Charles Schweger, and Diane Strand. 2004. Ethnographic and Archaeological Investigations of Alpine Ice Patches in Southwest Yukon, Canada. *Arctic* 57 (3):260–72.

Hare, P. Gregory, Christian D. Thomas, Timothy N. Topper, and Ruth M. Gotthardt. 2012. The Archaeology of Yukon Ice Patches: New Artifacts, Observations, and Insights. *Arctic* 65 (suppl. 1):118–35.

Haury, Emil W. 1988. Recent Thoughts on the Mogollon. *Kiva* 53(2):195–96.

Haynes, C. Vance Jr. 2008. Younger Dryas "Black Mats" and the Rancholabrean Termination in North America. *PNAS* 105:6520–25.

Haynes, C. Vance Jr., and Bruce B. Huckell (eds.). 2007. *Murray Springs: A Clovis Site with Multiple Activity Areas in the San Pedro Valley, Arizona.* Anthropological Papers of the University of Arizona, no. 71. Tucson: University of Arizona Press.

Haynes C. Vance Jr., J. Boerner, K. Domanik, D. Lauretta, J. Ballenger, and J. Goreva. 2010. The Murray Springs Clovis Site, Pleistocene Extinction, and the Question of Extraterrestrial Impact. *PNAS* 107(9):4010–15.

Haynes, Gary. 2002. *The Early Settlement of North America: The Clovis Era.* New York: Cambridge University Press.

———— (ed.). 2009. *American Megafaunal Extinctions at the End of the Pleistocene.* Dordrecht, Germany: Springer.

————. 2015. The Millennium before Clovis. *PaleoAmerica* 1(2):134–62.

Hegmon, Michelle. 2002. Recent Issues in the Archaeology of the Mimbres Region of the North American Southwest. *Journal of Archaeological Research* 10(4):307–57.

Hegmon, Michelle, and Stephanie Kulow. 2005. Painting as Agency, Style as Structure: Innovations in Mimbres Pottery Designs from Southwest New Mexico. *Journal of Archaeological Method and Theory* 12(4):313–34.

Hegmon, Michelle, James R. McGrath, E. Michael O'Hara III, and Will G. Russel. 2018. Mimbres Pottery Design in Their Social Contexts. In *New Perspectives on Mimbres Archaeology. Three Millenia of Human Occupation in the North American Southwest,* edited by Barbara J. Roth, Patricia A. Gilman, and Roger Anyon. Tucson: University of Arizona Press.

Hegmon, Michelle, and Margaret Nelson. 2003. The Archaeology and Meaning of Mimbres. *Archaeology Southwest* 17(4):1–2.

Hegmon, Michelle, and Will Russell. 2013. A Quantitative Method for Recognizing the Same Hands in Mimbres Black-on-White Pottery, Date of use: 10 December 2018. core.tdar.org/document/377853/a-quantitative-method-for-recognizing--the-same-hands-in-mimbres-black-on-white-pottery.

Hegmon, Michelle, Will G. Russell, Kendall Baller, Matthew A. Peeples, and Sarah Striker. 2021. The Social Significance of Mimbres Painted Pottery in the U.S. Southwest. *American Antiquity* 86(1):23–42.

Hegmon, Michelle, and Wenda R. Trevathan. 1996. Gender, Anatomical Knowledge, and Pottery Production: Implications of an Anatomically Unusual Birth Depicted on Mimbres Pottery from Southwestern New Mexico. *American Antiquity* 61(4):747–54.

Heintzman, Peter D., Duane Froese, John W. Ives, André E. R. Soares, Grant D. Zazula, Brandon Letts, Thomas D. Andrews, Jonathan C. Driver, Elizabeth Hall, P. Gregory Hare, Christopher N. Jass, Glen MacKay, John R. Southon, Mathias Stiller, Robin Woywitka, Marc A. Suchardl, and Beth Shapiro. 2016. Bison Phylogeography Constrains Dispersal and Viability of the Ice Free Corridor in Western Canada. *PNAS* 113(29):8057–63.

Heitman, Carrie C. 2015. The House of Our Ancestors: New Research on the Prehistory of Chaco Canyon, New Mexico, A.D. 800–1200. In *Chaco Revisited New Research on the Prehistory of Chaco Canyon, New Mexico,* edited by Carrie C. Heitman and Stephen Plog, pp. 215–48. Tucson: University of Arizona Press.

Hemmings, E. Thomas, and C. Vance Haynes Jr. 1969. The Escapule Mammoth and Associated Projectile Points, San Pedro Valley, Arizona. *Journal of the Arizona Academy of Science* 5:184–88.

Hernbrode, Janine and Peter Boyle. 2016. Petroglyphs and Bell Rocks at Cocoraque Butte: Further Evidence of the Flower World Belief Among the Hohokam. *American Indian Rock Art, Vol.42.* Ken Hedges, Editor. American Rock Art Research Association, pp. 91–105.

Herr, Sarah, Chris North, and J. Scott Wood. 2009. Scouting for Apache Archaeology in the Sub-Mogollon Rim Region. *Kiva* 75(1):35–62.

Hill, J. Brett. 2019. *From Huhugam to Hohokam. Heritage and Archaeology in the American Southwest.* Issues in Southwest Archaeology series. Lanham, MD: Lexington Books.

Hill, Jane H. 1999. Linguistics. *Archaeology Southwest* 13(1):8–9.

———. 2001. Proto-Uto-Aztecan: A Community of Cultivators in Central Mexico? *American Anthropologists* 103:913–34.

———. 2002. Toward a Linguistic Prehistory of the Southwest: "Azteco-Tanoan" and the Arrival of Maize Cultivation. *Journal of Anthropological Research* 58(4):457–75.

———. 2017. Historic Linguistics. In *The Oxford Handbook of Southwest Archaeology,* edited by B. Mills and S. Fowles, pp. 122–35. New York: Oxford University Press.

Hill, Matthew E., Jr. and Sarah Trabert. 2018. Reconsidering the Dismal River aspect: A review of current evidence for an Apachean (Ndee) cultural affiliation. *Plains Anthropologist* 63(247): 198–222.

Hilpert, Bruce E. 1996. The Inde (Western Apaches). The People of the Mountains. In *Paths of Life: Native Americans of the Southwest and Northern Mexico,* edited by T. E. Sheridan and N. J. Parezo, pp. 61–90. Tucson: University of Arizona Press.

Hoijer, Harry. 1938. The Southern Athapaskan Languages. *American Anthropologist* 40(1):75–87.

———. 1956. The Chronology of the Athapaskan Languages. *International Journal of American Linguistics* 22(4):219–32.

Holliday, Vance T. 2000. The Evolution of Paleoindian Geochronology and Typology on the Great Plains. *Geoarchaeology* 15:227–90.

Holliday, Vance T., Bruce B. Huckell, James M. Mayer, and Steven L. Forman. 2006. Geoarchaeology of the Boca Negra Wash Area, Albuquerque Basin, New Mexico. *Geoarchaeology* 21:765–802.

Huckell, Bruce B. 1996. The Archaic Prehistory of the North American Southwest. *Journal of World Prehistory* 10(3):305–73.

Huckell, Bruce B., and C. Vance Haynes. 2003. The Ventana Complex: New Dates and New Ideas on Its Place in Early Holocene Western Prehistory. *American Antiquity* 68(2):333–52.

Hughes, David T. 2012. Tierra Blanca: A Complex Issue. In *From the Land of Ever Winter to the American Southwest. Athapaskan Migrations, Mobility, and Ethnogenesis,* edited by Deni J. Seymour, pp. –36. Salt Lake City: University of Utah Press.

Hull, Sharon, and Mostafa Fayek. 2012. Cracking the Code of Pre-Columbian Turquoise Trade Networks and Procurement Strategies. In *Turquoise in Mexico and North America: Science, Conservation, Culture and Collections*, edited by J. C. H. King, Max Carocci, Caroline Cartwright, Colin McEwan, Rebecca Stacey, pp. 29–40. London: Archetype Publications.

Huntley, Deborah L. 2012. Pottery, Heritage, and Ideology in the Greater Upper Gila Region, 1200–1450. *Archaeology Southwest* 26(3–4):16–18.

Ilger, Wayne, Marian Hyman, John Southon, and Marvin Rowe. 1995. Dating Pictographs with Radiocarbon. *Radiocarbon* 37(2):299–310.

Irwin-Williams, Cynthia. 1979. Post-Pleistocene Archaeology 7000–2000 BC. In *Handbook of North Native Americans, vol. 9: Southwest*, edited by A. Ortiz, pp. 33–42. Washington, DC: Smithsonian Institution.

Iverson, Peter. 2002. *Diné: A History of the Navajos*. Albuquerque: University of New Mexico Press.

Ives, John W. 2014. Resolving the Promontory Culture Enigma. In *Archaeology of the Great Basin and Southwest. Papers in Honor of Don D. Fowler,* edited by N. J. Parezo and J. C. Janetski, pp. 149–62. Salt Lake City: University of Utah Press.

Ives, John W., Duane G. Froese, Joel C. Janetski, Fiona Brock, and Christopher Bronk Ramsey. 2014. A High Resolution Chronology for Steward's Promontory Culture Collections, Promontory Point, Utah. *American Antiquity* 79(4):616–37.

Jackson, William H., and William H. Holmes. 1981. *Hayden Survey, 1874–1876: Mesa Verde and the Four Corners*. Bear Creek Publishing, Ouray.

Janetski, Joel C., and Richard K. Talbot. 2014. Fremont Social Organization. A Southwestern Perspective. In *Archaeology of the Great Basin and Southwest. Papers in Honor of Don D. Fowler,* edited by N. J. Parezo and J. C. Janetski, pp. 118–29. Salt Lake City: The University of Utah Press.

Jett, Stephen C. 1991. Split-Twig Figurines, Early Maize, and a Child Burial in East-Central Utah. *Utah Archaeology* 4(1):23–31.

Jett, Stephen C., and Peter B. Moyle. 1986. The Exotic Origins of Fishes Depicted on Prehistoric Mimbres Pottery from New Mexico. *American Antiquity* 51(4): 688–720.

Johnson, C. David. 2003. Mesa Verde Region Towers: A View from Above. *Kiva* 68(4):323–40.

Johansson, Lindsay D. 2015. Coming Together: Fremont Communal Structures. *Archaeology Southwest* 29(4):6–8.

Johansson, Lindsay D., Katie K. Richards, and James R. Allison. 2014. Wolf Village (42UT273): A Case Study in Fremont Architectural Variability. *Utah Archaeology* 27(1):33–56.

Judd, Neil M. 1954. *The Material Culture of Pueblo Bonito*. Washington, DC: Smithsonian Institution.

Judge, W. James. 1989. Chaco Canyon—San Juan Basin. In *Dynamics of Southwest Prehistory*, edited by L. S. Cordell and G. J. Gumerman, pp. 209–61. Washington, DC: Smithsonian Institute Press.

Kantner, John W. 1997. Ancient Roads, Modern Mapping: Evaluating Chaco Roadways Using GIS Technology. *Expedition* 39(3):49–62.

———. 2004. *Ancient Puebloan Southwest*. Cambridge: Cambridge University Press.

Kantner, John W., and Ronald Hobgood. 2016. A GIS-Based View Shed Analysis of Chacoan Tower Kivas in the US Southwest: Were They For Seeing or to Be Seen? *Antiquity* 90(353):1302–17.

John Kantner, David McKinney, Michele Pierson, and Shaza Wester. 2019. Reconstructing Sexual Divisions of Labor from Fingerprints on Ancestral Puebloan Pottery. *Proceedings of the National Academy of Sciences* 116(25): 12220–25.

Kearns, Timothy M. 1973. "Abiotic Resources." In *An Archaeological Survey of the Orme Reservoir*. Assembled by V. Canouts and M. Grady. Report prepared by US Bureau of Reclamation. Central Arizona Project. Tucson: Arizona State Museum and University of Arizona.

Kelley, J. Charles. 2000. The Aztatlan Mercantile System. Mobile Traders and the Northwestward Expansion of Mesoamerican Civilization. In *Greater Mesoamerica. The Archaeology of West and Northwest Mexico*, edited by M. S. Foster and S. Gorenstein, pp. 137–154. Salt Lake City: University of Utah Press.

Kelley, Klara B., and Harris Francis. 2019. *A Diné History of Navajoland*. Tucson: University of Arizona Press.

Kelly, Robert L., and Lawrence C. Todd. 1988. Coming into the Country: Early Paleoindian Hunting and Mobility. *American Antiquity* 53(2):231–44.

Kemp, Brian M. 2006. Mesoamerica and Southwest Prehistory, and the Entrance of Humans into the Americas: Mitochondrial DNA Evidence. Unpublished PhD dissertation, University of California, Davis.

Kemp, Brian M., Angélica González-Oliver, Ripan S. Malhi, Cara Monroe, Kari Britt Schroeder, John McDonough, Gillian Rhett, Andres Resendéz, Rosenda I. Penaloza-Espinosa, Leonor Buentello-Malo, Clara Gorodesky, and David Glenn Smith. 2010. Evaluating the Farming/Language Dispersal Hypothesis with Genetic Variation Exhibited by Populations in the Southwest and Mesoamerica. *PNAS* 107(15):6759–64.

Kennett, Douglas J., Stephen Plog, Richard J. George, Brendan J. Culleton, Adam S. Watson, Pontus Skoglund, Nadin Rohland, Swapan Mallick, Kristin Stewardson, Logan Kistler, Steven A. LeBlanc, Peter M. Whiteley, David Reich, and George H. Perry. 2017. Archaeogenomic Evidence Reveals Prehistoric Matrilineal Dynasty. *Nature Communications* 8:14115.

Kenzle, Susan C. 1997. Enclosing walls in the Northern San Juan: Sociophysical Boundaries and Defensive Fortifications in the American Southwest. *Journal of Field Archaeology* 2 (24):195–210.

Kessell, John L. 2002. *Spain in the Southwest: A Narrative History of Colonial New Mexico, Arizona, Texas, and California*. Norman: University of Oklahoma Press.

James D. Keyser. 1975. A Shoshonean Origin for the Plains Shield Bearing Warrior Motif. *Plains Anthropologist*, 20(69): 207-215.

Keyser, James D., Kevin Conti, and David A. Kaiser. 2018. Finding Faded Fremont: Shorthand Anthropomorphs and Fugitive Pigment at Pipe Spring, Utah. In *Native American Rock Art*, edited by David A. Kaiser and James D.

Keyser, vol. 44, pp. 145–158. San Jose, CA: American Rock Art Research Association.

Kidder, Alfred V. 1962 [1924]. *Introduction to Study of Southwestern Archaeology*. New Haven, CT: Yale University Press.

———. 1927. Southwestern Archaeological Conference. *Science* 66:489–91.

Kidder, Alfred V., and Samuel Guernsey J. 1919. *Archaeological Explorations in Northeastern Arizona*. Bulletin 65. Washington, DC: Bureau of American Ethnology.

Kirschke, Barbara. 2005. Odzyskana kolekcja (A recovered collection). *Fontes Archaeologici Posnanienses* 41: 339–48.

Kloor, Keith. 2007. The Vanishing Fremont. *Science* 318:1540–43.

Kluckhohn, Clyde, and Paul Reiter (eds.). 1939. *Preliminary Report on the 1937 Excavations, BC 50–51. Chaco Canyon, New Mexico, with Some Distributional Analyses*. University of New Mexico Bulletin, No. 345. Santa Fe: University of New Mexico Press.

Kohler, Timothy A. 2000. The Final 400 Years of Prehispanic Agricultural Society in the Mesa Verde Region. *Kiva* 66(1):191–204.

Kohler, Timothy A., Sarah M. Cole, and Stanca Ciupe. 2009. Population and Warfare: A Test of the Turchin Model in Puebloan Societies. In *Pattern and Process in Cultural Evolution*, edited by S. Shennan, pp. 277–95. Berkeley: University of California Press.

Kohler, Timothy A., and Kathryn Kramer Turner. 2006. Raiding for Women in the Prehispanic Northern Pueblo Southwest? *Current Anthropology* 47(6):1035–45.

Kohler, Timothy A., Scott G. Ortman, Katie E. Grundtisch, Carly M. Fitzpatrick, and Sarah M. Cole. 2014. The Better Angels of Their Nature: Declining Violence Through Time among Prehispanic Farmers of the Pueblo Southwest. *American Antiquity* 79(3):444–64.

Kohler, Timothy A., and Kelsey M. Reese. 2014. Long and spatially Variable Neolithic Demographic Transition in the North American Southwest. *PNAS* 111(28):10101–6.

Kohler, Timothy A., Mark D. Varien, and Aaron M. Wright (eds.). 2010. *Leaving Mesa Verde: peril and change in the thirteenth-century Southwest*. Tucson: University of Arizona Press.

Kohler, Timothy A., Mark D. Varien, Aaron M. Wright, and Kristin A. Kuckelman. 2008. Mesa Verde Migrations. New Archaeological Research and Computer Simulation Suggest Why Ancestral Puebloans Deserted the Northern Southwest United States. *American Scientist* 96:146–53.

Kozłowski, Janusz K. (ed.). 1999. *Encyklopedia historyczna świata, tom 1: Prehistoria*. Krakow, Poland: Opress.

———. 2004. *Świat przed "rewolucją" neolityczną. Wielka Historia Świata tom 1*. Krakow, Poland: Wyd. Fogra and Świat Książki.

Kuckelman, Kristin A. 2002. Thirteenth-Century Warfare in the Central Mesa Verde Region. In *Seeking the Center Place: Archaeology and Ancient Communities in the Mesa Verde Region*, edited by M. D. Varien and R. H. Wilshusen, pp. 233–53. Salt Lake City: University of Utah Press.

———. 2008. An Agent Centered Case Study of the Depopulation of Sand Canyon Pueblo. In *The Social Construction of Communities: Agency, Structure and Identity in the Prehispanic Southwest*, edited by M. D. Varien and J. M. Potter, pp. 109–24. Lanham, MD: Altamira Press.

———. 2010. The Depopulation of Sand Canyon Pueblo, A Large Ancestral Pueblo Village in Southwestern Colorado. *American Antiquity* 75(3):497–525.

———. 2017. Cranial Trauma and Victimization among Ancestral Pueblo Farmers of the Northern San Juan Region. In *Broken Bones, Broken Bodies: Bioarchaeological and Forensic Approaches for Accumulative Trauma and Violence*, edited by C. E. Tegtmeyer and D. L. Martin, pp. 43–59. Lanham, MD: Lexington Books.

Kuckelman, Kristin A. (ed.). 2000. *The Archaeology of Castle Rock Pueblo: A Thirteenth-Century Village in Southwestern Colorado*. Date of use: 10 December 2018. www.crowcanyon.org/ResearchReports/CastleRock/Text/crpw_contentsvoume.asp.

Kuckelman Kristin A., Ricky R. Lightfoot, and Debra L. Martin. 2002. The Bioarchaeology and Taphonomy of Violence at Castle Rock and Sand Canyon Pueblos, Southwestern Colorado. *American Antiquity* 67(3):486–513.

LeBlanc, Steven A. 1989. Cultural Dynamics in the Southern Mogollon Area. In *Dynamics of Southwest Prehistory*, edited by L. S. Cordell, and G. J. Gumerman, pp. 179–208. Washington, DC: Smithsonian Institution Press.

———. 1997. A Comment on Hegmon and Trevathan's Gender, Anatomical Knowledge, and Pottery Production. *American Antiquity* 62(4):723–26.

———. 1999. *Prehistoric Warfare in the American Southwest*. Salt Lake City: University of Utah Press.

Lee, Craig M. 2012. Withering Snow and Ice in the Mid-latitudes: A New Archaeological and Paleobiological Record for the Rocky Mountain Region. *Arctic* 65:165–77.

Lekson, Stephen H. 1986. *Great Pueblo Architecture of Chaco Canyon, New Mexico*. Albuquerque: University of New Mexico Press and National Park Service.

———. 1999. *The Chaco Meridian. Centers of Political Power in the Ancient Southwest*, Walnut Creek, CA: Altamira Press.

———. 2006. *Archaeology of the Mimbres Region, Southwestern New Mexico, USA*. BAR International Series 1466. British Archaeological Reports. Oxford: Archaeopress.

———. 2007. Great House Form. In *The Architecture of Chaco Canyon, New Mexico*, edited by S. H. Lekson, pp. 7–44. Salt Lake City: University of Utah Press.

———. 2008. *A History of the Ancient Southwest*. Santa Fe, NM: School for Advanced Research Press.

———. 2014. Thinking about Fremont: The Later Prehistory of the Great Basin and the Southwest. In *Archaeology of the Great Basin and Southwest. Papers in*

Honor of Don D. Fowler, edited by N. J. Parezo and J. C. Janetski, pp. 109–17. Salt Lake City: University of Utah Press.

———. 2017. Narrative Histories. In *Oxford Handbook of the Archaeology of the American Southwest*, edited by B. J. Mills and S. Fowles, pp. 91–107. Oxford: Oxford University Press.

———. 2018. *A Study of Southwestern Archaeology*. Salt Lake City: University of Utah Press.

Lekson, Stephen H., Thomas C. Windes, and Patricia Fournier. 2007. The Changing Faces of Chetro Ketl. In *The Architecture of Chaco Canyon, New Mexico*, edited by S. H. Lekson, pp. 155–78. Salt Lake City: The University of Utah Press.

Lemke, Ashley K., D. Clark Wernecke, and Michael B. Collins. 2015. Early Art in North America: Clovis and Later Paleoindian Incised Artifacts From the Gault Site, Texas (41bl323). *American Antiquity* 80(1):113–33.

Lepofsky, Dana. 1986. Preliminary Analysis of Flotation Samples from the Turkey Pen Ruin, Cedar Mesa, Utah. Manuscript on file, Laboratory of Archaeology. University of British Columbia, Vancouver.

Lewandowska, Magdalena. 2019. Athapaskan Migration to the North American Southwest. *Contributions in New World Archaeology* 12:139–64.

Liebmann, Matthew J., Joshua Farella, Christopher I. Roos, Adam Stack, Sarah Martini, and Thomas W. Swetnam. 2016. Native American Depopulation, Reforestation, and Fire Regimes in the Southwest United States, 1492–1900 CE. *PNAS* 113(6):E696–E704.

Lightfoot, Ricky R. 1992. Architecture and Tree-Ring Dating at the Duckfoot Site in Southwestern Colorado. *Kiva* 57(3):213–36.

Lightfoot, Ricky R., and Kristin A. Kuckelman. 2001. A Case of Warfare in the Mesa Verde Region. In *Deadly Landscapes: Case Studies in Prehistoric Southwestern Warfare*, edited by G. E. Rice and S. A. LeBlanc, pp. 51–64. Salt Lake City: University of Utah Press.

Lipe, William D. 1974. A Conservation Model for American Archaeology. *Kiva* 39 (3/4):213–45.

———. 1995. The Depopulation of the Northern San Juan: Conditions in the Turbulent 1200s. *Journal of Anthropological Archaeology* 14:143–69.

———. 1999. Basketmaker II (1000 BC–AD 500). In *Colorado Prehistory: A Context for the Southern Colorado River Basin*, edited by W. D. Lipe, M. D. Varien and R. H. Wilshusen, pp. 132–65. Denver: Colorado Council of Professional Archaeologists.

———. 2002. Social Power in the Central Mesa Verde Region, AD 1150–1290. In *Seeking the Center Place: Archaeology and Ancient Communities in the Mesa Verde Region*, edited by M. D. Varien and R. H. Wilshusen, pp. 203–32. Salt Lake City: University of Utah Press.

———. 2006. Notes from the North. In *The Archaeology of Chaco Canyon: An Eleventh-Century Pueblo Regional Center*, edited by S. H. Lekson, pp. 261–314. Santa Fe, NM: School of American Research Press, Santa Fe.

Lipe, William D., and Bonnie L. Pitblado. 1999. Paleoindian and Archaic Periods. In *Colorado Prehistory: A Context for the Southern Colorado River Basin*, edited by W. D. Lipe, M. D. Varien and R. H. Wilshusen, pp. 95–131. Denver: Colorado Council of Professional Archaeologists.

Lipe, William D., and Mark D. Varien. 1999. Pueblo III (AD 1150–1300). In *Colorado Prehistory: A Context for the Southern Colorado River Basin*, edited by W. D. Lipe, M. D. Varien and R. H. Wilshusen, pp. 290–352. Denver: Colorado Council of Professional Archaeologists.

Lipe, William D., Mark D. Varien, and Richard H. Wilshusen (eds.). 1999. *Colorado Prehistory: A Context for the Southern Colorado River Basin*. Denver: Colorado Council of Professional Archaeologists.

Lister, Robert H., and Florence C. Lister. 1987. *Aztec Ruins on the Animas. Excavated, Preserved, and Interpreted*. Tucson: Southwest Parks and Monuments Association.

Loendorf, Larry. 2004. Rock Art and Southward Moving Athapaskans. In *Ancient and Historic Lifeways in North America's Rocky Mountains Proceedings of the 2003 Rocky Mountain Anthropological Conference Estes Park Colorado*, edited by R. H. Brunswig and W. B. Butler, pp. 94–109. Greeley: University of Northern Colorado.

Lyneis, Margaret M. 1995. The Virgin Anasazi, Far Western Puebloans. *Journal of World Prehistory* 9(2):199–241.

Lyons, Patrick D. 2012. Maverick Mountain Series and Salado Polychrome Origins. *Archaeology Southwest* 26 (3–4):13–15.

Mabry, Jonathan B. (eds.). 2008. *Las Capas: Early Irrigation and Sedentism in a Southwestern Floodplain*. Anthropological Papers No. 28. Tucson, AZ: Center for Desert Archaeology.

Madsen, David B., and Steven R. Simms. 1998. The Fremont Complex: A Behavioral Perspective. *Journal of World Prehistory* 12(3):255–336.

Magne, Martin P. R., and Michael A. Klassen. 2002. A Possible Fluteplayer Pictograph Site near Exshaw, Alberta. *Canadian Journal of Archaeology* 26(1):1–24.

Malhi, Ripan S. 2012. DNA Evidence of a Prehistoric Athapaskan Migration from the Subarctic to the Southwest of North America. In *From the Land of Ever Winter to the American Southwest. Athapaskan Migrations, Mobility, and Ethnogenesis*, edited by D. J. Seymour, pp. 241–48. Salt Lake City: University of Utah Press.

Malhi, Ripan S., Holly M. Mortensen, Jason A. Eshleman, Brian M. Kemp, Joseph G. Lorenz, Frederika A. Kaestle, John R. Johnson, Clara Gorodezky, and David Glenn Smith. 2003. Native American mtDNA Prehistory in the American Southwest. *American Journal of Physical Anthropology* 120:108–24.

Malotki, Ekkehart, and Ellen Dissanayake. 2018. *Early Rock Art of the American West: The Geometric Enigma*. Seattle: University of Washington Press.

Malotki, Ekkehart, and Henry D. Wallace. 2011. Columbian Mammoth Petroglyphs from the San Juan River Near Bluff, Utah, United States. *Rock Art Research* 28(2):143–52.

Malville, J. McKim. 2008. *A Guide to Prehistoric Astronomy in the Southwest Paperback*. Boulder, CO: Johnson Books.

Marden, Kerriann. 2011. Taphonomy, Paleopathology and Mortuary Variability in Chaco Canyon: Using Modern Methods to Understand Ancient Cultural Practices. Unpublished PhD dissertation, Department of Anthropology, Tulane University, New Orleans.

Marmaduke, William S., and Richard J. Martynec. 1993. *Shelltown and the Hind Site: A Study of Two Hohokam Craftsman Communities in Southwestern Arizona, vol. 1, parts 1–2*. Flagstaff, AZ: Northland Research, Inc.

Martin, Paul S. 1967. Prehistoric Overkill. In *Pleistocene Extinctions: The Search for a Cause*, edited by P. S. Martin and H. E. Wright Jr., pp. 75–120. New Haven, CT: Yale University Press.

Mason, Ronald J. 2000. Archaeology and Native North American Oral Traditions. *American Antiquity* 65(2):239–66.

Matheny, Ray T., Deanne G. Matheny, Pamela W. Miller, and Blaine Miller. 2004. Hunting Strategies and Winter Economy of the Fremont as Revealed in the Rock Art of Nine Mile Canyon. In *New Dimensions in Rock Art Studies*, edited by R. T. Matheny, pp. 145–93. Occasional Paper Series No. 9. Provo, UT: Museum of Peoples and Cultures, Brigham Young University.

Matthews, John A., and Keith R. Briffa. 2005. The 'Little Ice Age': Re-evaluation of an Evolving Concept. *Geografiska Annaler*. Series A, Physical Geography 87(1): 17–36 (Special Issue: Climate Change and Variability).

Matson, Richard G. 1991. *The Origins of Southwestern Agriculture*. Tucson: The University of Arizona Press.

———. 1999. The Spread of Maize to the Colorado Plateau. *Archaeology Southwest* 13(1):10–11.

———. 2002. The Spread of Maize Agriculture into the U.S. Southwest. In *Examining the Farming/Language Dispersal Hypothesis*, edited by P. Bellwood and C. Renfrew, pp. 341–56. Cambridge: McDonald Institute for Archaeological Research.

———. 2008 The Archaic Origins of the Zuni. *Archaeology Southwest* 22(2):7–8.

Matson, Richard G., and Brian Chisholm. 1991. Basketmaker II Subsistence: Carbon Isotopes and Other Dietary Indicators from Cedar Mesa, Utah. *American Antiquity* 56(3):444–59.

Matson, Richard G., and Martin P. R. Magne. 2007. *Athapaskan Migrations. The Archaeology of Eagle Lake, British Columbia*. Tucson: University of Arizona Press.

———. 2013. North America: Na Dene/Athapaskan archaeology and linguistics. In *The Encyclopedia of Global Human Migration*, edited by Immanuel Ness, pp. 333–39. Malden, MA: Blackwell Publishing.

Matsuoka, Yoshihiro, Yves Vigouroux, Major M. Goodman, Jesus G. Sanchez, Edward Buckler, and John Doebley. 2002. A Single Domestication for Maize Shown by Multilocus Microsatellite Genotyping. *PNAS* 99(9):6080–84.

McBrinn, Maxine E., and Bradley J. Vierra. 2017. The Southwest Archaic. In *The Oxford Handbook of Southwest Archaeology,* edited by B. Mills and S. Fowles, pp. 231–45. New York: Oxford University Press.

McCreery, Patricia, and Ekkehart Malotki. 1994. *Tapamveni The Rock Art Galleries of Petrified Forest and Beyond.* Petrified Forest, AZ: Petrified Forest Museum Association.

McEwan, Colin, Andrew Middleton, Caroline Cartwright, and Rebecca Stacey. 2006. *Turquoise Mosaics from Mexico.* London: British Museum Press and Durham, NC: Duke University Press.

McGuire, Randall H. 1980. The Mesoamerican Connection in the Southwest. *Kiva* 1/2(46):3–38.

McGuire, Randall H., Charles E. Adams, Ben A. Nelson, and Catherine A. Spielmann. 1994. Drawing the Southwest to Scale Perspectives on Macroregional Relations. In *Themes in Southwest Prehistory*, edited by G. J. Gumerman, pp. 239–65. Santa Fe, NM: School of American Research Press.

McGuire, Randall H., and Elisa C. Villalpando. 2007a. The Hohokam and Mesoamerica. In *The Hohokam Millennium*, edited by P. R. Fish and S. K. Fish, pp. 57–63. Santa Fe, NM: School for Advanced Research Press.

———. 2007b. Excavations at Cerro de Trincheras. In *Trincheras Sites in Time, Space and Society,* edited by P. R. Fish, S. K. Fish, and M. E. Villalpando, pp. 137–64. Amerind Studies in Archaeology no. 1. Tucson: University of Arizona Press.

McIntyre, Allan J. 2008. *The Tohono O'odham and Pimeria Alta.* Arizona Historic Society. Charleston, SC: Arcadia Publishing.

McKusick, Charmion R. 2007. Casas Grandes Macaws. *Archaeology Southwest* 21(1):5.

Metcalfe, Jessica Z., John W. Ives, Sabrina Shirazi, Kevin P. Gilmore, Jennifer Hallson, Fiona Brock, Bonnie J. Clark, and Beth Shapiro. 2021. Isotopic Evidence for Long-Distance Connections of the AD Thirteenth-Century Promontory Caves Occupants. *American Antiquity* 86(3):526–48.

Merrill, William L. 2012. The Historical Linguistics of Uto-Aztecan Agriculture. *Anthropological Linguistics* 54(3):203–260.

Merrill, William L., Robert J. Hard, Jonathan B. Mabry, Gayle J. Fritz, Karen R. Adams, John R. Roney, and Arthur C. MacWilliams. 2009. The Diffusion of Maize to the Southwestern United States and Its Impact. *PNAS* 106(50):21019–26.

Middleton, Emily S., Geoffrey M. Smith, William J. Cannon, and Mary F. Ricks. 2014. Paleoindian Rock Art: Establishing the Antiquity of Great Basin Carved Abstract Petroglyphs in the Northern Great Basin. *Journal of Archaeological Science*, 43:21–30.

Miller, Mary, and Karl A. Taube. 1993. *An Illustrated Dictionary of the Gods and Symbols of Ancient Mexico and the Maya.* New York: Thames & Hudson.

Mills, Barbara J. 1995. The Origins of Southwestern Ceramic Containers: Women's Time Allocation and Economic Intensification. *Journal of Anthropological Research* 51:149–72.

———. 2002. Recent Research on Chaco: Changing Views on Economy, Ritual, and Society. *Journal of Archaeological Research* 10:65–117.

———. 2018. What's New in Chaco Research? *Antiquity* 92(364):855–69.

Mills, Barbara J., and Thomas J. Ferguson. 2008. Animate Objects: Shell Trumpets and Ritual Networks in the Greater Southwest. *Journal of Archaeological Method and Theory* 15:338–61.

Mills, Barbara J., Matthew A. Peeples, Leslie D. Aragon, Benjamin A. Bellorado, Jeffery J. Clark, Evan Giomi, and Thomas C. Windes. 2018. Evaluating Chaco Migration Scenarios Using Dynamic Social Network Analysis. *Antiquity* 92:922–39.

Mimbres Pottery Images Digital Database—MimPIDD: core.tdar.org/collection/22070/mimbres-ceramic-database. Date of use: 11 March 2019.

Minnis, Paul E., and Michael E. Whalen. 1993. Casas Grandes: Archaeology in Northern Mexico. *Expedition* 35(1):34–43.

———. 2003. The Casas Grandes Community. *Archaeology Southwest* 17(2):1–3.

Minnis, Paul E., and Michael E. Whalen (eds.). 2015. *Ancient Paquimé and the Casas Grandes World*. Amerind Studies in Archaeology. Tucson: University of Arizona Press.

Mitchell, Douglas R. 1994. *The Pueblo Grande Project: An Analysis of Classic Period Hohokam Mortuary Practices*. Soil Systems Publications in Archaeology 7(20). Phoenix, AZ: Soil Systems.

———. 2003. Burial and Society. In *Centuries of Decline during the Hohokam Classic Period at Pueblo Grande*, edited by D. R. Abbott, pp. 107–27. Tucson: University of Arizona Press.

Mitchell, Douglas R., and Michael S. Foster. 2000. Hohokam Shell Middens along the Sea of Cortez, Puerto Penasco, Sonora, Mexico. *Journal of Field Archaeology* 27(1):27–41.

Mitchell, Douglas R., and M. Steven Shackley. 1995. Classic Period Hohokam Obsidian Studies in Southern Arizona. *Journal of Field Archaeology* 22(3):291–304.

Monagle, Victoria, and Emily Lena Jones. 2020. Dog Life and Death in an Ancestral Pueblo Landscape. In *Archaeology beyond Domestication*, edited by B. Bethke and A. Burtt, pp. 45–71. Gainesville: University Press of Florida.

Morales, Reinaldo. 2002. "The Nordeste Tradition: Innovation and Continuity in Brazilian Rock Art." ProQuest Dissertations and Theses.

———. 2005. The Angelim Style and Northeast Brazilian Rock Art. In *Making Marks: Graduate Studies in Rock Art Research at the New Millennium*, edited by Jennifer K. K. Huang and Elisabeth V. Culley, pp. 27–39. Tucson, AZ: American Rock Art Research Association, Occasional Paper No. 5, Tucson.

Morss, Noel. 1954. *Clay Figurines of the American Southwest*. Cambridge, MA: Harvard University Papers 49(1). Peabody Museum.

Moulard, Barbara. 1984. *Within the Underworld Sky: Mimbres Ceramic Art in Context*. Santa Fe, NM: Twelvetrees Press.

Munson, Marit K. 2000. Sex, Gender and Status: Human Images from the Classic Mimbres. *American Antiquity* 65(1):127–43.

———. 2011. *The Archaeology of Art in the American Southwest*. Lanham, MD: Lexington Books.

Nabokov, Peter. 1996. Native Views of History. In *The Cambridge History of the Native Peoples of the Americas, Vol. 1, North America, Part 1*, edited by B. G. Trigger and W. E. Washburn, pp. 1–59. New York: Cambridge University Press.

Neitzel, Jill E. 2007. Architectural Studies of Pueblo Bonito. The Past, the Present, and the Future. In *The Architecture of Chaco Canyon, New Mexico*, edited by S. H. Lekson, pp. 127–54. Salt Lake City: University of Utah Press.

Nelson, Ben A. 1993. Complexity, Hierarchy, and Scale: A Controlled Comparison between Chaco Canyon, New Mexico, and la Quemada, Zacatecas. *American Antiquity* 60(4): 597–618.

———. 2002. La Quemada, a Monument on the Mesoamerican Frontier. *Archaeology Southwest* 16(1):1–3.

———. 2006. Mesoamerican Objects and Symbols in Chaco Canyon Context. In *The Archaeology of Chaco Canyon: An Eleventh-Century Pueblo Regional Center*, edited by S. H. Lekson, pp. 339–71. Santa Fe, NM: School of American Research Press.

Nelson, Ben A., Paul R. Fish, and Suzanne K. Fish. 2017. Mesoamerican Connections. In *The Oxford Handbook of Southwest Archaeology*, edited by B. Mills and S. Fowles, pp. 461–79. Oxford University Press, New York.

Nelson, Margaret C., and Gregson Schachner. 2002. Understanding Abandonments in the North American Southwest. *Journal of Archaeological Research* 2(10):167–206.

Neves, Walter A., Astolfo G. M. Araujo, Danilo V. Bernardo, Renato Kipnis, and James K. Feathers. 2012. Rock Art at the Pleistocene/Holocene Boundary in Eastern South America. *PLoS ONE* 7(2), e32228. Date of use: 10 December 2018 dx.doi.org/10.1371/journal.pone.0032228.

Nials, Fred L., John R. Stein, and John R. Roney. 1987. *Chacoan Roads in the Southern Periphery: Results of Phase II of the BLM Chaco Roads Project*. Cultural Resources Series No. 1. Albuquerque: United States Department of the Interior, Bureau of Land Management.

Noble, David G. 2000. *Ancient Colorado. An Archaeological Perspective*. Denver: Colorado Council of Professional Archaeologists.

Nordenskiöld, Gustaf. 1990. *The Cliff Dwellers of the Mesa Verde*. Mesa Verde National Park, CO: Mesa Verde Museum Association.

Obregón, Baltazar de. 1584 [1988]. *Historia de los Descubrimientos Antiguos y Modernos de la Nueva España Escrita por el Conquistador en el Año de 1584*. Porrúa, Mexico.

O'Connor, Richard D., and Walter P. Parks. 2012. Rock Art in the Casas Grandes Region: Report of Seven New Sites and a Review of the Literature. *Journal of the Southwest* (special volume: *Forgotten Tributaries of the Palanganas: Untold Stories from Mata Ortiz*) 54(1):9–46.

Opler, Morris E. 1983 The Apachean Culture Pattern and Its Origins. In *Handbook of North Native Americans, Vol. 10: Southwest*, edited by Alfonso Ortiz, pp. 368–92. Washington: Smithsonian Institution.

Ortiz, Alfonso. 1969. *The Tewa World: Space, Time, Being and Becoming in a Pueblo Society*. Chicago: University of Chicago Press.

Ortman, Scott G. 2008. Action, place and space in the Castle Rock Community. In *The social construction of communities: agency, structure, and identity in the pre-Hispanic Southwest*, edited by Mark D. Varien and James M. Potter pp. 125–54. Lanham (MD): Rowman & Littlefield.

Ownby, Mary F., James M. Heidke, and Henry D. Wallace. 2015. New Insights into Hohokam Buff Ware Production and Distribution. *American Antiquity* 80(2):387–96.

Pailes, Matthew. 2017. Northwest Mexico: The Prehistory of Sonora, Chihuahua, and Neighboring Areas. *Journal of Archaeological Research* 25(4):373–420.

Palonka, Radosław and Kristin A. Kuckelman. 2009. Goodman Point Pueblo: Research on the Final Period of Settlement of the Ancestral Pueblo Indians in the Mesa Verde Region, Colorado, USA. The Preliminary Report, 2005–2006 Seasons. *Recherches Archeologiques, Nouvelle Serie 1:* 543–567.

Palonka, Radosław. 2011. *Defensive Architecture and the Depopulation of the Mesa Verde Region, Utah-Colorado, USA in the XIII Century AD*. Kraków, Poland: Jagiellonian University Press.

———. 2013. Pueblo Culture Settlement Structure in the Central Mesa Verde Region, Utah-Colorado in the Thirteenth Century AD. In *Environment and Subsistence—Forty Years after Janusz Kruk's "Settlement studies . . . ,"* edited by S. Kadrow and P. Włodarczak, pp. 193–224. Rzeszow, Poland: Institute of Archaeology, Rzeszow University .

———. 2017. Shamans, Spirals and Warrior: Rock Art in Castle Rock Pueblo Community, Colorado, USA through Native American Oral Traditions and Archaeological Interpretations. *Expression* 16:112–25.

———. 2019a. Rock Art from the Lower Sand Canyon in the Mesa Verde Region, Southwestern Colorado, USA. *Kiva* 85(3):232–56.

———. 2019b. Towers as an Architectural Element of Pueblo Culture in the Mesa Verde Region, Utah–Colorado, in the 12th–13th Century AD In *Tower Studies 3, Urbs Turrita–Urban Towers in Medieval and Renaissance Europe*, edited by Richard Oram, pp. 16–35. Donington, UK: Shaun Tyas.

———. 2021. Investigations of Ancestral Pueblo Rock Art in the Lower Sand Canyon Area of Canyons of the Ancients National Monument, Colorado. In *American Indian Rock Art*, edited by D. A. Kaiser, M. Greer, and J. D. Keyser,

47: 105–21. El Cajon, CA: American Rock Art Research Association (ARARA) and Sunbelt Publications.

Palonka, Radosław, Jakub Nawrot, and Anna Słupianek. 2015. Pueblo Community in the Lower Sand Canyon Locality, Colorado: Preliminary Report of the Sand Canyon-Castle Rock Community Archaeological Project, 2011–2014. *Contributions in New World Archaeology* vol. 9:69–92.

Palonka, Radosław i Kristin A. Kuckelman. 2009. Goodman Point Pueblo: Research on the Final Period of Settlement of the Ancestral Pueblo Indians in the Mesa Verde Region, Colorado, USA. The Preliminary Report, 2005–2006 Seasons. *Recherches Archeologiques, Nouvelle Serie* 1: 543–567.

Palonka, Radosław, Kathleen O'Meara, Katarzyna Ciomek, Zi Xu. 2020. Ancestral Pueblo Settlement Structure and Sacred Landscape at Castle Rock Community, Colorado. *Antiquity* 94(374):491–511.

Palonka, Radosław, Bolesław Zych, and Vincent M. MacMillan. 2021. Photogrammetry and 3D Laser Scanning as Methods of Digital Documentation of Ancestral Pueblo Sites in the Canyons of the Mesa Verde Region, Colorado (USA). In *Proceedings from the Computer Applications and Quantitative Methods in Archaeology (CAA) 2019 Conference,* edited by Ł. Miszk et al, pp. 17–33. Tübingen: Tübingen University Press.

Parr, Ryan L., Shawn W. Carlyle, and Dennis H. O'Rourke. 1996. Ancient DNA Analysis of Fremont Amerindians of the Great Salt Lake Wetlands. *American Journal of Physical Anthropology* 99:507–18.

Patterson, Carol. 2018. Cultural Affiliations of the Western Basketmaker II Style Petroglyphs of American Southwest: Keres. *Expression* 22:41–51.

Pederson, Joel L., Melissa S. Chapot, Steven R. Simms, Reza Sohbati, Tammy M. Rittenour, Andrew S. Murray, and Gary Cox. 2014. Age of Barrier Canyon-Style Rock Art Constrained by Cross-Cutting Relations and Luminescence Dating Techniques. *PNAS* 111(36):12986–91.

Piperno D. R., and K.V. Flannery. 2001. The Earliest Archaeological Maize (Zea mays L.) from Highland Mexico: New Accelerator Mass Spectrometry Dates and Their Implications. *PNAS* 98(4):2101–3.

Pitblado, Bonnie L. 1993. Paleoindian Occupation of Southwest Colorado. Unpublished master's thesis, University of Arizona, Tucson.

———. 1999. Late Paleoindian Occupation of the Southern Rocky Mountains: Projectile Points and Land Use in the High Country. Unpublished PhD dissertation, University of Arizona, Tucson.

———. 2003. *Late Paleoindian Occupation of the Southern Rocky Mountains.* Boulder: University Press of Colorado.

Pitblado, Bonnie L., Molly B. Cannon, Megan Bloxham, Joel Janetski, J.M. Adovasio, Kathleen R. Anderson, and Stephen T. Nelson. 2013. Archaeological Fingerprinting and Fremont Figurines: Reuniting the Iconic Pilling Collection. *Advances in Archaeological Practice* 1(1):3–12.

Pitezel, Todd A. 2003. The Hilltop Site of El Pueblito. *Archaeology Southwest* 17(2):10.

———. 2007. Surveying Cerro de Moctezuma, Chihuahua, Mexico. *Kiva* 72:353–69.

Plog, Stephen. 1997. *Ancient People of the American Southwest*. London: Thames & Hudson.

———. 2003. Exploring the Ubiquitous through the Unusual: Color Symbolism in Pueblo Black-on-White Pottery. *American Antiquity* 68(4):665–95.

Plog, Stephen, and Carrie Heitman. 2010. Hierarchy and Social Inequality in the American Southwest, AD 800–1200. *PNAS* 107(46):19619–26.

Plog, Stephen, Carrie C. Heitman, and A. S. Watson. 2017. Key Dimensions of the Cultural Trajectories of Chaco Canyon. In *The Oxford Handbook of Southwest Archaeology*, edited by B. J. Mills and S. Fowles, pp. 285–306. New York: Oxford University Press.

Potter, Ben A., Joshua D. Reuther, Vance T. Holliday, Charles E. Holmes, D. Shane Miller, and Nicholas Schmuck. 2017. Early Colonization of Beringia and Northern North America: Chronology, Routes, and Adaptive Strategies. *Quaternary International* 444:36–55.

Potts, Adreanne. 2011. A Typology for Fremont Figurines. (Unpublished papers) *All Student Publications 67*. Provo, UT: Brigham Young University. Date of use: 20 March 2019. scholarsarchive.byu.edu/studentpub/67.

Powell, Eric A. 2014. Tracking the Ancient Apache. *Archaeology* 67(1):11.

Powell, John Wesley. 1961. *The Exploration of the Colorado River and Its Canyons*. New York: Dover.

Powell, Mellisa S. (ed.). 2006. *Secrets of Casas Grandes, Precolumbian Art and Archaeology of Northern Mexico*. Santa Fe: Museum of New Mexico Press.

Powers, Robert P., William B. Gillespie, and Stephen H. Lekson (eds.). 1983. *The Outlier Survey: A Regional View of Settlement in the San Juan Basin*. Reports of the Chaco Center, No. 3. Albuquerque: Division of Cultural Research, National Park Service.

Prasciunas, Mary M. 2011. Mapping Clovis: Projectile Points, Behavior, and Bias. *American Antiquity* 76(1):107–26.

Preece, Shari J., Robert G. McGimsey, John A. Westgate, Nicholas J. G. Pearce, William K. Hart, and William T. Perkins. 2014. Chemical Complexity and Source of the White River Ash, Alaska and Yukon. *Geosphere* 10(5):1020–42.

Price, Douglas T., and Ofer Bar-Yosef. 2011. The Origins of Agriculture: New Data, New Ideas: An Introduction to Supplement 4. *Current Anthropology* (special volume: *The Origins of Agriculture: New Data, New Ideas*) 52(4):S163–S174.

Price, Douglas T., Stephen Plog, Steven A. LeBlanc, and John Krigbaum. 2017. Great House Origins and Population Stability at Pueblo Bonito, Chaco Canyon, New Mexico: The Isotopic Evidence. *Journal of Archaeological Science: Reports* 11:261–73.

Prudden, T. Mitchell. 1903. The Prehistoric Ruins of the San Juan Watershed in Utah, Arizona, Colorado, and New Mexico. *American Anthropologist, New Series* 5(2):224–88.

Purdy, Barbara A., Kevin S. Jones, John J. Mecholsky, Gerald Bourne, Richard C. Hulbert Jr., Bruce J. MacFadden, Krista L. Church, Michael W. Warren, Thomas F. Jorstad, Dennis J. Stanford, Melvin J. Wachowiak, and Robert J. Speakman. 2011. Earliest Art in the Americas: Incised Image of a Proboscidea on a Mineralized Extinct Animal Bone from Vero Beach, Florida. *Journal of Archaeological Science* 38:2908–13.

Rakita, Gordon F. M., and Gerry R. Raymond. 2003. The Temporal Sensitivity of Casas Grandes Polychrome Ceramics. *Kiva* 68 (3):153–84.

Raymond, Anan. 1986. Experiments in the Function and Performance of the Weighted Atlatl. *World Archaeology* 18(2):153–77.

Reed, Paul F. 2011. Chaco Immigration or Local Emulation of the Chacoan System? The Emergence of Aztec, Salmon, and Other Great House Communities. *Kiva* 77(2):119–38.

Reich, David. 2018. *Who We Are and How We Got Here: Ancient DNA and the New Science of the Human Past.* New York: Pantheon Books.

Renfrew, Colin. 2001. Production and Consumption in a Sacred Economy: The Material Correlates of High Devotional Expression at Chaco Canyon. *American Antiquity* 66:14–25.

Rice, Keren. 2012. Linguistic Evidence Regarding the Apachean Migration. In *From the Land of Ever Winter to the American Southwest. Athapaskan Migrations, Mobility, and Ethnogenesis*, edited by D. J. Seymour, pp. 249–85. Salt Lake City: University of Utah Press.

Richards, Katie K. 2015. Shared Style: Design and Fremont Painted Pottery. *Archaeology Southwest* 29(4):8–9.

Robins, Michael R. 2002. Status and Power. Rock Art as Prestige Technology among the San Juan Basketmaker of Southeast Utah. In *Traditions, Transitions, and Technologies: Themes in Southwestern Archaeology*, edited by S. H. Schlanger, pp. 386–400. Proceedings of the 2000 Southwest Symposium. Boulder: University Press of Colorado.

Rodriguez Garcia, Elsa. 2003. Instituto Nacional de Antropologia e Historia Chihuahua. *Archaeology Southwest* 17(2):4–5.

Roney, John R. 1983. Glossary. In *Chaco Road Project, Phase I: A Reappraisal of Prehistoric Roads in the San Juan Basin, 1983*, edited by C. Kincaid, pp. 1–12. Albuquerque: Bureau of Land Management.

Roosevelt Anna C., Marcondes Lima da Costa, C. Lopes Machado, M. Michab, Norbert Mercier, Hélene Valladas, James Feathers, William Barnett, M. Imazio da Silveira, A. Henderson, J. Silva, B. Chernoff, David S. Reese, J. A. Holman, Nicholas Toth, and Kathy Schick. 1996. Paleoindian Cave Dwellers in the Amazon: The Peopling of the Americas. *Science* 272(5260):373–84.

Roth, Barbara J. 2016. Agricultural Beginnings in the American Southwest. Lanham, MD: Lexington Books.

Rozwadowski, Andrzej. 2009. *Obrazy z przeszłości: Hermeneutyka sztuki naskalnej.* Poznań: Wydawnictwo Naukowe UAM.

———. 2017. *Rocks, Cracks and Drums: In Search of Ancient Shamanism in Siberia and Central Asia.* Budapest: Molnar & Kelemen Oriental Publishers.

Russell, Will G., Sarah Klassen, and Katherine Salazar. 2018. Lines of Communication: Mimbres Hachure and Concepts of Color. *American Antiquity* 83(1):109–27.

Samuels, David. 2001. Indeterminacy and History in Britton Goode's Western Apache Placenames: Ambiguous Identity on the San Carlos Apache Reservation. *American Ethnologist* 28(2):277–302.

Sapir, Edward. 1936. Internal Linguistic Evidence Suggestive of the Northern Origin of the Navaho. *American Anthropologist* 38(2):224–35.

Sánchez, M. Guadalupe, and John Carpenter. 2012. Paleoindian and Archaic Traditions in Sonora, Mexico. In *From the Pleistocene to the Holocene: Human Organization and Cultural Transformations in Prehistoric North Americass,* edited by C. B. Bousman and B. J. Vierra, pp. 125–47. College Station: Texas A&M University Press.

Sánchez, M. Guadalupe, and Vance T. Holliday. 2016. First Sonorans. *Archaeology Southwest* 30(3):7.

Sánchez, M. Guadalupe, Vance T. Holliday, Edmund P. Gaines, Joaquín Arroyo-Cabrales, Natalia Martínez-Tagüena, Andrew Kowler, Todd Lange, Gregory W. L. Hodgins, Susan M. Mentzeri, and Ismael Sanchez-Morales. 2014. Human (Clovis) Gomphothere (*Cuvieronius sp.*) Association ~13,390 Calibrated Yr BP in Sonora, Mexico. *PNAS* 111:10972–77.

Scarborough, Vernon L., Samantha G. Fladd, Nicholas P. Dunning, Stephen Plog, Lewis A. Owen, Christopher Carr, Kenneth B. Tankersley, Jon-Paul McCool, Adam S. Watson, Elizabeth A. Haussner, Brooke Crowley, Katelyn J. Bishop, David L. Lentz, and R. Gwinn Vivian. 2018. Water Uncertainty, Ritual Predictability and Agricultural Canals at Chaco Canyon, New Mexico. *Antiquity* 92:870–89.

Schaafsma, Curtis F. 1996. Ethnic Identity and Protohistoric Archaeological Sites in Northwestern New Mexico. In *The Archaeology of Navajo Origins*, edited by R. H. Towner, pp. 19–46. Salt Lake City: University of Utah Press.

———. 2002. *Apaches de Navajo: Seventeenth-Century Navajos in the Chama Valley of New Mexico.* Salt Lake City: University of Utah Press.

Schaafsma, Polly. 1963. *Rock Art in the Navajo Reservoir District.* Santa Fe: Museum of New Mexico.

———. 1980. *Indian Rock Art of the Southwest.* School of American Research Southwest Indian Arts Series. Albuquerque: University of New Mexico Press.

———. 1992. *Rock Art in New Mexico.* Albuquerque: University of New Mexico Press.

————. 1994. Trance and Transformation in the Canyons: Shamanism and Early Rock Art on the Colorado Plateau. In *Shamanism and Rock Art in North America,* edited by S. A. Turpin, pp. 45–71. San Antonio: Rock Art Foundation, Inc.

————. 1997 *Rock Art Sites in Chihuahua Mexico.* Office of Archaeological Studies: Archaeology Notes 171.

————. (ed.). 2000. *Kachinas in the Pueblo World.* Salt Lake City: University of Utah Press.

————. 2003. *Warrior, Shield, and Star: Imagery and Ideology of Pueblo Warfare.* Santa Fe, NM: Western Edge Press.

————. (ed.). 2007. *New Perspectives on Pottery Mound Pueblo.* Albuquerque: University of New Mexico Press.

————. 2009. The Cave in the Kiva: The Kiva Niche and Painted Walls in the Rio Grande Valley. *American Antiquity* 74(4): 664–90.

————. 2013 Petitions for Rain: Textile and Pottery Designs in Rock Art. In *International Newsletter of Rock Art*, Comite International d'Art Rupestre, edited by Jean Clottes, pp. 17–27. Foix, France.

————. 2018. Chaco Rock Art Matters. *Journal of the Southwest* 60(1):2–73.

Schaafsma, Polly, and Curtis F. Schaafsma. 1974. Evidence for the Origins of the Pueblo Katchina Cult as Suggested by Southwestern Rock Art. *American Antiquity* 39(4):535–45.

Schaafsma, Polly, and Karl A. Taube. 2006. Bringing the Rain. In *Pre-Columbian World*. edited by J. Quilter and M. Miller, pp. 231–85. Washington, DC: Dumbarton Oaks.

Schroedl, Alan R. 1977. The Grand Canyon Figurine Complex. *American Antiquity* 42(2):254–65.

Schwartz, Douglas W. Arthur L. Lange, and Raymond de Saussure. 1958. Split-Twig Figurines in the Grand Canyon. *American Antiquity* 23(3):264–74.

Schwartz, Christopher W., Stephen Plog, and Patricia A. Gilman (eds.). 2022. *Birds of the Sun: Macaws and People in the U.S. Southwest and Mexican Northwest.* Tucson: University of Arizona Press.

Schwindt, Dylan M., Kyle R. Bocinsky, Scott G. Ortman, Donna M. Glowacki, Mark D. Varien, and Timothy A. Kohler. 2016. The social consequences of climate change in the central Mesa Verde region. *American Antiquity* 81: 74–96.

Scotter, Troy. 2015. Fremont Rock Art. *Archaeology Southwest* 29(4):14–17.

Seymour, Deni J. 2004. Before the Spanish Chronicles: Early Apache in the Southern Southwest. In *Ancient and Historic Lifeways in North America's Rocky Mountains Proceedings of the 2003 Rocky Mountain Anthropological Conference Estes Park, Colorado*, edited by R. H. Brunswig and W. B. Butler, pp. 120–42. Greeley: University of Northern Colorado.

————. 2009. Comments on Genetic Data Relating to Athapaskan Migrations: Implications of the Malhi et al. Study for the Southwestern Apache and Navajo. *American Journal of Physical Anthropology* 3(139):281–83.

———. 2012. Gateways for Athabascan Migration to the American Southwest. *Plains Anthropologist* 57(222):149–61.

———. (ed.). 2012. *From the Land of Ever Winter to the American Southwest. Athapaskan Migrations, Mobility, and Ethnogenesis.* Salt Lake City: University of Utah Press.

Shackley, M. Steven. 1996. Range and Mobility in the Early Hunter-Gatherer Southwest. In *Early Formative Adaptations in the Southern Southwest*, edited by B. J. Roth, pp. 5–16. Monographs in World Archaeology No. 25. Madison, WI: Prehistory Press.

———. 2005. *Obsidian: Geology and Archaeology in the North American Southwest.* Tucson: University of Arizona Press.

Shafer, Harry J. 1995. Architecture and Symbolism in Transitional Pueblo Development in the Mimbres Valley, SW New Mexico. *Journal of Field Archaeology* 22(1):23–47.

———. 2003. *Mimbres Archaeology at the NAN Ranch Ruin.* Albuquerque: University of New Mexico Press.

Shafer, Harry J., and Robbie L. Brewington. 1995. Microstylistyc Changes in Mimbres Black-on-White Pottery: Examples from The NAN Ruin, Grant County, New Mexico. *Kiva* 61(1):5–26.

Sheridan, Thomas E., and Nancy J. Parezo (eds.). 1996. *Paths of Life: Native Americans of the Southwest and Northern Mexico.* Tucson: University of Arizona Press.

Sikora, Martin, Vladimir V. Pitulko, and Victor C. Sousa, et al. 2019. The Population History of Northeastern Siberia since the Pleistocene. *Nature* 570: 182–88.

Simmons, Marc. 1979. History of Pueblo-Spanish Relations to 1821. In *Handbook of North Native Americans, vol. 9, Southwest,* edited by Alfonso Ortiz, pp. 178–93. Washington, DC: Smithsonian Institution.

Simms, Steven R. 1999. Farmers, Foragers, and Adaptive Diversity: The Great Salt Lake Wetlands Project. In *Understanding Prehistoric Lifeways in the Great Basin Wetlands: Bioarchaeological Reconstruction and Interpretation,* edited by B. E. Hemphill and C. S. Larsen, pp. 21–54. Salt Lake City: University of Utah Press.

———. 2008. *Ancient Peoples of the Great Basin and Colorado Plateau.* Left Coast Press, Inc., New York.

———. 2010. *Traces of Fremont. Society and Rock Art in Ancient Utah.* Salt Lake City: University of Utah Press.

Slifer, Dennis. 1998. *Signs of Life: Rock Art of the Rio Grande.* Santa Fe, NM: Ancient City Press, Santa Fe.

Smiley, Francis E. 1997. The American Neolithic and the Animas-La Plata Archaeological Project. In *Early Farmers of the Northern Southwest: Papers on Chronometry, Social Dynamics, and Ecology,* edited by F. E. Smiley and M. R. Robins, pp. 1–12. Animas-La Plata Archaeological Project Research Paper 7. Flagstaff: Northern Arizona University.

Smith, Watson. 1952. *Kiva Mural Decorations at Awatovi and Kawaika-a: Reports of the Awatovi Expedition, with a Survey of Other Wall Paintings in the Pueblo South-*

west. Papers of the Peabody Museum of American Archaeology and Ethnology, vol. 37. Cambridge, MA: Harvard University.

Snyder, Ernest. 1966. Petroglyphs of the South Mountains of Arizona. *American Antiquity* 31:705–9.

Sofaer, Anna. 2007. The Primary Architecture of the Chacoan Culture. In *The Architecture of Chaco Canyon, New Mexico*, edited by S. H. Lekson, pp. 225–54. Salt Lake City: University of Utah Press.

Sofaer, Anna, Michael P. Marshall, and Rolf M. Sinclair. 1989. The Great North Road: A Cosmographic Expression of the Chaco Culture of New Mexico. In *World Archaeoastronomy*, edited by A. F. Aveni, pp. 365–76. Cambridge: Cambridge University Press.

Sofaer, Anna, Rolf M. Sinclair, and LeRoy Doggett. 1982. Lunar Markings on Fajada Butte, Chaco Canyon, New Mexico. In *Archaeoastronomy in the New World*, edited by Anthony F. Aveni, pp. 169–86. Cambridge: Cambridge University Press.

Sofaer, Anna, Volker Zinser, and Rolf M. Sinclair. 1979. A Unique Solar Marking Construct. *Science* 206:283–91.

Spence, Michael W. 2000. From Tzintzuntzan to Paquime. Peers or Peripheries in Greater Mesoamerica? In *Greater Mesoamerica. The Archaeology of West and Northwest Mexico*, edited by M. S. Foster and S. Gorenstein, pp. 255–61. Salt Lake City: University of Utah Press.

Spicer, Edward H. 1962. *Cycles of Conquest: The Impact of Spain, Mexico, and the United States on Indians of the Southwest, 1533–1960*. Tucson: University of Arizona Press.

Spielmann, Katherine A. 1994. Clustered Confederacies: Sociopolitical Organization in the Protohistoric Rio Grande. In *Ancient Southwest Community: Models and Methods for the Study of Prehistoric Social Organization*, edited by H. Wills and R. Leonard, pp. 45–54. Albuquerque: University of New Mexico Press.

———. (ed.). 1998. *Migration and Reorganization: The Pueblo IV Period in the American Southwest*. Anthropological Research Paper No. 51. Tempe: Arizona State University.

Stafford, Michael D., George C. Frison, Dennis J. Stanford, and George Zeimans. 2003. Digging for the Color of Life: Paleoindian Red Ochre Mining at the Powers II Site, Platter County, Wyoming. *Geoarchaeology* 18:71–90.

Stanford, Dennis, and Bruce Bradley. 2012. *Across Atlantic Ice: The Origin of America's Clovis Culture*. Berkeley: University of California Press.

Stein, John, Richard Friedman, Taft Blackhorse, and Richard Loose. 2007. Revisiting Downtown Chaco. In *The Architecture of Chaco Canyon, New Mexico*, edited by S. H. Lekson, pp. 199–224. Salt Lake City: University of Utah Press.

Stein, John R., and Stephen H. Lekson. 1992. Anasazi Ritual Landscapes. In *Anasazi Regional Organization and the Chaco System*, edited by D. E. Doyel, pp. 87–100. Anthropological Papers No. 5. Albuquerque, NM: Maxwell Museum of Anthropology.

Stevenson, Matilda Coxe. 1890. *The Sia*. Eleventh Annual Report of the Bureau of American Ethnology 1889–1990. Washington, DC: Smithsonian Institution.

Stoffle, Richard W., David B. Halmo, and Michael J. Evans. 1999. Puchuxwavaats Uapi (To Know about Plants): Traditional Knowledge and the Cultural Significance of Southern Paiute Plants. *Human Organization* 4(58):416–29.

Straus, Lawrence Guy. 2000. Solutrean Settlement of North America? A Review of Reality. *American Antiquity* 65(2):219–26.

Surovell, Todd A., Joshua R. Boyd, C. Vance Haynes Jr., and Gregory W. L. Hodgins. 2016. On the Dating of the Folsom Complex and its Correlation with the Younger Dryas, the End of Clovis, and Megafaunal Extinction. *PaleoAmerica* (thematic volume: *Exploring Variability in the Folsom Archaeological Record*) 2(2):81–89.

Swanson, Steve. 2003. Documenting Prehistoric Communication Networks: A Case Study in the Paquime Polity. *American Antiquity* 68(4):753–67.

Swidler, Nina, Kurt E. Dongoske, Roger Anyon, and Alan S. Downer (eds.). 1997. *Native Americans and Archaeologists, Stepping Stones to Common Ground*. Walnut Creek , CA: Altamira Press,–.

Taube, Karl. 2000. Lightning Celts and Corn Fetishes: The Formative Olmec and the Development of Maize Symbolism in Mesoamerica and the American Southwest. In *Olmec Art and Archaeology in Mesoamerica*, edited by J. E. Clark and M. E. Pye, pp. 297–337. Washington, DC: National Gallery of Art.

Tennesen, Michael. 2009. Earliest Canals in America. *Archaeology* 62(5).

Thibodeau, Alyson M., John T. Chesley, Joaquin Ruiz, David J. Killick, and Arthur Vokes. 2012. An Alternative Approach to the Prehispanic Turquoise Trade. In *Turquoise in Mexico and North America Science, Conservation, Culture and Collections*, edited by J. C. H. King, M. Carocci, C. Cartwright, C. McEwan and R. Stacey, pp. 65–74. London: Archetype Publications.

Thibodeau, Alyson M., Leonardo López Luján, David J. Killick, Frances F. Berdan, and Joaquin Ruiz. 2018. Was Aztec and Mixtec Turquoise Mined in the American Southwest? *Science Advances* 4(6):eaas9370.

Thompson, Ian M. 2004. *The Towers of Hovenweep*. Moab, UT: Canyonlands Natural History Association.

Thompson, Kerry F., and Ronald H. Towner. 2017. Navajo Archaeology. In *The Oxford Handbook of Southwest Archaeology*, edited by B. Mills and S. Fowles, pp. 481–94. New York: Oxford University Press.

Thompson, Marc, Patricia A. Gilman, and Kristina C. Wyckoff. 2014. The Hero Twins in the Mimbres Region. Representations of the Mesoamerican Creation Saga Are Seen on Mimbres Pottery. *American Archaeology* 18(2):38–43.

Tipps, Betsy L. 1994. *Barrier Canyon Rock Art Dating*. Washington, DC: National Park Service.

———. 1995. *Holocene Archaeology Near Squaw Butte, Canyonlands National Park, Utah*. Selections from the Division of Cultural Resources vol. 7. Rocky Mountain Region. Denver: National Park Service.

Toll, H. Wolcott. 1991. Material Distribution and Exchange in the Chaco System. In *Chaco and Hohokam: Prehistoric Regional Systems in the American Southwest*, edited by P. L. Crown, W. J. Judge, pp. 77–107. Santa Fe, NM: School for Advanced Research Press.

———. 2001. Making and Breaking Pots in the Chaco World. *American Antiquity* 66(1):56–78.

———. 2004 Artifacts in Chaco. Where They Came From and Why They Mean. In *In Search of Chaco. New Approaches to an Archaeological Enigma*, edited by D. G. Noble, pp. 32–37. Santa Fe, NM: School of American Research Press.

Toll, Oliver W. 2003 [1962]. *Arapaho Names & Trails. A Report of a 1914 Pack Trip.* Reprint. Estes Park, CO: Rocky Mountain Nature Association.

———. 2006. Organization of Production. In *The Archaeology of Chaco Canyon*, edited by S. H. Lekson, pp. 117–151. Santa Fe, NM: School of American Research Press.

Towner, Ronald H. 1999. Eighteenth-Century Navajo Defensive Sites in the Dinetah. *Archaeology Southwest* 13(2):8–9.

———. 2003. *Defending The Dinétah. Pueblitos in the Ancestral Navajo Homeland.* Salt Lake City: University of Utah Press.

Trask, Garrett Lee. 2016. Analyzing Style in Classic Mimbres Black-on-White Geometric Pottery Designs. Unpublished PhD dissertation, Department of Anthropology, San Francisco State University, San Francisco.

Trigger, Bruce G. 1989. *A History of Archaeological Thought.* Cambridge: Cambridge University Press.

Upham, Steadman, Patricia L. Crown, and Fred Plog. 1994. Alliance Formation and Cultural Identity in the American Southwest. In *Themes in Southwest Prehistory*, edited by George J. Gumerman, pp. 183–210. Santa Fe, NM: School of American Research Press.

US Census Bureau. 2013. *United States: 2010. Summary Population and Housing Characteristics 2010 Census of Population and Housing.* Washington, DC: US Department of Commerce Economics and Statistics Administration. census.gov/.

Vance, Meghann M. 2011. Stones without Bones: Reconstructing the Lime Ridge Clovis Site. Unpublished master's thesis, Northern Arizona University, Flagstaff.

Van Dyke, Ruth M. 2007. Great Kivas in Time, Space, and Society. In *The Architecture of Chaco Canyon, New Mexico*, edited by S. H. Lekson, pp. 93–126. Salt Lake City: University of Utah Press.

———. 2008. *The Chaco Experience: Landscape and Ideology at the Center Place.* Santa Fe, NM: School of American Research Press.

VanPool, Christine S. 2003. The Shaman-Priests of the Casas Grandes Region, Chihuahua, Mexico. *American Antiquity* 68(4):696–717.

VanPool, Christine S. Gordon F. M. Rakita, Rafael Cruz Antilló, and Todd L. VanPool. 2008. Field Guide to the Ceramic Types of the Casas Grandes Region. In *Touching The Past: Ritual, Religion, and Trade of Casas Grandes*, edited by G. Nielsen-Grimm and P. Savast, pp. 59–67. Popular Series 5. Provo, UT: Museum of Peoples and Cultures.

VanPool, Christine S., Todd L. VanPool, and Lauren W. Downs. 2017. Dressing the Person: Clothing and Identity in the Casas Grandes World. *American Antiquity* 82(2):262–87.

Van West, Carla R., and Jeffrey S. Dean. 2000. Environmental Characteristics of the AD 900–1300 Period in the Central Mesa Verde Region. *Kiva* 66:19–44.

Varien, Mark D. 1999. *Sedentism and Mobility in a Social Landscape. Mesa Verde and Beyond.* Tucson: University of Arizona Press.

———. 2000. Introduction. *Kiva. Journal of Southwestern Archaeology and History* 66(1):5–18.

Varien, Mark D., William D. Lipe, Michael A. Adler, Ian M. Thompson, and Bruce A. Bradley. 1996. Southwestern Colorado and Southeastern Utah Settlement Patterns: AD 1100 to 1300. In *The Prehistoric Pueblo World, AD 1150–1350*, edited by M. A. Adler, pp. 86–113. Tucson: University of Arizona Press.

Varien, Mark D., Scott G. Ortman, Timothy A. Kohler, Donna M. Glowacki, and C. David Johnson. 2007. Historic Ecology in the Mesa Verde Region: Results from the Village Ecodynamics Project. *American Antiquity* 72(2):273–99.

Vierra, Bradley J., Margaret A. Jodry, M. Steven Shackley, and Michael J. Dilley. 2012. Late Paleoindian and Early Archaic Foragers in the Northern Southwest. In *From the Pleistocene to the Holocene: Human Organization and Cultural Transformations in Prehistoric North America*, edited by C. Britt Bousman and Bradley J. Vierra, pp. 171–96. College Station: Texas A&M Press.

Vigliani, Silvina. 2019. La "personeidad" de la caguama: Arte rupestre, paisaje y agencia en la costa central de Sonora, México. *Contributions in New World Archaeology* 12: 119–38. DOI: 10.33547/cnwa.12.04.

Villalpando, Elisa M. 2000. The Archaeological Traditions of Sonora. In *Greater Mesoamerica. The Archaeology of West and Northwest Mexico*, edited by M. S. Foster and S. Gorenstein, pp. 241–53. Salt Lake City: University of Utah Press.

Villalpando, Elisa M., and Randall H. McGuire. 2017. Sonoran Pre-Hispanic Traditions. In *The Oxford Handbook of Southwest Archaeology*, edited by B. Mills and S. Fowles, pp. 381–396. New York: Oxford University Press.

Vint, James M., and Jonathan B. Mabry. 2017. The Early Agricultural Period. In *The Oxford Handbook of Southwest Archaeology*, edited by B. Mills and S. Fowles, pp. 247–64. New York: Oxford University Press.

Vivian, R. Gwinn 1990. *The Chacoan Prehistory of the San Juan Basin*. New York: Academic Press.

———. 1997a. Chaco Roads: Morphology. *Kiva* 63(1):7–34.

———. 1997b. Chaco Roads: Function. *Kiva* 63(1):35–67.

Vivian, R. Gwinn, and Bruce Hilpert. 2002. *The Chaco Handbook: An Encyclopedic Guide*. Chaco Canyon Series. Salt Lake City: University of Utah Press.

Wallace, Henry D. 1989. *Archaeological Investigations at Petroglyph Sites in the Painted Rock Reservoir Area, Southwestern Arizona*. Technical Report 1989-5. Tucson: Institute for American Research.

———. 2001. Time Seriation and Typological Refinement of the Middle Gila Buffware Sequence. In *The Grewe Archaeological Research Project, Vol. 2: Material Culture, Part I: Ceramic Studies*, edited by D. R. Abbott, pp. 177–262. Anthropological Papers No. 99-1. Flagstaff-Tempe, AZ: Northland Research.

———. 2007a. Keys to Time. *Archaeology Southwest* 21(4):6–7.

———. 2007b. Hohokam Beginnings. In *The Hohokam Millennium*, edited by P. R. Fish and S. K. Fish, pp. 13–21. Santa Fe, NM: School for Advanced Research Press.

———. 2014. Ritual Transformation and Cultural Revitalization: Explaining Hohokam in pre-AD 1000 Southeastern Arizona. In *Between Mimbres and Hohokam: Exploring the Archaeology and History of Southeastern Arizona and Southwestern New Mexico,* edited by H. D. Wallace, pp. 433–99. Anthropological Papers No. 52. Tucson and Dragoon, AZ: Archaeology Southwest, Desert Archaeology and The Amerind Foundation.

Wallace, Henry D., and William H. Doelle. 2001. Classic Period Warfare in Southern Arizona. In *Deadly Landscapes: Case Studies in Prehistoric Southwestern Warfare*, edited by G. E. Rice and S. A. LeBlanc, pp. 239–87. Salt Lake City: University of Utah Press.

Wallace, Henry D., and James Holmlund. 1986. *Petroglyphs of the Picacho Mountains, South Central, Arizona*. Anthropological Papers no. 6. Tucson, AZ: Institute for American Research.

Waller, Kyle D., Adrianne M. Offenbecker, Jane H. Kelley, and M. Anne Katzenberg. 2018. Elites and Human Sacrifices at Paquime: A Bioarchaeological Assessment. *Kiva* 84(4):403–23.

Washburn Dorothy K., William N. Washburn, and Petia A. Shipkova. 2011. The Prehistoric Drug Trade: Widespred Consumption of Cacao in Ancestral Pueblo and Hohokam Communities in the American Southwest. *Journal of Archaeological Science* 28(7):1634–40.

Wasley, William W., and Alfred E. Johnson. 1965. *Salvage Archaeology in Painted Rocks Reservoir, Western Arizona*. Anthropological Papers of the University of Arizona, no. 9. Tucson: University of Arizona Press.

Waters, Michael R., and Thomas W. Stafford. 2007. Redefining the Age of Clovis: Implications for the Peopling of the Americas. *Science* 315:1122–26.

Watkins, Joe. 2014a. Through Wary Eyes: Indigenous Perspectives on Archaeology. *Annual Review of Anthropology* 34:429–49.

———. 2014b. Working Internationally with Indigenous Groups. *Advances in Archaeological Practice* 2(4):366–74.

Watson, Adam S., Stephen Plog, Brendan J. Culleton, Patricia A. Gilman, Steven A. LeBlanc, Peter M. Whiteley, Santiago Claramunt, and Douglas J. Kennett.

2015. Early procurement of scarlet macaws and the emergence of social complexity in Chaco Canyon, NM. *PNAS* 112:8238–43.

Weaver, D. E. Jr, and B. H. Rosenberg. 1978. Petroglyphs of the Southern Sierra Estella, a Locational Interpretation. In *Native American Rock Art 4*, edited by E. Syder, pp. 108–23. Tucson, AZ: American Rock Art Research Association.

Webster, Laurie D. 2007. Ritual Costuming at Pottery Mound. In *New Perspectives on Pottery Mound Pueblo*, edited by Polly Schaafsma, pp. 167–208. Albuquerque: University of New Mexico Press.

Webster, Laurie D., Kelley A. Hays-Gilpin, and Polly Schaafsma. 2006. A New Look at Tie-Paint and the Dot-in-a-Square Motif in the Prehispanic Southwest. *Kiva* (thematic volume: *Recent Perishables Research in the U.S. Southwest*) 71(3):317–48.

Weiner, Robert S., and Klara B. Kelley. 2021. Asdzáán Náhodidáhí (Lady Picker-Up) at Fajada Butte: Astronomy, Landscape, and the Basketmaker III Origins of Chacoan Ceremonialism. *Kiva* 87(3):268–94.

Wernecke, D. Clark, and Michael B. Collins. 2010. *Patterns and Process: Some Thoughts on the Incised Stones from the Gault Site, Central Texas, United States.* Paper presented at IFRAO conference—symposium: L'art pleistocenedans les Ameriques (Pre-Actes)-Pleistocene art of the Americas(Pre-Acts), Foix, France.

Whalen, Michael E., and Paul E. Minnis. 1996. Ballcourts and Political Centralization in the Casas Grandes Region. *American Antiquity* 61(4):732–46.

———. 2001a. *Casas Grandes and Its Hinterlands: Prehistoric Regional Organization in Northwest Mexico.* Tucson: University of Arizona Press.

———. 2001b. Architecture and Authority in the Casas Grandes Area, Chihuahua, Mexico. *American Antiquity* 66(4):651–68.

———. 2012. Ceramics and Polity in the Casas Grandes Area, Chihuahua, Mexico. *American Antiquity* 77(3):403–23.

———. 2017. Chihuahuan Archaeology. In *The Oxford Handbook of Southwest Archaeology*, edited by B. Mills and S. Fowles, pp. 398–409. New York: Oxford University Press.

White, Leslie A. 1962. *The Pueblo of Sia, New Mexico.* Bureau of American Ethnology: Bulletin 184. Washington, DC: Smithsonian Institution.

Whitley, David S. 2000. *The Art of the Ahaman: Rock Art of California.* Salt Lake City: University of Utah Press.

Whittlesey, Stephanie M. 2007. Not the Northeastern Periphery: The Lower Verde Valley in Regional Context. In *Hinterlands and Regional Dynamics in the Ancient Southwest*, edited by A. P. Sullivan and J. M. Bayman, pp. 11–30. Tucson: University of Arizona Press.

Wilcox, David R. 1981. The Entry of the Athabaskans into the American Southwest: The Problem Today. In *The Protohistoric Period in the American Southwest, AD 1450–1700*, edited by D. R. Wilcox and W. Bruce Masse, pp. 213–56. Anthropological Research Papers No. 24. Tempe: Arizona State University.

———. 1991. The Mesoamerican Ballgame in the American Southwest, In *The Mesoamerican Ballgame*, edited by V. L. Scarborough and D. R. Wilcox, pp. 101–25. Tucson: University of Arizona Press.

———. 2005. Perry Mesa and Its World. *Plateau* 2(1): 24–35.

Wilcox, David R., Jonathan Haas. 1994. The Scream of the Butterfly. Competition and Conflict in the Prehistoric Southwest. In *Themes in Southwest Prehistory*, edited by George J. Gumerman, pp. 211–38. Santa Fe, NM: School of American Research Press.

Wilcox, David R., and Charles Sternberg. 1983. *Hohokam Ballcourts and Their Interpretation*. Arizona State Museum Archaeological Series, no. 160. Tucson: Arizona State Museum, University of Arizona.

Wildesen, Leslie E. 1980. Cultural Resource Management: A Personal View. *Practicing Anthropology* 2(2):10–23.

Willey, Gordon R. 1966. *An Introduction to American Archaeology, Vol. I: North and Middle America*. Englewood Cliffs, NJ: Prentice-Hall.

Willey, Gordon R., and Philip Phillips. 1958. *Method and Theory in American Archaeology*. Chicago: University of Chicago Press.

Willey, Gordon R., and Jeremy A. Sabloff. 1993. *A History of American Archaeology*. New York: W. H. Freeman.

Williams, Thomas J., Michael B. Collins, Kathleen Rodrigues, William Jack Rink, Nancy Velchoff, Amanda Keen-Zebert, Anastasia Gilmer, Charles D. Frederick, Sergio J. Ayala, and Elton R. Prewitt. 2018. Evidence of an Early Projectile Point Technology in North America at the Gault Site, Texas, USA. *Science Advances* 4(7):eaar5954.

Wills, Wirt Henry III. 1985. Early Agriculture in the Mogollon Highlands of New Mexico. Unpublished PhD dissertation, Department of Anthropology, University of Michigan.

———. 1988. *Early Prehistoric Agriculture in the American Southwest*. Santa Fe, NM: School of American Research Press.

———. 1991. Organizational Strategies and the Emergence of Prehistoric Villages in the American Southwest. In *Between Bands and States*, edited by S. A. Gregg, pp. 161–180. Occasional Paper No. 9. Carbondale: Southern Illinois University, Center for Archaeological Investigations.

Wills, Wirt Henry III, Wetherbee B. Dorshow, and Jennie Sturm. 2018. Chaco Farming in 3-D. *Archaeology Southwest* 32(2–3):11–12.

Wills, Wirt Henry III, and Thomas C. Windes. 1989. Evidence for Population Aggregation and Dispersal during the Basketmaker III Period in Chaco Canyon, New Mexico. *American Antiquity* 54(2):347–69.

Wilmsen, Edwin N., and Frank H. H. Roberts Jr. 1978. *Lindenmeier 1934–1974: Concluding Report on Investigations*. Smithsonian Contributions to Anthropology No. 24. Washington, DC: Smithsonian Institution Press.

Wilshusen, Richard H. 1999. Basketmaker III (AD 500–750). In *Colorado Prehistory: A Context for the Southern Colorado River Basin*, edited by W. D. Lipe,

M. D. Varien and R. H. Wilshusen, pp. 166–195. Denver: Colorado Council of Professional Archaeologists.

———. 2002. Estimating Population in the Central Mesa Verde Region. In *Seeking the Center Place: Archaeology and Ancient Communities in the Mesa Verde Region*, edited by M. D. Varien and R. H. Wilshusen, pp. 101–20. Salt Lake City: University of Utah Press.

Wilshusen, Richard H., and Eric Blinman. 1992. Pueblo I Village Formation: A Reevaluation of Sites Recorded by Earl Morris on Ute Mountain Ute Tribal Lands. *Kiva* 57(3):251–69.

Wilshusen Richard H., and Ronald H. Towner. 1999. Post-Puebloan Occupation (AD 1300–1840). In *Colorado Prehistory: A Context for the Southern Colorado River Basin*, edited by W. D. Lipe, M. D. Varien and R. H. Wilshusen, pp. 353–69. Denver: Colorado Council of Professional Archaeologists.

Windes, Thomas C. 1984. A New Look at Population in Chaco Canyon. In *Recent Research on Chaco Prehistory*, edited by W. J. Judge and J. D. Schelberg, pp. 75–87. Reports of the Chaco Center No. 8. Albuquerque, NM: National Park Service.

———. 2003. This Old House: Construction and Abandonment at Pueblo Bonito. In *Pueblo Bonito: Center of the Chacoan World*, edited by J. E. Neitzel, pp. 14–32. Washington DC: Smithsonian Books.

———. 2007. Gearing Up and Piling On: Early Great Houses in the Interior San Juan Basin. In *The Architecture of Chaco Canyon, New Mexico*, edited by S. H. Lekson, pp. 45–92. Salt Lake City: The University of Utah Press.

Windes, Thomas C., and Dabney Ford. 1996. The Chaco Wood Project: The Chronometric Reappraisal of Pueblo Bonito. *American Antiquity* 61(2):295–310.

Woodbury, Richard B., and Ezra B. Zubrow. 1979. Agricultural Beginnings, 2000 BC–AD 500. In *Handbook of North Native Americans, Vol. 9: Southwest*, edited by A. Ortiz, pp. 43–60. Washington, DC: Smithsonian Institution.

Woodman, Neal, and Nancy Beavan Athfield. 2009. Post-Clovis Survival of American Mastodon in the Southern Great Lakes Region of North America. *Quaternary Research* 72:359–63.

Woosley, Anne I. 2001. Shadows on a Silent Landscape. Art and Symbol at Prehispanic Casas Grandes. In *The Road to Aztlan: Art from a Mythic Homeland*, edited by V. M. Fields and V. Zamudio-Taylor, pp. 164–83. Los Angeles: Los Angeles County Museum of Art.

Woosley, Anne I., and Allan J. McIntyre. 1996. *Mimbres Mogollon Archaeology: Charles C. Di Peso's Excavations at Wind Mountain*. Albuquerque: Amerind Foundation Archaeology–University of New Mexico Press.

Wright, Aaron M. 2014. *Religion on the Rocks: Hohokam Rock Art, Ritual Practice, and Social Transformation*. University of Utah Press.

———. 2016. Reorientation in Understanding Hohokam Rock Art. *Old Pueblo Archaeology* (Bulletin of Old Pueblo Archaeology Center) 77:1–15.

Wright, Aaron M., and Todd W. Bostwick. 2009. Technological Styles of Hohokam Rock Art Production in the South Mountains, South-Central Arizona. In *Native American Rock Art, Vol. 35*, edited by J. D. Keyser, D. Kaiser, G. Poetschat and M. W. Taylor, pp. 61–78. Tucson, AZ: American Rock Art Research Association.

Wrobel, Gabriel D., Christophe Helmke, Lenna Nash, and Jaime J. Awe. 2012. Polydactyly and the Maya: A Review and a Case from the Site of Peligroso, Upper Macal River Valley, Belize. *Ancient Mesoamerica* 23:131–42.

Wyckoff, Kristina Celeste. 2009. Mimbres-Mesoamerican Interaction: Macaws and Parrots in the Mimbres Valley, Southwestern New Mexico. Unpublished master's thesis, University of Oklahoma, Norman.

Yoder, David T. 2015. Gazing Back at You: Fremont Figurines. *Archaeology Southwest* 29(4): 10–11.

Young, Jane M. 1988. *Signs from the Ancestors: Zuni Cultural Symbolism and Perceptions of Rock Art*. Albuquerque: University of New Mexico Press.

Young, Robert W. 1983. Apachean Languages. In *Handbook of North Native Americans, Vol. 10: Southwest*, edited by A. Ortiz, pp. 393–400. Washington, DC: Smithsonian Institution.

Index

About the Author

Radosław Palonka is associate professor in the Department of New World Archeology, Institute of Archaeology of the Jagiellonian University in Kraków (Poland) and Research Associate at the Crow Canyon Archaeological Center, Colorado (USA). He specializes in archaeology and anthropology of North America, particularly the US Southwest. Since 2011 he has been leading an archaeological project focusing on sociocultural and settlement changes in the thirteenth-century AD Ancestral Pueblo culture from the central Mesa Verde region, southwestern Colorado, within the Canyons of the Ancients National Monument. His research interest connects also with investigations of the pre-Hispanic Ancestral Pueblo and historic Ute and Navajo rock art. He cooperates with several American institutions as well as the members of the Hopi tribe from the Hopi Culture Preservation Office (Second Mesa, Arizona) in terms of the indigenous oral traditions and knowledges. He applies various digital techniques of documentation, analysis, and conservation of indigenous cultural heritage. He is also involved in popularizing archaeology and history of Native Americans in Europe and United States.

www.ingramcontent.com/pod-product-compliance
Lightning Source LLC
Chambersburg PA
CBHW022259280326
41932CB00010B/913